Writing the Early Americas

Anna Brickhouse and Kirsten Silva Gruesz, Editors

❧ Inkface

Othello and White Authority
in the Era of Atlantic Slavery

MILES P. GRIER

University of Virginia Press
Charlottesville and London

University of Virginia Press
© 2023 by the Rector and Visitors of the University of Virginia
All rights reserved

First published 2023

9 8 7 6 5 4 3 2 1

Library of Congress Cataloging-in-Publication Data

Names: Grier, Miles P., author.
Title: Inkface : *Othello* and white authority in the era of Atlantic slavery / Miles P. Grier.
Description: Charlottesville : University of Virginia Press, 2023. | Series: Writing the early Americas | Includes bibliographical references and index.
Identifiers: LCCN 2023026397 (print) | LCCN 2023026398 (ebook) | ISBN 9780813950365 (hardcover) | ISBN 9780813950372 (paperback) | ISBN 9780813950389 (ebook)
Subjects: LCSH: Shakespeare, William, 1564–1616. Othello. | Shakespeare, William, 1564–1616—Dramatic production. | Shakespeare, William, 1564–1616—Stage history. | Blackface. | Race in the theater.
Classification: LCC PR2829 .G75 2023 (print) | LCC PR2829 (ebook) | DDC 822.3/3—dc23/eng/20230615
LC record available at https://lccn.loc.gov/2023026397
LC ebook record available at https://lccn.loc.gov/2023026398

Publication of this volume has been supported by *New Literary History*.

Cover art: Othello, act 5, scene 2, engraved by W. Leney after J. Graham, 1799. (Folger Shakespeare Library)

Theatre historians err by failing to appreciate the differing semantics of stage and study.

—Charles B. Lower, "Othello as Black on Southern Stages, Then and Now"

If racial construction is . . . the creation of a virtual human reality from another psychic realm, its greatest provenance will be in the theater.

—Imtiaz Habib, "Racial Impersonation on the Elizabethan Stage: The Case of Shakespeare Playing Aaron"

Theatre is an incubator for the creation of historical events—and, as in the case of artificial insemination, the baby is no less human.

—Suzan-Lori Parks, "Possession"

Contents

Acknowledgments

It is daunting to confront the task of writing acknowledgments after writing a book concerning the reduction of human character to writing—a process that potentially mars the reputation of the subject and of the author. Nevertheless, the opportunity to garner collective applause for some of the people who made this book possible is worth the risk.

I would like to thank the institutions that funded the research undergirding *Inkface*. The Colonial Williamsburg foundation awarded me the Gilder-Lehrman Fellowship to conduct research at the Rockefeller Library. I am particularly grateful to Inge Flester, Cathy Hellier, Marianne Martin, Doug Mayo, Linda Rowe, and George Yetter. I would also like to acknowledge the helpful staff members at other archives I visited, including the Massachusetts Historical Society, the American Antiquarian Society, the British Library, the Folger Shakespeare Library, the British National Archives, and the Houghton Library at Harvard University. Dale Stinchcomb of the Houghton deserves special kudos for engaging me in the most delightful and encouraging conversation about my research and then locating the uncataloged playbills I had sought in vain. I want to thank my unofficial sponsors, who allowed me to stay with them when I was conducting research on a limited budget: Arthur Knight, Dawn Peterson, Adam Schickedanz, and Neil Wade.

I want to thank to my colleagues in the ad hoc dissertation writing group in NYU's American Studies—Richard Blint, andré carrington, Miabi Chatterji, Andrew Cornell, Kerwin Kaye, and especially Dawn Peterson, whose careful attention and extended conversation bettered this project in its first years. I would be remiss not to praise my former partner in early modern racial representations, from the visual side—the dynamic Dacia Mitchell. Jan Padios made a great downstairs neighbor and unparalleled conversation partner in those years. I had the good fortune of a harmonious and all-Black dissertation committee: Jennifer L. Morgan, Kim F. Hall, G. Gabrielle Starr, Tavia Nyong'o, and Philip Brian Harper. I am grateful to Jennifer for her faith that this literary scholar is indeed "historically minded" and her continued support and counsel. Before I knew her, Kim kicked down the archival doors to this kind of research and demonstrated the pervasiveness of racial imagery in early modern English literature and culture. Her expertise, advice, and support across early modern and African American studies is unparalleled. Although she was not on my committee, Lisa Duggan made tremendous contributions to my thinking when I was her student and continues to serve as a trusted guide.

I appreciate the generous funding I received from the Provost's Postdoctoral Fellowship at Duke University. Robyn Wiegman was one of the first scholars outside my graduate program to express excitement about this project. Her belief buoyed me. She welcomed me warmly to Duke and introduced me to incisive interlocutors, including Srinivas Aravamudan, Ian Baucom, Karla Holloway, Thavolia Glymph, Ranjana Khanna, Kimberly Lamm, and Fred Moten. I am also grateful for Kelvin Black, Mary Caton-Lingold, Alex Greenberg, Darren Mueller, Beth Perry, and Matthew Somoroff. Extended conversations with them propelled the project forward, and we also formed durable friendships that are among the treasures I carried with me from Durham.

In 2018 the Folger Library sponsored a colloquium on gender and race, which introduced me to a wonderful and varied community of scholars and to the indispensable Owen Williams. Urvashi Chakravarty, Mira Kafantaris, Carol Mejia-Laperle and I began a deep academic and personal engagement there. Now they are three of my favorite thinkers and most cherished friends in the field.

I would like to thank CUNY and the Mellon Foundation for funding the costs of research and publication through two generous PSC-CUNY grants. CUNY also sponsored two helpful writing groups: the Faculty Fellowship Publication Program (FFPP) and the CUNY Mellon Faculty Diversity Career Enhancement Initiative (CFDI). I thank the FFPP cohort, composed of Anita Baksh, George Fragopoulos, Daly Guilamo, Robert Higney, Lucia Cedeira Serantes, Tanya Zhelezcheva, and our indefatigable (cheer)leader, Carrie Hintz. The Mellon CFDI group included our leader Rich McCoy, who gave constructive, encouraging feedback and threw the most delicious dinner party, Susan Davis, Regine Joseph, Bill Orchard, Rebecca Taleghani, and Laura Villa. I would also like to thank an ad hoc writing group that invited me in and workshopped several chapters together: Grégory Pierrot, Lily Saint, and Bhakti Shringarpure.

A number of scholars had long talks or email exchanges with me about the project at various stages, including Kevin Dawson, Jenna Gibbs, and Farah Griffin. Very special thanks to John Archer and Patricia Parker, who made an interloper from American studies feel like a legitimate early modernist during moments of doubt. From getting the book organized and completed to navigating the profession, Erika Lin is a supreme tactical thinker, a great adviser as well as a friend who has invited me to everything from dinner at home to nights of theatre and masked jam sessions during the early days of Covid.

I owe a special debt to the reviewers for the University of Virginia Press, who pored over the manuscript twice and offered constructive and pragmatic feedback. It has been so nice to come "home" to UVA Press and the Writing the Early Americas series, where this project was always wanted. Eric Brandt,

Anna Brickhouse, Kirsten Silva Gruesz, Wren Myers, Angie Hogan, Clayton Butler, and Fernando Campos have all been tremendously helpful while answering the anxious questions that accompany a first book.

While I am fortunate to have many friends in the fields my work touches, I must highlight several who, in their scholarship and by their friendship, frame the total context in which this work is even possible: Nicole Aljoe, Hamit Arvas, Dennis Britton, Lara Cohen, Matthieu Chapman, Katherine Gillen, Jim Greene, Robert Hornback, Nick Jones, JohnPat Leary, Sabina Lenae, Jason Shaffer, Cassander Smith, Steven Thomas, Christine Varnado, and Sydnee Wagner. I got into academia to have meaningful conversations with smart people. These folks exceed that hope.

At a meeting of the Shakespeare Association of America, three people approached me and said they wanted to form a group to help me finish *Inkface*. Did they know that my faith in my ability to corral this project was faltering? What angel sent me Patricia Akhimie, Mario diGangi, and Will Fisher, I will never know. But I do know that, without their dedication to reading multiple drafts of nearly every chapter, it is highly unlikely that I could have brought it all together. Kudos to Mario and Will for bearing the full load when Patricia took her rightful maternity leave and to Will for generosity and encouragement above what I could have imagined. This writing coven saved the project, and I cannot repay them—though I intend to pay it forward.

When I talk about my department at Queens College, people typically disbelieve my idyllic description of the intellectual environment and camaraderie. During their terms as chair, Glenn Burger, Steven Kruger, and Karen Weingarten all took significant time to engage my writing and to offer insightful advice for organization and completion. I could not have asked for more consistent and tailored support as a junior faculty member. Many other colleagues took time out for long conversations and to attend talks, including Natalie Léger, John Weir, Andrea Walkden, Rich McCoy, Jeff Cassvan (who also provided me a trove of secondary sources), Talia Shaffer, Duncan Faherty, Cliff Mak, and Sian Silyn-Roberts. Some went farther, reading late drafts during the final push. Andrea Walkden read an ancient draft of chapter 2 and the gestures of a new one and encouraged me to light out for the new territory. Duncan Faherty and Karen Weingarten helped me wrestle an unruly Melville chapter into shape. (Duncan was also the crucial reader of an early draft of chapter 4.) Ryan Black entered into the spirit of this project and read nearly every word of the final version with a poet's care. My debt to him is profound and incalculable.

While the Covid pandemic precipitated great fear and the loss of some relationships, it brought some surprising additions to my world. Brandi K. Adams and I had a very pleasant first meeting at the Modern Language

Association conference in January of 2020. Then the world shut down. We haven't seen each other in person since, but she has nonetheless become a most valued reader, a font of sources, and the first call on many matters. Brandi's kindness, intelligence, and humor are a treasured gift. Ambereen Dadabhoy has been not only an incomparable host on my visit to LA but a dear friend and intellectual comrade in the truest sense. I marvel at Ambereen's breadth of knowledge, fierce commitment, unmatched hospitality, and deep kindness. I also want to thank Joey Gamble here—how often does one get the benefit of a superlative listener, a brilliant interlocutor, and a person of great human sympathy in one?

Of all my new friendships, the one with Joshua Calhoun surprised me the most. Thanks, I think, are due to the Winans for sewing the seeds of our meeting sometime in the early '90s. But, for a right-on-time invitation to flee the epicenter of Covid for the lakes and trails of the Adirondacks, a welcome place at table, and a thoughtful reading of my book manuscript—and, indeed, for much more—I thank Josh (and Arden for sharing her Fother with me).

Kim Smith and I took our friendship to another level during the pandemic, when she became not just my emergency contact but my sister. I have yet to find the thing we can't do together, but I haven't let her try to teach me TikTok dances yet.

Although once I was recruiting Elliott Powell to the graduate program in American Studies, the younger has outpaced the elder. I am not sure how he can be both younger than I am and senior to me at the same time, but this is just one of his magic tricks. I have grown so much as a person and scholar from his insights from both of those vantage points. Our friendship has been easy, durable, and absolutely essential.

Dylan Yeats has accompanied me across so many areas of life for the better part of twenty years. I've slept on his couch while apartment hunting, and he has read drafts of articles and job talks on the shortest notice . . . and then there are the trips to see Shaw's *Saint Joan* and the rooftop parties. Niles to my Frasier (or is it the other way around?), he is an endless font of hospitality, historical knowledge, political wisdom, emotional insight, care, and good cheer.

While I've met many new people in my career, those rest on the bedrock of lasting friendships. I picked up Andrew Breving, Kevin Cooney, David Olinger, Rob Olinger, and Alex Smith in high school in Cincinnati. Jealool Amari, Orion Baker, Ellen Ketels, Jeanné Lewis, Travis McAlister, David Rentz, Adam Schickedanz, Matthew Schneider, Crystal Simon, Mariam Williams, and Windsor Williams all date to undergraduate days at Washington University in St. Louis. Eric Madison dates to the year following. I met Derek McPhatter and Aymar Jean Christian during early graduate school days in New York. While space won't permit me to elaborate on each of them individually here, suffice it to say: almost everyone on this list has been in my life for more than twenty years. I joke, sometimes, that I am single now because these friends have set too high a standard. I do want to make special note here of Ken Ferrigni, who has shared his home and family with me, as well as his singular verve for guitar, acting, playwriting, exercise. Ken somehow manages to be a most reliable friend while also being full of surprises.

There are some academics I need to thank whose influence preceded graduate school and made it possible. At Washington University in St. Louis, I like to say I majored in English and minored in Erin Mackie, as I took three separate eighteenth-century courses with her. Although Erin was always quick to announce that the early modern period did not interest her, I hope she will read this book as a *very* long eighteenth-century project born in her seminars. Joe Loewenstein was a delightfully impossible Shakespeare professor. I will never forget his comparison of Iago's "sew nettles" speech to Diana Ross's overture on "Ain't No Mountain High Enough." I doubted that anyone could pull *that* off, but when he stuck the landing I was a convert.

Alison Francis and the late, beloved Jonathan Smith were the dazzling, brilliant Black graduate instructors who diagnosed me as a future academic and made that life seem exciting, worthy, and attainable. The late Garrett Albert Duncan, an unparalleled scholar of African American language and education, profoundly shaped my thinking about the role of literacy in racial hierarchy. I strive to be for others what these three Black scholars were and are to me.

I also want to acknowledge here Brian Haggenmiller, Jarvis DeBerry, Keri McWilliams, N'Jai-An Patters, whom I met at Wash U, and who, in different ways, set a standard of excellence while offering unconditional friendship and encouragement that continues to resonate even when some time elapses between contact. The Ervin Scholars program, run by the incomparable figures James McLeod and Dorothy Elliott, made Washington University possible and changed my life permanently.

Lynn Weiss was my mentor for two years in the Mellon Minority (now Mays) Undergraduate Fellowship, a program for aspiring scholars from groups that are historically underrepresented in academia. She taught me how to research literature and has been a chief counsel and supreme advocate ever since. Lynn handed me to Rafia Zafar to advise my senior thesis on representations of masculinity in post-Emancipation African American literature. To be claimed by Rafia is an eternal boon; she keeps tabs on all of us and calls situations as she sees them.

Nancy Pope has probably had the most lasting influence on me, as she taught me the fundamentals of literary analysis. I couldn't have known how invaluable those tools would be in the interdisciplinary days to come, nor how indispensable Nancy would become as a guide through many challenging periods of my life. I am endlessly grateful that she has invited me to be a part of her family and that we can now enjoy a season of calm and celebration. Now, as ever, the mutual admiration society continues.

Surrogate mother the first, however, is Joan Pipkins. Her love and support have been a constant since I was about twelve or thirteen years old, playing tennis with the Inner City Tennis Project, run by the legends Tony Pack and Rachel Fair. I joke sometimes that, as an adoptee, I have always been good at attracting potential parents. Ms. P's love and contribution exceed whatever I could have asked for: they are all that and a bag of her homemade chocolate chip cookies.

My dear aunt Janet bought me the Macbook on which I completed the entirety of the dissertation project and then read every word of it when I finished. To hear her say *my nephew*! with such pride was one of the best elements of earning a doctorate.

I dedicate this book to the memory of a woman who loved all of me from the moment she began taking care of me: my grandmother, Corine Grier, also known as Mama Corine. There were many people in my life who told me I was smart. She was the first person I knew who cared about all of me. Along with Leslie Grier, Annie Mae Jones, and Horace Jones, these elders showed generosity, openness, concern and humility. I miss them all terribly, but their examples live in me.

Finally, I want to thank Métra Gilliard. Thanks is, of course, insufficient—as is "friend." No one could ask for a better advocate and champion, a shrewder tactician, a wiser counsel, a more loyal ally. Thank you, Métra, for keeping our friendship tended and watered, for keeping the main thing the main thing, and for ensuring that when I ask, "You there, sister?" the answer is always "yes." May we reach that higher ground.

Author's Note

For quotations from Shakespeare plays, I have opted for *The Riverside Shakespeare* (1974), except when early textual variants are germane to the argument. Throughout the text, I have purposely chosen to leave "moor" uncapitalized, except when quoting from texts in which it is capitalized, such as *Othello: The Moor of Venice*. By this unconventional spelling, I aim to deter readers from the habitual search for a single ethnic population called Moors and point them instead to the multiple ethnic, religious, topographical, and nautical referents of moor at play in *Othello* and in the broader culture.

Inkface

The Residue of Inkface

In fall of 2015, as I was engaged in the research and writing that produced this book, New York's Metropolitan Opera staged Giuseppe Verdi's *Otello* (1877) with an innovation. For the first time at the Met, the lead tenor would not wear makeup to darken his skin. Although the Met was not the first major opera house to eschew blackface for their *Otello,* their decision seemed to indicate a tipping point.[1] Verdi's operatic moor was the last direct descendant of Shakespeare's Othello whom twenty-first-century audiences could encounter in dark makeup.[2] *Othello* was not the first English play featuring a blackfaced character, but it has been the most influential. From its 1604 debut, *Othello* has been a mainstay of the professional stage. In addition, it spawned tragedies and minstrel parodies in the eighteenth and nineteenth centuries—as well as cinematic experiments into the twentieth.[3] For over four centuries, blackface *Othello* pervaded high, low, and middlebrow cultures, with allusions and retellings in every media form.[4] Now, as more opera houses abandon dark makeup, it appears that blackface will not be seen on elite stages: Verdi's moor will be cleansed and, with him, Shakespeare's legacy.

Bartlett Sher, director of the 2015 opera, proclaimed the gospel: "[Otello] at his core, [i]s an outsider uncomfortable in Venetian society who is manipulated into a kind of jealous madness that leads to tragedy—all of which can be communicated without makeup."[5] Sher contended that simply omitting the makeup would allow aesthetic enjoyment to continue undiminished by the "[negative] historical resonance" of blackface.[6] Omitting conspicuous dark paint becomes a veritable *un-mooring,* resurrecting Verdi's Shakespearean moor as a white protagonist primed to confront the universal themes of jealousy and alienation unbound by the ostensibly limiting frame of racism.[7] Although Sher's expressed purpose is to avoid causing modern audiences unnecessary offense, eliminating blackface also projects a sanitized version of the cultural past—in which great Western thinkers (and the societies that birthed them) were too concerned with "eternal verities" to care much about "ephemeral" modern-day preoccupations, such as "racism, homophobia, colonialism."[8]

Edward Pechter presents readers with precisely such a past in his introduction to the most recent Norton edition of *Othello:* "The relative inconsequence of race to eighteenth-century audiences is one of those astonishment-inducing

revelations ... that make for critical self-consciousness."[9] Pechter expends significant energy discouraging readers from "approach[ing]" the earliest *Othello*
"in racial terms" (xi, 147). Although he claims historical fidelity when arguing
that early modern audiences would have interpreted Othello's skin color in the
solidly "pre-racial" terms of "sin and redemption," he admits that this analysis
cannot account for "the blacked-up Richard Burbage audiences saw on the
Globe stage" (144, 147). To resolve this problem, he suggests that audiences
"might have sensed [something] in and around" the black stage paint, available
only to "their mind's eye" (147.) Pechter and Sher, the editor and the director,
would both do away with blackface lest it trap *Othello* and its playwright in
what they view as the morass of race. Together, they offered the wide world
of Shakespeare lovers an innocent past and future, encouraging them to wash
their proverbial hands of the blackface in *Othello,* as if it had always been superfluous, "as if [the] offense ... were long ago remitted, were never truly *real.*"[10]

Actors, on the contrary, have always found Othello's blackface difficult
to remove or do without. The "change of dress" was a simple enough matter, but players essaying the titular moor found a tedious labor in "wash[ing]
off the last tint of Othello's swarthy hue."[11] As late as 1930, the actor Frank
Benson reminisced that after staining his face with permanganate of potash,
he "remained of dusky hue for weeks on end."[12] The foremost actor of his
day, eighteenth-century superstar David Garrick might have rather not applied the paint for his 1745 performance. Legend explains Garrick's failure as
Othello as a function of the required makeup: "when his face was obscured,
his chief power of expression was lost; and then, and not till then, was he reduced to a level with several other performers." Dressed in a Venetian style but
topped with a turban, the blacked-up Garrick was reportedly taunted as less
than Othello and less than himself. The joke circulated that Garrick resembled
not Othello but a "negro servant" in Richard Hogarth's satiric series *The Harlot's Progress:* "*jet black* with rolling white eyes, and dressed in laced coat and
knee-breeches, and with a disproportionately large turban on his head sur-
mounted by an aigret."[13] Rather than having his stellar career tainted by such
comparisons, Garrick abandoned the blackface role.

Theatre lore is full of stories of Desdemonas smeared with Othello's
paint—or carefully protected from it.[14] The staining effects of kissing a blackfaced Othello were already an inside joke for theatre people by the debut of
Isaac Jackman's *All the World's a Stage* in 1777. The character playing the heiress Kitty Sprightly merely describes her rehearsal of *Othello*'s final bedroom
scene with a servant slathered in goose grease and soot, and knowing laughter
ensues.[15] This joke became more pronounced over the centuries, until it was
finally suppressed in the second half of the twentieth century by the eschewal
of blackface. In the late nineteenth century, New York star Louis James used

his paint to draw inconspicuous facial hair on Desdemona during the final murder scene. The actors who saw a blonde Desdemona "disfigured by apparent hirsute tufts over her mouth and chin . . . were convulsed with laughter and the effect of a great tragic scene was ruined."[16] James might have been imitating the legendary Edwin Booth, who is depicted with pillow in hand, preparing to smother a Desdemona whose face is half black with his paint and also imprinted with his moustache.[17] This image of uncertain provenance contradicts a promise Ellen Terry says that Booth made her and kept: "I shall never make you black. . . . When I take your hand, I shall have a corner of my drapery

MR. BOOTH, AS " OTHELLO," SMUDGES THE FACE OF
THE FAIR " DESDEMONA " IN KISSING HER.

"Mr. Booth, as 'Othello,' Smudges the Face of the Fair 'Desdemona' in Kissing Her," insert in *The Life and Art of Edwin Booth,* by William Winter, New York: Macmillan, 1893. (Folger Shakespeare Library, Washington, D.C.)

in my hand. That will protect you."[18] Laurence Olivier offered Maggie Smith no such protection. She remembered that during a scripted struggle onstage, Olivier "did knock me out. . . . I was left with some black marks on my face."[19] In the film made of that production, after Othello kisses her in Cyprus, Smith turns away from the camera and walks upstage. Desdemona has no reason to feel shame at that moment. I suspect that the director instructed Smith to hide a blackened face from the camera, as it does not comport with a sense of Desdemona's innocence or the gravity Shakespearean tragedy had accumulated by the twentieth century.[20]

Beyond Desdemona, other players also absorbed Othello's blackness in scenes that became a part of stage tradition over the centuries. Performing opposite Charles Macready in the mid-nineteenth century, John Coleman remembered that despite taking care to wipe his hands, he "left the marks" of all ten of his fingers "in [Iago's] beautiful white cashmere dress."[21] Actors and crew could not have ignored the obtrusive residue of this easily transmissible makeup. Anything a painted Othello touched would potentially need cleaning: Cassio's shoulder, Desdemona's clothes, Emilia's hands, Iago's neck, orders sent from Venice, the couple's bedsheets. With a blackface Othello, when the general's "occupation's gone"—when, as Macbeth would say, his "hour upon the stage" is concluded—the white actor reemerges, as if from a sleep, to see the evidence of his crimes on the set and on his own face.[22] These are performance remains indeed.[23]

Far from superfluous, blackface was apparently essential to the first centuries of Othello's performance. The great nineteenth-century impressionist Charles Mathews could not imagine performing or viewing Othello without it. In his one-man shows, an unpainted Mathews would use his voice and body to slip into Africanist persona, yet he did not dare attempt Othello without blacking up. In fact, he viewed Shakespeare's dramatic texts as fundamentally incomplete without stage prosthetics: "No one, I presume, will deny, that Shak[e]speare would have *written* in vain . . . had actors attempted to play Othello with a fair face or Richard the Third without a hump."[24] His confidence in his assertion was not misplaced. Fair-faced Othellos are all but unheard of to this day, as directors and audiences have generally agreed that Othello must have his tint, by any means necessary.[25]

Though some may want to overlook how integral dark makeup once was to *Othello,* painted players mediated audiences' engagement with Shakespeare's script. A primary encounter with a clean, modern, printed edition tempts the scholar to restrict investigation of early modern racial thinking to an archive containing intertextual echoes of *Othello*'s overt propositions about moorish character. Yet, performance can enact events and relationships that cannot be achieved in any other medium. Everyone knows that reading and viewing a play are not equivalent experiences, but with *Othello* in particular, there seems a persistent urge to disregard the significant difference that performance makes—to recur to textual matter rather than to sweat, breath, and smeared paint. For example, the literary scholar Mary Floyd-Wilson turns to a "long line of classical, medieval, and early modern [medical] texts" that, she says, supplied "foundational knowledge" Shakespeare's audience employed in distinguishing Othello "from people of cooler climates."[26] Yet climate could not have determined ethnic character and temperament in performances in which other characters, especially Desdemona, acquire blackness through amorous and abusive touch. Therefore, I argue that access to the racialized world early *Othellos* constructed must come through the messy materiality of blackface.[27]

Scholars such as the theatre historian Charles Lower cautioned four decades ago that scholars searching for "the Moor of Venice" had been misled by prioritizing the "semantics of the . . . study" over those of the stage.[28] More recently, the performance scholar Ayanna Thompson has urged critics to "attend to *how* actual performance techniques affect constructions of race."[29] Imtiaz Habib puts the case more forcefully still: "If racial construction is . . . the creation of a virtual human reality from another psychic realm, its greatest provenance will be in the theater."[30] These exhortations suggest that, through its deployment of bodies, objects, and representational conventions such as blackface, performance produces a racial reality that is unique to its media. Those whose primary encounters with Othello have been in the literature classroom or on the contemporary stage have likely met a moor with a rich interior life informed, in part, by his presumed awareness of Venetian racism. I would argue that the psychological depth of the literary Othello springs from habits of extrapolation honed while reading novels, a genre that offers extensive access to characters' unvoiced thoughts.[31] Contemporary casting solicits an allied projection by featuring actors whose non-white identities audiences recognize as congenital and enduring rather than cosmetically produced for the occasion. I have argued elsewhere that viewers' ensuing perceptions of Othello as a man conscious of a racial predicament stem not from Shakespeare's sympathies but from productions that capitalize on actors' social identities to stage confrontations with racial taboos of the audience's world.[32]

Across *Othello*'s four centuries of performance, the play has become subject to increasing pressures of historical and psychological realism, especially as pertains to casting. Yet, there is no reason to conclude that realism was artists' consistent stylistic priority in earlier periods, that audiences always demanded it, or that such demands had to be filled in the same way. In fact, the expectation that *Othello*'s characters must be historically accurate and psychologically plausible may well make it more difficult to access early *Othellos* and their racial systems that do not aim to produce coherent, recognizable persons. Surveying early modern performances in black paint or cloth, Ian Smith demonstrates a pattern: "racial prosthetics evinced blackness as material object devoid of interiority."[33] Smith continues: "the black African on the stage is presumed to be immediately *knowable*" covered in a "chromodermal signifier" that requires "no decoding."[34] Smith identifies blackness as a readable complexion; hence, my proposal that early blackface can fruitfully be understood as *inkface*. Black stage moors, then, were known less for a coherent history or worldview than for bearing an inky meaning beyond their capacity to shed, contain, or decipher.

Both African American and postcolonial literary theorists have informed my conception of inkface. In the overture of "Mama's Baby, Papa's Maybe"—her legendary exploration of gender, racial blackness, and property law in the Atlantic World—Hortense Spillers surveys the long span from the transshipment of the first African captives to the post–civil rights era. She observes that the discourses of race have covered the descendants of Africans with "markers so loaded with mythical prepossession that there is no easy way for the agents buried beneath them to come clean."[35] Spillers's metaphor conjures the stubborn paint of an early Othello, an Africanist figure par excellence, overlaid with what Toni Morrison has called "the denotative and connotative blackness that African peoples have come to signify, as well as the entire range of views, assumptions, readings, and misreadings that accompany Eurocentric learning about these people."[36] In the light of Spillers and Morrison, early modern blackface reveals itself as the trace of an origin, as if the strange race of stage moors were born of the ink of European maps, histories, medical treatises, travel narratives. Meanwhile, postcolonialist Jyotsna Singh observes that such overwritten black figures "can only gain access [to their] own origins through the *ascriptions* of European colonial discourses."[37] The inky allusion in her "ascriptions" proves a felicitous description of peoples whose words, signs, and flesh Europeans forced to speak within the symbolic orders of Christianity, capitalist calculation, and the Roman alphabet. Composed of the ink that Europeans use to make (themselves) believe, these blackened figures could not express anything for which Western thought lacks symbols.[38]

These theorists suggest how epochal an overwriting inkface executed. The whitewashing of *Othello* with which I began this introduction has functioned to conceal an enduring project: supplying blackened characters to be read in intramural debates, the conduct of which both presumes and reproduces whiteness as interpretive authority. Inkface bequeaths a blackness to latter centuries that is not so much a fixed biological category as a position defined by both legibility and obvious cultural incompetence, toward which anyone might be pushed. In this book, I take the convergence of blackface and literacy seriously in the hopes of grasping deep roots of white supremacy in an asserted monopoly on reading, which functioned as a synecdoche for legitimate assessment in every realm of social life. Blackened characters' repeated failures to read their own inky bodies and other textual objects suggest that the staging of literacy was designed to install an exclusively white interpretive community.

Inkface in Early Modern English Culture

This book begins near the turn of the seventeenth century, when the English stage repertoire featured a parade of moors whose painted blackness was crucial to their business onstage. The performance scholar Erika Lin would classify stage blackness as an aspect of the "materiality of performance," which encompasses physical matter onstage, stage conventions, and the "codes of intelligibility" required to grasp their significance.[39] Playwrights and actors knew that black paint on the face was a performance convention, an aspect of costuming that could signal a wide array of foreign types. In the lexicon, moor could accommodate many peoples under its umbrella. Applied with inconsistent modification to inhabitants of northern and sub-Saharan Africa, the Indian subcontinent, and the Americas, the category had no positive content; it guaranteed only that the person referenced was neither Christian nor European.[40] My interest, however, is not in finding the real-world population designated by "moors" but in examining the materiality of their stage representation. As Dympna Callaghan theorized, black stage moors were constituted by paint, and this constitution involved them in business such as staining that no offstage moor—however defined—could execute.[41]

Beyond conveying their taint, blackface moors were subjected to a curious code of intelligibility: audiences and readers were often asked to think of their coating as an ink. The association of blackness with ink seems both longstanding and fundamental. Etymologists contend that the English word "black" derives from Middle Dutch, Old Saxon, and Middle Low German words for "black ink," "dye," and "color."[42] Apparently, ink predates the word black and serves as its source and epitome. Either knowingly or unwittingly, early modern dramatists, poets, and scientists elaborated upon this conceit, making ink both an aspect of blackamoor constitution and a sign of exclusion from matters of social business.[43] Composed of ink and covered in it, stage blackamoors were clearly not meant to be readers but to be read.

For example, Ben Jonson's *The Masque of Blackness* (1605) presents Queen Anna and eleven ladies as sun-blacked nymphs. These painted "nigritae" bemoan their complexion and long to be made fair. One night, while cooling themselves in a moonlit lake, they all simultaneously spy in the water a face inscribed with poetic couplets. The lines instruct them to seek fairer faces in a land that, when rendered in Greek, ends with the suffix -TANIA. Jonson is at pains to inform the audience that this unwashable, underwater face is no hallucination, since "Aethiops never dream."[44] The mystery is resolved when the goddess Aethiopia descends to inform the nymphs that it was her face reflected in the water—a revelation that reinforces the association of blackness with ink, since her name comes from the Greek term for Africans, "burnt face." Once this racist fantasy of a people incapable of imagination is accepted, the conflation is complete: the black nymphs have a fate beyond their control spelled out on their faces. They are destined to wander until they happen on Britannia, figured as a temperate clime where a king versed in classical and Christian texts can eventually restore black moors to full humanity by miraculously removing the indelible ink of their blackness.[45]

In *Lust's Dominion*, purchased for public performance some five years before the queen's masque,[46] the villainous moor Eleazar speaks of "digest[ing] the gall" of banishment—a metaphor that suggests swallowing one of the essential ingredients that makes black ink.[47] Soon after he consumes the figurative gall, he begins to speak of his black face as expressing what he ingested. The transformation culminates in his predicting the ruin of an adversary: "Cardinal, this disgrace / shall dye thy soule as Inky as my face."[48] The blotted face of Eleazar offers the pattern after which the Cardinal's otherwise inaccessible soul will be read.

Sometimes the figurative link of black moors with ink is astonishingly literal. When he rediscovered *Mr. Moore's Revels* (1636), John Elliott Jr. described "the main conceit of the work" as "an elaborate, not to say tediously extended, pun on the name 'Moore.'"[49] Through verbal and visual puns, the *Revels* plays upon the linguistic imprecision and geographical eccentricity of moor and illustrates the affordances of different means of producing stage blackness in early modernity. The first material metaphor for the skin of the masque's six "blacke" moors is a textile prosthetic.[50] They enter wearing "black buckram coats laced with yellow straw."[51] Although the terms black and moor are both employed, these figures have no singular ethnic designation or homeland. The peoples of Africa, India, and perhaps the Americas merge when the six are called, variously, "negroes" and "*sutty* visag'd Indian[s]" (24–25, my emphasis). Soot serves as a second covering, distinct from the black coats—closer to the skin than clothing, but removable by ordinary washing. Uninterested in differentiating what we might now think to be unmistakably distinct populations, the text and performance of *Revels* blithely subsume Africans north and south of the Sahara, not to mention American Indians and those of the subcontinent, under the single sign of a sooty "blacke" prosthetic skin (30).[52]

In the *Revels*, blackness signifies wildly and widely. The ends of the earth meet under its sign, as do the contrary natures of bellicosity and tractability.

The moors are depicted as alternately warlike and submissive, as they arrive bearing javelins but lay down these arms at the feet of the mock king presiding over the revels.[53] Disarmed, the moors exit to remove their black coats. They will return to perform "a country dance" (71). During this interlude, the performance offers another material through which to think of the surface of blackness. The stage directions recount that, while the moors are offstage,

> ffoure litle
> boyes drest ffor apes stole a way
> ffoure of their coates who soe soone
> As ye moores left ye stage each of
> the Apes had an inkehorne in his
> hand to blacke themselves
> To resemble ye moores and yat they might
> see to doe it exactly one of them
> had a lookinglasse. (ll. 72–80)

With whatever pigment was in the horn, the English boys mimicked the process by which professional players blacked up to transform into surrogates of the departed moors in buckram.[54] The allusion to blackface as an ink does not prioritize establishing a specific ethnicity but positioning blackness as indelible and readable—an indication of *character* whether the ink has been formed into letters or not.[55]

The buckram coats—and the coat*ing* of a black tincture—constitute an accumulation of black layers that prompts questions in an audience: is blackness clothing easily doffed to reveal an original fair skin, or would one remove one overlay only to find another? In a bravura chapter, Matthieu Chapman argues that *Revels* stages "a shift of the occupant of the black position from the religious abject of the Moor [i.e., a Muslim] onto the human abject of the black [i.e., negro]."[56] While Chapman's argument is powerful, I tend to doubt that performances of white authority maintain racial distinctions so faithfully, or that they need to do so. In my view, the masque positively revels in all the geographic, sartorial, and cosmetic possibilities of an inky complexion that whites alone can read. Although *Revels* lacks the hyper-canonicity of Shakespeare or Jonson, it powerfully displays what other early modern English plays imply: in the theatre, opportunities to read the black moor's inky constitution facilitated the emergence of a white interpretive community of varying levels of literacy. While knowledge of classical texts, geography, and natural history required a high level of literary attainment, inkface offered interpretive authority to a white English race across social differences such as class, region, and gender. Alphabetical literacy was not necessary.[57] All that was needed was cultural fluency in the significance assigned to the colors of the contemporary page—primarily black, white, and red.[58]

Clearly intrigued by the dramatic and intellectual possibilities of a readable complexion, Shakespeare made repeated use of inkface throughout his career. Shakespeare's first moor, Aaron in *Titus Andronicus* (1594), hands his pale mistress Tamora "a fatal plotted scroll" as one of his first consequential acts onstage (II.iii.47). This object with black overlaid on white becomes the emblem of their illicit contact and, eventually, its product. In far less than nine months' time, a nurse hands Aaron "a joyless, black and dismal issue" (IV.ii.66). In accordance with early modern stage convention, he would have received not an infant or even a doll but a bundle of linens.[59] In that sense, he would hold bedsheets destined to become linen rag paper, the most common writing surface of the day.[60] The nurse's language racializes textual metaphors, conflating the child's inherited color with a "stamp" or "seal" on a white page (IV.ii.69). This language suggests that the forged scroll Aaron hands off in his first speaking scene is miraculously returned to him as the undeniable product of his liaison with a white mistress.[61] Maintaining the social order of Rome requires that paternity is expressed in the legible form that Aaron's indelible black "stamp" provides.

Reversing the genders, Shakespeare revisits this nexus in *Antony and Cleopatra* (1607), in which Octavius Caesar refers to "all the unlawful issue" that the titular couple's "lust . . . / hath made between them" (III.vi.7–8). A lovesick Cleopatra calls repeatedly for "ink and paper" to write an absent Antony (I.v.65, 76). In an ironic turn, the delivery of letters has the opposite effect of the black-white copulation the missives presumably narrate and materially represent: instead of reproduction they accomplish a depopulation of Egypt's messengers (I.v.78). These love letters emblematize Cleopatra atop Antony. The historical couple's children never appear. Instead, a mass of pornographic pages is all the fruit of black (with its inky etymology) pressed into white. It should come as no surprise that, in *The Tempest,* the purported son of an Algerian and a devil, Caliban, has been so coated in blackness that no "print of goodness" can be made upon him (I.ii.352) or that the Prince of Morocco leaves Belmont without the biracial progeny he wanted to beget with Portia but with, instead, a scroll pronouncing him a gullible reader (II.vii.65–75).

Other members of Shakespeare's company also enjoyed playing at this nexus of ink and racial blackness. After severing his association with Shakespeare and the Lord Chamberlain's Men, William Kemp made a nine-day tour dancing from London to Norwich. In his dedication to Queen Elizabeth's maid of honor, he calls upon the inky associations of blackface:

> A sort of mad fellows, seeing me merrily dispos'd in a Morrice, haue so bepainted
> mee in print since my gambols began from London to Norwich, that (hauing

but an ill face before) I shall appear to the world without a face, if your fayre hand wipe not away their foule coulors. . . . In a word, your poore seruant offers the truth of his progresse and profit to your honorable view: receiue it, I beseech you, such as it is, rude and plaine; for I know your pure judgment looks as soone to see beauty in a Blackamoore, or heare smooth speech from a Stammerer, as to finde any thing but blunt mirth in a Morrice dauncer, especially such a one as Will Kemp, that hath spent his life in mad Iigges and merry iestes.[62]

It is not an accident that Kemp's fear of being designated a "Blackamoore" stems from his public performance in a dance associated with Spanish moors. The cultural historian Robert Hornback notes that a reader seems to have aided Kemp's metaphor for these character attacks by placing an ink blot over the clown's face.[63] Kemp hoped that switching venues from the stage to the print marketplace and establishing himself as an author with a powerful patron would earn him readmittance into a white corporate body.

When Kemp's successor, Robert Armin, went to press six years later with his play *The History of the Tvvo Maids of More-Clacke* (1606), he seems to have anticipated this attempt to denigrate the wit of clowns. He distinguished himself as an artificial fool—an intellectual comedian rather than one who relied on physicality—by appearing on the frontispiece with inkhorn on his hip.[64] He would not have to beg a patron to restore his fair face by clearing up his reputation. Armin would not wear ink on his face but imprint his name and work on paper in a public performance of authorship.

For dramatists and performers, ink and paper transcended their functions of conveying information and upholding rank through literary performances of deference.[65] Pages became surrogates for children, documents of sexual contact, and props for distinguishing sophisticated readers from illiterates and gulls. These page-props formed part of the aforementioned "materiality" of performances that distributed authority to those who could maintain a claim to whiteness. According to Ian Smith, the stage moor's blackness and inked pages shared a "chromatic materiality": the product of an English imagination in which "Africans figure[d] neither principally nor solely as persons but [were] construed . . . based on the shared feature of color with specific objects."[66] Blackness became a sign of subjection to interpretation.

Poets also played in this field where ink served as the etymological root and the literary destiny of blackness.[67] John Cleveland might well have taken inspiration from inkface plays of transferable blackness when he wrote a poem of racial amalgamation five years after Parliament mandated the closure of the theatres in 1642.[68] In his "A Fair Nimph Scorning a Black Boy Courting Her," the titular nymph refuses to couple with a blackamoor for fear that, even in lawful marriage, he will publicize her dishonor:

Thy ink, my paper, make me guess
Our Nuptial bed might make a presse
And in our sports, if any came,
They'll read a wanton epigram.[69]

In a poem of gratitude to Chancellor Bacon, George Herbert presents himself as a man turned black by late night reading: "Schollers Habitt & Obscurity." Appearing before Bacon transformed into "a meane & humble Blackamore," Herbert begs pardon for the poem's extended play on blackness: "Perhaps some other subiect I had tryed / But that my Inke was factious for this side."[70]

If poets employed an imaginative conceit, emerging empiricists suspected that African persons and ink might share a composition. Using his knowledge of alchemy, the Norwich physician Thomas Browne hypothesized in 1624 that a black epidermis is the result of "an atramentous condition or mixture, that is a vitriolate or copperose quality conjoyning with a terrestrious and astringent humidity, for so is *Atramentum scriptorium,* or writing Inke commonly made."[71] Browne would appear to be the source for fellow physician John Bulwer's speculation seven years later. Bulwer wrote that lighter "*Moores* might possibly become *Negroes* by receiving atramentitious impression, by the power and efficacy of imagination."[72] Although Browne seeks a purely chemical explanation and Bulwer reserves space for the legend that maternal imagination could impress a child, they employ the same figuration. To conceptualize black complexion, both require the properties of indelible ink and the ideas and practices associated with inscription and impression.

Whatever the Bible or medical treatises said about the origins of blackness, the theatre offered the only *place* in which blackened people could be dramatized as sharing physical properties with ink—a material equivalence that allowed for human being to be transformed into textual material and subjected to interpretive protocols of the page. While one historical method attempts to identify what early modern English people consciously thought, believed, or knew, I seek to be historical in another way—namely, by analyzing what white subjects *entertained,* regardless of whether another, more official, discourse corroborated the entertainment.[73] The crucial question is not whether literate early moderns (whose textual traces too often serve as the basis for speculation about common knowledge) would have avowed *belief* that black moors had ink in their bodies or on their faces. Rather, what matters is that they *enjoyed* staging a metaphor that was useful for social business related to assigning, interpreting, and removing stigma.

In defending his focus on Shakespeare's puns, the scholar Arthur Little offers a lucid formulation of the method I employ: "The real stuff of culture may be gotten at by massaging the ongoing interchange between seemingly more objective, public, and empirical signifying processes and those more insular and metonymically driven."[74] The performance of inkface both exemplifies and feeds upon the (dirty) jokes and extravagant wordplay that Little analyzes. The knowing grin of the person who gets the joke—and his fellows— constitutes a private realm deemed of no significance to the public history of race. Yet, as Kim Hall so thoroughly demonstrated, the linguistic and visual repertoires idealize social relations in ways that abet the gender and racial structures of empire.[75]

Contemporary moves to ban blackface as offensive overlook that inkface exceeded ridicule to accomplish work across the terrains of literacy, commerce, diplomacy, and sexuality, as I demonstrate throughout this book. As James Howell put it in an ode to the epistle, mastery of the page was foundational to the establishment of an international brotherhood of white men: "Letters *as* Ligaments the *World do tie, / Else all commerce and love 'twixt men would die.*"[76] While one could argue that a pan-European affiliation of whiteness had not yet been achieved, the body Howell articulates with these ligaments is unmarked and literate—key components of the imagined white community to come.[77] Although fractious and unstable, the regional, national, and imperial affiliations that a scholar might now call white racial formations aspired to a monopoly on the realm of written representation as an aid to accumulation. In the fantasy conjured by inkface, blackened figures were brought under the jurisdiction of alphabetical and numerical operations. Being characters themselves, they failed to master the operations of character—that is, they could not decipher signs placed before them nor make their own textualized bodies unreadable to authorities.[78] Overwritten or functionally illiterate—and sometimes both—blackened characters were portrayed as incapable of mastering alphanumerical characters—or their own characters—in the very centuries in which free white citizens used literacy, numeracy, and self-fashioning to redistribute the privileges of the aristocracy downward to unpropertied white men but not outward to the rest of the disenfranchised.[79]

Racial Difference and the Capacity for Legitimate Knowledge

I have coined the term *inkface* to draw attention to blackface as it appeared in England's earliest professional theatres of the late sixteenth and early seventeenth centuries. Inkface allowed the English to constitute and circumscribe black/moorish personhood by staging racially stratified scenarios of virtuosic and inept handling of characters alphanumerical and dramatic. Before the racial categories of high scientific racism were elaborated in the late eighteenth century, a functional white racial community was being forged through the shared exercise of interpretive authority over inky black figures. The stage offered a place in which control over symbols and their interpretation could be celebrated as if it were already a fait accompli, rather than a tense, ongoing battle.[80] Blackened characters could be shown as at once the ground of character— the bearers of a transferable, stigmatizing ink—and as incompetent assessors of character whether alphabetical, theatrical, numerical, or metaphysical.

In watching these errors, a white audience riven by hierarchies of status, ethnicity, and gender could assemble and regulate a community based on what the sociologist Étienne Balibar identifies as a narrow "linguistic . . . competence" that becomes an indicator of "a specific family origin and an hereditary disposition."[81] Balibar helps to illuminate that a presumed mastery of character in its written or dramatic form has been a precondition of inclusion in a white racial community. This maldistribution of capacities of interpretation and impersonation endows Europeans with a "flexible positional superiority" that Edward Said identifies as a crucial element of that Eurocentric discourse of Orientalism.[82] The prohibition of blackface Othellos has been undertaken in the name of sensitivity to Black people, but it serves to maintain the epistemic injustice that early modern blackface presumed and propagated—a distinction between persons treated as reading material and persons who claim dominion over the entire sphere of interpretation.[83]

The blackness operating in these performances is unconcerned with any rigid distinction between race and religion, race and class, or race and gender as social categories. Rather, inkfaced figures permitted audiences to make an *epistemological* distinction between those who could, at least potentially, master character and an elastic category of blackened people—American indigenes, sub-Saharan Africans, Muslims, and disreputable Europeans—deemed both eminently readable and laughably media illiterate.[84] By the nineteenth century, when the negro dialect we now associate with blackface was cemented, explicit dramatizations of reading and of imprinting had become optional. Yet, inkface became even more powerful as a dead metaphor, as blackened peoples' racialized incapacity for text and other mediations of urban life became an assumption that did not require explicit staging. Embodying textuality but performing illiteracy, the inkfaced moors of the seventeenth century laid the groundwork for babblers and spendthrifts, the foolish blackface minstrels of the nineteenth century.[85] The precondition of black rapists, welfare queens, Zip Coons, and so-called race hustlers is, arguably, the inkfaced stage moor who has always already been drawn outside the circle of those who may credibly establish value or testify to injury.

The philosopher Miranda Fricker offers the term "epistemic injustice" to encompass projects designed to maldistribute credibility or willfully impoverish common language, so that certain injuries, lacking a name, cannot be addressed.[86] Like any social hierarchy, racial order cannot survive without a necessary mechanism for failing to conceive of injury and dismissing the victim who speaks (of) it. The epistemic injustice perpetrated through blackface persists to this day, when racialized subordinates remain the seen and not the seers—especially when what we have witnessed threatens to disrupt official business.[87]

Why Inkface Matters Now

The cultural history of inkface performance matters now because it offers an account of the materials of race-making—one needed to supplement the intellectual histories of the race-*concept* in law, science, and philosophy.[88] If histories of racist ideas had grasped racial authority by the root, then the discrediting of scientific racism and the dismantling of legal apartheid in the twentieth century should have terminated the mechanisms of social maldistribution that attend racial hierarchy. These admirable, painstaking efforts have not uprooted racism precisely because they miss that an *epistemological* divide between knowers and known must be established before legislators and experts can systematically articulate a category called "race."[89] Each elaboration of racial character—or any other kind of character—presupposes that a so-called expert already has possession of the (symbolically freighted) materials and interpretive protocols necessary to articulate the content and parameters of the category. Every articulation of character—fixed or mutable, inherited or acquired, physical or cultural—relies on a prior accumulation of interpretive authority. Both forerunner and constant helpmeet, epistemic injustice lies at the concealed and protected core of social inequality. It is a quotidian element of racialized society that is rarely treated by academics outside philosophy and has never been undertaken as a systematic social project.[90]

In part because there has been no broadscale attempt to address racism as an epistemic injustice, the great majority of us sit befuddled at the refusal of a postracial age to arrive. The fledgling candidacy of Democratic candidate Barack Obama bore the affective weight of this desire to declare *the race problem* resolved. His 2008 victory was hailed both within the United States and internationally as portending a new day of equality at the global level. With the insights of the Human Genome Project, the precepts of race-neutral law, and a white populace both chastened and enlightened, many believed individual merit could finally be perceived in a body racialized as black. Through diligent efforts of scientists, scholars, and activists, legal and scientific racism had been defeated. Private misconceptions and malice were sure to follow. The shining example of the smooth, accomplished president of the United States seemed to herald an epoch in which people could finally be assessed without the distortion of racial bias. Obama himself encouraged people to see his election as the fulfillment of Dr. Martin Luther King's widely repeated wish: "I have a dream that my four little children will one day live in a nation where they will not be judged by the color of their skin, but by the content of their character."[91]

The content of their character. Here, in a phrase, is the horizon of the postracial dream: a millennial jubilee when the error or prejudice of racial generalization will be left behind and individual merit will emerge as the sole and legitimate means of social judgment.[92] Yet, the shift from the character of a group to that of a single person does not undermine white interpretive authority. Instead, it permits those who control the means of legitimate representation to slide from the exceptional to the typical. Such slippage is evident in the telling definition of character, offered in the OED: "The sum of the moral and mental qualities which distinguish an individual *or a people, viewed as a homogeneous whole.*"[93] The racial type is an appositive of the individual in this definition, showing their uneasy relationship in character determinations. The practice of characterization includes determining both the singular and the prototypical—the instance that is like no others and the one that is like all of its kind.[94] The authority to establish both equivalence and distinction facilitates both instantaneous exchange and social reproduction across time. Hence, racial essentialism proves compatible with both capitalism's mercurial exchange-value and scientific nomenclature, with its pretenses of transhistorical permanence. In the end, the business of character oscillates from collectives to single persons—and from exemplars to exceptions—always authorizing both typification and individuation.

The project of redeeming character from its entanglement with a global project of white supremacy has proceeded through refined legal and scientific terminology, as well as prohibitions against hate speech and generalizations.[95] Yet, this attempt to rescue character from color relies on suppression of cultural memory that the conceit of peoples with their character written upon them fueled the epistemic injustice that sustains the social hierarchy of race. Many indicators signaled character; color was only one of its signifiers. Character could be conveyed as easily by religious practice, economic system, sexual and marital practices, or speech—the wide array of self-management techniques Patricia Akhimie classifies as conduct.[96] The most important function of race discourse has *not* been to fix meaning to the skin color of the target but rather to secure the propositions that metaphysical character exists and that Europe's alphanumeric system is the means for accessing it. Acquiring a monopoly on the means of symbolic representation precedes and enables the forms of racial naming in law and science that have been confused for the origin of racial hierarchy.[97] *Inkface* offers an opportunity to grasp the problem at this cultural root, before it is concealed in the rush to save Shakespeare and the West by prohibiting blackface.

Propositions and Provocations

This book contains 250 years of battles about what constitutes a mark and by what procedures such marks could be assessed. It is an episodic history of literacy, sociality, and capitalism in their mutually productive relationships with the material cultures of reading, writing, and performance. It is a history of Anglophone white interpretive community and its attempts to determine social status, economic value, and textual meaning in ways that would serve an imperial maldistribution of property, pleasure, and protection. Inkface inheres in practices of performance and interpretation across imperial geography. Therefore, the book spans time, genre, and space. I have chosen case studies that flout the geographic and temporal boundaries that separate early modern (British) studies from early American studies to demonstrate a continuity that persists despite change: the attempt to maintain a monopoly on the means of representation via the racialized semiotics of inkface.[98]

The texts of Greek and Roman antiquity bequeathed early modern Britons a troubling schema for dividing the free from barbarous slaves, with somatic, cultural, and metaphysical aspects.[99] Their system was triangular, with those of the northern Mediterranean at the apex while paler northern Europeans and darker Africans occupied the base. These lower designations were distinguished by skin tone and, often, by their practice of body art—tattooing—which became the basis of the Greek mark *stigma,* an indicator of enslaveability.[100] Pan-ethnic affiliations within Europe—white coalitions of national or transnational scale—emerged from reconfigurations of the classical map of civility and slavish barbarism, which entailed a redistribution of stigma. The new poetic geography served as an early pan-ethnic accord, transforming peoples that had suffered under the Roman yoke of slavery (such as those in England) into inheritors of Rome's imperial prowess.[101] At the same time, while practices of tattooing and branding continued in Atlantic slavery, an array of cultural practices were deployed to conjure an aura of stigma that would hover over those designated black.

The scholars Barbara Fields and Karen Fields refer to this collective conjuration as racecraft, which encompasses "what goes with what and whom (sumptuary codes), how different people must deal with each other (rituals of deference and dominance), where human kinship begins and ends (blood) and how [members of one community] look at themselves and each other (the gaze)."[102] As the Fields sisters make clear, racial stigma can be envisioned even when it is neither epidermal nor anatomical. The "stamp" of inferiority, which supplies the title of Ibram Kendi's celebrated history of racist ideas, was not always merely a figure of speech. Near the turn of the seventeenth century, the stamping of an elastic category of blacks was a theatrical preoccupation. The specific conceit of inking Africans receded after successful repetition made racial stigma visible even in the absence of a supplemental character mark.[103]

I turn to the broader cultural arena of inkface to pose important challenges to two common deployments of the term "ideology" in histories of race and racism. Scholars who locate the origin of race in law, philosophy, or the natural sciences treat ideology as a system of thought elaborated in a text, usually written by a political elite or a professional expert.[104] While this approach succeeds in demonstrating that written propositions about race have changed over time, it often lacks a demonstration of whether and how a broader population adopted and adhered to the particulars of expert racial discourse. The study of culture arose to provide this account. Students of culture often derive popular ideology by interpreting popular culture as a reflection or mystification of successive modes of production, forms of government, scientific epistemes, or legal precedents.[105] Though this second approach aims to center culture as the mechanism of popular embrace, its treatment of ideology as a direct response to the immediate social context risks making the study of culture redundant. The field of history would have no need for the study of literature and performance if cultural developments invariably indicate changes happening in areas thought to be more socially determining, such as law, science, or economics.[106]

A different conception of ideology, however, reveals ways in which the student of literature or theatre can enrich the historical study of racial ideology. Louis Althusser argues that ideology operates more as an immersive performance than a philosophical proof. He writes, "Where only a single subject (such and such an individual) is concerned, the existence of the ideas of his belief is material in that *his ideas are his material actions inserted into material practices governed by material rituals which are themselves defined by the material ideological apparatus from which derive the ideas of that subject.*"[107] Althusser's conception is particularly helpful in accessing the ways in which ideology operates more as lived performance than systematic text. If, according to his dictum, "ideology represents the imaginary relationship of individuals to their real conditions of existence," then it accomplishes this representation through compelled, repeated action.[108]

From Althusser's formulation, it follows that ideology is not necessarily an elaborated system of thought, the historical development of which can be traced in successive legal pronouncements or scientific paradigms. In addition, if ideology is an *imaginary* relationship, one could argue that it is not a mere reflection but, rather, a virtual reality acculturated persons inhabit together.

Slavoj Žižek describes the encompassing nature of such ideological fantasies. "The function of ideology," he writes, "is not to offer us a point of escape from our reality but to offer us the social reality itself as [an] escape" from "'antagonism,' a traumatic social division that cannot be symbolized."[109] Or, in Raymond Williams's terms, aesthetic forms and conventions are "a true and integral element" of the construction of a society, which is not "completed . . . before the cultural practice begins."[110] If ideology does not stand apart from social reality but constitutes it, then the material stuff of racial ideology would not have its origin in a series of self-conscious attempts to define race *ex situ*. Rather, it would be found in the everyday performance of ritualized activities that assume and perpetuate imaginary relationships with racialized characters—the hands-on management of consumption, deference, kinship, and looking that the Fields sisters enumerated.

The recurrence of racial ideology's manufactured characters suggests that they were not anchored in or restricted to the periods or regions that demarcate traditional scholarly areas of specialization. Yet, acknowledging the reproduction of these figures does not suggest that they have an eternal existence outside history. Instead, it invites a historical account of the vehicles and occasions of their revival. As vehicles of ideology, the alphabet and stock theatrical characters change, albeit at their own pace; and occasions for fantasy have been as fleeting as a single night at the theatre and as durable as the long careers of slavery and settler colonialism.[111] Therefore, it would be inaccurate to map a media history or the rituals of social relationships onto a timeline punctuated by changes in law, science, or economic production. As a ritual that literalized the overwriting of bodies and naturalized the maldistribution of epistemological authority, inkface met the ideological needs of a white interpretive community.

Inkface fueled an ideological fantasy by facilitating a characterology of the invisible. The utility of this metaphor, in which human character appears in readable form, does not diminish over the two and a half centuries I cover. These framings persisted—despite the emergence of the United States or scientists' gradual abandonment of climate theory for bioracism—because the underlying premise was essential for reproducing social exchanges and hierarchies. Unequal distribution of property, pleasure, and protection could not be maintained or justified unless the beneficiaries asserted sole control of the mechanisms of economic and moral assessment. They had to insist on transcendent knowledge of the value of things and the essence of justice.

With its own form of embodied character and its capacity to bridge the written and the unspoken, theatre was a fitting location to enact racial ideology. I would add that this ideology might be conceived as enduring folk racism, which rarely features in scholarship focused on the intellectual history of race. However, the presuppositions of this racial habitus or disposition undergird the laws and treatises that intellectual historians consult. Inkface furnishes the sine qua non of a racial epistemology: selected objects—including human persons—made signifying figures available to another's protocols of valuation and interpretation. As such, insubstantial or anticipated qualities—such as culture, motivations, market price, capacities—become subject to calculation and assessment as they are translated into the symbols of an alphanumeric system that benefits imperial accumulation.[112] Of course, the people translated into nonsentient bearers of meaning and value—walking, breathing characters—possessed ethical and evaluative systems that Europeans dismissed, effaced, and overwrote. The repetition of these processes of ascription and discrediting makes the inkfaced moor a site where the imperatives of racial capitalism, sexual reproduction, and social reproduction converge. With these imperatives in mind, I offer four propositions on the functions of the stage moor:

1. By bearing black complexion as an overlay of ink, the stage moor serves as a moor, indeed—a referential tether, the place where textual system and human body meet. It is in this sense that the moor is a monster, which medieval encyclopedias defined as "Monstra vero a monitu dicta, quod aliquid significando domstrent, sive quod statim monstrent quid appareat" (Monsters, in fact, are so called as warnings, because they explain something of meaning, or because they make known at once what is to become visible).[113] The monster de-*monstrates;* its purpose is to show. The key aspect of the monster is that it is sign, warning, omen; it is an impetus to read, to probe for a meaning intimated but not directly revealed by what is already visible.

2. Specifically, the stage moor bears a *stigma,* that is the dishonorable mark of enslaveable persons.[114] This external mark, of course, is a token of the crucial difference of soul or capacity. The imposed tattoo facilitated the creation of vulnerable and deprived people since at least the time of Aristotle while also revealing that these differences had no origin in the spirit or constitution of the enslaved.[115]

3. When stage moors are painted, they can convey dishonor to their fair-skinned lovers, transforming the shame of captivity into that of sexual exposure. In this fated transfer, racial slavery and gendered reputation are organized not by precedence but by endless conversions of one into the other.

4. Finally, the stage moor performs an incapacity for the media forms of the modern, urban economy. Textual materials typically befuddle stage moors, as do any objects treated as analogous, such as their inky

faces or the marked faces of their lovers. In addition, this inability to distinguish inherent value from appearance was extended from textual materials to commodities and to theatrical performance. Whether expressed in interactions with text, performance, or commodities, inkfaced people commit *visual errors,* born of a hopeless literalism that takes appearance for essence.[116]

These forces combine to produce and maintain a white interpretive community, one drawn together not by internal cohesion or even orthodoxy of belief but by presumed co-possession of privileged interpretive protocols. The term "character" encompasses the object and the end of this interpretive activity, while the assignation of ink to certain faces distributes the power to know unevenly, as a precursor to a justifiable maldistribution of material necessities.[117]

Structure of the Book

What kinds of simulations does this conception of blackface as telltale stain or alphanumeric inscription allow the playwright and audience regarding the origin, permanence, and legibility of blackened character? This is the fundamental question that animates *Inkface,* in which I compile case studies from a disremembered history of *Othello* as a play that summoned a white interpretive community. *Inkface* is divided into three parts. In the first part, I imaginatively reconstruct *The Moor of Venice,* the name by which most seventeenth-century viewers referred to stage productions of the play. I argue that the particularities of these early performances have been occluded by scholars' and performers' reliance on the print edition of *Othello,* itself a product of editors' pruning of Shakespearean text. Escaping the editorial tradition's preoccupation with the plausibility of *Othello,* I explore an unrealistic play.[118] One of the first fruits of this approach is a new understanding of Othello's blackness as indicative not of a specific ethnicity but of an inky constitution. Establishing ink as Othello's essence and its expression establishes him as the object of a white interpretive community extending from the white cast onstage to the broader audience. Subsequent chapters consider the ways in which this volatile interpretive community fashioned a somewhat flexible sense of whiteness to regulate its membership in a period in which subjected Europeans reconfigured hierarchies of sex and birth to allow for their own upward mobility while severely restricting that of racial subordinates.

In chapters 2 through 5, I reconsider episodes in *Othello*'s first 250 years in the Atlantic World, revealing a play through which white audience members attempted to join a selective interpretive community keen to dismiss the testimony of those who employed dissident sign systems or reached forbidden conclusions. In assembling rich cases ranging across traditional historical periods, I aim to show that the desire to maintain a monopoly on interpretive authority remains the defining end of racial characterization across historical breaks such as national founding, shifting legal premises, and emerging scientific paradigms. Beneath these elite and expert maneuverings, the potent metaphor of the face as a readable object—exemplified by inkfaced characters—persisted as a sort of folk knowledge available at all strata of white society.

Although race, gender, and rank are concerns throughout the book, I have arranged the chapters in pairs rather than chronologically. This structure allows me to bracket the familiar straightforward narratives of great transitions in race thinking: from climate to biology, flexibility to rigidity, religion to science. Instead, my pairings reveal the recurrence of the struggles to produce and maintain authority over the interpretation of character, especially as it plays out in the assessment of women's sexual honor and white men's urgent attempts to maintain interpretive authority.

Part 2 contains two chapters involving Anglo women struggling to escape offstage versions of dilemmas Desdemona faces onstage, including the fact that she does not own her sexuality or her reputation and cannot speak on her own behalf. While Aphra Behn attempts to solve these problems by inventing a black Desdemona in her 1688 novella "Oroonoko," a century later the actress Sarah Siddons and US Founding Mother Abigail Adams instead endeavor to maintain a stainless whiteness in the 1780s. These chapters reveal continuities and departures in the maneuvers made by white women confronting their position as subject to white male characterization. Rather than being a function of legal or scientific racism, their tactics come from the materials afforded by different media, such as theatre, printed books, and familiar epistles—and the audiences summoned to each of them.

Part 3 features the textual and theatrical machinations of white male brothers who strain to maintain a monopoly on interpretation in the face of challenges that expose the impossibility of the endeavor. In the fourth chapter, I use an interrupted performance of *Othello* in colonial Virginia to detail a transatlantic attempt to portray Cherokees as media illiterates, as well as the Cherokees' efforts to assert alternate means of interpretation and bases for diplomacy. In the final chapter, *Othello* is brought to crisis in the wake of the Haitian Revolution and on the eve of the U.S. Civil War, as Herman Melville imagines a white fraternity sentenced to muteness by a mutinous African captive. Melville's Senegalese mastermind exploits the fact that, for Euro-American literary cultures, blackness is the color of legibility. When he forces them to read *white* character—written in chalk instead of black ink—the possibilities for white male interpretive community, and indeed for a government founded upon it, disintegrate. I end with Melville's novella not because it is the last time in history that the figure of inkface was deployed in relation to *Othello*. Rather, Melville's fiction arrives at the conceptual (though not historical) conclusion of the relations of inkface, revealing white interpretive mastery as always an inverted power relation, in which all signifying power resides with blackness, and whiteness is comparatively vulnerable, imprintable, and mute. Although his story is not as much a championing of the African mutineer as some literary critics have contended, Melville's attempt to make whiteness the object of scrutiny, without the aid of figurative blackness or African illiteracy to provide moorings for assessments of character, remains the challenge before us today.

Throughout the project, I am interested in aspects of the performance and reception of *Othello* that do not adhere to the legal codes and scientific paradigms mistaken for the origin and engine of racial hierarchy. As these cases indicate, actors and audiences did not follow the rules of archival fidelity and cartographic accuracy that have constrained academic inquiry. For precisely this reason, their socially efficacious behavior offers glimpses of racecraft as practiced by everyday folk. At the folk level, Othello and Desdemona functioned as object lessons in the promise and peril of the technology of character—as the name for both a domain of invisible essences and the representational system of alphanumeric marks. In the first centuries of an Atlantic economy, the motley members of a white interpretive community in fitful emergence were fighting about whether and how economic exchange and social relationships should—or should not be—governed by the page.[119] This contest becomes visible when scholars view Othello and Desdemona not as a realistic couple but as a fantasy of the marriage of ink and paper twisted into a terrifying nightmare of textual indeterminacy.

❧ Part I

The Moor of Venice Reconstructed

❧ 1

"O Bloody Period"
Reconsidering Othello's Constitution and Iago's Motive

The controversy of Othello's precise ethnicity—an attempt to specify what Eldred Jones called "Othello's countrymen"—began at the end of the seventeenth century and has proceeded along false premises to the present.[1] To pinpoint the identity of "the Moor of Venice," generations of scholars have dutifully pored over dictionaries, maps, medical treatises, and travel literature, a textual archive that they hope will situate stage moors within the "historical linguistic context" of seventeenth-century England.[2] Yet, they have never been able to establish that audiences clamored for the makers of theatre to bring the moor of ethnographers and lexicographers to life—or that available theatre technologies were capable of faithfully reproducing what these authorities wrote.[3] Genre, mode, and medium exert a meaningful force: race is functionally different depending on the materials through which it is expressed and attendant interpretive protocols.

In the introduction, I argued that blackface performance in the first professional theatres of London owed more to a deep cultural association of blackness and ink than to systems of human variety being worked out by ethnologists. From that premise, the fact that English stage moors share no single, consistent homeland means that they cannot be found solely by pinpointing the precise referents of terms such as Turk, Moor, or Saracen. For the same reason, attempts to map Othello onto historical personages—Abd el-Ouahed ben Messaoud ben Mohammed Anoun (the Moroccan emissary to Elizabeth I), Trayvon Martin, Tamir Rice, and even O. J. Simpson—founder on Othello's purely fictional origins.[4] Neither the archival realism of New Historicists nor the psychological realism of Stanislavski's acting method leads to the source of the earliest Othellos. A serious consideration of the materiality of *Othello* in performance offers an escape from the various realisms that bar access to the black stage moor's origins in inkface, the cultural zone in which blackface performance and the conventions of reading intersect. As I will demonstrate in this chapter and the interlude that follows, this approach also recovers perhaps deliberately buried understandings of Iago's motive and Desdemona's voice.

Attending to the stickiness and significance of inkface illuminates both familiar and forgotten moments in *Othello*'s cultural career. I return here to Isaac Jackman's *All the World's a Stage* (1777), which I mentioned briefly in the introduction. Jackman's burlesque follows the plot of two urban scoundrels who seek to wed themselves to wealthy heiresses. The occasion of this fortune hunting is the staging of a play at a country estate; the men woo the ladies by suggesting they rehearse various scenes that will allow the men to say self-aggrandizing things and, perhaps, to kiss the women. This premise allows Jackman to place dialogue from Shakespeare and other crowd-pleasers of the eighteenth-century London stage in the mouths of these confidence men.

Othello proves a particularly helpful resource in their attempts to seduce. A spate of unattributed allusions culminates in a monologue about a rehearsal of the signature scene of Othello's smothering Desdemona.[5] One of the eligible ladies, Kitty Sprightly, explains that she has been entertaining herself after dinner by having a servant perform "the speech where the blackamoor smothers his wife."[6] The servant makes an impression as Othello: "He was black as old Harry, that's certain. He had black'd all his face with soot and goose dripping. . . . When [the servant] Cymon kissed me in bed, he blacked my left cheek so abominably, that when I came down to breakfast in the morning, the family were all frightened out of their wits. . . . I told them the whole story. And do you know, that I am locked in my room every night since."[7] Jackman could make such farcical fun out of Othello's communicable tint because cast and spectators experienced stage blackness not as an inert indicator of racial identity but as a material substance known to spread. Jackman could expect laughter at this image—described but not presented—because the sight was not novel. Audiences of *Othello* would seem to have come to expect it.[8]

The stain on Kitty's cheek exemplifies the reason that I refer to blackface as *inkface* throughout this book. While the servant plays Othello in a homemade black paint, blackface does significant work here beyond demeaning Black people. Ultimately, this paint is important for its meaningfulness. Soot and goose grease function as an ink, a black residue that prompts interpretation and oral performance.[9] In this case, it spawns two narratives: one Kitty's family infers from the telltale imprint of kissing lips and then the corrective she offers (i.e., "I told them the whole story"). The subjects of my subsequent chapters—Aphra Behn, Abigail Adams, colonial American governors, Cherokee diplomats, and Herman Melville—would have caught this metatheatrical joke. They, too, saw blackface as inkface: a deeply significant transferred impression.

From scenery to the casting of women instead of boy actors, Shakespearean performance changed significantly from the 1590s to this late eighteenth-century spoof. However, the use of blackface for moors remained consistent, as did the impetus to read blackness as a mark of character. The stability of the cosmetic conventions allows for some intelligent speculation about the seventeenth-century *Othello* that bequeathed inkfaced moors to the eighteenth century.

The Dyeing Moor of Venice

In the final moments of *Othello,* the eponymous moor moves toward the beloved wife he murdered on suspicion of her infidelity and says, "I kissed thee ere I killed thee, no way but this / Killing myself to *dye* upon a kiss."[10] This suggestive pun is memorialized in the Second Quarto (Q2) of *Othello,* printed in 1630. "Dye" would not seem to be a mere variant of "die," since Q2 distinguishes "to dye upon a kiss" from the italicized stage direction "*he dies*" printed on the same line. The invocation of dyeing draws attention to stagecraft that readers now miss when modern editions supply "to *die* upon a kiss" as the unmistakable and definitive words accompanying the suicidal general's last utterance. Under original performance conditions, audiences could have heard and envisioned that Othello's final act was not only to die (expire) but also, while doing so, to dye (stain) Desdemona with his kiss.[11] Unlike a Moroccan ambassador to Queen Elizabeth's court in 1600 or a towering African American actor committed to eradicating the color line in the second quarter of the twentieth century, the Renaissance stage moor had this unique capacity to mark, conveyed in a macabre pun on dye.[12]

In a rare audience reaction to early seventeenth-century blackface, an audience member demonstrated awareness of the potential for color transfer. The nobleman and diplomat Dudley Carleton attended *The Masque of Blackness,* which Queen Anna commissioned from Ben Jonson for the Twelfth Night festivities of 1604. He admired the sumptuous costumes of the queen and eleven other ladies painted as Moors while registering a lingering unease: "Their appearance *was rich,* but too light and courtesan-like for such great ones. Instead of visors, their faces and arms, up to the elbows, were painted black, which was disguise sufficient, for they were hard to be known; but it became them nothing so well as their own red and white; and you can not imagine a more *ugly* sight than a troop of lean-checked Moors." Beyond what he could see beneath diaphanous clothing (likely the queen's pregnancy), he was concerned with the physical interactions between the ladies and the male guests. He watched a Spanish ambassador who "took out the Queen [for a customary dance], and forgot not to kiss her hand, though there was danger it would have left a mark on his lips."[13]

In anticipating the spread of dark makeup through the vehicle of a kiss, Carleton occupies the position of a viewer of *Othello,* which debuted eleven months later. The pun in "to dye upon a kiss" would prompt an audience member to envision the imprint of Othello's lips on Desdemona's face, even if the audience member could not see a stain or the actor's makeup did not rub off. When his destination was this dyeing kiss, Othello's blackness referred more to a dramatic function than to a discrete ethnoracial identity and attendant consciousness. No living moor—black, white, or tawny—could make such an impression; neither could the medieval Vice figure, whose blackness was usually achieved with a vizard.[14] The material properties of paint offered unique affordances that include but exceed the concerns of scholars who compare the morality and spirituality of stage figures who appear in black onstage. As scholars of cosmetics and stage paint have shown, this particular prosthetic demands a distinctive approach.[15] The theatrical creation of the early modern English stage blackamoor is sui generis, "a body," as Gwendolyn Brooks once wrote,

> like no other
> On any hill or plain or crawling cot
> Or gentle for the lillyless hasty pall.[16]

This stage moor was the product of a very particular convention in England's early professional theatres. Therefore, care should be taken not to conflate it with depictions of Africans in travel literature, with blackface achieved with cloth or vizards, or with blackface personages whose coloring is not a prompt for reading. From the late sixteenth century, theatre companies restaged scenarios in which black paint worked as a readable sign of character, both for the moor covered in it and for the moor's lovers, who receive it. These staged simulations in which insubstantial qualities become both external and legible summon an implicitly white audience to exercise authority as potential readers of inward character rendered visible and legible.[17] The whiteness of this interpretive community is less a function of a single, shared ethnicity than of an assumed epistemic advantage over an elastic category of blackened people. The spectacle of transferable blackface allowed the staging of scenarios that fulfilled or unraveled dreams that the elusive character of wives, servants, and strangers might be translated into the visible and rationalized realm of alphanumerical character, where it could be subjected to imperial geography, demography, jurisprudence, and economics.[18]

Alphanumeric characters enter here because the mark on Desdemona is not represented as an amorphous stain. As I demonstrate later in this chapter, the phrase "to dye upon a kiss" suggests a circular impression that, especially because of its blackness, constellates with the letter *O*, the numeral zero, and the end stop of punctuation, the period. Scholars have remarked on

Shakespeare's obsessions with these circular symbols in plays such as *Henry V,* *King Lear,* and *Twelfth Night.*[19] These recur with particular intensity in *Othello,* in which the circular mark potentially serves an additional purpose. Rather than simply providing a geographic origin or aligning the titular moor with the devil, the residue of this kiss serves perhaps as Othello's signature mark, his initial.[20] Catholics are reminded on Ash Wednesday that humans are dust and will return to it. Othello bears out his origins in another register, a man who originated in ink and leaves only ink behind. It is no wonder that after he stabs himself, an onlooker screams, "O bloody period!" The blackface Othello is not only covered in ink but suffused with it—so much so that he bleeds punctuation.

The *Othello* I am proposing may strike my readers as preposterous, but I prefer to think of it as disremembered stage history. Scholarship, schooling, performance tradition, and popular allusions deliver audiences to *Othello* confident that we know the story. We have been primed to expect the tragedy in which an interracial couple is doomed by racism that pervades their society and even their own psyches; or, alternately, the one in which the racial subordination is incidental, and the couple is, instead, haunted by the monster of unfounded jealousy. Whether or not they think racism is the prime engine of the characters' downfall, theatregoers who have any information at all arrive expecting to see plausible human beings on stage confronting recognizable social and psychological obstacles.

The bed and the handkerchief—recurring objects artists and publishers have used as *Othello's* emblems throughout the centuries—encourage this presumption of realistic characterization. The bed focuses interest on Desdemona's honor, Othello's capacity for violence, and the couple's potential offspring, whom her father fears will take seats in the Venetian government. The plot turns on the handkerchief, a gift from Othello to Desdemona that he suspects she has given to a new lover. Yet, paper recurs more often during the play's duration than the bed or the handkerchief, which unsettles the solemn realism with which some believe Shakespearean tragedy must be approached.

Momentum stalls on three different occasions for characters to scrutinize paper. In act 1, the senators compare urgent oral and written messages from the war front of Cyprus. Later, in act 4, Othello receives, kisses, and then reads a missive from Venice that enrages him. Onlookers speculate about the letter's effect on his temperament. Finally, in act 5, the revelation of Iago's murderous plots comes from not one or two but *three* letters produced from his dead co-conspirator's pocket. In addition to these moments of onstage reading, literary metaphors abound for nontextual materials. The handkerchief Othello gives Desdemona as a love token is first the property of an Egyptian charmer who "could almost read / the thoughts of people" (III.iv.57–58). Othello calls Desdemona's face a "goodly book" but perceives that "whore" has been scrawled upon it (IV.ii.71–72).[21] Iago suggests that the scene of Cassio kissing Desdemona's hand is "an index and obscure prologue / to the history of lust and foul thoughts" (II.i.257–58). Illustrators, directors, and scholars have focused on the conjugal bed and the purloined handkerchief, a visual legacy that has obscured the page, one of *Othello*'s prominent motifs and props.

As a corollary to my contention that early modern theatre mobilized a specific form of blackface best understood as *inkface,* I would also propose that seventeenth-century performances of *Othello* need to be distinguished from the increasingly sanitized performance and print traditions of the following centuries. In a 2016 essay, Gerald Baker finds historical evidence for precisely such a distinction: From its premiere in 1604 until the late 1680s, "what people *read* was [*The Tragedy of*] *Othello,* but what they *saw* was *The Moor of Venice.*"[22] Baker argues that, by designating a genre and featuring the moor's proper name, the print title tips readerly expectations away from the absurd humor of the play in performance toward contemplation of a grand tragedy with a psychologically complex protagonist at its center. Inspired by his suggestion that *The Moor of Venice* potentially provides its audience a substantively different experience, I will employ this forgotten title to imaginatively re-create seventeenth-century performances. *The Moor of Venice* invites an attempt to reconstruct a play not overdetermined by its hero's name—a play of puns and props, in which the doomed couple at the center is mediated through the materiality and metaphorical significance of ink and paper.

To accept the page as an emblem of *The Moor of Venice* is to grasp a performance of dramatic character in its textual form, a story that does not involve psychologically credible people but instead enacts the conditions of legibility that establish the authority of a fraternity of white male interpreters. In its time, *The Moor of Venice* unfurled a dream about the infallibility of ink and paper as instruments for assessing human character—a wish that Iago turns into a nightmare of indecipherability. It is the kind of dream that an insular, patrilineal society could stage as a sort of inoculation, a rehearsal for what happens when character becomes illegible and, consequently, social reproduction becomes imperiled. Of all the parts available in the dramatic repertoire, only an ink-faced moor and a paper-based ingenue had the properties required.

To consider that *The Moor of Venice* once staged the potential of using techniques borrowed from writing culture to assess people opens the historical imagination. Our modern *Othello* is, in many ways, an absurd play made plausible by successive changes that cumulatively established realism as the end of performance: casting women instead of boys to play the female parts in the Restoration, employing a lighter brown makeup to specify that moor referred only to North Africans, assigning the role to Black men in the latter half of the twentieth century.[23] The pursuit of ethnographic accuracy and insistence upon the identity of actors and roles have transposed the play into a register of social and psychological realism that would not necessarily have been the presiding ethos under original conditions, including a performance title in which Othello is unnamed. The scholar John Bernard's observations resonate with this impulse. He argues that "the action transcends the represented character, Othello, and embraces the representing theatrical apparatus itself, that is, the entire panoply of production, including the audience, that constitutes the play's ultimate interpretive authority."[24] Decentering Othello's name makes a world of difference. In place of an exposé of women's psyches under patriarchy or Black men's under white supremacy, the play becomes a potential exploration of the political unconscious of white men who entrusted the reproduction of social relations to the legibility of "character." Although the rest of *Inkface* will be dedicated to that white fraternity and those anxious to join it, for now I want to focus on the fundamental distinction between white interpreters and textualized blackness. This distinction was enabled by Othello's reduction to ink, the essential racializing act of *The Moor of Venice*.

Othello's Constitution and Significance

In Aleppo *Once*

Before Othello kills himself, Venetian agents strip him of his sword, relieve him of command, and place him under arrest. Distraught at his own infidelity, the moor responds by usurping the state's role and executing himself. While the emissary Lodovico utters the rueful summation "O bloody period," Othello's successor, Cassio, is puzzled. The Florentine who will assume leadership of Venice's forces remarks of the suicide: "This did I fear, *but thought he had no weapon*" (V.iii.422, my emphasis). Given the attempts to prevent this precise outcome, how does Othello manage to kill himself and with what instrument?

Centuries of actors' and directors' invented solutions screen a clear view of how the suicide might have been handled in the earliest performances. Yet, the recurrence of literary paraphernalia and metaphors suggests that the coincidence of Othello's blood and a mark of punctuation may reveal the mysterious weapon.[25] The moor is portrayed as consanguineous with ink. One might surmise Othello's inky nature from the fact that he calls wife "fair paper, this most goodly book" (IV.ii.71–72). After all, ink is not only the proverbial partner of paper; it also "tops" it—a fact that gives another set of associations for Iago's infamous representation of Othello and Desdemona's union as a "black ram / . . . tupping [a] white ewe" (I.i.88–89).[26] However, Othello bears those associations even without his wife.

One indicator of Othello's inky nature is that the materials used to make blackface overlapped with those that produced inks. One could find peach stones, ivory, and eggs in receipts (i.e., recipes) for writing ink and face paint.[27] In addition, printers' ink and blackface share physical properties. Print was becoming the dominant form of textual production while urban professional theatre and its painted black moors were emerging. The ink required for printing was considerably heavier than that used in writing and covered ink makers in a thick coating. These stage moors might have resembled printer's devils, described later in the century by Joseph Moxon: "The Press-man sometimes has a Week-Boy to Take Sheets as they are Printed off the Tympan: These boys do in a Printing-House, commonly black and Dawb themselves; whence the Workmen do Jocosely call them *Devils*."[28] Emilia declares that Othello is "the blacker devil" after she discovers him as the murderer of Desdemona (V.ii.131). While this epithet has been discussed in terms of stereotypes of African immorality, it also potentially aligned the English actor with the printer's devil, also smeared in a stubborn black substance. The diabolical stage moor, so often remarked by scholars, should be understood not merely as a descendant of the medieval Vice figure but also as kin to the printer's devil. In the composition, connotation, and consistency of his makeup, Othello and his ilk become stage personages filled with ink and covered in it. This inky essence earns the bitter pun contained in the cry of "O bloody period" after Othello stabs himself.

The "bloody period" is arguably an apotheosis for the moor of Venice. Othello uses his final monologue to resign himself to the status of ink, to make his body the guarantee of the truth of the written representation of his story.

> Soft you, a word or two before you goe;
> I haue done the state some service and they know't:
> No more of that: I pray you in your letters,
> When you shall these vnlucky deedes relate,
> Speake of me as I am; nothing extenuate,
> Nor set downe ought in malice: then must you speake,
> Of one that lou'd not wisely, but too well:
> Of one not easily iealous, but being wrought,
> Perplext in the extreame: of one whose hand,
> Like the base *Indian,* threw a pearle away,
> Richer then all his Tribe: of one whose subdued eyes,
> Albeit vnused to the melting moode,
> Dropped teares as fast the *Arabian* trees,
> Their medicinall gum: Set you downe this;
> And say besides, that in *Aleppo* once,
> Where a Malignant and a Turband *Turke,*

Beat a *Venetian,* and traduc'd the State;
I tooke bi'th throate the circumcised dog,
And smote him thus.   *He stabs himself.*[29]

The Second Quarto's text, which I cite here, offers the sole period of this monologue at its conclusion. At this moment, the Venetian emissary Lodovico declares: "O bloody period." I have already stated that this "period" suggests that moorish blood is ink. This hypothesis is strengthened by the dead general's description of his own constitution, which contains crucial ingredients for an ink receipt.

Petrus Maria Caneparius, who gained renown as the most outstanding ink scientist of the seventeenth century, referred to gum arabic, a crucial ingredient in writing ink, as "the tears of Arabia." Caneparius devoted to inks a large part of his *De Atramentis,* a text that, incidentally, followed the fictional moor's own trajectory: first published in Venice in 1619, then imported and translated in London in 1660.[30] Caneparius's term "tears of Arabia" clearly echoes Othello's confession that he dropped *tears* "as fast as the Arabian trees their medicinall gum."[31] The existence of this term in Venice, specifically— before the translation of Shakespeare's works into Italian—suggests that Shakespeare may have employed an existing designation rather than inventing the evocative image for Othello's tears himself. In fact, gum arabic resembles mucus more than human tears. According to the ink historian William Barrow, gum oozes from a species of the acacia tree and hardens into round, yellowish white drops about the size of partridge eggs.[32] Gum arabic helps bind ink permanently to the page. Othello desires this adhesive quality. The sound and sense of his final command convey as much—an imperative in emphatic spondees: "set you down this."

Shakespeare signaled ink production again through the general's mention of Aleppo. Early modern travel writing links ink to this Syrian city. In Hakluyt's propaganda for imperial expansion, *The Principal Navigations* (1599), Arthur Edwards's entry describes Aleppo as a city "wherein continually are many Venetians dwelling, besides other that come yeerely and there buy wools, gals, tallow, saffron, skins, cotton wooll, and other wares, and great store of spices."[33] Englishmen interested in trade understood galls to be one of Aleppo's signature exports, made more desirable because Aleppo exported nut galls with acid twice as concentrated as that of galls harvested in Europe. A nineteenth-century ink manufacturer who endeavored to write the first history of ink, Thaddeus Davids, notes that this great discrepancy in quality created a demand for galls from "Persia, Mesopotamia, Syria, and Asia Minor" in the "manufactories of Europe."[34] After iron, "galls [are] the second most important ink ingredient, contain[ing] tannic and gallic acids which combine with the iron in the copperas to form a black pigment."[35] Writing ink made with Aleppo galls would become blacker over the years rather than fading or turning rusty brown as would inferior inks.[36]

In Gainsford's *The Glory of England,* another text championing commercial expansion, Aleppo serves as the site of fatal conflict over galls. *Glory* contains an anecdote about an English merchant residing in Aleppo circa 1610 who joins with a Frenchman to buy "12000 dollers" worth of galls from a Moor. According to the English source, the Moor is convinced he has been "a great gainer in the traphique" until a Turk intervenes to persuade him that the galls were weighed to his disadvantage. To satisfy an alleged hatred of Christians, the local Ottoman ruler (or Bashaw) breaks on the wheel the official who weighed the galls and sets his eye on executing both European merchants. Ostensibly revealing Ottoman character, English consul Paul Pindar averts the murder of his countryman by convincing the Bashaw to accept a fine of ten thousand silver dollars in lieu of the execution.[37] The texts of Hakluyt and Gainsford suggest that invocations of Aleppo could conjure many elements present in Othello's final monologue: ink ingredients, fraught international commerce, and interfaith battles.

In addition to their association with a deep and lasting blackness, Aleppo galls were used in tanning. As their name suggests, tannic acids were first employed to darken hides, a parallel practice that could call to mind the backstage preparations of the actor playing Othello: "[Aleppo galls] contain the vegetable astringent principle called tannin in greater abundance than any other known substance. . . . All the woods and barks employed in the manufacture of leather by the tanning of hides contain this astringent matter in various degrees."[38] Whether in tanning hides, adding script to vellum (a paper made of animal skin), or imprinting ink on the cheaper paper made from linen, Aleppo astringents were famous for their capacity to "dye"—reflected in Q2's pun.[39] In summary, Aleppo may surface in Othello's final monologue to signal the famously wandering stranger's poetical origin. At the instant when he commits his blood to serve as a period on an imperial Venetian document, he returns imaginatively to the city of galls and gum arabic.

A Pen(knife) in Othello's Throat

Through the course of *The Moor of Venice,* the page becomes not only the metaphor but also the site of reputation. That the page is the repository of, as well as the sign for, character becomes most apparent in Othello's insistence that the Venetians write his story fully and accurately with neither elaboration nor omission ("set you down this . . . nothing extenuate"). It becomes inevitable that a man who insists upon his own fidelity and accuracy could be poised to stab himself in the throat with a goose quill pen—a weapon small

enough to have gone unnoticed but (theoretically) sharp enough to successfully puncture him.

Regarding the location of the wound, evidence of the likelihood that early
Othellos stabbed themselves in the throat comes from Aphra Behn's 1688
novella "Oroonoko." In my second chapter, I argue that "Oroonoko" could
indicate that Behn not only studied Shakespeare's text but also saw *The Moor
of Venice* in performance. Consequently, her depiction of Oroonoko's suicide
may reveal early stage practice. After all, Behn was a playwright first—and
one steeped enough in the repertoire to have been accused of plagiarism.[40]
Unlike his literary model, Oroonoko does not die by suicide, declaring self-
mutilation evidence of "a sort of courage too brutal to be applauded."[41] He
does, however, engage in one moment of self-injury, at precisely the moment
that Othello does—namely, after the discovery of the wife that he has murdered. Oroonoko, tellingly, "cut[s] a piece of flesh from his own throat and
thr[ows] it at [the onloookers]."[42] At the least, Behn's novella provides a suggestion that early Othellos stabbed themselves in their throats.[43] However, I
am going to argue that, unlike Oroonoko, Othello may have employed a literary weapon and not a dagger to puncture his larynx.

The idea of literary instruments as murder weapons had enough currency
for Shakespeare to include it in the non-mimetic play *The Moor of Venice.* The
Roman historian Suetonius recounts that Julius Caesar stabbed one of his as-
sassins in the arm with a stylus. Although Shakespeare's tragedy of Caesar's
assassination would seem to follow Plutarch in omitting this detail, Jonathan
Bate has argued that Shakespeare's acting would have familiarized him with
Dio Cassius, Juvenal, and the pertinent passage in Suetonius.[44] Shakespeare
could have specifically encountered a dramatic death by penknife in *The Spanish Tragedy,* one of the theatrical sensations of the 1590s and model for his
revenge plays.[45] Given these precedents in Shakespeare's reading, acting, and
spectatorship, it is entirely possible that he wanted to experiment with his version of death by writing implement.[46] The elaborate disarming of Othello earlier in the scene, and Cassio's remark that he thought no weapons were present,
draw attention and suggest the extraordinary nature of the instrument of suicide. Before the triumph of realism that gave us white women as Desdemona,
Black men as Othello, and a motiveless Iago, audiences may have witnessed
an impossible sight: a dead black moor with a white quill protruding from his
throat as if he were a human inkwell.

The scholars who pay attention to props in *Othello* have not contemplated
the possibility of literary paraphernalia as weapons of self-injury in *The Moor
of Venice.*[47] Perhaps following the practice of more recent productions, most
now imagine Othello wielding a dagger or a small knife. However, the stage
business of Othello's locating a concealed weapon under the bed, under his

own turban, or in his jewelry has no support in written or implied action. These innovations, like that of the bronze Othello, did not become canonical until the nineteenth century.[48]

Some might object that a goose quill is too dull and brittle to puncture the throat. While true, this objection carries less weight in an *Othello* unmoored from realism. Jonathan Goldberg shows in his cultural history *Writing Matter* that during early modernity some artists depicted the quill as equal in sharpness to the penknife that hones it.[49] Moreover, early modern terms for punctuation—referred to as pointing or pricking—summon the pen's capacity to puncture.[50] Given Othello's commitment to full and faithful self-disclosure, it is fitting that he die plunging a pen in his very own larynx. This act would ensure that his voice and bloody essence would be incorporated in the text that will represent him after death.[51] It is tempting to imagine death by sharpened pen or penknife as a grim inside joke in Shakespeare's company. Perhaps this stage practice was lost from 1642 to 1660, when Parliament outlawed public stage plays. When the theatres reopened, the practice might have been forgotten or, like the boy actress, rejected. In any case, the methods of suicide invented for Othello have no firmer grounding than my pen/knife, save that they satisfy the dictates of realism.

Through the offices of inkface performance, the first audiences of *The Moor of Venice* had the opportunity to see Othello not as a realistic man but as mere material for literary production. Their response might have been divided, as that of Lodovico, the ambassador who pronounces Othello's blood a period. He issues contradictory imperatives, first to Iago and then to the rest of the embassy: "Look on the tragic loading of this bed; / This is thy work. The object poisons sight, / Let it be hid" (V.ii.363–65). Overhearing these directives voiced to Iago and the Venetian retinue, audiences receive irreconcilable instructions to look at the bloody period writ large and to avert their eyes from a poisonous sight. I would argue that Lodovico's quick order to conceal the human page initiates centuries of denial of the deeper implications of this scene.

In many ways, the use of a quill for suicide would indicate the violence underwriting *character* as a site where alphanumeric characters such as ordinal rank, actuarial value, or reference letters represent human capacity and delimit social possibilities.[52] In this respect, the moor's service exceeds the militaristic to encompass the semiotic. As an ink-filled, signifying character, Othello aims desperately to restore the transparency and efficacy of signs not for himself but for another—the Venetian state. "I must be found," he says confidently in his first appearance: "My parts, my title, and my perfect soul / Shall manifest me rightly" (I.ii.30–32). One could supply the elided prepositional phrase "manifest me rightly" *to them,* to the same audience of Venetian senators to whom all of Othello's submissions and performances are addressed.

When appearing before the Senate, he proclaims with a confidence born of guilelessness:

> That I have ta'en away this old man's daughter
> It is most true; true, I have married her:
> The very head and front of my offending
> Hath this extent, no more. (I.iii.78–81)

Summarizing seventeenth-century English lexicographers' translations of Latin rhetoricians, Bruce Smith concludes that the metaphor of the body is indispensable to explaining punctuation: "If commas are the bones of the hands and feet, if colons are thighbones, periods figure as the head."[53] Thus, Lodovico's cry of "O bloody period" could refer to Othello's wounded head, if indeed he stabbed himself in the throat as I contend. While any person has these joints that could be articulated as marks of punctuation, they take on a special resonance in the print era when a blackface character is thus represented.

In this early speech, the head appears as period, a full stop—after which, "no more." In addition, Othello emphasizes the period's circular uniformity. The "head and front" of his actions is their full "extent." One need not view the rear of his offense, for it will be identical; there is nothing other, *no more,* as he says. The head becomes a geometric figure instead of a container of thought.[54] Viewed from any angle, Othello believes his black head should display the same significance to his ultimate readers—unlike Iago, who invokes the two-faced Janus (I.ii.33). Othello's suicide is a desperate attempt to restore an easy interchangeability among speech, writing, and social identity upon which the state relies. In this regard, his vain attempt to imbue official documents with his essence indicates a failure of the state project to know and to deploy inky subjects like himself. The failure of Othello to reestablish his identity with official, written knowledge of him poses such a grave threat to the project of Western knowledge that, I will argue, literate audiences and critics have taken Lodovico's directive to "hid[e]" the sight and suppress their knowledge of it.

Reading the O in Othello

I chose the Second Quarto's rendering of Othello's suicidal monologue because its punctuation points (to) pauses in his speech, sparing any grammatical periods until the bloody conclusion. A close examination of Renaissance understandings of punctuation reveals that beyond the ink-on-paper motif, the "bloody period" has a sonic and physical impact. In a classic essay on early modern punctuation, Bruce Smith provides a relevant genealogy of the period. The period—an unvoiced but meaningful character—is an abstraction of the prick, an Anglo-Saxon word referring to that which is there, "a prick is *there*—on the page, marked with the nib of a pen, impressed with a piece of metal type." This prick calls for a pause. This older term, associated with a medieval sense of such marks as regulating the speaker's breathing, is joined by a more recent addition—the point. "Literally a punctum is a prick or a dot made on paper; figuratively it is an opening made in space or time."[55] Smith's definition of the point or punctum encapsulates the ambiguity of the self-injury in *The Moor of Venice*. In the abstract, the period is the culmination of Othello's monologue, his life, and the play's major action—a "signifying but not sounding" character.[56]

Yet, the materiality of this mark cannot be dismissed. The period can also be the circle of blood that issues from Othello, the gasping breath the player has to take before executing the violent act, the hole he gouges when he plunges the quill or penknife into his own thorax. It is the pause in the action, as players and audience respond to this turn. In *The Moor of Venice,* punctuation punctures. In this figurative world, ink and paper fuse: Desdemona becomes inked over the course of the play, and Othello becomes a page subject to pricking. The black period would seem to be the emblem of this final scene, dotting the dictation, imprinted on Desdemona's face, and gouged in Othello's throat.

Attention to this emblem allows a new view of the preponderance of O in the sound design and typography of *Othello* observed by the psychoanalytic critic Joel Fineman and book historians Gary Taylor and John Jowett.[57] The repetition of O sometimes reaches absurd proportions, as in Othello's lament over his dead wife's body: "O Desdemona, Desdemona dead, O, O!" (V.ii.332). I would contend that Othello's repeated O is a testament to this scene's proliferating, ambiguous circular marks—even a last attempt to read Desdemona's face, spotted with many kisses since they met at Cyprus. However, Lodovico's exclamation "O bloody period" transforms the majuscule O into a punctuation mark and renders Othello's reading that of an incompetent. Just as he mistakes his kisses as evidence of whoredom; he mistakes the period for the O and gives voice to a silent mark. This misreading secures his racial denigration as a poor reader.

Othello's last wish, as I have argued, is that the blood and air from his own throat could serve as his signature, authenticating his suicide note with his sign and circular seal. As the Shakespearean Howard Felperin succinctly puts it: "Othello lives and moves and has his being within an allegorical mode in which sign and significance are inseparable, words and deeds magically and instantaneously joined."[58] However, that enchanted allegorical structure crumbles when his signature becomes an indication of self-alienation. Although he would have the blood from his throat form an indisputable link between his voice and its written representation, the entire dictation translates him into terms that are not his own but those of the Venetian state. Othello's key concern at the beginning of this monologue is that he be recorded in a faithful way—with nothing omitted or elaborated, with the kind of circular perfection of the period, so complete as to obviate the need for future speech.

Othello begins the play by thinking of blackness as the sign of linguistic fullness—inked character as self-identical, fully revealing, and completely efficacious. It is not until he is put in mind of a *dis*honorable mixture of white and black, as figured in the conceit of the page as sexual record, that he can no longer think of himself or of Desdemona as fair or noble. In this sense, Othello proves himself too credible a believer in Protestant scriptural semiotics, too ready to believe the prophet Jeremiah that Ethiopian skin is an indelible marker of sinfulness. Imprisoned in this moral framework, Othello ends up a helpless reader.

While Othello oscillates helplessly between irreconcilable meanings of inked imprints, he establishes this quality as peculiar to blackened people. Desdemona—spotted with Othello's black kisses—misreads her husband's complexion in thinking he is incapable of jealousy. "I think the sun where he was born / Drew [jealous] humors from him," she muses (III.iv.31–32). Although the scholar Mary Floyd-Wilson suggests that Desdemona echoes the scientific "knowledge" of the era, the Venetian offers a mere conjecture that the implicitly white audience, and her unblackened maid Emilia, recognize as erroneous.[59] Othello ultimately compares his own misreading of his wife's face to the error of "a base Indian," who discards "a pearl . . . / Richer than all his tribe" (V.ii.407–8). *The Moor of Venice* positions its knowledgeable audience at a remove from base Indians, blackamoors, and marred white daughters—figures in an elastic category of blacks united less by precise complexion or geographic origin than by a figurative blackness and its attendant incapacity for assessing character.

The racial rhetoric of blackness as legibility and illiteracy creates the potential for an interpretive fraternity of literate white men. All others, it would appear, were created to be fodder for calculation and archival material for the state. In this readable and communicable blackness is a hidden history of blackface, one more profound and more insidious than ridicule or cultural appropriation. To engage it, we must see early modern blackface in its material and figurative specificity—as a transferable paint represented as a telltale ink.

"Let It Be Hid": The Scholarly Refusal to Read Othello's Pages

Scholars of nineteenth-century performance culture have noted that performances of blackface in the theatre and in the streets facilitated aspiring Europeans' acquisition of the psychic and economic wages of whiteness. The historian David Roediger writes of the nostalgia immigrant industrial workers could express for agrarian rhythms of life through idealized (and patently absurd) portrayals of the ceaseless leisure of darkies on Southern plantations.[60] If Irish migrants to industrializing North American cities indulged in a romance of a pastoral past while in blackface, what might be said of those seventeenth-century players and audiences engaged in what I have been calling inkface?

Roediger argues that the cavorting figures of the minstrel stage expressed white mechanics' longing to escape the regimented time of the industrial age. The seventeenth-century counterpart to the industrial clock may have been the urban page. Migrants to early modern cities entered a world increasingly mediated by writing and print. This transition occasioned both opportunities and restrictions. On the one hand, the capricious demands of manorial lords would increasingly have to be committed to fixed terms—a potentially advantageous development for laborers who, previously, "were bound to do whatever work was set them, and who 'knew not in the evening what was to be done in the morning.'"[61] On the other hand, as Walter Ong says, "There is no way directly to refute a text. After absolutely total and devastating refutation, it says exactly the same thing as before."[62] Consequently, the face-to-face negotiations that may have been possible in a manorial situation were converted into written contracts that, once subjected an official's interpretation, could not easily be overturned. For those who chose to flout their contracts—and others who refused to work for wages—there was always the threat of being sentenced to forced, unpaid labor.

Migrants to London, then, were enclosed within a veritable matrix of alphanumeric characters: vagrancy laws, contracts, wages, property leases, and the unstable prices of labor and of goods. Considering these roiling changes in post-feudal relationships, Jean-Christophe Agnew observes that landlords were so treacherous that "to change one's copy" (i.e., the spirit and letter of the contract) became an expression for any sudden reversal in demeanor or intention.[63] As oral and literate culture coexisted and cooperated, as Adam Fox has demonstrated, the transition from embodied oral authority to disembodied textual authority was a fraught contest with unpredictable positions and maneuvers.[64]

In a world in which treachery was mediated by letters, the illiterate stage blackamoor seems to serve as an object of nostalgia, as was the succeeding plantation stereotype. A figure like Othello exhibited an idealized, integral self-assertion in which the body was a perfect indicator—in fact, a guarantor—of internal capacities. Othello's willingness to stand or fall as the man he is elicited the sympathy European men, in particular, sometimes showed. One nobleman identified Thomas Betterton's Othello with a noble ideal of manly integrity. In 1709 Sir John Perceval, the Earl of Egmont castigated "insensible" viewers as uncivilized women: "Those who cannot be moved at Othello's story so artfully written by Shakespeare and justly played by Betteron, are capable of marrying again before their husbands are cold, of trampling on a lover when dying at their feet, and are fit to converse with tygers only."[65] While it is true that blackness does not preclude Perceval's gendered sympathy with Othello, that sympathy is not extended to moors but routed through the genius of Shakespeare and Betterton. At the same time, Othello could serve as an object of ridicule, as did his minstrel successor. When stable feudal obligations were being transformed into contractual agreements of uncertain value in fluctuating market contexts, the inked-up blackamoor represented persons too gullible to anticipate those who would exploit linguistic ambiguities in texts—and too unimaginative to reinvent themselves in step with mercurial market value.

The downtrodden and ambitious may have found Iago, the subversive semiliterate servant, a more appealing ego-ideal than Othello, the aristocratic man of unshakable sincerity. In every performance over its storied early Atlantic history, Othello's sincerity—so dependent upon his inky, all-revealing blackness—indicated that mastery of the characters of the page and stage was reserved as a racially exclusive potential. Othello need not have been evil or lowborn, what some of my recent peers and predecessors might deem a negative *stereotype,* for this work to proceed. He simply needed to lack capacities for interpretation and self-expression that even the lowliest white characters claim, including Malvolio and Phoebe in the comedies and Iago, to whose motives I now turn.

"Letter and Affection," or Iago's Motive

It has become one of the truisms of Shakespeare scholarship that Iago, the great villain of Shakespeare's *Othello,* lacks a motive. Critics have adopted Samuel Taylor Coleridge's famous phrase—"the motive-hunting of motiveless malignity"—to describe Iago's shifting rationales for his destructive project: hatred of Othello, envy of Cassio's promotion to lieutenant, suspicion that Othello, Cassio, or both men have slept with Iago's wife, Emilia.[66] Special pressure has been placed on Iago's final invention—"For I fear Cassio with my nightcap too" (II.i.307)—a worry for which the text supplies no basis. Thus, it has been easy to conclude that all of Iago's motives are invented to serve an evil design he wishes to fulfill for its own sake. Iago's motive and his scheme appear completely self-generated, as in Emilia's description of jealous souls as proceeding without "cause," since jealousy is a "monster" begotten "upon itself" (III.iv.160–62).[67] Although jealousy is undoubtedly one of the play's engines, Iago's *initial* complaint that "preferment goes by letter and affection" demands an investigation of the ways that literacy becomes implicated in matters of love and social advancement in *The Moor of Venice.*

In the final scene, Othello famously refuses to name the cause of his honor killing of Desdemona. In the bookend of the play's first scene, however, Iago is quite voluble in articulating his causes of action. Contrary to the notion that he lacks motivation or that his entire motivation is sexual, he outlines precise grievances regarding a lost military promotion.[68] Consequently, Iago might well be put alongside other characters with urgent social and economic motivations. In his willful self-assertion in the face of a social order that leaves him dispossessed with no foreseeable possibility of advancement, Iago is reminiscent of the illegitimate son, Edmund, in *King Lear*. The two men vow to make themselves vindictive deceivers as a response to experiences of undeserved dispossession. In his biting analysis, Edmund indicts the "curiosity of nations," the customs of primogeniture and disinheritance of children born out of wedlock (I.ii.4). Edmund finds nothing in his figure deserving of abjection. He dismisses "bastard" and "base," the epithets attached to him, as ascriptions of the world (I.ii.6). Iago is similarly debased in relation to Cassio. As the ensign ruefully states of his new lieutenant, "he hath a daily beauty in his life / that makes me ugly" (V.i.19–20). In rejecting congenital explanations for behavior, Edmund reframes his disinheritance as a social wrong, sparking an elaborate, improvised scheme to get Edgar's land. Iago is another version of this villainous type: not one who lacks motive but one who must use improvisation and cunning to obtain upward social mobility. Each enlists a social superior—his father or his commander—to reverse a dispensation and prior decisions about "preferment," with attendant increases in status and wealth.

This Shakespearean type, an unpropertied but socially ambitious villain, must infiltrate the fraternity of literate men to achieve this "preferment." In *Lear*, Shakespeare has Edmund win legitimacy and land through the agency of a dishonest letter that turns his father's heart against his legitimate son, Edgar. Iago confronts a similar conspiracy of letter and affection, yet this villain subverts his dispossession without employing the medium of writing. Moreover, Iago aims not at his own father but at a much larger structure of affectionate camaraderie shared by literate men.[69] Iago decides to engage in "double knavery," to obtain promotion from a lettered fraternity while also confounding the medium that forms its affective ties (I.iii.394).

In Iago's situation, the usurping rival is not a blood brother but a competitor in a professional fraternity. To Iago's surprise, the magic of the epistle and the ledger has intervened to override the embodied system of rank that he once believed governed both. Herein lies the germ of Iago's plotting: Cassio's promotion has left the soldier socially stagnant—"beleed and calmed" (I.i.30). Othello rejects Iago's bid to become a lieutenant, assigning him the lowly rank of ensign, a post with a presumable pittance of a salary. This stalled social advancement gives him not only motive but also perhaps an urgent need to leech money from his mark, the nobleman Roderigo. Iago never pleads that the lieutenancy should have been his birthright. Instead, he argues that he has earned it through valorous deeds Othello witnessed in person.[70] Iago describes himself as "I of whom his eyes had seen the proof / At Rhodes, at Cyprus and on other grounds / Christened and heathen" (I.i.28–30). Yet, Othello devalues the sign of the ensign's unfurled body—word transformed to the flesh of valorous deeds—in comparison to Cassio's capacities for paperwork.

Iago fumes that the Florentine Cassio "never set a squadron in the field / Nor the division of a battle knows / More than a spinster—unless the bookish theoric" (I.i.22–24).[71] The play never contradicts the accusation. In fact, Cassio's quick demotion for drunken behavior during peacetime suggests that his pen is better trained for the schoolroom than his will and body are disciplined for the battlefront.[72] Cassio may be, in Iago's disdainful words, a "great arithmetician" (I.i.20), but the skills of a "debitor and creditor" (25)—involving tables and ledgers—are precisely those that would be in favor in a society in which (to give the full quotation) "Preferment goes by letter and affection / and not by old gradation, where each second / Stood heir to th' first" (1.1.38–40). Iago's insistence here on ordinal value suggests that he cannot perform numerical operations that require further schooling to master. Othello prefers Cassio's grasp of the specialized operations of bookish abstraction and mathematical manipulation to Iago's naturalized sense of number as a measure of magnitude or seniority.[73]

While Edmund takes up the pen to forge a letter that sways paternal affection and property, Iago departs from this example. He pursues the path of Jack Cade, as imagined in Shakespeare's *History of Henry VI Part 2*.[74] The book historian Roger Chartier describes Cade as a foe of "any form, any presence, any use of the written word" who opposes the "tyrannical power of writing" as part of a larger battle against "private appropriation of land, . . . [the] monetary economy, and . . . inequalities of status."[75] This rebel from one of Shakespeare's earliest plays objects to the written word for reasons that prefigure Iago's criticisms: writing has come to supersede "oral testimonies."[76] This shift tended disproportionately to benefit those from wealthy families in an age in which writing was not taught universally but was, instead, the elite boy's penultimate preparation for participating in the market.[77] Jack Cade anticipates Iago's status-based animus when he snarls during an inquisition of a clerk: "Dost thou use to write thy name? Or hast thou a mark to thyself, like an honest, plain-dealing man?" (IV.ii.102–4). The clerk responds: "Sir, I thank God, I have been so well brought up that I can write my name" (105–6). If he had the power to do so, Iago would certainly enact on Cassio Cade's sentence for the upwardly mobile man of letters: "Hang him with his pen and inkhorn about his neck" (109–10).

Unlike Edmund, who reverses his disinheritance with a forged letter, Iago adheres to Cade's code, in which honesty and writing are incompatible—just as letters are, to their minds, inimical to "plain-dealing." Iago's deploys voices, bodies, and objects as paraliterary tools that vex would-be readers with multiple meanings that cannot be reduced. Iago's proper epithet "honest," then, is not (as most editions have it) only an indication of rank tinged with dramatic irony, since he lies so often. By linking "honest" with the inability to sign one's name, Cade reveals an ethics of the unlettered. In such a world, Iago's credibility depends on his status as a commoner who eschews the written, a realm of forgeries and falsehoods.[78]

One could say that Iago capitalizes on the residual credibility still accorded to speech, especially as a reaction to the rise of paper agreements that submit to a different protocol of authentication than does the speaking witness. From the perspective of Cade's real-world counterparts, Iago's spoken words are either honest—or, at least, potentially verifiable—because they come from the mouth of a living witness instead of from a text that cannot be made to reply to interrogation in the moment. Iago embodies the ensign not merely because, in his words, he displays a deceptive "flag and sign of love," but because his signs *are* flags (I.i.156). He quite purposely flaunts textiles and other surrogates that tempt the alphabetically inclined to deploy text-specific reading practices. Beyond his own speech, he employs bodies and objects as signifiers: handkerchiefs, bedsheets, Othello's always already begrimed face, and Desdemona's increasingly marred one. A descendant of Jack Cade, Iago works in textual analogues but never with alphabetical writing.

Despite the school of critics who take Emilia's part and believe that Iago has no cause, that souls such as his are "jealous for they're jealous," Iago's "cause" extends beyond the psycho-emotional concerns of the tormented husband (III.iv.160–61).[79] For him, affection is interfering with his social advancement—and this interference has been abetted by the medium of writing. Thus, when Iago laments that he lives in a time in which "preferment goes by letter and affection," he is positioning himself from the very first scene as an antagonist of both love *and* literacy, not the kind of person motivated primarily by marital jealousy.[80]

To think sexual jealousy Iago's primary motive is to restrict interpretation to his wife's prism of marital fidelity. Although Iago conjoins "letter and affection," Emilia considers affection alone and, thus, does not illuminate Iago's substitution of textiles for text. While scholars and performers want to highlight her powerful condemnation of Iago at the play's end, risking her life in the act, this forthrightness should not be confused with omniscience.[81] Emilia, after all, is completely blind to Iago's reasons for wanting the handkerchief that Othello gave Desdemona. She regards it as a love token, overlooking what

Iago sees: a textual surrogate that Othello, enthralled to textual suggestion, will credit as if it were "holy writ" (III.iii.324). Like the flag most closely associated with Iago's role as ensign, handkerchiefs are textiles, and Iago exploits that they have a material and functional kinship with texts.[82] Flags, handkerchiefs, and pages were all made of a fabric dyed and decorated with images and letters—and all these features held significance.[83] Therefore, Emilia's observations about Iago's jealousy constitute only a partial analysis of Iago's motive and his scheme, which targets fully literate men of the elite. Emilia is ignorant of the campaign against "bookish theoric," an essential element that shapes Iago's revenge.

Extending beyond Emilia's defining interest in jealousy illuminates Iago's conjoined disdain for "letter and affection"—indeed the curdling effect of letters upon his affection. To recognize the kinship of Iago and Jack Cade, whose strategies for social advancement emanate from their inveterate loathing of the written word, has momentous implications for interpretation of the play. Perhaps most important, it clarifies the ultimate target of Iago's vengeance. To the extent that blackface performances of *The Moor of Venice* ask their audiences to take the moor for ink and his wife for fair paper, the two become the *instruments* of Iago's malice and not his targets. Iago uses and disposes of them to achieve a victory against the "letter[s] and affection[s]" he believes have skewed an embodied, ordinal system of preferment "where each second stood heir to the first."

Iago before the Senate

In one of his rare, true remarks, Iago says he does not have the "conscience" to commit "contrived murder" (II.i.2–3). Strictly speaking, he adheres to this morality, as he induces others to consent to murder, and the only ones committed by his own hand (Roderigo's and Emilia's) are improvised rather than "contrived" in advance. Yet, using the textuality ascribed to Othello and Desdemona's coupling, he does successfully reverse his fortunes, like Edmund, and "serve his turn upon" not only his superior, Othello, but also upon the senators, to whom his commander Othello is subject (I.i.42).[84] Iago expands the compass of his revenge to include these high priests of Venetian literacy, one of the systems he deems responsible for his dispossession. Although commentary has ascribed his plots against Cassio and Othello to social envy and racism, these adversaries are part of the body of governing men who determine preferment by the letter.

Indeed, Iago reviles the Venetian state so much that the mere word "senator" is, to him, an insult. In the play's first scene, Brabantio makes a class-coded moral judgment in saying to a voice addressing him in the darkness: "Thou art a villain" (I.i.118). Iago, who has not revealed his name, nearly gives away his presence when he blurts out the impertinent phrase that completes Brabantio's line of verse: "you are a senator."[85] Although Iago repeats that he "hate[s] the moor," moments such as this one suggest an antipathy toward the state that seethes unvoiced beneath the scenes he has with senators and ambassadors (I.iii.366). Iago's rage toward his government, a precursor of the bureaucratic state, deserves attention equal to that devoted to his jealousies, his racism, and his misogyny.[86]

Iago's seditious side surfaces in the bitter quip that "the togèd consuls can propose / As masterly as" Cassio in matters of war (I.i.25–26). He compares this literate coterie's knowledge of war to that of a spinster. Iago figuratively diminishes reading, accounting, and other paperwork to the devalued activities of spinning women.[87] Despite the fact that Iago never again directly "traduce[s] the state," an audience's view of the Senate's eventual arrival onstage can be colored by his depiction (V.ii.354). In Iago's elaboration on the character of senators, the Duke and senators appear as clones of Cassio and all as analogues of spinning women involved with their text(iles).[88]

To save time, many productions now pass over the Senate's war preparations. Laurence Olivier would have approved such a choice because it restricts the scene to Othello's turn as a star witness, defending himself against Brabantio's charge that Desdemona was won by means of witchcraft.[89] Although this cut both speeds and focuses the plot, it obscures the extent to which Othello's impromptu trial is framed by the Senate's comparative assessment of oral testimony and writing. In the process, Othello's proud self-narration takes the place of the Senate's flexible and self-serving hermeneutical method as the factor that determines their decision to favor the general over the senator.[90] From Iago's vantage point, act 1, scene 3 illustrates the swaying of affection by letters. While watching, silently, he sees firsthand (perhaps for the first time) that the Senate functions as the command center of the textual order that blocks his advancement.[91]

The scene opens during the Signiory's gathering of intelligence on the movements of the Turkish fleet. What follows is not, perhaps, the most gripping action, but it does permit a view of senators' protocols for assessing oral and written reports from the war front. The Duke and two senators enter, each carrying a piece of paper that aligns them, like Cassio, with "bookish theoric." The Duke establishes the motif: "There's no composition in these news [t]hat gives them credit" (I.iii.1). In this statement, he voices the play's obsession with textual assessment in both its economic and evidentiary senses.[92] The senators are trying to assess the truth of reports that refer to differing numbers of Turkish ships bearing toward the Venetian outpost of Cyprus isle. Despite the varying reports of the size of the fleet, the senators are able confidently to glean from the correspondence that the Turks, in some number, aim for

Cyprus. However, once the written texts have been reconciled, an oral report immediately arrives to contradict the resolution: a sailor reports that the Turkish fleet bears instead toward Rhodes (I.iii.14–15). One of the senators emphatically rejects the report in language that will prove telling: "'Tis a pageant / To keep us in a false gaze" (I.iii.18–19). This senator warns that the pageant of embodied performance should not be allowed to distract the eye. The Senate distrusts the oral and embodied signifiers that Iago elevates, subjecting them to the scrutiny of the lettered.[93]

The senator's skepticism is rewarded immediately—another messenger announces that the Turks visited Rhodes only to augment their fleet before rushing back to Cyprus. A messenger confirms that "now they do restem / Their backward course, bearing with frank appearance / Their purposes toward Cyprus" (I.iii.37–39). This scene establishes a narrative arc in which moorish types behave in ways that seem calculated to deceive but those actions eventually reveal an appearance "frank" enough to quell doubt.[94] In other words, despite changing contexts and situations, Turks ultimately have a consistent, readable character that will show itself. The master code for the senators comes from alphabetical thinking, with its fixed set of characters that may appear changed to the unwise but have a consistent, legible identity to the initiated.

When not cut, the rather tedious business of the field reports regarding the Turks can establish that the Venetian Senate is a white male interpretive community that prizes textual evidence and hermeneutics.[95] The most urgent state matters—including those that require military action and not merely philosophical deliberation—are determined by textual precept. Oral testimony is subordinate to that which is written; indeed, the senators consider the theatre of the world a deceptive "pageant" and return to the page to give it order.[96] This interpretive community of literate white men has sidelined Iago and welcomed Cassio, whom they will eventually promote over even Othello, once there is no military need for a moorish general. Florentine or not, Cassio is one of their own, a literate, Christian nobleman.[97]

It is unexpected that this interpretive fraternity should prefer Othello to Brabantio, even temporarily.[98] After all, Brabantio enters the Senate chamber with absolute confidence that his "brothers of the state" will "feel the wrong" of Othello's elopement with Desdemona as if she were their daughter instead of his (I.ii.96–97). Brabantio appears at the Senate in person, confident in the power of his "*voice* potential as double as the Duke's" (I.ii.15–16).[99] Unaware that the Senate is meeting to discuss military strategy, the influential senator has come making allegations of that sexual crime that is also a crime against a father's property, rape.[100] Without knowing that the accused rapist is Othello, the Duke initially defers to Brabantio's stature and promises to allow his "brother" to "read the bloody Book of law" according to his own "sense," or interpretation (I.iii.66, 68).[101] In fact, he promises to yield up "even his proper son" to Brabantio's legal vengeance (68). The Duke employs these speech acts to reassure Brabantio of their fraternal ties to the book, the medium that is both the emblem of their social distinction and the technology they use to reproduce it.

With this assurance, Brabantio accuses someone who is not only outside the Duke's family but also outside his ethnos and, therefore, presumably even more easily expelled from the Venetian fraternity than a native son would be.[102] Brabantio has articulated these stakes as both familial and political: by Othello's entry into an elite family and (presumably) with his stamp upon Desdemona's children, "bond-slaves and pagans" could become "statesmen" of Venice (I.ii.99).[103] Were it not for the threat to Venice's overseas possession, Brabantio could have expected swift and bloody sentence against Othello. However, the exigencies of the impending battle for Cyprus suddenly make general Othello dearer than a son—although bereft of the protections that kinship might offer.[104]

Hoping to find a way to avoid losing a peerless commander at the hour his services are most needed, the Duke invites Othello to defend himself. Yet, before he offers his exculpation, Othello asks that Desdemona be sent for. Othello offers an ambiguous defense against accusations of witchcraft. He confesses that he told her stories of his mythical homeland and suspenseful adventures: "this only is the magic I have used" (I.iii.169). This indirect denial falls short of "I used no witchcraft," a declaration that would constitute a definitive rebuttal. In stating, directly, that he used "only this magic," Othello defends himself while refraining from calling Brabantio a liar. Far from Olivier's star turn, Othello's self-defense is inconclusive, since he cannot engage in insubordination against senators, like Brabantio, whom he takes care to address as his "very noble and approved good masters" (I.iii.77). If Othello's speech were so successful, Desdemona's would not be required. However, the subsequent addition of Desdemona's permits the Duke to forswear his promise to execute a man accused of the theft of her body and its value.[105]

The Duke does not reverse himself to uphold colorblindness as an ideal, nor out of any peculiar affection for Othello.[106] Rather, he elects to value the combined testimony of Othello and Desdemona as textual material—and to grant it more weight than he grants Brabantio's voice. "I do beseech you, / Send for the lady," Othello has asked. "If you do find me foul in her report, / . . . let your sentence / Even fall upon my life" (I.iii.114–15, 117, 118–19). In what may be a play on fair and foul papers, Othello offers the first hint of what I have already argued in previous sections of the book: the relationship between black stage moors and their fair-skinned lovers is inscription personified, with Desdemona as the paper and Othello as the ink source. In wagering that she will not offer a "foul . . . report," Othello is already implicitly relying on his wife to serve as "fair paper"—the term he uses for her in act 4. Desdemona's spotless fairness is the source of his confidence that he will not be found "foul in her report."[107] Unlike "foul papers"—marred by unsightly ink blots—she indeed gives Othello a "fair" report, as beautiful and unblemished as her skin is before the two have kissed and the moor's makeup has been transferred to her.[108]

The dictates of realism governing modern productions of *Othello* make it difficult to convey the Duke's recognition of the couple as personifications of the page. However, in seventeenth-century productions of the *Moor of Venice,* the Duke may not observe Othello's and Desdemona's faces but, rather, hear them while thumbing "the bloody book of law" he invokes when Brabantio makes the initial accusation (I.iii.66). This kind of substitution would prefigure the later scene in which it is unclear whether Othello's outbursts are directed at Desdemona or at a communiqué from the Venetian Senate. Perhaps the Duke refers ceremoniously to a blank page before he pronounces—even writes—his sentence and his dispatch to Othello. Perhaps Othello has already gestured to unmarked pages during his "foul report" line. Perhaps the Duke thinks of this attraction of paper and ink again and looks back and forth from his page to the couple. It is difficult for us, now, to know how the Duke's knowledge of the literary nature of Othello and Desdemona's coupling would be signaled—or indeed whether it would require any overt signaling in a theatre culture that recurred to this language often.

In any case, he and the other senators find a way to divorce the needs of their domestic fraternity from the requirements for protecting the empire. Without objection from any other senator, the Duke dismisses Brabantio's problem as personal and psychological.[109] Reenacting the earlier preference for written reports from the field, the Duke and senators elevate the textualized voice over the embodied one—paper above pageant. They dismiss Brabantio as if his character, housed in his body, means nothing in the face of Othello's black character foregrounded on the paper of Desdemona's fair report.

Othello's success in the textual field will be short-lived, as the Duke will, by some miracle, dispatch a letter cashiering Othello seemingly upon the instant that news of the Turks' defeat is known. Virtues and service aside, the threat Othello poses to the governing fraternity is too grave. Of course, the Duke's admission that Othello's tale "could win [his] daughter, too" indicates that he never forgets the threat should "the Turk" graduate from seizing overseas possessions to infiltrating the domestic arena. Thus, the Senate turn against the General the very medium that granted him temporary status. This easy severing of ties reveals that Othello was only the ink of their dispatches—a means of execution, a speech act brought to life. He was never a member of their literate fraternity, never a brother of state.

Iago is present but silent when Brabantio's suit is denied. Brabantio's failure unveils the politics of Othello's rejection of Iago's bid for promotion:

> Three great ones of the city
> In personal suit to make me his lieutenant
> Off-capp'd to him.
> . . . .
> But he, as loving his own pride and purposes
> Evades them with a bombast circumstance
> . . . .
> And in conclusion nonsuits my mediators (I.i.8–10, 12–13, 16)

This scenario mirrors the Senate deliberations, in that the voice of a high-ranking man is set aside by a proud and a prolix commander in favor of a kind of textual proficiency. The parallels are, of course, not perfect: Othello and Desdemona are textual surrogates, while Cassio has a knowledge of actual books. Nevertheless, both Cassio and Othello prove to be inept judges of character, while the interpretive fraternity of the Senate never errs in such assessments.

Iago observes the Senate's surprising rebuff of their brother Brabantio's suit, a scene of wordless witness that permits him to compare it to his own failed bid for promotion. This comparison reveals to him that he is suppressed in a society that has elevated the textual as the master code for assessing character. Moreover, he sees that the shared conceit of Desdemona as paper personified allows his betters to coordinate the various forms of character—racial, moral, and textual.

Iago's Revenge: Tools and Target

Subsequently, on the shore of Cyprus, Iago observes Cassio engaging in some overly familiar gestures with Desdemona, involving elaborate and repeated kissing and touching of her hands. As befitting his own literate status, Cassio engages in these courtly gestures after having repeatedly cast Desdemona as the personification of a page. He calls her "a maid / That paragons description and wild fame; / One that excels the quirks of blazoning pens" (II.i.61–63). Quirk here is a pen stroke, a flourish—thus, Cassio is referring to Desdemona's fair and still unmarked complexion.[110] Yet, Desdemona's resemblance to paper extends beyond fair skin to include her fated pairing with any inky moor.[111] This female page is unique among the play's women in her irresistible desire to be inked. For example, when Iago composes misogynist rhymes, his wife retorts, "You shall not write my praise." Her quip demonstrates an understanding that slander, though unwritten, publishes character in making it public. Desdemona, though, cannot resist the lure of being written upon and asks: "What wouldst write of me, if thou shouldst praise me?" (II.i.117). As an antagonist of the written, Iago engages in his signature banter, but the fact that Desdemona imagines this oral performance as a "writ[ing]" suggests how primary that frame is for her. Iago does his best to denigrate women with bawdy rhymes, but his words alone cannot besmirch Desdemona.

Indeed, nothing sullies her until Othello arrives and Iago witnesses their passionate engagement—the first time that the play gives an incontrovertible indication that the lovers kiss. These kisses in Cyprus materialize a page—the kisses of the painted moor and the Venetian woman on whose papery complexion the state has based (or pretended to base) an impromptu criminal decision. Where the besotted Roderigo sees nothing amiss in Cassio's kissing Desdemona's hand, Iago suggests that kisses leave a pornographic imprint. To Roderigo's claim that Cassio's kisses were "but courtesy," Iago responds by reframing the exchange as "Lechery, by this hand; an index and obscure prologue to the history of lust and foul thoughts" (II.i.256–58). Iago asks Roderigo to substitute a figuration for what he sees, to make of Desdemona's hand a lewd book, complete with index and prologue.[112] Iago now thinks of Desdemona in terms of paper and men's amorous contact with her as potentially blotting. He has gained a crucial insight in observing the difference between contact with Cassio, which leaves no mark, and contact with Othello, which covers and stains.[113]

This moment of seeing Desdemona's face physically overlaid with blackness for the first time offers Iago a way of turning Othello and Desdemona into instruments of his revenge against the text-obsessed fraternity that refused to promote him. Even after these scenes, Iago has not entirely cemented his plot, confessing: "'Tis here, but yet confus'd" (II.i.311). Iago's plan has the qualities scholars have attributed to the unwritten: performed in time and, therefore, subject to improvisation.[114] Iago will never exercise the judicial authority Jack Cade wields for a brief time, never sentence anyone to be hung with his pen and inkhorn around his neck. Yet, in the play's final act he will create a tableau—a theatrical scene in which black and white faces take the place of ink and paper—that confounds any attempt at a written report. This unreadable scene functions as his triumph.

To defeat Othello is a petty victory, compared to overturning the entire regime of visual epistemology of which writing is the emblem—that is, the entire relationship between seeing (a sign) and believing (in something beyond the materiality of the sign itself). In this quest, Iago takes every visible and invisible form of character available to seventeenth-century audiences and turns it into an object of undecidable meaning. Moreover, he confounds any distinction between oral testimony and textual evidence, precisely as he promises in one of his scheming soliloquies: "Trifles, light as air / Are to the jealious confirmations strong / As proofs of holy writ" (III.iii.322–24). Iago gets Othello to place his faith in airy words mistaken for infallible scripture.[115] The materialization of those words—the trace of salacious innuendo in black marks on Desdemona's face—desacralizes the parchment of her skin, which Othello has treated as an analogue for the Bible, "a most goodly book" (IV.ii.71).

The play directs audience attention in the third and fourth acts to the poisoning of Othello's imagination and his growing suspicion that his wife, Desdemona, has been unfaithful with Cassio. Scholarship that focuses on cognition describes Iago's mental capacities and Othello's psychological change; yet, under original performance conditions, Iago accomplishes his work not deep in Othello's interior but on Desdemona's surface, turning "her virtue into pitch" with his touch (II.iii.360).[116] While Iago manipulates Othello and Desdemona as human personifications of tacky blackness and absorbent whiteness, the play's dialogue continues to refer to his target, beyond them.[117] One illustrative moment is when Othello becomes so enraged by the thought of his wife's infidelity that he strikes her publicly. The emissaries from Venice respond incredulously: "This would not be believed in Venice," one says (IV.i.242). He continues later, "Is this the noble moor whom our full Senate call all in all sufficient?" (264–65). Shakespeare engages here in subtle punning on moor. For, if all state activity relies upon the recognizable character of moors, as I discussed above with Turks specifically, then Othello's uncharacteristic behavior would doubly *unmoor* the state's confidence in written reports.[118] Moors would not be moors, signs would come untethered from referents—and even lose their self-identity. Othello would not be Othello; O would not be O.

Othello's errant behavior threatens the way that he has been characterized in state discourse, the terms (such as "noble moor" and "all in all sufficient") by which the Senate identifies him. The emissaries in Cyprus replay the business of the war room, imagining carrying to Venice an incredible oral report while the "fair paper" of Desdemona has now been befouled by Othello's blackened and blackening hand.[119] Desdemona's oral testimony never varies. Even on her dyeing bed, she asserts that she is chaste and Othello noble. However, because of acts that Iago provoked, bodies have invalidated any prior texts, real or imaginary, concerning Othello. Iago's paraliterary work appears in this published discordance: the simultaneous marring of speech and the dis-abling of text's epistemological basis. Consequently, Othello's "occupation" as moor, as anchor in the field of signification, is indeed, as he famously wails, "gone" (III.iii.357).

In this unmoored world, Iago, too, gets to make his escape from consistent identity. His own body remains the sign only of itself, with no textual corollary. He defeats writing in his refusal to confess for posterity. Even as Iago sounds the Spanish name of a moorslayer, it also suggests a pun that troubles the archive: "I-ago"; I of the past.[120] Iago's famous self-description "I am not what I am" insists that he is not self-identical, in this instant or from moment to moment (I.i.65).[121] He is not who he is; nor who he once was some time ago.[122] I does not equal I. It is this lack of identity that makes it impossible for him to enter the state archive, in which stable reference is so crucial to identifying culprits and passing sentence.[123]

Understanding Iago's antiliterary aims sheds new light on his incessant iteration "I have told thee often, and I retell thee again and again, I hate the Moor" (I.iii.364–66). In a later exchange with Emilia, Othello poses the question most pertinent to interpretation of Iago's repetition: "what needs this iterance?" (V.ii.150).[124] When taken as something other than dull repetition, "Moor" begins to resonate beyond its ethnoracial valence to include the sense of moor as tether.[125] Othello the anchoring moor is the identity principle of signification brought to life, the fully "sufficient" man whose outward character and inward character align. In that sense, he is a transcendent sign, in which signifier, material referent, and idea are indissolubly fused. His sufficiency inheres in this nexus, where idea, word, thing, and deed are one. Thought and incarnation in him are linked, which quality makes him a desired soldier and lover, appealing to the state that requires him to fulfill their military designs—and to Desdemona, who knows that his amorous aims (or hers) will also be fulfilled to the letter. Desdemona wishes "heaven had made her such a man" as the one Othello describes in his reminisces (I.iii.163). Although his purposes are public and official instead of private and romantic, the Duke might well echo Desdemona's fantasy.

In "hat[ing] the moor," Iago declares antipathy toward that which secures the referentiality of language. He stakes a position opposed to the black characters of the alphabet, those conventional forms that the educated manipulate in order to attach themselves to an inflated, virtual identity. Through manipulation of his social identity via letters, Cassio has been able to claim the aura of a potentially worthy lieutenant. Meanwhile, Iago, who has performed the role of a good soldier, has been unable to convert his demonstrated service into the rank he desires and, arguably, deserves. Hence, he vows not to be what he is and to untether all identities. For Iago to destroy "the moor," is not only to unseat Cassio and undo Othello, but to engage in "double knavery" (I.iii.394) against a Senate that elevates the textual over the embodied. Iago is utterly opposed to the moor of Venice, that which anchors the literate fraternity who call themselves "brothers of state." Thus, he attempts to set the Venetian ship of state adrift from its epistemological anchors.[126]

The state uncovers Iago's triumph over character-literacy in the play's emblematic bed scene. The bloody maidservant, pale gentlewoman, and blackamoor repeat the pattern of ink and blood on the letters Lodovico bran-dishes revealing Iago's plot. In addition, they recall the figurative "bloody book of Law" the Doge suggested Brabantio could level against his daugh-ter's (then-unnamed) rapist (I.iii.66). Despite his inability to sway the state via alphanumeric paperwork, Iago weaponizes orality. Throughout the play, he successfully fabricates lies to superiors without compunction, then refuses to speak truth when commanded. Beyond the flag, his signifier is the "rag-ing tooth" (III.iii.471), which recalls Jack Cade's declaration "my mouth shall be the parliament of England" (*2 Henry VI* IV.vii.14–15). The primary differ-ence, of course, is that Cade invents for himself a claim to rule, while Iago contents himself with exercising his fury through speech that tears as teeth do.

Beyond his orality, Iago weaponizes the textile against the text. Iago's shrewd recognition of Othello and Desdemona as surrogates for ink and paper allows him to see that letters do not function entirely in the world of objective assess-ment, a pretense the Senate must maintain to legitimate the exercise of their pleasures. Instead, letters are tied up with hopes, beliefs, hungers, and, as Iago bitterly notes, "affection[s]." This insight allows him to undermine the founda-tion of writing upon which the knowledge and legal pronouncements of the state are based. Barred from escaping from "the curse of service" (I.i.35) into a liberated pan-European elite, Iago chooses to bring down the social structure by undermining the symbolic conventions on which it relies.[127]

In this light, Othello appears just a tractable animal, hardly a worthy op-ponent of so virtuosic a villain.[128] There is an indication of this performance, which we might call *Othello* without Othello, in the early performance title, *The Moor of Venice,* which does not center Othello by his proper name. In-deed, one of the wailing laments at the end of the play—"all that's spoke is marred" (V.ii.357)—indicates that Othello, however injured and undone, is not Iago's target. "All that's spoke" refers to the entire realm of representa-tion that the begrimed Othello unwittingly helps in sullying. Perhaps, Iago consumes and exhausts Othello as a black character, a fortuitously apt means by which to vanquish the ensign's ultimate enemy, the letters that determine preferment. In attacking the blackamoor, Iago attacks the authority and reli-ability of the writing the literate classes relied upon for deliberations they proclaimed to be rational but are truly distributed by affection.

The laments in the final scene—"all that's spoke is marred," and "this object poisons sight / let it be hid"—refer not only to the immediate problem of the tragically loaded bed but also to the apparent impossibility of communicating this scene to Venice in a credible way. It is no accident that the play does not return to the Senate, so confident in its assessment of pages—both missives and messengers—arriving from abroad. There is no route home from the un-mapped world that Iago has stripped of its mooring symbols.

If a racial bar prohibits Othello's entry into the literate fraternity that employs his black figure to execute their commands, Desdemona becomes ostracized by accruing stains of sexual shame through contact with him. Iago occupies a strange position, lacking the cultural capital of literacy but perhaps more interested in unmooring his society than in upward mobility. Across the next two and a half centuries, ambitious Anglos—men and women in theatre, government, and the arts—show the triumph and the tragedy of achieving a place in the circle that Iago sought to disable. I would argue that scholars, inheritors of the project of alphanumeric mediation of all life, have made nonsense of Iago's mission rather than confront that we stand in for the "togèd spinsters," his ultimate targets. The inordinate time spent attempting to establish Othello's faith, color, and ethnos has, in that sense, served as a desperate distraction. For, in confronting Othello's mooring function, scholars would also risk confronting how thoroughly the imperative to maintain white authority has predetermined our methods—limiting not so much our conclusions as the questions we can begin to posit. The Senate, the state, and dutiful scholars have indeed needed "the Moor" to provide moorings.

To unsettle that tendency, I have ventured to present *The Moor of Venice,* a play unloosed from the anchor of *Othello*'s verisimilitude. This play concludes with the in-credible double-speak of characters who voice irreconcilable truths beyond any but an omniscient reader's capacity to confirm or deny. The blackness of Othello's face is the sign of both inherent nobility and stigmatized slavery; while Desdemona acquires a blackness that is at once the sign of holiness and of profanation. Neither can be resolved, as the very character conventions on which the brotherhood of state relies has authorized both significations. Because of the indissoluble link of ink and paper, Desdemona has served as much as Othello to moor analysis of the play. The question of her guilt has served to establish the mood and moral of the play. In the interlude following this chapter, I argue that a nonhuman Desdemona, a personification of paper, functions far differently than would a plausible woman. On the one hand, she acquires a text's remarkable ability to speak after death. On the other hand, this textual voice is really that of her readers and, tragically, never her own. This consignment to paper turns out to have critical consequences for real women of the long eighteenth century, as women such as Aphra Behn, Abigail Adams, and Sarah Siddons discover in the chapters of part 2.

Part II

Women on the Verge of Whiteness

Interlude

Desdemona's Guilt, or "The Farce of Dead Alive"

In the previous chapter, I argued that seventeenth-century blackface renders Othello a character composed of ink by situating the painted black moor in scenes governed by textual metaphors. Consequently, his interiority, psychological depth, cognition, and capacities—what he thinks and what he enacts—are limited less by factors of human identity than by this inky constitution. Before black actors take over the role, ink is Othello's essence and its outward expression, an origin and a signature. Early blackface versions of the play would have drawn attention to blotting ink in multiplying images that cluster around what one witness of the murder-suicide calls a "bloody period," including the end stop on the missive Othello dictates and the circular imprint of his "dye[ing]" kiss. In this section, I turn to Desdemona, whom Othello explicitly calls "fair paper" amid his agonizing attempts to read her for signs of dishonesty. I aim to unfold the implications of the conceit that she personifies paper. I argue that the textual Desdemona conjures a virtual reality in which sexual contact does leave a readable trace. With these stains transferred through amorous contact, blackface theatre offered a unique opportunity to fulfill a patriarchal wish that a woman's sexual character would appear in legible marks impressed upon her face. Yet, *Othello* presents a nightmare scenario in which this fantasy is fulfilled in black marks with a vexing, undecidable meaning.

This interlude establishes the terrain of the next two chapters, which feature historical women who confronted the patriarchal overwriting that *Othello* attempts to literalize in equating Desdemona with paper. Following feminist scholars, I argue that Shakespeare's Venetian maid is circumscribed by an economy of honor in which a woman's chastity is represented by a figurative page, with inked marks as sexual experiences.[1] As she becomes increasingly blackened, Desdemona assumes the form of a page Othello has imprinted. The transformation produces her as the bearer of a sign meant not for herself but for another to read. In the process, she loses her voice in a redoubling of the discourses that speak on and through her.[2] European patrimony does not protect this strange(r) Desdemona, for by the play's end, she has been reconstituted by the same Africanizing materiality that renders Othello himself as marked and illiterate. Desdemona's arc dramatizes the transposition of the stigma of blackness from what sociologist Orlando Patterson calls "[general] dishonor" to sexual shame.[3]

The strange(r) Desdemona I have described was known to audiences before realism became the dominant mode of production for *Othello*. In this interlude, I summon this paper Desdemona—an impossible character, pronouncing her version of the impossible sentence "I am dead."[4] On her journey from "fair paper" to "dye[d]" whore, her character—her sexual reputation—is derived more from confounding logics of the sexualized page than from the plausible experience or psyche of a historical woman. The repeated alignment of Desdemona with paper imbues her with a page's ability to speak—an uncanny agency demonstrated in the miracle of her speech after being smothered. Yet, at the same time, this undying voice threatens to tip the play from tragedy to farce, as one insightful eighteenth-century wit intuited. To the gallery of eccentric seers in *Inkface,* I would like now to introduce this unnamed heckler.

In the final moments of a performance of *Othello* at London's Haymarket theatre, a "quarrel" erupted in the upper boxes.[5] Desdemona had already been smothered, and Miss Woollery (first name unrecorded), who played the part on that September night in 1785, lay at still as she could. However, a shout of "Fire!" reportedly brought her out of bed and out of character. According to one amused spectator: "she instantly got upright in the bed to see what was the matter; at which a wit from the gallery said aloud—'Do you call this a *tragedy*? Why, d—me, it is the *farce* of *Dead Alive*!'"[6] This outburst strikes me not so much as a breach of decorum but as exposure of a genre problem latent in a tragic denouement that relies on incredible, even laughable, revivals of Desdemona and reproductions of her voice.

Determination of the genre and effect of the play often come to rest on Desdemona even though she is not the title character (Othello) nor the one with the most lines (Iago). The earliest surviving response to the play comes from a 1610 letter of an Oxford student, Henry Jackson, who responds piteously to the victim of an elevated tragedy: "the celebrated Desdemona, slain in our presence by her husband, although she pleaded her case very effectively throughout, yet moved (us) more after she was dead, when, lying on her bed, she entreated the pity of the spectators by her very countenance."[7] For this male viewer, Desdemona's entreaty is more effective when she is dead and he can speak for her. His Desdemona is a page in the sense that others must state the message her surface bears. John Quincy Adams considered the play a secular parable: "When Othello smothers [Desdemona] in bed, the terror and the pity subside immediately to the sentiment that she had her just deserts."[8] He concluded, "The great moral lesson of The Tragedy of Othello, is that black and white blood cannot be intermingled in marriage without a gross outrage upon the laws of nature, and that in such violations nature will vindicate her laws."[9] Here, Adams refuses the "pity" the Oxford student extended to Desdemona, reading the tableau of the play's death scene as an interdiction against interracial marriage.

Jackson's catharsis and Adams's philosophical deduction reach opposite ends, but each requires the dead silence of Desdemona. The temptation for the literary scholar is to argue whether the play endorses the judgmental or the empathic response. Yet, I would argue, the masculinist perspective of the play is not moral but structural. The play invites a gathering to determine Desdemona's character as a daughter and wife, and her self-expression cannot override their authority. The moments when she revives to speak again threaten to become a feminist interruption, but they ultimately fail to disperse the putatively white synod gathered to assess her. Although he concluded that Othello is neither a piteous tragedy nor a moral exemplum, the unnamed wit in Woollery's audience designated the play a farce as a member of the interpretive fraternity that the play summoned before the long feminist project of its revision.

Woollery's reported resurrection could count as at least the fourth time that the audience senses that Desdemona has returned to life. Perhaps, then, the legendary heckler was aiming his barb as much at the play's own structure as at Woollery's alleged rupturing of dramatic illusion. The idea of Desdemona revived once more apparently exceeded his sense of the bounds of tragic decorum. His outburst reveals that, for him, act 5 edged into absurdity even before Woollery reportedly bolted up in bed. In the shell of solemn affect and conventional realism, he saw a glimpse of a farce based on a nonhuman character, which he calls "dead-alive."[10] This veritable zombie opens the path to encounter a Desdemona whose character and psyche (such as it is) are delimited by the attributes and capacities of paper. This person is necessarily paper-thin, no more than a surface her culture scans to derive her character.

This Desdemona, as flat and overwritten as a page, is not known today partly because of a relentless drive to make Othello realistic. From the Restoration—when the first woman replaced the boy actress in the reopened theatres—to today's Desdemonas who typically speak up and fight back, the general trend has been to make Desdemona plausible, autonomous, insightful, and political. Much like Othello, Desdemona has acquired the historical and political consciousness of the actors playing her. While I have seen some remarkable Desdemonas in this vein, my aim here is to recover an earlier conception in which the character is reducible to a stage persona with no more dimension than that of an imprinted page.

≱ᵉ

Act 5, scene 2 offers three remarkable opportunities to hear Desdemona's voice after her apparent death. The first time involves misdirection. Emilia's loud calls of "my lord" from beyond the door immediately appear to a reader as her lines. The typographical conventions of the modern Shakespeare edition fetishize each Shakespearean syllable and therefore fail to convey simultaneous or overlapping speech. Emilia's line has her speech prefix and occurs subsequent to Desdemona's. Therefore, a reader expects the two women to speak in succession. Yet, the performance of this script could easily confuse a theatre-goer, as it does Othello. Theatre historian Julie Hankey notes that the 1995 Oliver Park film has Emilia mimic Desdemona's voice, an echo that confuses Othello.[11] This approach, however, is not new. It has roots in earlier theatre practice.

Theatre historians Tiffany Stern and Simon Palfrey would observe that this possibility is integral to the parts once distributed to each actor. Under original conditions, actors did not receive the whole script but simply a roll containing the lines and cues of one part. The actor playing Emilia has studied a part in which the word "Lord" is her cue. However, Desdemona will cry out "O Lord! Lord! Lord!" an indeterminate number of times until the strangulation is complete (V.ii.84). The actor playing Emilia would not know how many times Desdemona might scream this last word. Thus, the women's voices could overlap, especially because Emilia's "What, ho!" picks up on the "O" in Desdemona's cry, just as "My Lord" would seem to specify or complete Desdemona's truncated "Lord" (85).[12]

The coinciding sounds and repeated cues suggest that Emilia and Desdemona should match the volume and pitch of their voices as much as possible. The voices must be coordinated to induce confusion, since Othello's next actions indicate that he mistakes the source of the cries. Duped by what seems a duplicate of Desdemona's voice, Othello engages in overkill, smothering an already silenced Desdemona again to ensure her death. The audience's experience is, at first, aligned with Othello's. Presumably the audience discovers the error before Othello does, as Emilia's unmuffled voice rings out while he smothers Desdemona a second time. Once convinced that the repeated cries of "my Lord" do not come from Desdemona, Othello asks the question that provides Emilia her next cue: "Who's there?" (89). When Emilia's answer comes, it is clearly from beyond the chamber. After a bit of musing aloud to himself, Othello summons Emilia to enter.

Yet, within fifteen lines of Emilia's onstage arrival, which would appear to confirm Desdemona's suffocation, Othello and the audience find the ingenue temporarily revived to offer cryptic answers to Emilia's inquest about the manner of death. Desdemona wakes from apparent death with some potentially farcical lines. Her ambiguous outburst "O falsely, falsely murdered" refers to the wrong inherent in Othello's deed (117), but it is also a macabre joke about the deceptive appearance of her death. When Emilia asks her to name her murderer, Desdemona replies, "Nobody, I myself, farewell; / Commend me to my kind lord; O, farewell" (124–25). These lines are not only improbable and incoherent, but also contain a false ending: the first "farewell" cues Othello's next line, which Desdemona must interrupt to speak yet *again*. Skeptical audience members would be forgiven for asking themselves if she would finally stay down this time.

Miss Woollery's heckler dismissed the tragedy as a farce after the trick of reviving Desdemona had been played three times. His agitated quip offers us the opportunity to focus on a structural problem already present in the play's final scene: how is Desdemona capable of speaking after death? A realist performance tradition attempts to preserve decorum through a rational solution: Othello's first attempt at murdering his wife simply fails. Yet, rational solutions presume that Shakespearean tragedy has always been an occasion of high solemnity—or should have been.[13] This eighteenth-century performance recalls a time before his tragedies were sacred. The gallery wit's exasperation illuminates the potentially absurd business in the final scene: the aural trick of Desdemona's voice seeming to come from outside the room; Desdemona's resurrection, not after Othello's first attempt to smother her, but after his *second;* her return to silent death after words that clarify nothing.

Today's performances *almost* fully manage unruliness to produce an uninterrupted serious tragedy.[14] Yet, contemporaries of the gallery wit were still trying to figure out how to make Desdemona's death plausible and generically fitting. In the 1790s some commentators engaged in a brief dispute about the staging of the murder. In 1797 the *Oracle and Public Advertiser* included a piece in which "a correspondent lately expressed a doubt of the propriety of Kemble's stabbing Desdemona." The unnamed correspondent marshaled as support Othello's vow that he will not "shed her blood."[15] Yet, a subsequent response refers to the commentary of editor George Steevens to argue that "nothing but his stabbing her can reconcile her death after speaking; for if, after an attempt to suffocate her, she could recover her voice at all, she would not have died."[16] The manner of Desdemona's death cannot be reconciled with realism, given the information in the script. Innovations such as stabbing make realism the dominant aesthetic, but I would like to recover what logic allows the Desdemona of a farce to speak after Othello—and, presumably, the audience—are certain that she has breathed her last.

One clue is offered in the manner of the murder. What if I were to stipulate that Othello chokes her? Although choking does not make postmortem speech any more likely, it has a remarkable resonance in the world of ink and paper. Joseph Moxon's early modern guide to printing offers suggestive language: "If a Form be not Washt in due time, the Inck will get into the Hollows of the Face of the Letter: And that getting in of the Inck is called *choaking* of the Letter."[17] Its face covered with too much ink, this letter might blur or fail to make a full impression. Choking a letter does not kill it; choking mars the letter's expression on the page, as with Desdemona's final lines, delivered when she has absorbed Othello's color from his kisses and this struggle on their bed. This additional sense of choking comports with Othello's vow not to shed Desdemona's blood and repositions the play as a surreal it-narrative—not as Rymer's *Tragedy of the Handkerchief* but as "The Tragedy of Ink and Paper."[18] Before realism became the dominant mode, the inkface *Othello* could always unfold as "the *farce* of *Dead Alive*" because Desdemona's status as inked paper endows her with the uncanny—indeed, inhuman—capacity to speak after being choked.[19]

Inheritors of *Othello* as realistic tragedy have barely asked how Desdemona could speak after being smothered. Consequently, few have noticed that Othello's errors regarding Desdemona—so ridiculous they potentially tip the play into farce—often occur in scenes when paper is either present or invoked. The problems with Desdemona's doubled and alienated voice stem from the ultimate source of Desdemona's vocal problems—her reduction to paper.

Desdemona's testimony in the Senate relies implicitly on what Othello will later name as her status as "fair paper." In the early scene, he asks that she be summoned, confident that he will not be found "foul in her report."[20] As Othello wagered, Desdemona speaks against her father—and, therefore, in what seems to be her own voice. This antipatriarchal voice establishes herself and Othello as officially blameless.[21] The spotless report that Desdemona offers on her first appearance corresponds to the actor's face, enhanced to a cosmetic ultra-whiteness.[22] One could argue, however, that Desdemona does not speak autonomously. Rather, the culturally assigned meaning of her fair skin speaks for her and for her husband—for their union. She attempts to perform both parts of what she calls "a divided duty," to father and to husband, but filial duty cannot be fulfilled in a patriarchal society when the father disapproves of the marital choice. Fatally split even in the moment in which she avows her desire, Desdemona will prove powerless to master and deploy the contradictory meanings assigned to the blackness the painted Othello transfers to her.

Under original performance conditions, Desdemona risks acquiring blackness from both erotic and abusive contact with her painted husband over the course of the play. This discoloration is figured as a black ink that inscribes Desdemona with enigmatic writing that simultaneously signals the sacred and the profane.[23] Once Othello has become convinced of his wife's infidelity, he encapsulates his problem in a dense metaphor: "Her name, that was as fresh / As Dian's visage is now begrim'd and black / As mine own face" (III.iii.386–88) Scholars have tended to fixate on the end of this simile, the visage of Othello. However, to understand the blackness that is most central to this passage, it pays to bracket Othello's face temporarily and to attend to the women invoked. This reorientation draws attention to the name of his wife and the visage of a Roman goddess.

The color-coded public estimation of Desdemona's name is the occasion of these comparisons to the epitomes of chastity (figured as white and feminine) and uncleanness (figured as black and masculine). Although it is tempting to think of "name" as merely a metonym for reputation, the full conceit disallows pure abstraction. In this figuration, a name is an artifact that cannot shed its material qualities. In fact, the dialogue grounds the "[bad] name" circulating in gossip in an inked name set down in records or, indeed, in the biblical Book of Life.[24] Desdemona's unsullied character has a freshness exemplified by the visage of the Roman goddess of chastity, Diana. Othello serves as the agent of befoulment. The face of an early modern stage moor, painted as it would have been, defiles the imagined face of Diana as well as the figure of Desdemona's printed name.[25]

This conceit is notable not only for its insistence on materiality but also for the dueling functions of blackness. Othello figures good name as a legible black inscription or impression. Its letters are presumably well-formed and impervious to fading or smearing—which qualities render this deep black name figuratively "fresh," un-degraded. Clean and uncorrupted, these letters wind up sharing associations with whiteness in a semiotic universe in which white complexion was usually deemed original and white objects deemed unmarked. Yet, the virtual whiteness of this undefiled name can become black again through a "begrim[ing]" defacement, an overwriting such as a smudge or lewd marginalia.[26] Here are the knotted conundrums of blackness in *The Moor of Venice:* black is of the face and of the text; it is the sign of the faithful document and of malicious (mis)representation. Blackness is inescapably doubled. Once imprinted, Desdemona becomes double-voiced, a quality that accounts for her speech—so prolific that the prospect of death cannot focus its connotations, nor death itself prevent it from sounding again.

As Desdemona becomes increasingly blackened, her speech becomes increasingly ambiguous.[27] Interpretive problems arise first because white paper cannot speak for itself. Although whiteness has significance in Christian terminology as virtue never blemished or miraculously restored, in Western writing cultures, white paper is voiceless. Only black marks signify. Once Desdemona has been blackened, her voice is overtaken by that of black marks which are forever caught between sanctioned imprint and profane addition.

The material representation of her reputation, her inked name, is black in its original state *and* in its sullied form—hence the strange doubling of "black and begrim'd" in Othello's phrasing, as if one would not suffice. Othello conjures a black name that was cleanly impressed but is later befouled.

The agony of Othello's attempts to read Desdemona lies in this dual significance of blackness as a color both original and acquired and, therefore, either unadulterated or defacing. Thus, he finds himself imagining two inscriptions after he has marked her with his kisses (and perhaps his blows) in Cyprus: "Was this fair paper, this most goodly book / Made to write whore upon?" (IV.ii.71–72). This image contains the confusion of Protestant patriarchalism: the metaphors for Desdemona's unmarked face are both blank paper and page from the Good Book, already inked. If Desdemona is "fair paper," then any black mark mars. However, if she is a biblical page. the blackness of a sanctioned imprint does not befoul her. With the two images combined, Othello imagines a divine impression has been supplemented by another black inscription—whore. He envisions a profane human hand has scrawled whore *over* biblical text or beside it in the white margins.

In the semiotics of print and script, black ink has two clashing significances beyond any reconciliation. Therefore, Othello's inability to determine Desdemona's fidelity has a cultural cause: the culture that educated him cannot answer whether black ink is a goodly mark or a foul one.[28] Can the unseemly associations of blackness be disregarded, as one does when reading the black text of the scriptures? Or is all blackening profane, like a stain on a white textile, or an obscenity defacing an authorized text? In early *Othello,* semantic content, the source of the inscription, the material properties of printing and writing inks, and the values ascribed to the color black become conjoined in a text that is both visible and invisible, irresistibly meaningful but resistant to interpretation.[29] Irrespective of the words that issue from her mouth, what Desdemona's blackened face says is inherently multifold.[30] This confluence of suggested meanings manifests in the multiple, conflicting voices that are attributed to Desdemona.

In the strange logic of this play, Desdemona's voice is always divided between her own desires and those of her male readers. However, her capacity to express her will voluntarily declines precipitously after she is overwritten by Othello's kisses and blows in Cyprus. After these markings, her meaning becomes increasingly visible on her surface. Words issuing from her own throat are subsumed by what has been prescribed and inscribed. This process begins after her first appearance, when she offers Othello an unblemished report in her own voice. Subsequently, she begins to accrue the black marks that speak for her.[31] On the shore of Cyprus, Cassio also refers to her status as an unmarked page, saying that she "excels the quirks of blazoning pens" (II.i.63).

As Iago spins his impromptu verses, impugning women's character, Emilia responds, "You shall not write my praise" (II.i.116). Desdemona, as the embodiment of paper, cannot resist the potential to be paired with ink and, thus, asks how Iago "wouldst praise" her (II.i.117).[32] As Emilia and Cassio have fused praise with the written, Desdemona's request for praise constitutes a request that Iago (over)write her.[33] Desdemona achieves her desire to be written upon just after her interactions with Cassio and Iago. While these men leave no impression, the painted Othello apparently marks her with passionate kisses at their seaside reunion. From the time that she acquires these black marks on (and against) her character, Othello follows an overdetermined cultural imperative to doubt it.[34]

The equation of Desdemona with paper also becomes a part of the play's sound design, in that her voice becomes entangled with the disembodied voice of pages that appear onstage. When messengers arrive carrying papers from Venice, Othello kisses "the instrument of their pleasure," as he has kissed and will kiss only one other object, the face of his wife (IV.i.218). More important, it is impossible to determine whether the words he says while his face is buried in the paper are directed to the missive from Venice or to Desdemona. Modern editions clarify the confusion by inserting stage directions such as "reading" to indicate that Othello's words come from the paper. Yet, the effect of the scene relies on an inability to determine whether he is addressing the dead (inanimate, unresponsive) letter or Desdemona. Adding to the confusion, as Othello's lips move while he reads, it can appear as if he is continually whispering to—or even kissing—the paper. The paper, then, acquires Desdemona's erotic charge: it is, as Othello says, the "instrument" of the state's "pleasure[s]" and not, merely, of its command. The metaphorical speech that has long been ascribed to paper—the casual way of asking what a paper or its absent author *says*—has been conflated with Desdemona's proper, human voice. When he speaks to the paper, she answers.

> *Desdemona:* Cousin, there's fall'n between him and my lord
> An unkind breach, but you shall make all well.
> *Othello:* Are you sure of that?
> *Desdemona:* My lord?
> *Othello: (reading)* "This fail you not to do, as you will"—
> *Lodovico:* He did not call; he's busy in the paper.
> Is there division 'twixt my lord and Cassio?
> *Desdemona:* A most unhappy one. I would do much
> T' atone them, for the love I bear to Cassio.
> *Othello:* Fire and brimstone!
> *Desdemona:* My lord?

Othello: Are you wise?
Desdemona: What, is he angry?
Lodovico: May be the letter moved him. (IV.i.224–35)

This fusion of the marked Desdemona and the page recovers *Othello* as the "farce of Dead Alive." Desdemona vocalizes after death in the same way that paper speaks on behalf of its author. However, Desdemona's posthumous speech conjures the nightmare version of the timeworn literary conceit of the texts that speak for eternity. Authors relinquish their human voice when they leave behind textual traces, despite our conventional tags: *Aristotle says; Shakespeare says.* Their message always arrives in the voice of the person reading it. Therefore, Desdemona does not project a unique, expressive self into eternity but, rather, *loses* her own voice to its paper mediation. Consequently, she speaks with the ambiguity of the forgery. While Othello authenticates the life he dictates with blood from his own throat, Desdemona is forever represented by marks made (and subsequently read) by another.[35] This lack of authenticity condemns her to die as an oxymoron: a faithful harlot. Desdemona cannot speak over telltale black marks against her character, and patriarchal culture cannot resolve imperatives to read them as both signs of sin and traces of contact with her lawful husband.

I arrive, then, at the heart of "the farce of dead-alive": Desdemona's paper—whether unmarked or stamped with her husband's imprint—always has a cultural meaning that she has no part in constructing and can only attempt to speak through. Dead Desdemona is the tragic fulfillment of a dream of patriarchal knowledge and control—a dream that *The Moor of Venice* reproduces but did not originate. As the Atlantic World system expanded in the long eighteenth century, *Othello* remained relevant because the play already encoded imperatives of patrilineality and racial hygiene crucial to the maldistribution of property, pleasure, and protection characteristic of that system. The next two chapters feature white women who sensed precisely why *Othello* remained resonant throughout the long eighteenth century. These women confronted social forces that would stake the reproduction of racial capitalism on the fidelity of white women but also exclude them from the political administration of the commercial empires in which they lived. Desdemona's suspect and revocable whiteness, as well as her inability to speak credibly on her own behalf: these were conundrums of character that would be achingly familiar to Aphra Behn, Abigail Adams, and Sarah Siddons. Their successful bids for membership in male-dominated white interpretive communities—and the unexpected costs thereof—are the subject of the next two chapters.

🕮 2

"Be Thus When Thou Art Dead"
Aphra Behn's Remediation of *Othello*

Aphra Behn's short novel "Oroonoko" (1688) supplies a wealth of evidence of how its author, a feminist writer and critic *avant la lettre,* felt about the popular seventeenth-century tragedy *The Moor of Venice,* which we now call *Othello.* She had ample opportunity to read and see a play at least eight decades old that was a sensation once again in the Restoration—no doubt, in part, because of the recent, titillating innovation of a real live woman playing Desdemona, rather than a boy in white paint.[1] It has become a commonplace of scholarship to note that Behn echoes *Othello* in writing of a noble African warrior—the titular Oroonoko—who, under great duress, murders his wife. However, Behn's decision to convert the white wife Desdemona into Imoinda, a black African woman, begins to suggest the many ways that the author refused to reproduce with her own pen *Othello*'s literal and metaphorical staining of fair-skinned Desdemona. To track Behn's refusals requires focused attention on her choices of medium and metaphor, which aim to convert a patriarchal stage play into literary property that could serve women—or, at least the female author.

Whether she ever saw *The Moor of Venice* performed, Behn was clearly familiar with what I have been calling inkface, theatrical codes treating black paint as both transferable and legible. Thus, when encountering the Shakespearean source of "Oroonoko" in print or on stage, she would have been able to envision the telltale marks that convey dishonor from black, moorish slaves to their white lovers. From the pun on fair papers when Othello assures the Senate they will not "find [him] foul in her report" (I.iii.117) to the final scene in which Othello "dye[s]" her "upon a kiss," Desdemona's journey to death is marked by her blackening at the hands of her husband.[2] Her exercise of sexual volition against her father's choice, as well as her erotic experience, manifests as black marks against her character, impressed upon her person.[3] The double valence of the marks of Othello's kiss and touch becomes apparent on her deathbed when he thunders, "[T]hink on thy sins" and she answers, "[T]hey are loves I bear to you" (V.ii.39–40). According to the symbolism of the play's real or threatened cosmetic transfer, the love she holds for Othello is her sin, a love she "bears" as burden and as discoloration.[4] For the white wife of a stage moor, even *fidelity* leaves the black mark of sexual shame.

As if the tedious elaboration of this trope were not galling enough, Behn also would have had to endure hearing (or reading) women demeaned as a class in Iago's banter on the shores of Cyprus.[5] The kinds of women Iago names exemplify extreme types, from fair skinned to dark, witty to foolish. However, Iago informs his wife, Emilia, and Desdemona that these attributes are inconsequential: women, whatever their physical or mental character, all amount to nothing more than lusty vessels for reproduction. Desdemona earlier solicits his misogyny, asking, "What wouldst write of me if thou shouldst praise me?" (II.i.117). Emilia then rejects Iago's authority to establish her character, announcing, "You shall not write my praise" (I.ii.116). The literary critic Lynda Boose would note that the potential text that Emilia forbids epitomizes *pornography,* specifically "a written story of whores." In Boose's argument, *The Moor of Venice* "construes all women as insatiably carnal" and "rallies its followers into a male bond formed around time-honored misogyny."[6] Aphra Behn could not have failed to notice that each of the play's three women—Desdemona, Emilia, and Bianca—spends most of her time desperately defending her sexual reputation.

Iago's savage denigration of all women, regardless of color or intelligence, seems to have inspired Behn to conduct an experiment: could a woman writer take hold of means of characterization to produce a narrative in which the women of *Othello* could avert the literal marks and the aura of stigma that Iago conjures? More specifically, would it be possible for a woman writer to accept *Othello*'s premises about character, the materials that signify it, and the play's tragic mode—and yet produce triumphant women whose character is not assassinated?[7]

These questions regarding the materiality of print and theatre reframe the political inquiries that have shaped the powerful scholarship on "Oroonoko." The first wave of Behn scholars, whom Srinivas Aravamudan calls "Oroonokoists," celebrated the novel as a simultaneous indictment of patriarchy for metaphorically enslaving women and of slavery for metaphorically feminizing the noble hero.[8] They saw the great sympathy the narrator has for the hero and celebrated the power of this pioneering woman writer to contribute to Abolition.[9] A subsequent wave of scholars, whom Aravamudan terms "Imoindaists," noted the narrator's comparative disregard for—and even rivalry with—Oroonoko's black wife, Imoinda, and indicted the white author for a failure to work for the liberation of women of color alongside that of white women.[10]

The bulk of "Oroonoko" scholarship has bypassed Behn's primary facility as a dramatist—a theorist of gender and genre—in order to assess where this prose fiction belongs in the history of the novel.[11] This tremendous outpouring of ideological critique has been enabled by the presumption that Behn's text is essentially a novel.[12] By accounting for the ways in which Behn's selection of media and symbolic materials is itself an ideological choice—one that *precedes* and *conditions* the racialized and gendered relations in the text that follow from it—I aim to enrich the existing conversation on "Oroonoko." The politics of Behn's novella are inextricably bound up with her choices of genre, material, and metaphor—and insufficient attention to those authorial choices potentially yields distortions of her intertextual project.

Though opting for fiction instead of drama, Behn largely restricts herself to character types and materials supplied by the blackface theatre of *Othello*. She accepts the major character types (general, lieutenant, mistress, maid, interfering father) from *Othello* and the materials through which moral character is conveyed (ink, stone, and paper). It is, therefore, difficult to ascribe aesthetic concept or political responsibility to Behn alone, as her critics and champions do, when much of the matter that "Oroonoko" works comes from *Othello*. The materials and premises of Behn's novella are not necessarily a guide to *her* unique mind or a direct window to contemporary metropolitan or imperial thought, as ideological critique sometimes has it. What they do reveal about Behn's mind and other contemporary mentalities appears in a new light when "Oroonoko" is understood as an experiment with medium. Behn seems to have designed her short fiction to test whether the paradigm exemplified by *Othello* could be re-mediated (through print) to disable the tragic choice it poses between women's chastity (sexual dispossession) and sexual experience on their own terms (as a fatal blackening of character).[13]

Prefiguring the answer songs popularized centuries later by R&B girl groups, "Oroonoko" relies on its predecessor, redeploying existing materials to contest some unacceptable premises. In fact, the politics of "Oroonoko" look quite different when the critic looks backward to *Othello* onstage and not only forward to the emergent form of the English novel. From that vantage, Behn's text emerges as an idiosyncratic reading that is historically situated without making it a representative text of the period. Artistic production plays out real, social conflicts in the chosen medium of the artist, and the choice of medium itself indirectly reveals Behn's calculations about how much authority print, speech, and performance might yield her. Instead of speaking an imperial discourse undifferentiated from that of her fellow Britons, Behn becomes visible as a particular woman who took up available materials and chose desirable venues in which to stake a claim to social authority.

In this chapter, I consider ideological, aesthetic, and historical questions anew, bracketing the relationship of "Oroonoko" to the history of the novel and treating it, primarily, as a retort to the still-popular *Othello*. In the very gap that Aravamudan describes as the critical impasse between Imoin-daists and Oroonokoists, I aim to produce a historically sensitive analysis of Behn's engagement with *The Moor of Venice*—one that does not sacrifice the fiction's prominent feminist experiment to accommodate a racial critique. I pursue this renegotiation of an intersectional approach to "Oroonoko" by fo-cusing on the ways in which both Desdemona figures—the novella's young narrator *and* Imoinda—claim "eternal Empire over" black Oroonoko.[14] I con-tend that both Oroonoko and Imoinda become opportunities to resignify and redistribute the damning blackness Desdemona absorbs in *The Moor of Venice* and, in so doing, imagine her as the virtuous victor in a tragic plot.

Rather than simply an early novel, "Oroonoko" is the work of a writer comfortable in diverse media who specifically chose print for what it afforded (i.e., her ownership of a male figure) and what it denied (i.e., the physical presence of *any* body).[15] The novel's conception of media such as painting, sculpture, speech, and writing is set against the spectacle of female blackening ritually enacted in the all-white (but no longer all-male) theatre, with *Othello* being the foremost example. The choice of prose fiction allows Behn to frag-ment the male prerogatives that structured the character economy that *Othello* drew upon and perpetuated. In the end, Behn's multiplication and partial re-distribution of character traits and prerogatives from *Othello* do not result in a consistent philosophy, yet the (proto)feminist project propelling it is every-where visible.[16]

The Published Voice of Behn's Prefaces

This section is concerned with Aphra Behn's deft manipulation of voice in her printed prefaces. The tonal effects and social frisson Behn skillfully pro-duced open the possibility for reading "Oroonoko" as a deadly serious parody of *Othello*. Behn was adept at infusing the paratexts of her printed works with breaches of decorum that strike us as genuine personality. The paradigmatic book ("The Book," in fact) is the Bible—and orthodox Protestant imagined the voice emanating from it to be grave and somber, a voice without what we think of as personality, unshaped by human sociality, issuing edicts and proc-lamations from a time and place beyond that of its readers.[17] Behn scandalizes the idea of the *good book* with her solicitations—now coy, now brazen—of a prurient gaze. The content of her plays and her framing remarks about them bank on the appeal of a calculated insouciance, a tempered outrageousness. Aphra Behn wrote *bad* books.

For example, in the epistle to the reader that opens *The Dutch Lover*, she so-licits her readers with appealing flattery: "Good, Sweet, Honey, Sugar-candied READER. (Which I think is more than any one has call'd you yet.) I must have a word or two with you before you do advance into the Treatis."[18] She moves smoothly from this self-conscious fawning to a thrilling combination of self-aggrandizement and apology. The word that she demands is "not," she insists, "to beg [the reader's] pardon" for interrupting our pursuit of our affairs with what she confesses is her "idle pamphlet." Rather, she contends that her readers are the idle ones, whom she might be saving from "worse imployment," by offering relatively innocuous reading material. Should her readers not be idle, she encourages them to "get . . . gone about [their] business" or to excuse her and "lay the fault upon [them]sel[ves]" if they "mis[s]pend" their time. Fluctuating from self-deprecating to imperious, solicitous to demanding, Behn here shows shades of both personae that Catherine Gallagher attributes to her—prostitute-playwright and author-monarch.[19] It is the performance of a queen, or perhaps that of a diva.[20] Whatever epithet we use, Behn's paratexts demand careful attention, as their slippery, improvised quality suggests a rhetorical address as supple as it is crafty. The electrifying effects of her works often result, as here, not purely from salacious content but also from transgressive ways of mixing the conventions of different media, such as using the disembodied voice of print to say what no proper woman could say publicly in her own person and, simultaneously, lending somber print the lively, unpredictable aspects of a witty voice. Behn learned the lesson of Desdemona's failure to intervene in her own characterization and used an impressive array of tactics to render the page a site of feminine self-fashioning.

This insinuating Aphra Behn arguably lurks in the apology in the dedication to Lord Maitland that precedes "Oroonoko" (121–22):

'Twill be no Commendation to the Book to assure your Lordship I writ it in a few Hours, though it may serve to Excuse some of its Faults of Connexion, for I never rested my Pen a Moment for Thought: 'Tis purely the Merit of my Slave that must render it worthy of the Honour it begs; and the Author of that Subscribing herself,

> My Lord
> Your Lordship's most oblig'd
> and obedient Servant
> A. Behn

Most scholars have approached this preface as a means of investigating matters of historicity or genre.[21] Are the "Faults of Connexion" an indication that Behn was never in Surinam, despite her claims that she was?[22] Or do they indicate the pressures imposed by the aesthetic ideologies of different genres, such as travel narrative, romance, and the emergent novel?[23] These questions assume a greater generic distinction than I would. I view the Behn of "Oroonoko" as a drama queen on the page, experimenting with how voice and spectacle might translate from theatre to print.

Scholars in the 1990s reminded us of Behn's dramatic flair by establishing that *Othello* is the primary model not only for Aphra Behn's short fiction but also for the numerous versions of "Oroonoko" that proved theatrical hits for the next two centuries.[24] I intend to show that a study of the characterizing materials that "Oroonoko" shares with *Othello* gives us good reason to think of Behn's confession of her text's "faults of connexion" as a retrospective snipe by an author who spent significant time studying, inhabiting, and rethinking Shakespeare's popular tragedy. Behn seems to have concluded that if one is going to rewrite *Othello* faithfully—particularly if that person is a self-respecting woman—she must do it without resting her pen for thought.[25] The alleged faults of *her* text would seem to be supplied at least as much by the inconsistencies of her source as by some flaw in her own conception.[26]

Behn was accustomed to writing significant revisions of her male predecessors' texts. While she established her reputation first as a dramatist, by the 1688 publication of "Oroonoko," this first English woman to make her living as a professional writer (and perhaps the first professional writer full stop) had added poetry and epistolary novels to her repertoire.[27] These included translations from Latin and French and reworkings of Spanish stories.[28] Sometimes these engagements were so close that they resulted in charges of plagiarism.[29] One of her early successes, her 1676 play *Abdelazar,* staged six years into her career, faced such accusations. The play was, notably, a revision of Dekker's *Lust's Dominion.* In the introduction, I mentioned that Dekker's villain Eleazar the moor drinks the key ink ingredient of gall and then begins to refer to his face as inky. Behn chose to revive what I have been calling inkface plays, preposterous productions in which moors and their white paramours lay together to produce pages instead of offspring.[30] She wrote "Oroonoko" in a state of financial distress: the consolidation of theatres in the early 1680s had diminished the demand for new plays, and her specialty (the bawdy comedy) was out of favor—as was her political support of the absolutist Stuart monarchs.[31] These developments pushed her to increase her writing in genres outside drama.[32]

Through print, she solicited book buyers and elite patrons rather than the sustained mass attendance required for her to make money from plays.[33] Reworking *The Moor of Venice* in printed form would seem a potentially ingenious way to navigate her financial conundrum: even the play's fiercest critic, Thomas Rymer, allowed that *Othello* was tremendously popular during the Restoration. The desire for moorish plays—so strong around the turn of the seventeenth century—survived the shuttering of the playhouses from 1642 to 1660. Therefore, adapting *Othello* as a short fictional tale of her own might offer a quick infusion of cash from a patron and sell well in print. We can imagine that adapting a play with such cultural purchase would not tax her capacities: without directly criticizing Shakespeare or lovers of *Othello,* she implied that she could write the tale without pausing to think.

This attention to Behn's printed prefaces provides an alternative to Jonathan Elmer's recent proposition regarding Behn's choice of medium: "Perhaps [Behn's] decision *not* to make a stage drama of ['Oroonoko'] indicates her conviction that the new world of deterritorialized and racialized sovereignty was no longer expressible in terms of the theatrical unities [of action, place, and time], but leeched and drifted into ambiguous spaces and twilit times, only graspable by a spasmodic—'I writ it in a few hours'—and 'inglorious' prose."[34] While Elmer may well be correct about the pressures that the Atlantic World system placed on dramatic representation, Behn did not endeavor to uphold the classical unities in her plays. In a preface written fifteen years earlier, she declared that she had no use for the "musty rules of Unity," replacing them with the simple rules of "making [plays] pleasant, and avoiding scurrility."[35] By this light, her declaring that she wrote her version of *Othello* "in a few hours" seems more an audacious commentary on her source than a confession that her writing emerged from involuntary spasms.

If Behn meant to expose the incongruities of *Othello,* she would not have been alone in noticing them. Indeed, the implied mock in her fidelity to *Othello* anticipated Thomas Rymer's scathing remarks on the play half a decade later: "Nothing is more odious in Nature than an improbable lye; And, certainly, never was any Play fraught, like this of *Othello,* with improbabilities. . . . For the unraveling of the Plot, as they call it, never was old deputy Recorder in a Country Town, with his spectacles in summoning up the evidence, at such a puzzle: so blunder'd, and bedoultefied: as is our Poet, to have a good riddance: And get the Catastrophe off his hands."[36] Rymer's attack was designed to dislodge *Othello,* with what he deemed improbable characters engaged in a trivial plot about a handkerchief, from the loftiest genre of tragedy. Although implicit, Behn would appear to have conducted a reading of *Othello* as thorough and bruising as Rymer's.[37] She identified inconsistencies of form, crucially linking these contradictions to the color-coded materials through which *Othello* produced gendered character and imbued it with social meaning and value. From Behn's point of view, any play in which a kiss is a sign of fidelity *and* infidelity—or ink is tied both to Holy imprint and profane scribble—is profoundly disconnected.

Behn seems to have been simultaneously entranced and enraged by the means of gender characterization realized onstage in *Othello.* Thus, her approach to "versioning" *Othello* was two-pronged: she inhabited its absurdities, accepting its premises about human character, color, and legibility; yet, she approached them all in ways that thwart the play's patriarchal premises.[38] In the first chapter, I argued that *Othello* offered audiences patriarchy's wish fulfillment and its nightmare. Through the agency of the stage moor's paint, a woman's sexual history appears in telltale black marks on her face. Male audience members were invited to enjoy and be dismayed by the problem of Desdemona's literally marked sexual reputation. In "Oroonoko," Behn conjures a space beyond the patrilineal property relations undergirding both the monarchical Old World and the mercantilist New—a realm of love in which women achieve "eternal empire" over men who willingly submit to them.[39]

A quick review of the forms of memorializing in Shakespeare's play gives a sense of the materials Behn decided to employ. Othello promises not to shed his wife's blood, "nor scar her skin as white as monumental alabaster." In memory of her former unspotted reputation, he intends to leave her a corpse, a white statue, an object that he can "love ... after" (V.ii.20–21) he ends her deceitful life. Desdemona asks for her wedding sheets to be laid on her bed the night of her death. She asks to be shrouded in the linens; Othello associates white cloth with her chastity, calling her "pale as [her] smock ... cold like [her] chastity" (V.ii.273, 276). Last, Othello's final words are to be "set ... down" in ink and conveyed back to the Senate (V.ii.412). Othello's "bloody period" (V.ii.418) invokes a martial masculinity "round [and] unvarnished" (I.iii.105), "all in all sufficient" (IV.i.300).

Behn gathers these same materials of gendered characterization but redistributes them. Oroonoko—a warrior modeled after Othello—is the figure in her text associated with statuary in lieu of Desdemona. Behn's Imoinda, called a "fair Queen of Night" (132), resembles Desdemona in beauty but not in complexion, and both women's skin matches their clothing. Imoinda bears dark tattoos over her entire body which the narrator compares to "high Poynt," a lace pattern (160).[40] Last, her narrator carries on long after Oroonoko refuses to speak; it is her pen and not her hero's blood that forms the text's final period.

This brief overview of the modes of memorializing her text's major figures lets us know how much Behn studied and retained *Othello's* methods of characterization. In fact, I would argue that the qualities of the various media—the hard brittleness of stone, the externality of clothing, the indelibility of the ink tattoo—supplied her with character information and determined the fates of the novella's major characters.[41] Behn's figures—as I argued in the previous chapter regarding Shakespeare's—are shaped by the qualities of the materials with which they are associated, rather than by deep, psychological interiority or fidelity to historical persons.[42] The only fidelity Behn exemplifies in this text is in remaining true to the materials of characterization given in *Othello,* though she turns them to unexpected ends. Viewed in this light, "Oroonoko" emerges as an experiment or an étude, designed to ascertain whether one could adhere strictly to her source's materials and metaphors—as well as its tragic mode—and yet have a Desdemona figure who is triumphant in her death. "Oroonoko" constitutes a protofeminist experiment with self-possession—woman's control of her characterization, especially in the arena of sexual desire and marriage.

The Page as a Site of Remediation

One might well ask why Aphra Behn did not create a dramatic version of *Othello* to rival Shakespeare's, if she found his play so flawed. Although Behn could not have known it, "Oroonko" was destined for theatrical success. When demand for new plays picked up again after her death, her hastily written no-vella spawned a series of stage adaptations that were perennial hits into the first quarter of the nineteenth century.[43] Indeed, alongside other sensations such as *The Revenge* (1721), *The Padlock* (1768), and *Othello* itself, these *Oroonoko*s were among the most bankable plays of the era, prompting one scholar to make the punning observation that moorish plays put theatre companies "in the black."[44]

Thomas Southerne, the first dramatist to rework "Oroonoko," in a 1695 adaptation, inaugurated the search for Behn's motivations in choosing print over performance, musing: "[Behn] had a great command of the stage, and I have often wondered that she would bury her favorite hero in a novel when she might have revived him in the scene. She thought either that no actor could represent him; or she could not bear him represented."[45] I will return to South-erne's misperception of which characters most engaged Behn's affections. For now, I want to note that the alterations in his play, which premiered approxi-mately seven years after Behn's novella, indicate that "reviv[ing]" "Oroonoko" in the theatre would have pushed toward a straightforward restaging of *Othello* rather than the Desdemona-redeeming version Behn had in mind.

The frontispiece of Southerne's *Oroonoko,* an emblem drawn from stage practice, resembles nothing so much as Othello's murder of Desdemona, albeit outdoors and, thus, without its signature bed.[46] Each of the subsequent stage adaptations followed Southerne and reinserted Behn's story in the governing framework of *Othello*'s plot and premises. The image depicts the climax of the play's high plot, in which Oroonoko murders his wife Imoinda to prevent her from becoming the sexual prey of slaveholders. The black husband hesitates in performing an honor killing on a *white* woman who welcomes the stabbing with open arms.[47] While Shakespeare's Desdemona has occasional moments of defiance and resistance that elude Southerne's Imoinda, the hero's pained reluctance and the goal of preventing the ruination of white female virtue are consistent with *Othello*.[48]

Maintaining the dual heroism of Oroonoko and white Imoinda, their elevated status as tragic lovers, required a radical alteration of Behn's concept. Southerne's Oroonoko comports visually with the dominant representation of Othello across the long eighteenth century, as performed by such luminaries as John Phillip Kemble.[49] There is no attempt to liken him to a princely warrior of Coromantien or a maroon leader, his two most prominent roles in Behn's novella. In the playhouse, the elevated, romantic Othello is, in George Schuyler's memorable twentieth-century phrase, merely a "lampblacked Anglo-Saxon."[50] Even more glaring than the costuming of Oroonoko is Southerne's alteration of Imoinda: a "*Black Venus*" in Behn's novel becomes a white woman onstage (131), as numerous scholars have remarked.[51]

Faced with Southerne's remarkable substitution of a white Imoinda, the scholar Felicity Nussbaum speculates that the desire for a black heroine must have prompted Behn's option for page over stage.[52] According to Nussbaum,

A reluctant Oroonoko holds a dagger midair while hesitating to kill his wife, Imoinda, who would welcome the death stroke. Frontispiece from *Oroonoko,* by Thomas Southerne, London, 1735. (Houghton Library, Harvard University, TS 931.2)

the London stage recruited no black actresses until the nineteenth century, all but proscribed blacking up for women, and created "no central black parts for women comparable to Othello's or Oroonoko's roles until late in the century."[53] Therefore, Behn had to abandon theatre for print in order to explore a character such as her black Imoinda. Although justly influential, Nussbaum's hypothesis has one significant weakness.

It is difficult to imagine that not a single woman would have been willing to black up if such a paid role were available. As Nussbaum herself has noted, actors typically did not hail from families of independent means and, therefore, needed work.[54] If we were to find testimony of women saying they did not wish to play blackface parts or that they faced social, judicial, or financial sanctions for doing so, then we might conclude there was no desire to play any of the moorish women involved in the bed tricks of the early seventeenth century.[55] Absent such evidence, the search for potential explanations for Behn's choice of medium and of heroine must continue.

One enticing clue lies in the fact that Restoration and eighteenth-century actresses were blackened *on*stage even if they did not black up *back*stage.[56] The dramas with stage blackamoors and their lovers typically revolved around whether or not the paint from the male characters would stain these English actresses' skins, names, reputations, and progeny.[57] Throughout this book, moments of concern about Desdemona's person and reputation reliably follow physical contact between the painted stage moor and his fair-skinned wife. Behn's use of an already black woman in "Oroonoko" strongly indicates that she did not want to stage another drama in which the female figure's entry into erotic experience was symbolized by a shameful denigration. Like Shakespeare before her, Behn shows relatively little interest in cultural accuracy or psychological realism when it comes to her Imoinda. The primary goal seems to have been to produce a female partner for a blackamoor who would be exempted from the inevitable dramatic narrative of staining and shame. The fact that Southerne's white Imoinda ruled the stage for over a century suggests that the theatre culture could produce and consume an even more bathetic and sentimental *Othello* but had little appetite for the protofeminist tale that Behn created by disabling patriarchal plot machinery with an already black Desdemona figure.

The scholar Lara Bovilsky recently established that, on a textual level, the foul blackness imputed to women, to the vaginal canal, and to women's character is essential to Desdemona's downfall.[58] Bovilsky's claim that Desdemona's blackness—and not only Othello's—is central to the tragedy was novel in scholarship. Arguably, Behn's "Oroonoko" anticipated Bovilsky's insight. Behn's text trades in every commonplace of *Othello*—women whose skin is the color of their clothing, who are covered in an inky blackness, called fair warriors, compared to monuments; women who are brave, honest, desired and desiring, conquering and mutilated. A turn from Shakespeare's ideas to the materials of early modern textual and theatrical craft makes Behn's understanding available to us again.

In a virtuoso, offstage performance, Behn redeems womanhood by fracturing and redistributing the character-defining qualities of *Othello*'s dramatis personae, including blackness, which she resignifies as a mark of constancy, rather than infidelity. If indeed she considered her "Oroonoko" an étude, the thought experiment revealed that *Othello* could be *written* as a tragedy with a triumphant Desdemona but not staged. Moreover, it would turn out that even achieving a change of venue for Desdemona's case—from theatre to print—would provide Behn a protofeminist victory that also had grave unanticipated costs.[59]

In order to understand the project of Behn's revision, I will look not only at Imoinda but also at the narrator and indeed Oroonoko as Behn's attempts to reassign the materials and qualities out of which Shakespeare builds Desdemona's character. Behn pursued her re-vision of *Othello* by making twinned Desdemonas, as it were: the always already black Desdemona and the young white narrator, whose whiteness of character the narrative valiantly attempts to preserve.[60] The historicity of "Oroonoko" is not only that Aphra Behn renews her claim on authorship—in the famous and much-remarked references to the "Reputation of" her "Female Pen" (189, 156). "Oroonoko" is also, implicitly, an assertion of Behn's authority as a reader of *Othello*. In fact, the composition of the novella depends on a deep, transformative encounter with *Othello* that involves several strategies: mimicking, inhabiting, reorienting, and disputing Shakespeare's play and its gendered and racialized strategies of characterization.

The first of Behn's projects that I will engage is the creation of a white Desdemona in the young narrator. In this section, I revisit Laura Rosenthal's insight that Aphra Behn the young narrator in Surinam and Aphra Behn the aged professional writer should be distinguished by arguing, in brief, that the young character is the author's attempt to create a white Desdemona who will not be doomed by men's characterizations of her.[61]

Behn reveals her strategy in textual echoes that are radically resituated. Emilia's aforementioned retort to Iago "You shall not write my praise" (II.i.116) appears in "Oroonoko" as: "Thus died this great Man, worthy of a better Fate, and a more sublime Wit than mine to *write his Praise*" (189, my emphasis). This apparently trivial echo takes on far greater significance when understood as integral to the project undergirding Behn's intertextual engagement. In saying "you shall not write my praise," Emilia objects to her obscene, misogynistic characterization by Iago, a man who (as I argued in the first chapter) hates books and uses insinuating speech to render all forms of character maddeningly ambiguous. On the one hand, her retort is made in vain: she cannot prevent Iago from dimming women's virtue over the course of the play. On the other hand, her command suggests that she is confident in Iago's alienation from a literate elite. Iago will not *write* her praise, though he may (and does) *speak* quite ill of all womankind.

In "Oroonoko," conversely, the (black) male hero is subjected to having his praise written by a white woman to whom he would no longer entrust the story of his life. After his failed rebellion and subsequent whipping, he refuses to speak to the narrator and his erstwhile white friends among Surinam's colonial elite: "All we cou'd do cou'd get no more Words from him" (182). Over the course of the narrative, in the part of character and author, Aphra Behn exemplifies the opposite of Iago's antipathy toward literacy. She is not only a lover of writing but also a master of classical literature, a captivating raconteur, a state informant. Further, the mature woman (unlike the young woman purportedly experiencing these events in Surinam) has become, as I have said, a published author. Consequently, she can override Oroonoko's silent refusal to provide her what she calls "the whole Transactions of his youth" (123); she succeeds in writing his praise—and, more important for the indebted writer, publishing it. The triumph of Behn the author in this world of *Othello*'s racial and gender hierarchies inverted tells us something of Behn's project: a feminist experiment with the color-coded tropes and media of gender characterization—one that preserves the tragic mode but dares to imagine Desdemona victorious.

Shakespeare associates Desdemona with a passive, absorbent page; she is the unwitting receiver of the ink of Othello's "black and begrim'd . . . face" (III.iii.387). Behn pinpoints Desdemona's dilemma: there is no way for her to express her choice in husband and to remain fair, chaste, and reputable. Fidelity to a stage moor is rhetorically and physically blackening. Behn's strategy is to divide Desdemona into a black figure and a white one and, surprisingly, to attempt to redeem them both.[62] "Oroonoko" features a younger Behn as a white female narrator who is the subject of characterization and not its object: she writes and is not written upon. Having established herself as such, she Desdemonizes the male hero by making of his body both a statuary and a literary monument (the latter being more complex as it not only feminizes but also fulfills Othello's dying injunction to write his epitaph). Finally, she invents a novel figure in Oroonoko's wife Imoinda: a female figure whose character cannot be shamefully blackened because black is her original color. However, in the process of making these changes, Behn discovers terrible things: first, that the death of the beloved is the gruesome precondition for the active female narrator's authorial voice and love; second, that she must collude with villainous state power to ensure that death. Behn's dim awareness of this precondition does produce one character who briefly illuminates a comic path: a black female Iago, who uses her unruly tongue to foster the lives and the sexual union of the erotic couple, specifically by championing women's sexual choice. I will deal with each of these strategies in turn.

Behn's Pledges to the Fraternity of Literate White Men

One of the foremost Behn specialists, Janet Todd, warns that "what is known securely about Aphra Behn could be summed up in a page."[63] Scholars have turned to the first-person narrator of "Oroonoko" to supply the missing biographical details.[64] For example, in the text, the young narrator's father "dy'd at Sea, and never arriv'd to possess the Honour was design'd him, (which was Lieutenant-General of Six and thirty Islands, besides the Continent of *Surinam*)" (164). Biographers have not been able to establish that Behn was the daughter of such a high-ranking official. Yet, this textual detail reads differently if "Oroonoko" is approached as Behn's versioning of *Othello*. Desdemona, we will recall, is the daughter of one of Venice's most "beloved" senators: he "hath in his effect a voice potential / as double the Duke's" (I.ii.15–16). Behn's narrator has just such a father. Upon his death, the narrator ascends in his place. She claims that "as soon as I came in to the Country, the best House in it was presented me, called St. John's Hill. It stood on a vast Rock of white Marble" (165). In this moment, Behn occupies Desdemona's position before her fatal undoing. Both have taken voyages across the seas that separate them from fathers who do not survive: Desdemona hears that her marriage to Othello "was mortal" to her father (V.ii.245). Both are hailed on shore by noble men who immediately defer to them: Cassio calls Desdemona "a maid / That paragons description and wild fame" (II.i.67–68), a goddess whom the elements obey: "Tempests themselves, high seas, and howling winds / The guttered rocks and congregated sands . . . / As having sense of beauty do omit their moral natures, letting go safely by / The divine Desdemona" (II.i.75–76, 78–80); and finally a supreme authority, "our great captain's captain" (II.ii.82). Behn elevates her narrator to the same peerless position, writing of her younger self, "I had none above me in that country" (121).

For Desdemona as for the young narrator, this ascension to an unequaled status is specifically tied to the voyage away from the paternal home and, indeed, the death of the father. While scholars have expended tremendous effort trying to locate Behn's father, they have not considered that her aims in this text and theirs as biographers may not be aligned.[65] That is, she may not have intended for "Oroonoko" to provide verifiable biographical information about herself. If the narrator and the historical Aphra Behn are not the same person, the narrator emerges as a persona. More critic of *Othello* than memoirist, Behn uses this persona to replay Desdemona's scenarios with a difference: the narrator is a young white woman who masters the character economy that assists in the murder of her predecessor.[66]

The narrator achieves this victory by exceeding the aforementioned positions of subordinate daughter and even of acting queen. Instead, she transitions into a virtual "brother of the state"—Brabantio's term for his male fellows in the aristocracy (I.ii.96). The narrator's acceptance into the literate white male governing body has unexpected effects. It brings a fair Desdemona into the Senate's fraternal deliberations and aligns her with the state's interest in exerting mastery over black character, in the inked persons of Oroonoko and Imoinda. This position might not be troublesome in a memoir of Behn's adventures as a white woman in colonial Surinam. However, by implicating a Desdemona-figure in the Senate's betrayal of the Othello-figure, this tactic threatens to undermine Behn's goal of redeeming Desdemona. The narrator's literacy assures that no Iago will overwrite her in "pitch" the color of ink (II.ii.360), but it will also pit this white Desdemona's authority against the black one's liberty. The London writer will discover that the strategy of splitting Desdemona into a hyperliterate white woman and an already overwritten black one creates unexpected conflicts.

Yet, early in the novella, there are appears to be no contradiction. The narrator claims to receive "from the Mouth of the chief Actor in this History . . . the whole Transactions of his Youth" (123). In this moment, she usurps the paternal position. Desdemona's father, Brabantio, according to Othello, "oft invited me" and "questioned me the story of my life / . . . even from my boyish days, / To th' very moment he bade me tell it" (I.iii.129–33). Desdemona is a secretive eavesdropper in *Othello*. In "Oroonoko," the young Behn appears the leading figure in a house of women with no patriarch and thus may issue invitations and demand stories without threat to her honor.[67]

The elder author Behn accepts the fantastic notion that her hero could convey his life to her in an all-encompassing story—that narrative passes from his mouth to being her literary property.[68] In publishing it, she not only exceeds Desdemona, who is written upon, but exceeds Iago, whose ability to characterize Desdemona is only oral and not written. In "Oroonoko," she insists that she, as a judicious author, "shall omit, for Brevity's Sake, a thousand little Accidents of his Life, which, however pleasant to [the narrator and her circle of women in Surinam], where History was scarce, and Adventures very rare; yet might prove tedious and heavy to my Reader, in a World where he finds Diversions for every Minute, new and strange" (123). By this maneuver, she sustains the fiction of the moor's capacity to supply what Othello calls "a round, unvarnished tale" for the purpose of claiming credit for having produced, in ink, a true *bios-graphe,* a writing equivalent to the life it memorializes (I.iii.90).[69] At the same time, Behn highlights her intervention in the story that she wishes to have perceived as "all in all sufficient" (IV.i.264–65) despite its omissions.

Behn owns her authorial intervention to exceed the passivity Shakespeare assigned to Desdemona in the face of Iago's vicious mischaracterization of her. Desdemona's most assertive action in the play's economy of characterization is to "seriously incline" to hear Othello and "with a greedy ear / Devour up [his] discourse" (I.iii.145–46). Outside of that moment, she is all hint and importuning—even when she is pressuring Othello to reconcile with Cassio, her mode is to ask him questions, not to seize the prerogative of command. Although Behn is as hungry a listener as is Desdemona, the narrator's capacity to spin the oral into the written and then transport it to market places her beyond Desdemona's subjection to being the object of others who write about or upon her. In violating her station, the narrator arguably incorporates the capacities of Iago to "write [another's] praise," if the villain were cured of his inveterate opposition to writing.[70]

The short eulogy Behn offers at the novel's close transforms these "Transactions" of Oroonoko's life first to the work of her "pen"—the "writ[ing]" of "his praise." Her transcription establishes "Oroonoko" not as his story but, rather, as *her* authorial property. Behn then turns the marketable text into a literary monument, as the thick paste of printers' ink and the cultural prestige afforded the book can combine to "make his glorious Name to survive to all Ages" (189). In correcting for Desdemona's passive consumption of Othello's narrative—and, indeed, her aforementioned inability to write her own praise—Behn transforms the Venetian lady into a bibliophilic Iago.

This alteration makes of Iago something that character adamantly refused to be: an asset of an imperial government. Although Behn rails against the corruption of the colonial authorities in Surinam, scholars have always noted that the Tory Behn was a proponent of *royal* authority.[71] Therefore, her narrator does not collude in Iago's ultimate goal: she does not set out to disable the textual authority on which the state relies in *Othello*.[72] Iago ensures that *Othello* ends with bloody pages that vex the medium the senators use to collect information on their overseas territories. In fact, their representative in Cypress looks upon the bed and concludes: "The object poisons sight. / Let it be hid" (V.ii.364–65). He subsequently refuses to produce a written report. Confirming that writing has been ruined, he opts to make an oral report: "Myself will straight aboard, and to the state / This heavy act with heavy heart relate" (V.ii.370–71).

Conversely, Behn attempts to frame her book—her own report on bloody murders in a colonial outpost—as the fulfillment of a literary project intended by Oroonoko's master, Trefry, who "was carry'd into those Parts by the Lord-Governor, to manage all his Affairs" (154). Behn laments that "the

Dutch ... kill'd, banish'd and dispers'd all those that were capable of giving the World this great Man's Life, much better than I have done. And Mr *Trefry,* who design'd it, dy'd before he began it, and bemoan'd himself for not having undertook it in Time" (156). Thus, in a strange way, Behn joins a fraternity of literate men as the replacement for the governor's deceased manager. Simultaneously, she returns herself to a quasi-filial position, with the deceased and sainted Trefry a substitute for her father. Although she obtains this unofficial position as Trefry's surrogate through service to the state as an informant on Oroonoko—and through a mastery of both Roman history and modern publishing—the narrator does end the narrative as a white Desdemona who, also like Iago, has wrangled an unofficial promotion. Were "Oroonoko" a stage play, a female character might join such a fraternity temporarily, through an act of cross-dressing.[73] However, a novelist does not have to claim property in her person. She achieves it by claiming authorship of a story set in and reproduced through the *disembodied* medium of print—a fact that makes print an appealing medium to people who carry less social power in (their) person.[74]

The product, this romantic book, is a rare commodity ostensibly *of* the New World. But its vendibility depends on its form: an oral narrative or manuscript correspondence would not have the same economic value to the author.[75] Thus, Behn transforms the stories that she claims Oroonoko told her into a media form for London's print market. Behn invested in patronage and the print market, which required not the ephemeral sensation of a play in repertoire but the objectified form of the book. Indeed, I will argue below that her attempt was to make of "Oroonoko" a new *Lives of the Romans.*

White Authorship and Slave Names

If the narrator represents Behn's attempt to create a white Desdemona who is not at the mercy of a man who "writes her praise," the novella becomes an experiment in distributing to a (black) male character that helplessness in the hands of someone else's characterization. Behn assigns Oroonoko Desdemona's position as an object of others' characterization, producing a text that may be considered Plutarch's *Lives of the Romans* translated to the New World.[76]

I have already mentioned the pathos of Behn's well-remembered "praise" for Oroonoko, but here I would like to complete the eulogy: "Thus died this great Man, worthy of a better Fate, and a more sublime Wit than mine to write his Praise: Yet, I hope, the Reputation of my Pen is considerable enough to make his glorious Name to survive to all Ages, with that of the brave, the beautiful and the constant *Imoinda*" (189). In her source, Othello attempts to participate in—even direct—the writing of his epitaph, issuing the laconic command to Venice's emissaries, "set you down this" (V.ii.351). By contrast,

Behn composes her peroration on Oroonoko's name in the absence of her hero and against his expressed wishes. Yet, under the circumstances of his refusal, the narrator cannot bring herself to produce any proper name. Neither his birth name, Oroonoko, nor his slave name, Caesar, appears here. The narrative of the novelistic experiment grinds to a halt because Behn no longer has a name that suits her purposes: "Oroonoko" is now associated with violent rebellion against the white Desdemona's "brothers of the state," while "Caesar" recalls the narrator's betrayal of the black Desdemona, Imoinda.

The narrator faithfully calls the hero Oroonoko, the name of his royal birth, during the novella's African section. After he has arrived in Surinam, having been kidnapped by treacherous, unscrupulous English traders, she claims that she is incapable of using any but his slave name: "For the future . . . I must call *Oroonoko, Cæsar;* since by that Name only he was known in our Western World, and by that Name he was receiv'd on Shore at *Parham-House,* where he was destin'd a Slave" (156). Yet, Oroonoko eventually rejects the name, vowing to effect his revenge on slaveholders. "You shall see," he thunders, "that *Oroonoko* scorns to live with the Indignity that was put on *Cæsar*" (182). Behn's attempt to expand Desdemona's territory to include fairness, Iago-like oral manipulativeness, and senatorial bookishness would work but that the aristocratic code of martial honor she lends Oroonoko makes him unsuitable for narrative domestication.

Although Oroonoko does not claim it for himself, the name of Rome's great antagonist, Hannibal, is implied in his attempts to inspire his band of maroons. Behn has positioned the "glorious name" that "survive[s]" (189), as the one given Oroonoko by his master Trefry: "[Caesar], which name will live in that Country as long as that (scarce more) glorious one of the great *Roman*" (156). Consequently, the hero's attempt to play Hannibal and his rejection of the name Caesar constitute a serious problem for Behn's project of claiming literary property in a black male figure. How can an author own that which has no proper name? His narrative body is divided among those names, which eventually manifests in the fate of his quartered body. Recall that the narrator flees rather than confront the "earthy Smell" (187) and "extraordinary Melancholy" (188) that would attend the dismembered body—the macabre souvenirs that Governor Byam later calls "frightful Spectacles of a mangl'd King" (189).[77] Perhaps subconsciously driven by a similar dread of fragmentation, Behn the London author can supply only an ellipsis where the hero's name should be. That is to say, she would appear to recognize that her own narrative strategies contribute to the quartering of Oroonoko and align her with colonists she decries as regicides.

In order for Oroonoko to become Behn's textual property, the name must become improper to the hero, to whom she claims unending allegiance and loyalty. Her hero has been severed from his name so that her book may bear it. Dismemberment is Oroonoko's literal and figurative fate, while in *Othello* that punishment is one Othello contemplates but does not impose on Desdemona. "I will chop her into messes," he thunders (IV.i.200). Instead, he makes of her a statue—which would have been Behn's preferred ending for the character of Oroonoko.

Composing Oroonoko: Ink and Statuary

One of Behn's consistent strategies is to subject her Othello (i.e., Oroonoko) to the kinds of material characterizations that are typically applied to women. To aid in illuminating this tactic, I suggest looking anew at a notorious passage, the narrator's blazon of Oroonoko: "His Face was not of that brown, rusty Black which most of that Nation are, but a perfect Ebony, or polish'd Jett. His Eyes . . . were like Snow, as were his Teeth. His Nose was rising and *Roman,* instead of *African* and flat. . . . The whole Proportion and Air of his Face was so noble and exactly form'd that, bating his Colour, there cou'd be nothing in Nature more beautiful, agreeable, and handsome" (12). This passage has occasioned copious commentary on its racialized aesthetics, but its subtle redeployment of the materials and presumptions of *Othello*'s inky character economy remains to be elucidated.[78]

Given the underlying structure of the hero's face, it appears that Oroonoko is fundamentally Roman with a black veneer. Words such as "instead" and "bating," suggest that the African and the Roman do not easily inhabit the same space. Behn might well have derived this antagonism from the opposition in the theatrical repertoire between black and Roman characters. For example, Othello juxtaposes the face of Diana—the Roman goddess of chastity—with his own "begrim'd and black" face (III.iii.387).[79] Aaron the black moor is the eternal scourge of Rome in *Titus Andronicus.*[80] Behn takes these stage antagonisms back to their roots in classical texts such as Plutarch when she likens Oroonoko's action in leading the slave rebellion to that of the Carthaginian general Hannibal. In creating a New World version of *Lives of the Romans,* Behn seeks to raise her own status to that of Plutarch, while also trafficking in the novelty appropriate to the novelist. To assume the role of Plutarch, she has to suppress the historical opposition between African subjects and European empire in its Mediterranean or Atlantic eras. The use of the stones ebony and jet in her description of Oroonoko aids in this effort, as it produces less a Roman in blackface than a Roman fashioned from black material.[81]

Yet, there is a third African population excluded from this unstable unity of Rome and Africa in black Caesar, a collective distinguished by color.[82] Behn informs us that "most of that Nation"—that is, most captive Africans—have "brown, rusty Black" faces. In one sense, this image suggests that only a skin of "*perfect* Ebony" can house the virtues associated with the Roman Empire, the legendary apotheosis of European civilization. Behn insists, then, that "perfect Ebony" can house (male) virtue as well as Othello thinks that "monumental alabaster" can represent idealized female virtue (V.ii.5). The reference to polished jet represents honorable manhood as the proper material for the idealized sculptures of the ancient world—carved from white marble or from ebony.[83] Through the monumental figures of Caesar, Oroonoko, and indeed England's Charles I, Behn expresses a pronounced nostalgia for a classical code of honor being eroded, she claims, by the avarice and duplicity of the emergent merchant adventurer.[84]

At the same time, the "brown, rusty Black" has a reference that exceeds the bounds of human complexion. Just as ebony and jet conjure the world of the plastic arts, the image of rusty blackness refers to literary paraphernalia—ink, specifically. Catherine Gallagher famously argued that blackness in "Oroonoko" is the color of monarchy, exchangeability, and—most important for this chapter, ink. However, Gallagher's interest is in the modes of dissemination of manuscript and print more than the physical properties of the inks used for each. That is, she is interested in the commodity of the book, not the substance of ink.[85] After Gallagher's brilliant—if somewhat ungrounded—suggestion, I wanted to know through what habits of language and performance were skin and ink being yoked and brought into the same field of significance.

When Behn makes Oroonoko the epitome of blackness, she associates him not only with sculpture but also with writing ink of the highest quality, distinguished by its color saturation and durability. His countrymen, by contrast, represent a cheap, impermanent, oxidated ink. Their blackness, like that of a substandard writing ink, has not retained its richness but rusted. Writing inks of the early modern period were primarily made of "copperas, galls, gum Arabic, and a solvent such as water, wine, vinegar, ale, or beer." If mixed in the right proportions, the ink achieved "a high black luster" like the "polished Jett" of Oroonoko's complexion. However, the iron in poorly mixed batches "turned rusty brown or faded out completely."[86] Although the ink chemist who supplies these phrases wrote more than two centuries after Behn, both coincidentally employ the same locution of a "rusty brown." Behn's aforementioned desire to "make Oroonoko's glorious name last to all ages" would require a durable black ink, either a printer's ink or a writing ink of a very fine quality.[87] The novel as a form relies on both the author's scribal labor and the technology of the press.[88] Consequently, it is fitting that Oroonoko's colorfast blackness signals *both* media in which Behn invests: the labor of "[her] pen" and the print marketplace that brings her "diver[ting]" tale to "readers."

Regarding this indelible blackness, Chi-Ming Yang argues that the narrator wishes to embalm both Oroonoko and Imoinda in lacquer, a technology invented by the Japanese and imitated by eighteenth-century English ladies.[89] Without disputing Yang, I would argue that more needs to be said about ink before moving away from texts to a wider field of luxury commodities, as she does.[90] When it comes to her hero, Behn considers a number of media for his re-mediation—that is, the transformation of his body and the transport of his story beyond Surinam. Oroonoko's face is figuratively composed of material befitting high sculpture, while simultaneously being the apt color for inked, literary memorial. These materials are notable even though they do not pursue a consistent aesthetic of print or sculpture. Rather, they are aligned in that they further Behn's redirection of the arrows of character assassination aimed at Desdemona.

Before he murders her, Othello finds that, but for its "balmy breath" (V.ii.16), Desdemona's sleeping body perfectly resembles a statue. The stillness and whiteness of her body suggest to him an unblemished ideal of female virtue—one frozen at a temperature that is "cold, like . . . chastity"—the very virtue he insists she has violated (V.ii.275–76). Along with the coldness and hardness of stone, Othello also emphasizes unadulterated whiteness as proper to statuary. He has vowed to murder her in a way that will "not shed her blood / nor scar that whiter skin of hers than snow / and smooth as monumental alabaster" (V.ii.3–5). He imagines that this transformation of the living and therefore potentially treacherous wife into the lifeless (though lifelike) statue would render her, finally, safely lovable: "Be thus, when thou art dead," he says to her sleeping body, "and I will kill thee first and love thee after" (18–19).[91]

It is certainly arguable that the play does not take Othello's side in imagining the only good woman as a beautiful corpse.[92] However, it is difficult to locate in the play any case for allowing Desdemona to live, had she been *un*faithful. In other words, we are presented a tragedy that hinges on Othello's grievous mistake, whereas, for Behn, tragedy begins because women do not own their sexual selves. Even with Emilia's bravura monologue, asserting that women's sins are the product of men's "instruct[ive]" examples (IV.iii.103), one cannot say that *Othello* advocates for women's full sexual autonomy.

Behn appears to have detected that lacuna and made Imoinda's sexual self-determination—the subject of my next section—integral to her remediated *Othello*. For now, I would like to note that the metaphor of Oroonoko's face as a polished black work of sculpture reallocates the gendered distribution of virtue she found in her Shakespearean source. While Eve Sanders found that early modern men were to actively emulate virtue and women to passively embody it, Behn opts to represent male virtue frozen in immobile stone.[93] Of course, Behn will later transform Imoinda's face into a sort of death mask. This reassignment of stony qualities suggests that Behn does not entirely reverse the gendering of media in *Othello* and the larger culture. Rather, she redistributes property, pleasure, and protection through a number of disparate experiments with the mediation of gender. For example, the association of Oroonoko with ink (extended by the ink tattoos at his temples) brings him into Desdemona's orbit. Desdemona's smudges are an addition, an acquired stigma that Othello associates with damnable mutability and publicized dishonor. The tattoos of Oroonoko and Imoinda, however, partake of the culture of marking as a sign of distinction. In this case, Behn has the ink mark indicate "Quality" and, therefore, in-born aristocratic honor (160). Although the tattoo is not a congenital feature of the body but an artificial transformation, Behn's feminist imagination refuses to accept that such enhancements must always be either exclusively feminine or intrinsically degrading.[94]

In addition, one could also argue that (despite her insistence that she would have saved his life), the narrator wishes for Oroonoko to be a statue—an amour who is, in Othello's late words, "kill[ed] . . . first and loved . . . after." In this scenario, her irrational fears insert her in an ambiguous place—at once the vulnerable "white ewe" (I.i.89), Desdemona, and Othello, who cannot suppress his recurring suspicions of betrayal. Behn tries to incorporate Iago's skills as the supplier of secret intelligence on the object of surveillance—but she soon finds herself mired in Othello's predicament: being overtaken and unsettled by oral reports of Oroonoko's plans for rebellion. The final encomium to Oroonoko, therefore, resembles Othello's dying kiss, a belated realization of what it really means to achieve the wish of possessing the "transactions" of another life. For a time, she claims possession of a (living) statue, at the cost of a life of greater value than a pearl—in *Othello's* language—or "polished Jett," in Behn's.

Beyond stone, the business of the name is even more disturbing for Oroonoko. While Imoinda's name miraculously remains intact, Oroonoko's is fragmented and scattered—a shattered statue like his quartered body, living only in ephemeral talk until incompletely reassembled in Behn's treacherous tribute. The successive transitions from Plutarch's and Ovid's texts to Oroonoko's self-narration to the writer's ink and finally into print here are seriously troubled, as each re-mediation inevitably alters the material and its cultural associations. Yet, the surmises of a suspicious reader should not be confused with the official position taken by the narrator, who does not achieve the self-awareness necessary to acknowledge or ameliorate the damage she has caused. After all, these are not people but characters—narrative devices in an intermedia experiment. Like Plutarch's Romans, ink they are and to ink they return.

Composing Imoinda: Lace, Tattoo, and Flowers

In these last sections, I turn to the text's most prominent black women: Imoinda, the subject of tremendous scholarly outpouring and, finally, Onahal—the subject of almost none. While most scholars treat the "black Venus" Imoinda as if she were a real person to whom the historical Behn could have had allegiances, I want to think of her as, primarily, a formal experiment with the character of Desdemona. Imoinda is a literary figure designed to test whether the association of women with blackness can be redirected toward aims other than producing stains as evidence for prosecution within patriarchal culture.

As I argued in the preceding interlude, Shakespeare's Desdemona is not so much a thinking person as the personification of fair paper. She receives kisses from a painted Othello, which leave marks the significance of which she cannot establish. Moreover, her speech—like the visual evidence of a written document—remains eternally undecidable. Her famous answer to the question of her murderer's identity is "Nobody; I myself" (V.ii.124). It might as well have been Iago's "what you know you know" (V.ii.303)—talk that manages the feat of accumulation without reproduction. It doubles, while still amounting to nothing.

Theatre lore has it that in 1660 Desdemona was the first female character performed by a cisgender woman. Given the play's aforementioned popularity, we can imagine that, by 1688, Behn had ample opportunity to consider—and to identify with—the way that Desdemona is undone by the character industry. For this doomed woman, to be penetrated sexually—even touched or kissed—is to be permanently marked as unchaste and, therefore, disreputable. Behn makes two formal innovations to create an alternative to this vulnerable, unknowing, feckless womanhood. First, the device of the novel—which allows her to remove the moor's wife from the stage and enables Behn to occupy the Iago position as a narrator. Second, by creating a black Desdemona, she creates a woman who is *constant*—whose sexual activity cannot denigrate her, since black is her original shade. The color black, in this case, is not a stigma but, rather, a sign of unchanging character. Imoinda has received literal stigmata—tattoos all over her body—but Behn transforms these into an indication of inviolability. The narrator describes them as raised "Poynt[s]" resembling lace, an overlay or addition that denotes rank but not sexual history.[95] Moreover, the lacy tattoos form a sort of permanent clothing, endowing even her naked skin with a covering that conveys modesty while offering protection.

Behn's project of vindicating Desdemona required an acute familiarity with the semiotic constellation that brings ink, tattoos, slave character, and female honor into a formation I have been calling the *character economy*. This industry produces alphanumeric texts and theatrical types and instructs readers and audiences that invisible personal traits—such as racial essence and gendered virtue—can be accessed according to the same conventions one uses to read letters and stage personae.[96] Through the offices of complexion, stigmata, and lace, Behn is able to reinvest female figures with the dignity and inviolability stripped from them in *Othello*. The irony is that blackness becomes the color of this redemption.

Ending with Imoinda allows us to return to Southerne's question, with which I opened: why did Behn opt to mount her *Othello* on the page instead of the stage? The consensus has been that the stage would not afford Behn a black heroine. But, why should a black woman be able to appear on the page and not onstage? Scholars have suggested that Behn scapegoated this black woman, subjecting her in sequence to ravishment, sequestration, and murder.[97] Yet, considering Imoinda (and not just Oroonoko) as a creature of ink suggests Behn's connection to the heroine was ambivalent and only dimly conscious, rather than straightforwardly competitive.

The inky blackness that Behn would have known from plots of moors and adulteration recurs in the famous description of Imoinda's body:

> From her being carv'd in fine Flowers and Birds all over her Body, we took her to be of Quality before, yet, when we knew *Clemene* was [Oroonoko's beloved] *Imoinda,* we could not enough admire her. I had forgot to tell you, that those who are Nobly born of that Country, are so delicately Cut and Rac'd all over the Forepart of the Trunk of their Bodies, that it looks as if it were Japan'd; the Works being raised like high Poynt round the Edges of the Flowers: Some are only Carv'd with a little Flower, or Bird, at the Sides of the Temples, as was *Cæsar;* and those who are so Carv'd over the Body, resemble our Ancient *Picts* that are figur'd in the Chronicles, but these Carvings are more delicate. (160–61)

Recent cultural histories of the tattoo can clarify for us that to race or to raze in the seventeenth-century sense refers not only to cutting but specifically to tattooing, a coloring procedure that produced permanent marks, akin to those of a fine writing ink or a printers' impression.[98] Although the narrator insists that these tattoos are marks of the "Nobly born," those "of Quality," she is also the expert in ancient Rome, a culture in which tattoos marked—indeed, effected—the degradation of enslaved persons.[99]

The religious studies scholar Susanna Elm explains the strange recuperation of stigma as an elite property: "Only in a society where torture and physical degradation were ever present realities feared by most except for those of the highest status, who alone could display bodies 'without a gash' or 'any physical defect,' can marking with an indelible sign of extreme dependence and weakness [the stigma] become an all-powerful symbol."[100] An elite body bearing such a mark becomes, in her word, "unassailable," which would certainly explain Imoinda's ability—remarkable for an early modern woman of any color—to disarm male assailants.[101] It would appear that Oroonoko's stigmata, on the contrary, re-mark him as both royal and slave, prefiguring his Christological sacrifice—one that requires a humbling assault on the body, the more to distinguish it from the sovereign and transcendent soul.[102] Blackening constitutes a telltale change in Desdemona's public character. In imagery that conjures the imprint of a painted Othello's kisses, Desdemona's body transforms from "fair paper" to pages befouled with "misogynist discourse."[103] Imoinda forms an absolute contrast to Desdemona's model. The African woman begins as black: her overwriting therefore cannot alter her original coloring. Moreover, her tattoos do not manifest a private shame publicized. Instead, her society has conferred stigmata that indicate her honor and are, in fact, integral to her person.

Behn was not the first in the English tradition to align blackness with the virtue of constancy. In Ben Jonson's *The Masque of Blackness* (1605), Niger, the father of the twelve black nymphs, boasts of his daughters:

> That in their blacke the perfectst Beauty growes;
> Since the fixt cullor of their curled hayre
> Which is the heighest grace of Dames most fayre,
> No cares, no Age can chandge, or there display
> The fearfull tincture of abhorred gray.
> Since death him self (him self being pale, & blewe)
> Can never alter their most faithfull hew.[104]

Behn shares Jonson's interest in aggrandizing the purported fixity of unalterable blackness, in what seems an early version of that African American boast: "Black don't crack."

Kim Hall has noted that, beyond Jonson, English male sonneteers made a sport of using verse to beautify black complexions that their culture deemed ugly.[105] Behn enters that field to perform a feminist revision. The constancy that Jonson applies to blackness in his masque for Queen Anna reverberates in Behn's praise for the "the brave, the beautiful, and the *constant* Imoinda."[106] In her case, black is both her original color and that deriving from her husband's touch. Therefore, Imoinda maintains a kind of privacy and purity even after having sexual contact. Seizing upon the discourse of constancy, Behn transforms blackness from a sign of lasciviousness to one of fidelity. Imoinda, who never marries Oroonoko officially, offers Behn the opportunity to envision constancy as Imoinda's fidelity to her own desires, rather than to those of any man—thus, redeeming Desdemona, whose punishment ensues from following her own desire despite paternal disapproval.

Perhaps presaging magical realism as a literary mode in the New World, Behn specifies that Imoinda's tattoos depict "fine flowers"—a detail that establishes a miraculous incapacity to be deflowered. An African woman who has been subject to threatened violation nearly since her introduction in the text has flowers permanently in bloom on her exterior. These tattooed blooms manifest in the natural world after Oroonoko has fulfilled their agreement that he kill her and their unborn child: "As soon as he had done, he laid the Body decently on Leaves and Flowers, of which he made a Bed, and conceal'd it under the same Cover-lid of Nature; only her Face he left yet bare to look on."[107] Contrary to Southerne's aforementioned question about Behn's burying Oroonoko between book covers, the figure of Oroonoko receives no burial and suffers the distribution of his quartered remains as grisly souvenirs. Imoinda is the only person whose burial the text details, and her interment is festooned with flowers: "He pointing to the dead Body, sighing, cry'd, *Behold her there.* They put off the Flowers that cover'd her, with their Sticks, and found she was kill'd, and cry'd out, *Oh, Monster! that hast murder'd thy Wife.*" If Oroonoko is born in ink and returns to it; Imoinda emerges marked by flowers and is buried again among them. This remediation is Behn's most masterful. It is impossible to "deflower" Imoinda, because, as this scene demonstrates, even when blossoms covering her body are removed, flowers remain embedded in her skin. Here is Behn's ultimate retort to the patriarchal understanding of women's nonrenewable sexual value that Othello voices: "When I have plucked the rose, / I cannot give it vital growth again. / It must needs wither" (V.ii.14–16). "Put[ting] off the flowers that cover'd" Imoinda is only to reveal the ever-blooming flowers embedded in her skin.

No matter how much she is inked, she betrays no change of color and she—unlike Desdemona and the other besmirched white lovers of moors who haunt the stage—remains unadulterated.[108] The cultural historian Felicity Nussbaum has argued that the essential foundational color of theatrical *maleness* was white—and blackface a mere overlay.[109] In that context, Behn's audacious tactic was to employ the medium of print to experiment with blackness as the foundational color of female virtue—as opposed to the theatrical and proverbial color of women's ruination.

In making this argument, I am in tension with much of the current of scholarship that emphasizes Behn's need to subordinate Imoinda and force her into the background.[110] Surely, there is much truth here. It is quite telling that while Behn tells Oroonoko stories of Roman heroes, she tells Imoinda stories of nuns, urging quietude, pacifism (and perhaps sexual abstinence) on a woman who eventually proves herself capable of fighting alongside her husband and even wounding a colonial official.[111] Yet, critics should not set Imoinda apart from the self-possessed comic heroines in Behn's other texts entirely.[112] While a third-wave feminist lens may position Imoinda as the young narrator's rival, viewing Imoinda as a black Desdemona changes the political calculus. I say so not to suggest that racial politics are absent from "Oroonoko," but rather to clarify Behn's project. Put most charitably, one might say that Behn is interested in the liberation of all women. Put least charitably, it might be said that she displayed little interest in or knowledge of actual African women because the symbolic materials of their color interested her more than any ethnographic, experiential, or psychological realities. Therefore, the key difference between Imoinda and Behn's stage heroines results more from the mode (tragedy) than from a particular prejudice Behn has. Behn's "black Venus" has a clandestine affair, courts being called a whore, but ends up with the man of her heart's choice and unstained by the process. Imoinda, like the other Behn heroines, *wins*—albeit in a tragic mode rather than a comic one. I would not define winning in this way myself, but Behn agreed to these terms when she decided to take up *Othello*'s materials and premises.

Not only does Imoinda emerge unblemished; she is granted imperial status. Scholars have often pointed out the chivalric overtones of the African section of the novella,[113] but they may have glossed over, as mere convention, narration that offers Imoinda absolute and eternal power:

> [Oroonoko] made her vows she should be the only woman he would possess while he lived; that no age or wrinkles should incline him to change; for her soul would be always fine, and always young; and he should have an eternal idea in his mind of the charms she now bore; and should look into his heart for that idea, when he could find it no longer in her face. . . . After a thousand assurances of his lasting flame, and *her eternal empire over him, she condescended to receive him* for her husband; or rather, received him as the greatest honor the gods could do her. (14, my emphasis)[114]

Though the language of being a slave to love renders captivity a mere metaphor, in this novel that metaphor takes on a stark reality. Readers must conclude that the "eternal empire" of women over men would be infinitely preferable to the bonds of chattel slavery.[115] Oroonoko certainly has no complaint about Imoinda's empire: he resents "being the sport of women" only when it is a part of his captivity in Surinam (176).

Moreover, this female leadership is infinitely better for women. I have mentioned that Imoinda is victorious, despite the story's tragic mode. Unpalatable though it may be to us, Imoinda's death is a victory when considered as a reworking of Desdemona's. Desdemona is murdered against her will, after begging for her life. Imoinda, on the contrary, begs her husband to kill her. When he shrinks from the task, she imposes *her* will and insists that he do it. Thus, she manages another uncanny feat: just as she is incapable of being deflowered, so, too, is she incapable of being *defaced*. This claim sounds strange considering that Oroonoko "severs her still-smiling face" from her body. However, this image preserves her face as a *whole;* it is not the disfiguring act described in *Othello* of dirtying "Dian's visage" (III.iii.387). Nor is it the rigidifying gesture of turning Desdemona's entire body into "monumental alabaster." Instead, it is the creation of a remarkably plastic death mask, one that preserves the life and smiling warmth of the deceased woman. Imoinda's constancy is not "cold" like male-imagined chastity but emblazoned with a smile that allures and a tattooed skin that prevents deflowering. Informed by feminist scholarship on the misogynist tropes of rape genres like the snuff film, a modern reader may recoil when Imoinda is subjected to uxoricide and post-mortem surgery. However, a comparison of Imoinda's demise to Oroonoko's demise suggests that Behn did not intend to reproduce those tropes in the fiction's macabre denouement. Crucially, Imoinda's face remains whole, while Oroonoko later suffers having his ears and nose hacked away. Despite what Southerne and his successors presume, Behn employs her powers of narration to spare the "Queen of Night" and not the Coromantien prince.

Far from being locked into simple opposition to Imoinda, the author Behn is aligned with this imaginary African woman's capacity for "eternal Empire."[116] In fact, Behn makes Imoinda's power in the realm of love parallel to the power of the "female pen." Behn writes in the preface, "A Poet is a Painter in his way; he draws to the Life, but in another kind; we draw the Nobler part, the Soul and Mind; the Pictures of the Pen shall out-last those of the Pencil, and even Worlds themselves" (119–20). She returns to the eternal in the novella's final words, which I have already quoted: "I hope, the reputation of my pen is considerable enough to make his glorious name to survive all the ages, along with the beautiful, the brave, and the constant Imoinda" (189). Yet, if Behn and Imoinda are co-mistresses of the eternal in the preface, Behn dramatically subordinates herself to Imoinda in the last sentence. The author has assumed the position of Oroonoko making his aforementioned vows of love, as it is she who is to paint and maintain the idea of Oroonoko and Imoinda for all ages.[117] In the novel's final redemptive (and obfuscatory) stroke, the racial slavery of the Atlantic World disappears behind the screen of service. Oroonoko's chivalric service to his lady Imoinda and the author's artistic labors on behalf of her characters overshadow slavery with its opposite, the "perfecte fredome" of the willing.[118]

While I have argued against a premature assumption that Behn was the first white Anglo feminist to fail her sisters of color, I want to reiterate that the novella is simply not unified in its stance, toward the black hero or toward black women. On the one hand, Imoinda represents a sort of feminine ideal—already constituted by blackness and therefore immune to stain—and Behn the author certainly admires her. On the other hand, the political interests of the young narrator cannot quite be reconciled with those of Imoinda. The African woman wants freedom and is willing to fight alongside her husband to gain it, while young Behn tries to acclimate the couple to a luxurious enslavement with no end in sight.[119] To apprehend Behn's complicated relationship to her black female figures, it is necessary to augment our critical attention to Imoinda by attending, finally, to a lost black female character, the one most closely aligned with Behn the author.

Iago, Briefly Redeemed in a Black Female Form

Arguably, the elderly Onahal, who facilitates the consummation of Oroonoko and Imoinda's sworn love in Coromantien, is a stand-in for the aged writer. Onahal, she writes "had not forgot how pleasant it was to be in Love: And though she had some Decays in her Face, she had none in her Sence and Wit; she was there agreeable still" (139). An idealized version of the authorial Behn, Onahal is a spy and mediator, a clever woman who, with well-maintained beauty and court connections, can still seduce and wield influence.[120] Associating herself with her witty pen rather than with her decaying face, the aging Behn aligns herself with Onahal, an older woman of indestructible sense, status, and eloquence.

In her navigation of the embitterment and gendered service that accompany her status as the cast-off mistress of the Coromantien king, Onahal proves herself an African composite of Emilia and Iago. Like Desdemona's maid, Onahal controls access to the "Bed of State" she once occupied, where the king intends to consummate a marriage he is imposing on Imoinda, in spite of her prior betrothal to Oroonoko (138).[121] She resembles Iago in avenging her loss of status by pretending to do others' service—operating within the letter of decrees while employing an unruly orality. Yet, where Iago famously fabricates a scene in which his bedmate Cassio confesses in his sleep to a clandestine affair with Desdemona (III.iv.413–26), Onahal reveals to Behn's African prince that he should "not lose a Moment in Jealousie" of a king she "kn[o]w[s]" is impotent (138). Beyond disclosing this secret truth, she ensures that Oroonoko and Imoinda have time and privacy to have a sexual union that, though consensual, cannot achieve legitimacy. For her pains, Onahal is sold into slavery but not to Surinam, it would appear, as she is never heard from again.

The novel follows a careful pattern, wherein the plot in Coromantien is repeated with a crueler twist in Surinam.[122] In Surinam, the young Behn fulfills a negative version of Onahal's function in detaining Oroonoko and Imoinda with stories. Through her tales of warriors and nuns, the young Behn aims to split the transported African couple into gender-segregated pursuits of adventure and chaste contemplation. Behn's strategy is to interrupt the pair's conjugal life, as if she intuited what would occur: the expectation of a child who would be born into slavery makes the quest for gendered honor unsatisfactory and sets the couple a revolutionary path. Unlike Onahal, she does not deceive the government on Caesar's behalf but informs on him. The tragedy at the heart of this novella does not appear to be the triumph of mercantilism over monarchy, the dismemberment of noble kings, or even the thwarted love of Oroonoko and Imoinda.[123] Perhaps the secret tragedy is, instead, the disappearance of the Onahal figure.

In Coromantien, Imoinda's comrade is an older African woman set in opposition to the young lady by an age-based sexual system. Onahal is willing to play a loyal Emilia, which earns Imoinda a temporary union with her betrothed. In Surinam, Imoinda lacks a co-ethnic double. The closest analogue to Onahal is the young Behn, who defers and betrays Oroonoko and Imoinda's quest for freedom, as a white female Iago figure who has been accepted in the literature white fraternity. Behn would have liked to have been a different kind of narrator, to have used her wit like the self-revising narrator of Toni Morrison's *Jazz:* "Liking, loving [them] is not useful. I have to alter things. I have to be a shadow who wishes [them] well . . . I want to dream a nice dream for [them], and another of [them]. I want to be the language that wishes [them] well, speaks [their] name, wakes [them] when [their] eyes need to be open."[124] As the author Behn looked at the results of her experiment—a lifelike death mask, a shattered statue, a literary commodity, and a treacherous version of herself—Onahal suggests the faint wish that it could have gone another way.[125]

❧ 3

"Pale as Thy Smock"
Abigail Adams in Desdemona's Whites

Seizing a rare opportunity for enjoyment in a city she disliked, Abigail Adams purchased tickets a week in advance for opening night at London's Royal Theatre in Drury Lane. The entertainment on September 17, 1785, was *Othello,* but Adams was drawn less by Shakespeare than by a desire to see Britain's premiere tragedienne, Sarah (Kemble) Siddons, who would play Desdemona. Siddons was a sensation. In her famous correspondence, Adams observed: "You must make as much interest here to get a box when [Siddons] plays, as to get a place at Court; and they are usually obtained in the same way. It would be very difficult to find the thing in this country which money will not purchase, provided you can bribe high enough."[1] Adams tolerated these unseemly dealings to procure box seats, befitting the wife and daughter of the first American minister plenipotentiary to England. It would have been humiliating to appear in more affordable gallery seats, alongside those without titles—and the less expensive prostitutes. Of course, the utmost propriety would have required that mother and daughter appear with the family patriarch, but John had already seen Siddons, and his meager salary apparently would not stretch to accommodate a third seat. Thus, that night a pair of American women assumed their perch in a side box, enjoying a privileged view of Siddons while being exposed to the gaze of audience members eager to have a look at representatives of the rebel colonies.

In portraying Desdemona, the tall and commanding Sarah Siddons undertook a role that, in the eighteenth century, was slight in every sense. The part had been cut during the Restoration when boy actresses ceded the stage to women. This revision was in keeping with social expectations that Desdemona appear a paragon of innocence and obedience.[2] Biographers note that Siddons shrank her voice and body to fit the part, a feat made more remarkable by the fact that the statuesque actress was pregnant at the time.[3] Abigail Adams concluded that Siddons was "interesting beyond any actress I have ever seen," while her daughter, Abigail (called Nabby), found her more pleasing "than any person I ever saw upon any theatre."[4] Yet, both were dissatisfied. They did not doubt that Siddons could undertake Desdemona; they were uncertain that Desdemona was befitting of Siddons's character.

By H. MAJESTY's COMPANY,

The Theatre-Royal in Drury-Lane,
WILL BE OPENED
This prefent SATURDAY, Sept. 17, 1785.
With the TRAGEDY of

OTHELLO.

Othello by Mr. KEMBLE,
Roderigo by Mr. DODD,
Caffio by Mr. BANNISTER jun.
Brabantio by Mr. AICKIN,
Lodovico by Mr. PACKER,
Duke by Mr. CHAPLIN,
Montano by Mr. R. PALMER,
Gratiano by Mr. WRIGHTEN,
And Iago by Mr. BENSLEY.
Æmilia by Mrs. HOPKINS,
And Defdemona by Mrs SIDDONS.

To which will be added

The QUAKER.

Steady by Mr. BANNISTER,
Solomon by Mr. PARSONS,
Eafy by Mr. WRIGHTEN,
And Lubin by Mr. SUETT,
Gilliam by Mifs FIELD,
Cicely by Mrs LOVE,
And Floretta by Mrs. WRIGHTEN.
Places for the Boxes to be taken of Mr. FOSBROOK at the Theatre.
The Doors to be opened at Half after Five o'Clock.
To begin at Half after Six.   Vivant Rex & Regina.

On Tuefday, the Comedy of The SCHOOL for SCANDAL,
With (by Defire) the Dramatic Entertainment of The CRITIC.

Playbill from the night of September 17, 1785, when Abigail Adams and her daughter saw John Philip Kemble and Sarah Siddons play the doomed couple in *Othello*. (Houghton Library, Harvard University)

The story of Abigail Adams's investment in Siddons has never been thoroughly pursued. The United States' second First Lady is, of course, best known for her famous exhortation that her husband and other male legislators "remember the ladies" when apportioning rights in the New Republic.[5] Nevertheless, her response to the London performance of *Othello* has its own minor notoriety. Scholars are fond of quoting an edited version of her letter of March 1786: "Perhaps it could be early prejudice, but I could not separate the African color from the man, nor prevent that disgust and horror which filled my mind every time I saw him touch the gentle Desdemona." The author of this confession appears to be a privileged white woman declaring that Black people are inferiors unfit to marry white people. The lines have become a referendum on her racism. Historians have considered her actions toward Black people as well as the laws relating to interracial marriage and fornication in Massachusetts, hoping to ascertain whether this reaction was typical of Adams and, indeed, of her contemporaries.[6] However, these approaches fix Adams's gaze on Othello

The only known contemporary rendering of the layout of Drury Lane.
From the perspective of the pit, the boxes alongside the stage where Abigail Adams and her daughter sat are nearly as open to view as the stage
itself. "A Peep Behind the Curtain at Drury Lane," James Sayers, etching
and aquatint, 1780. (National Portrait Gallery)

when, arguably, the blackened character who most horrified her was not the
general but the wife marred by his touch.

By tracking Adams's prior experience as a reader of the play, her female circle's fanatical interest in Siddons, and the uncertain whiteness of US-American
womanhood in the metropole, I offer new insights to Adams's biographers
and to whiteness studies more broadly. Attention to these minute particulars
suggests that Desdemona's (character) assassination offered Adams pointed
lessons about how to maintain unspoiled identity as a woman abroad.[7] In my
view, the intensity of both her desire to see Siddons and her disgusted response
to *Othello* indicates that, even in the 1780s, whiteness was not guaranteed for
all women of European descent. This chapter tracks the canny maneuvers by
which Adams established and, when necessary, recaptured whiteness in a
variety of disparate Anglo-Atlantic settings. This interpretation of Adams's
sojourn in London has been nearly inconceivable in part because legal and

scientific chronologies have been allowed to set the historical mentality out of which Adams supposedly responded.[8] Reactions such as Adams's have been thought to emanate from a shared system of beliefs articulated in law, science, or—less often—religion. Yet, a medium has its own unique effects, as the difference between Adams's private reading in her family home and her public spectatorship in a metropolitan playhouse attest.

Throughout this book, I have bracketed those legal determinations and scientific publications typically used to narrate the history of racialization. My goal has been to demonstrate that racial fabrications in literary and theatrical realms do not merely echo official, systematized racial knowledge but produce a racial habitus of their own. I have been pursuing an extended argument that people do not simply infuse media with racist narrative content but, rather, that writing, printing, face painting, and tattooing each have distinctive sensuous properties that shape whether legibility, permanence, or transferability becomes the salient features of racial character. In the case of Adams, the influence of medium is evident in her incommensurate responses to *Othello* as a text and as a dramatic performance. If text and performance are not equivalent, then medium itself must be accounted for as possessing historical agency.

In addition to the undue emphasis on law and science, there has been a tendency to consider Adams's racial politics as divorced from those of gender. In scholarship, the protofeminist Adams is not conscious of her whiteness, while the Adams who makes statements about slavery and social segregation speaks as a white person of no specific gender.[9] By focusing on Desdemona, Sarah Siddons, and the network of female kin and friends with whom Adams corresponded, I attempt to unite these strands, to recover an Adams whose particular situation was determined by the specific forces producing white American womanhood at home and abroad.

When she attended *Othello* in London, Abigail Adams was a figure on a foreign itinerary, possessed of a sullied, minoritized American womanhood, struggling to make a mobile, reputable figure out of the character technologies available to her. Like Aphra Behn a century before, Adams was preoccupied with the problem of how to establish and maintain honorable femininity. However, unlike Behn (the subject of the previous chapter), Adams did not imagine that a congenital blackness might be made to signify a constant female character, impervious to black marks of dishonor. In fact, Adams emphasizes that she possesses a mutable complexion, susceptible to visible blushing and blanching. Behn's other solution—substituting the text for her speaking body—was available to Adams in the limited circle of her correspondents, rather than in the market of literary publication. Instead, since Adams was the wife of the US minister plenipotentiary, she was compelled to present herself in person at both formal and informal events. Therefore, Adams engaged what seemed possible to her: a mania for policing whiteness of character. Adams was on perpetual guard against that which may—to borrow a phrase from Othello—"scar that whiter skin of hers than alabaster," any external mark that might serve as a visible sign of a denigrated virtual identity. In order to unfold Adams's concerns about the public character of white women, I consider two decades of opportunities for her to recognize Desdemona's vulnerabilities as her own, her first experiences seeing women onstage, and the techniques of character management Adams brought with her or borrowed from the example of Sarah Siddons. This formerly submerged story begins with an abandoned wife and ends with a spectacular, layered white dress.

"The Rites for Which I Love Him Are Bereft Me": Marital Separations

Though Abigail Adams never wrote of it directly, the story of Desdemona's "heavy interim" apart from Othello shadowed the long separations that marked her marriage. Desdemona's father, Brabantio, tries to divorce Othello and Desdemona by accusing Venice's Moorish general of entrancing his daughter. Desdemona's testimony before the Senate that she was "half the wooer" negates her father's charges but does not dissipate the forces driving the new couple apart, since Othello is to be dispatched immediately to a distant war. Desdemona, again, prevents their being parted in a plea that owns her ardor: "dear lords, if I be left behind / A moth of peace, and he go to the war, / The rites for which I love him are bereft me, / And I a heavy interim shall support / By his dear absence. Let me go with him" (I.iii.290–93). Othello later calls Desdemona "frank," a perfect word for this unashamed insistence on the fulfillment of "the rites for which I love him."

However, once transposed to the battleground of Cyprus, Desdemona's finds herself transfigured. No longer covered by her esteemed father and his "brothers" of the Venetian state, she is, as she puns, "abhor[red]" (IV.ii.167)— that is, turned into a whore—for the sins she herself describes as "loves" she bears to Othello. Iago's slanderous insinuations eventually overwhelm her when a credulous Othello decides to strangle her for her alleged adultery. She dies at his hands, though she refuses to blame him by naming her murderer as "Nobody. / I myself." In her contextual history of *Othello,* Virginia Mason Vaughan offers an acute summation: "Respectable women would have been content to stay at home, . . . especially since military codes seldom distinguished between wives and prostitutes."[10]

In the early years of their marriage, when they both resided in Massachusetts, the text of *Othello* offered both Abigail and John Adams opportunities to consider approaches to various predicaments. It certainly raises the prospect of ardent lovers who might be separated, and their separations would only grow more prolonged. In 1766 Adams confessed that her husband's traveling—a result of his devotion to his budding career in law—left her at home feeling, if not bereft, then hungry for his company: "My Good Man is so very fat that I am lean as a rail. He is such an Itinerant, to speak [. . .] that I have but little of his company. He is now at Plymouth, and Next week goes to Taunton.—Butt is dinner time, and I must bid you good by, may be I shall find time to add more than that I am your affectionate Sister—[.]"[11]

Two years into their marriage, John Adams was already becoming a round man, but Abigail was not accusing him of gluttony when she said that his excess was the cause of her deprivation. According to Abigail, when the ambitious attorney was away for months following the circuit of the Massachusetts court, he kept the greater portion of himself for himself. Meanwhile, she starved on "but little of his company." The tableau calls to mind a gender-inverted Jack Sprat: While Abigail presided over family meals at the home in Braintree, she nonetheless grew thinner. In contrast, John engaged in a peculiar—and mysteriously fattening—form of self-ingestion. Though confusing—even hyperbolic—on its face, the talk of food contained a truth: later letters confirm that she did lose weight during her husband's extended absences from home.[12]

Increasingly professionalized and prominent, the field of law presented itself to John in the years before his marriage as a likely path to honor and position, dependent more on integrity and efficiency than on the inherited wealth his family lacked.[13] As disputes involving debt and property became more complex in North America, litigants increasingly sought advice rather than simply appearing before the magistrates on their own behalf. The itinerary Abigail described—with John trekking from Plymouth and Taunton—comprised stops on the Massachusetts court circuit. Throughout the colonial era, court was held seasonally, when weather permitted safe passage of magistrates from outlying areas to the center of each county—a location chosen for centrality, not for urban prominence.[14] John followed the winding circuit of the court in search of the opportunity to stamp the Adams name on these institutions.

Contrary to Abigail's narrative of his physical consolidation and growth, John characterized his travels as scattering his intellectual capacities.[15] In assessing the effect of this dispersal, John found an apt analogue for himself in *Othello*, a play he likely knew only as a text:[16] "Is it possible to pursue a regular Train of Thinking in this desultory Life?—By no Means.—It is a Life of Here and every where, to use the Expression, that is applyed to Othello, by Desdemona's Father. Here and there and every where, a rambling, roving, vagrant, vagabond Life. A wandering Life."[17] While John testified that his travels did not augment but diminished him, Abigail's underlying assessment retains its insight: in this same diary entry, John all but admitted that fame was more important to him than was his family. Setting up the problem, he wrote: "Am I planning the Illustration of my Family or the Welfare of my Country? These are great Questions." Yet, when he postulated the potential fruits his work could bear, he collapsed the formerly opposed beneficiaries of family and country. He envisioned a concentric circle, a circuit, emanating from "Friend, Parent, Neighbour" to embrace "Country and next all human Race." This image cleverly obscured the deprivation of his family by suggesting that in embracing country or the world he was, by definition, embracing the smaller circle of family.

In the early years of their marriage, Abigail, too, was fond of citing the text of *Othello*.[18] In the letter with which I began—concerning John's lengthy absences—Abigail cited *Othello* to offer her sister advice: "[M]ethinks your S[ale]m acquaintance have a very odd kind of politeness. By what I have heard of them, they have well learnd the lesson of Iago, to Rodorigo, 'put money in thy purse.' It is the Character of the whole people I find, get what you can, and keep what you have got. My advice to you is among the Romans, do as the romans do. This is a selfish world you know."[19] Although Abigail did not identify her husband with the mercenary moor, she did treat the play as a sort of commonplace text, from which to copy moral examples.[20] Beyond this citation of Iago's wisdom, Abigail's tendency to suggest that John return home rather than that she join him suggests she may have interpreted Desdemona's fatal departure from her Venetian home as a cautionary tale.

If she reached a moral conclusion, Adams would not have been alone among her colonial neighbors. David Douglass circumvented the ban on theatre in Newport, Rhode Island, by presenting *Othello* in 1762 as a "moral dialogue."[21] He solicited the audience's sympathy for Desdemona: "Reader, attend, and ere thou goest hence / Let fall a tear to hapless innocence." Despite this ode to Desdemona's blamelessness, once in the framework of extracting lessons, nothing would have prevented an audience from construing Desdemona as a flawed character whose demise offered object lessons. Desdemona takes two extravagant steps—a secret marriage to the blackamoor Othello and a sea voyage following him to war. As I suggested at the outset of this section, Desdemona sees these steps as identical, since she claims, "I love the moor to live with him" (I.iii.248). As such, to marry a moor is already both to be expelled from the paternal home and to embrace the moor's own itinerant life.[22]

Although some scholars presume *Othello* must have always served as a referendum on interracial unions and Africans' capacities, Adams was perfectly capable of thinking about and quoting from *Othello* without having to pause to indicate her strong distaste for mixed-race couples or her assessment of African character. Nevertheless, the fact that she does not question whether

Desdemona's exogamous marriage makes her complicit in her own murder is notable, as both Thomas Rymer and, later, her son John Quincy considered the matter crucial.[23] Though the play would mean differently to her when she saw it staged in London, during her moments of private reading in Massachusetts, it still remained a text to consult for moral advice.

For as long as she could bear it, Mrs. Adams rejected Desdemona's decision to follow her husband, remaining within a narrow compass, covered by John Adams's name and accomplishments but longing for his physical presence. By 1784 she had spent nearly ten years deprived of her husband—except for his four-month return home to Braintree in 1779. First, the attorney went to Philadelphia as one of Massachusetts's representatives to the First Continental Congress. Then, in 1778, he was sent as part of a three-man commission to France. After the aforementioned respite, John was dispatched again as minister plenipotentiary to England in late 1779. However, as England was not ready to treat for peace, John found himself in prolonged negotiations with France and the Netherlands, seeking alliance, diplomatic recognition, trade, and loans for the debt-saddled New Republic. John's actions had demonstrated that his primary commitment was to his quest for honor. During a lull in postings, as he waited for an honorable discharge or a new post from the US Congress, he neither returned nor arranged for his remaining family to join him in Europe.[24] Still, rather than follow John abroad, Abigail expended her energies trying to get her "Good Man" to return home.

Abigail chose to emphasize her rootedness, writing her husband using the pen name Portia, the loyal wife who waited at home for the Roman senator Brutus.[25] She pursued a safe characterization: the faithful wife, sending epistles from a domestic sphere she managed expertly.[26] Yet, eventually, starving in the character of Portia would fail to satisfy Abigail Adams. She resolved to risk departure. Realizing that her husband would never abandon a post for his family, she elected to undertake a voyage like Desdemona's, across the chasm separating the protections of her father's country from the exposed site of her husband's foreign errand. Abigail sent her two sons to finish their schooling at her brother-in-law's and set sail for England with her favorite companion, daughter Abigail. Nabby would turn nineteen during the thirty-day voyage that ended July 23, 1784. For her part, Abigail Senior, nearly forty, was amazed the ship did not prove the death of her.

Adams and the London Character Industry

From the moment of her boarding the ship through the duration of her European sojourn, *Othello* became for Abigail Adams more than a text to mine for proverbs. During her years in France and England, the text of *Othello* animated the materials of literature and theatre, as well as life outside their boundaries. Adams saw the play performed and reprised the role of Desdemona herself, though she triumphed where her model failed. Desdemona is the object of characterization. If she wishes to remain a faithful (and, implicitly, obedient) wife, she can neither stop the marks that come from a blacked-up Othello's touch nor control the interpretation of them. On the contrary, Abigail Adams—while cognizant of the restrictions of gender propriety—took unto herself the power to deploy visible characters, on the page and in person. When attending theatre for the first times in her life, selecting clothing for royal audiences, and corresponding with Americans abroad and Stateside female kin, the materials of theatre and literary culture provided her the vehicles by which to seize an honorable character—to establish rank and reputation in a hostile mother country.

Abigail Adams arrived in London in 1785 a proficient reader, a competent correspondent, and an inexperienced playgoer—as one would expect of a woman of her class and region. In the Massachusetts Bay Colony, Adams was part of a literate elite who imported books and magazines from London sellers. Public commercial theatre was unavailable because the descendants of Puritan emigrants maintained a Cromwellian ban lifted a century earlier in England.[27] While Abigail was taught to write, she was never taught proper penmanship or orthography, instilled in boys to equip them to conduct business correspondence.[28] At home in Massachusetts, advantages of wealth and race gave Abigail Adams uncommon access to the means of character production, yet gender propriety made circulating beyond the home, in person or on paper, an invitation to slander.[29] Adams was profoundly aware of the dangers of having her character exposed, but there was no other way to reunite with her ambitious husband than to follow him abroad.

A summer of discontent had exposed Adams to the great productive capacity of London's character industry, predisposing her to make the connection between Desdemona's public shaming and the publication of unflattering portraits. After reading ink-stained newsprint deriding her husband John's first audience with King George, she picked up her pen to retaliate among the coterie of intimates who read her letters. It was three months before her audience with Desdemona that Adams wrote her elder sister: "The Tory venom has begun to spit itself forth in the public papers, as I expected, bursting with envy that an American minister should be received here with the same marks of attention, politeness, and civility which are shown to the ministers of any other power."[30] In another letter to her allies in back in Massachusetts, Adams encompassed the dizzying array of attacks, including one directed at her. In an exhaustive list, she indicated the equivalences drawn as Britons demeaned John's title and reception by other diplomats, US independence, the value of

US currency, American illiteracy—even the announcement of "Mrs. Adams's" carriage at a state event:

> Tho treated by the Court with as much civility as could have been expected, it has not Screened us, or our Country from the base falshoods, and bilingsgate of hireling Scriblers or the envenomd pen of Refugees. Their evident design has been to get Mr. A. to notice them, and to replie to their peices. They have tried every string. Sometimes they will not even allow him the Rank of Minister, then they will represent the title in a ridiculous light, calling him commercial Agent, proscribed Rebel . . . Sometimes they have asserted that the king treated him with the utmost disdain, at others that Lord Carmathan and the American plenipo, were at the utmost varience, that the foreign ministers would not associate with him, that he could not give a publick dinner because Congress paper would not pass, and tradesmen would not credit, that the Secratary to the Legation could neither read or write, but that his principal had sent him to an evening school to qualfy him, that Hearing the Honble. Mrs. Adams's Carriage call'd was a little better than going in an old chaise to market with a little fresh butter; in short the publication which they have daily publishd have been a disgrace to the Nation. Now and then a peice would appear lashing them for their Scurility, but they are callous, and refuse to publish in favour of America, as I have been told or rather demand such a price for publishing as to amount to a prohibition. Mr. A has never noticed them.[31]

I have quoted at length because Adams provides a verbatim summary of the most vicious attacks against John Adams. Moreover, her catalog constitutes a primer on the jurisdiction of character. As opponents of the fledgling United States invented insults, they could not help but correlate the refusal to grant John's lofty rank as minister plenipotentiary with the image that the envoy's office was populated by illiterates. Character deficiency is multiplied and linked, as illiteracy and unscrupulousness merge. The degradation of Abigail worked through a version of character dependent upon comportment rather than literacy: the scene is of a woman whose carriage is announced at Court but, upon her disembarking, shows herself to be a dairywoman, carrying a bit of butter to sell at market.[32] As Elaine McGirr has discussed, country girls out of place in the city were stock characters in eighteenth-century fiction and drama.[33] Taken together, these attacks provided a bombastic display of the muddying, bruising, and bloodying that London's character machinery could perform upon that virtual identity known as reputation.

US-American national character was an unstable figure in the Atlantic character industry, and much of that instability had to do with its racial content.[34] Was its spirit wild and Indian? Were its blemishes indelible, like the blackamoor's unwashable blackness? Would these traits prove mutable over time?[35] The range of properties, meanings, and values of US character were in flux, not least because of dueling national representations and media with separate audiences and character properties. However, it was clear that when *women* represented the nation, their labor and consumption would be read as especially significant indicators.

Adams longed for privacy and a respite from the exposed life of the ambassador's wife: "We could not exchange our Lodgings for more private ones, as we might and should; had we been only in a private character."[36] She had foreseen it all two years prior from her farm in Braintree, Massachusetts: "To think of going to England in a publick Character, and resideing there; engageing at my time of life in Scenes quite New, attended with dissipation parade and Nonsense; I am sure I should make an awkward figure."[37] However, John had not satisfied her request to return to an enclosed "Domestick circle," thus she had to brave the formidable threats to personal and national character posed by London's mass media machinery.

In front of the British, Abigail hoped a look of "silent contempt" would show the family's true and noble nature despite these portraits in print's oily ink. Yet, when in her own chambers, she took a more combative stance, relishing the chance to counter these attacks in her own hand. Her private letters to her family promulgate ideas of national character as much as do her Tory rivals' printed columns. If they used printing ink to deride her as a dairywoman, she would dip them in the neologism she coined, "news-liars."[38] Failing print circulation, these letters still would have reached a limited public, as letters were in this period read aloud for gatherings of intimates and, also, circulated to absent or sympathetic parties.[39] Abigail could not do battle with the "news-liars" in the public sphere of print and retain her feminine propriety. Yet, she found a way to confront them in a field available to her. While the presses stamped their tacky ink on page after page, Abigail dipped her goose quill in gum-based, fluid writing ink to meet their smears with her own. Though her letters did not circulate as widely, the intelligent self-defense she employed there served as an antidote to the "venom" in the London papers.

Adams, French Opera, and American National Character

The year before she saw Siddons's Desdemona, Abigail Adams had a theatrical experience that taught her what was at stake for women and, indeed, for national character in the playhouse. After witnessing a titillating dance performance at a French opera, she confessed to her censorious older sister, Mary Cranch: "I have found my taste reconciling itself to habits, customs, and fashions which at first disgusted me."[40] Here, Adams called upon a language inherited from expansionist and nationalistic Europe, wherein habits and customs made the distinctions among nations, races, and stations.[41] Performing the feminine modesty appropriate to members of civilized nations, Adams continued: "No sooner did the dance commence, than I felt my delicacy wounded, and I was ashamed to be seen to look at them. Girls, clothed in the thinnest silk and gauze, with their petticoats short spr[ang] two feet in the air . . . and show[ed] their garters and drawers." This shame was not mere prudishness, for it had a genuine external source. For Adams to enjoy without reserve this shameless performance was to risk having audience members—or even her pious elder sister back in Massachusetts—judge her deficient in character. Uncharitable viewers would have seen that failure as a transgression against laws both temporal and divine, because the Puritan ban on public theatre remained in effect in Massachusetts in 1784. Paralleling judgments based on her possession of literacy (the characters of the alphabet), determinations of Adams's moral character at the theatre would have been based upon her reaction as a *viewer* of stage characters.

The dilemma was, in Abigail's apt phrase, how to manage "be[ing] seen to look"—how to accomplish being both seer and seen in the visual field, the subject and the object of character judgment. In her letter to Mary Cranch, Adams shrewdly presented herself as delicate, wounded, "ashamed." One image is of Adams blanching, the color draining from her face as she becomes increasingly mortified. Or perhaps she wanted to be seen to blush: the appearance of redness on her face could have preempted any accusations that she was like a brazen African who, as folk wisdom had long held, could sin without detectable shamefacedness.[42] Terrified or embarrassed, Adams's face would represent a virtuous inner character, far from that of the French opera girls, whose exposure of their translucent undergarments revealed that their inner character was, despite their pale skin, as black as a moor's. This analogy—suggesting that a Frenchwoman has a moral complexion like that of a licentious negress, though her epidermis is like that of an Englishwoman—rested on common, if unvoiced, tropes. Here, black character is a visible, detectable, but not epidermal trait of a morally compromised, publicly disdained *Frenchwoman*. The figure of the unblushing African serves to establish an intra-European distinction between national characters based upon the sexual reputations of women.

In the same summer of vicious press attacks on her family and nation, Abigail Adams encountered a portrait of herself that made all its readers see red:

Yesterday John Adams, Esq; the American Plenipotentiary, with his lady and daughter were presented to her Majesty at the drawing-room. . . . This gentleman, who was formerly proscribed as a rebel to this country, now appears invested with all the privileges and rank annexed to the representative of a free state; and the title of Excellency is now substituted by those persons who formerly called him traitor. The closet-scene on a late introduction at St. James's must have been curious. It is thought on one side the blush was of as deep a die, as the flush on Eve's cheek when she first saw Adam.[43]

Her Majesty Queen Charlotte features prominently here. Concerns about her swarthy Portuguese complexion conveniently tossed aside, she embodies England as a blushing Eve, embarrassed by John Adams as the *biblical* Adam, parading his naked ambition about St. James Court. However, the minister plenipotentiary is not the only target of this attack. In an implied comparison to the blushing queen, Abigail and her daughter are found lacking good character as well. As Kathleen Wilson argues in *The Island Race,* the "moral standing of Englishness came to rely upon English women's demonstration of domestic virtue and refinement."[44] Part of the distinction in the newspaper column, then, is a national one: metropolitan English female virtue is defined over and against that of the colonial woman, who is on a national "side" incapable of the natural shame of blushing. For the Adams women to be depicted as *not* blushing puts American whiteness into question on the levels of complexion and morality. The American women are portrayed much as were the French dancers in Abigail's letters—as shameless and therefore not quite white. Although blush is itself an ambiguous sign that seems to manifest both illicit carnal knowledge and an innocent capacity for shock, it can only arise on the face of one capable of both feeling and registering shame—specifically, a member of that contested, unstable category: white. Even as scientific nomenclature comes to prominence in the late eighteenth century, a folk index—the visibility of blush—continues to command recognition and determine difference.

US-American membership in a pan-European history or alliance (i.e., white civilization) was not at all assured. As E. Fleming noted in the 1960s, artists had been employing an Indian queen or princess to represent the Americas in general—and North American colonists, in particular—since the sixteenth century. The colonists and their British antagonists inflected this durable icon amid their conflict. The Creoles seized upon this noble savage as a beloved symbol of their own dignity and freedom; thus, it appeared in Paul Revere's celebration of the repeal of the Stamp Act in 1766 and on congressional medals and pattern coins commissioned by Washington and Jefferson in the 1780s and '90s.[45] As Fleming summarizes, "When it became necessary to identify an American interest distinct from the British interest, the Atlantic community turned to the symbolic figure of the Indian Princess."[46] One cartoon from the year of the Declaration of Independence shows the interchangeability of Indians and English Creoles in the character industry of the last quarter of the eighteenth century.[47] The term "American" had been used, at different times, to describe both populations. In the debate over the proper relation-ship between colony and metropole, one London printer thought the image of a civilized English mother chastising her wayward Indian daughter best captured the dispute. Tattooed and bare-breasted, this Indian figure indicates that the "special relationship" that would develop after World War II was not in effect. Creoles from the provinces would not be guaranteed recognition as inheritors of white British civility but could be depicted as savage and un-ruly. Clearly, Abigail Adams could not rely upon anything so obvious as her skin color to ensure that she, an American woman, would be perceived as a white compeer in London.

During the first two years of her European sojourn, Adams paid close at-tention to public women, while trying to discover how to engage with the

A London etching satirizing the escalating conflict between North American colonists and the British Crown as a fistfight. A bewigged woman in sumptuous clothing stands for England and demands obedi-ence of a bare-chested Indian woman with feathers in her hair and at her waist, the representative of the colonists fighting for liberty. "The Female Combatants, or Who Shall," hand-colored etching and engraving, 1776. (Lewis Walpole Library, Yale University)

materials of characterization without suffering denigration in the process. In an ingenious move, she crafted an American character that blended the unpretentious style of French women and the decorum of English women to mutually tempering effect.[48] Though she could not mass produce her opinions via print, Adams accrued positive value for white American womanhood by contrasting it with unflattering examples of English snobbery and French licentiousness. Her letters and gowns show an expert weaving of French and English sources to portray Republican womanhood as not only a combination of the best of contrasting European traits but also a unique essence of its own.

As she made her reluctant foray into "publick character," Abigail Adams had to enter the visual arena while somehow avoiding the stained reputation that she imputed to opera girls. While the actress playing Desdemona in 1785 did not engage in writing, Sarah Siddons did provide a template for how to be a public icon without losing honor. As Abigail sailed the currents of Anglo-American relations, it was Siddons's rigging of whiteness that she emulated.

Siddons's American Fans

From the Parisian suburb of Auteil, Abigail Adams wrote her friend, the political writer Mercy Otis Warren in Massachusetts, mulling the prospect of seeing the British actress Sarah Siddons a full year before she was able to bring it to fruition.[49] While John and John Quincy also participated in the discussion and correspondence about Siddons, reporting among female kin took on the status of an obligation—fulfilled joyfully and without fail. Daughter Nabby made certain to keep her cousin Lucy apprised when the family's transition from Auteil to London made a Siddons sighting a real possibility: "I considered myself a little unfortunate in not arriving soon enough to see the universally Celebrated Mrs. Siddons whose fame has extended to so many parts of the World, and of whom every Person without exception, I beleive, are equally delighted.... I have not yet seen her ... [w]hen I have my Cousin shall know my opinion, but she may be assured beforehand that I shall not dare to disent from all the World."[50] The letter stokes interest by noting that Nabby reserved the right to her own opinion but also that she could not contradict universal acclaim. Even if the verdict was inevitable, she did not falter in sending her reports.

Nor did her mother. As the season opener approached, Abigail Adams wrote her younger sister: "This week the Theatre at Covent Garden opens and Mrs. Siddons appears in the Tradigy of Othello in the Character of Desdamony. We have sent a Week before to engage places. I promise myself high entertainment from this admired and celebrated actress."[51] The next year, Adams remembered this vow as an obligation: "I think in one of my letters to you last fall I promised to give you some account of the celebrated actress Mrs Siddons, who I was then going to see."[52] That Adams thought the mere mention of Siddons entailed a promise suggests that the interest was not hers alone but distributed among her female kin.[53]

In this copious communication, all the women focused their attentions on Siddons's purported genius on the stage. Even once the play was announced, neither mother nor daughter recorded any hesitancy to see a story about a black-white marriage.[54] However, both women later reported disliking Sarah Siddons in this role. One must conclude, then, that something about the translation from page to stage changed the women's relationship to the play. A look at the facial, textile, and textual means of fashioning character suggests that Adams found harrowing the play's dramatization of the vulnerability of a woman's originally white character to fatal blackening.

In one of the play's numerous references to transferable stains on character, Othello laments that Desdemona's name has become as "begrim'd . . . / As [his] own face" (III.iii.387–88). By referring to the process by which the actor John Phillip Kemble put on the moor's color, this line signaled that this smeared-on makeup might have been transferred to the Desdemona character. The text's reference to sullying (which may, of course, have been omitted by a forgetful actor) was nevertheless an inescapable element of the performance: Siddons's famous brother received top billing as the eponymous moor; the audience knew they were not seeing a real blackamoor but a painted English celebrity.

In fact, theatre lore has it that when John and Sarah's brother Stephen played Othello two years before opposite his new wife, he killed his career: "Never was the heroic Moor so literally murdered. Many [of his] exclamations excited laughter; and so fond was he of Miss SATCHELL, the gentle *Desdemona*, that in embracing her he *would* have a kiss; the collision left one side of her face quite black, much to the entertainment of the audience."[55] John Kemble and Sarah Siddons did not make their first attempts at Othello and Desdemona until after their brother's flop. Perhaps they meant to redeem the name of their famous theatrical family. Playing Desdemona was certainly of no advantage to Sarah Siddons, who received the lowest billing and, as I have mentioned, a drastically reduced part. The casting of a brother-sister duo suggests a desire to minimize color transfer between actors whose passion in character would reflect a genuine sexual interest in each other. Abigail Adams's testimony indicates that reassigning parts may have reduced smudging but did not eliminate it. The conversion is somewhat ironic: to leave Desdemona's face "quite black" apparently induced laughter, but to make it only a little black opened the door to horror and disgust.

Besides the moments they embrace onstage—and the time he slaps her for denying his allegations—the maximum opportunity for transfer of blackface would occur during the climactic scene in which Othello repeatedly kisses Desdemona and then smothers her in their bed. In the play's cosmetic logic, there is no difference between the kisses Othello and Desdemona share and their deaths. In fact, Othello conflates them through ritual action in his final lines: "I kiss'd thee ere I kill'd thee: no way but this; / Killing myself, to dye upon a kiss" (V.iii.358–59).[56] As Abigail accurately perceived, every time he *touches* Desdemona, Othello can mar her skin with the outward representation of moral corruption. Adams seems to have been particularly mortified at the sight of Sarah Siddons, an honorable woman, being blackened before her eyes—receiving a mark of moral failure that was as indelible as the color of a blackamoor, at least for the duration of the performance.[57]

The text of *Othello* figures this blackening not only as an amorphous stain but also, specifically, as the application of profaning letters. Despondent at his wife's perceived infidelity, Othello wonders aloud: "Was this fair paper, this most goodly book, / Made to write 'whore' upon?" (IV.ii.71–72). In front of Adams's eyes, the blank page of Desdemona's reputation receives a profane mark and becomes a lewd publication. No longer a goodly book, like the Bible, her character becomes an unholy writ, a text that does not circulate as print (i.e., the letters of "whore" do not actually appear) but exceeds print in that its marks are legible even to the illiterate. Whether appearing in indelible ink as "whore" or in telltale smudges, the begrimed character of Desdemona was becoming public knowledge. After having her own character begrimed in the newspapers, there is little wonder why Abigail Adams responded with such intensity to this analogue for her own potential fate.

In her letters, Adams does ponder the nature of Othello's character, as well as the source of her reaction to it. She writes, for instance, that Othello's famous speech bidding farewell to his tranquillity and to his military career "lost half its force and beauty" because she "could not separate the Colour from the man."[58] While this line points to what Adams calls "prejudices of education or natural antipathy" toward persons of African descent, the letter also positions the character of Othello as something beyond a mimetic representation of a living person. "Othello," Adams writes, "was represented *blacker than any African.*" I would argue that this statement suggests that Adams perceived Othello as exceeding African humanity and, therefore, less an African person and more a conduit for blacking a white woman's character.[59]

In this consciousness of Othello as a dramatic construction, Adams aligned with a major stream of English theatre culture. Adams's references to the "sooty More" and "the sooty appearance of the moor" suggest an awareness of Kemble's makeup. Moreover, her emphases on the times that she saw him "touch the gentle Desdemona" highlight the potential transfer of Othello's makeup to Desdemona's character. As I mentioned in the first chapter, soot and goose grease served to make a homemade blackface in Jackman's *All the World's a Stage,* a parody of actors and popular plays like *Othello* that premiered in 1777 and was still in the repertoire eight years later. In fact, Adams could have attended Jackman's play in March before the theatres closed or, coincidentally, the week after she saw Siddons's Desdemona—and on the very same stage with some of the same players.[60] Jackman never brings forth the Moor or shows the black splotches on the heiress who playacts as Desdemona. Nevertheless, the play elicits knowing laughter from an audience that understands her character has been revealed even in her desire to play the bedroom scene with her servant.

For Adams, Othello's communicable blackness provided an occasion to fret over the precarious nature of white women's reputations. She trains her focus there in her most extensive commentary on Siddons. While some pieces of her two letters on Siddons's Desdemona are consistent—prejudice, sooty moor, horror at the touch—the content of the second letter focuses extensively on the question of Siddons's character. With the advantage of having "seen Siddons in several characters," Adams stepped back from Desdemona to make a larger pronouncement on the actress's reputation: "What adds much to the merit of Mrs. Siddons, is her virtuous character, Slander itself having

Sarah Siddons, playing Desdemona, sits up in bed and raises a hand to ward off Othello's advance during her death scene. Etching by Charles Sherwin after Johann Heinrich Ramberg, 1785, printed by J. Bell. (Houghton Library, Harvard University)

never slurd it." In an era in which actresses were often portrayed as prostitutes by definition, for Siddons to have achieved such a feat would have been remarkable, indeed.[61] Adams continued on the theme, "She is happy in having a Brother who is one of the best tragick actors upon the Stage, and always plays the capital parts with her, so that both her Husband, and the virtuous part of the audience can see them in the tenderest scenes without once fearing for their reputation."

Considering this abiding concern with Siddons's good name, it is unsurprising to read Adams's verdict on Siddons's Lady Macbeth: "She supported her part with great propriety, but She is too great to be put in so detestable a Character." In this assessment, Adams departed from the primary British response, as Lady Macbeth was Siddons's most celebrated role. Adams's deviation from the mainline view of Siddons may be explained by the messy materiality of performance: both Desdemona and Lady Macbeth find themselves doomed by an indelible mark, a sign of a deed they committed. While Siddons's Lady Macbeth perpetually washed a bloodstain long disappeared, her Desdemona bore visible marks of the kisses and touches she shared with Othello. Though Adams may not have said so explicitly, the characters' commonality was clear: these were women whose deaths followed the graphic marring of their characters. The resemblance of this predicament to Adams's own difficulties as a marked woman could not have escaped her.

Siddons as the Adams Muse

American Abigail Adams and her female kin were fascinated by a British star who became an emblem of national pride rather than an object of state suppression.[62] A celebrity in her own right, Sarah Siddons might appear "in the Caracter of Desdamony," as it was said in the parlance of the day, but her name remained an attraction by itself.[63] Her name was such a draw, in fact, that she was able to exceed her appellation as the premiere British tragedienne and venture into comedy.[64] Managers of theatre companies would not have risked a loss of audience, nor courted the ire of ousted comediennes, without a strong sense that Siddons would prove an attraction in any role.

Though she was a critical darling in 1785, Sarah Siddons was not likely to have forgotten that in 1777, barely three years into her career, the manager at Drury Lane had fired her. She performed on the provincial circuit, in such towns as York and Bath, for the next six years. Her exile ended two years before Abigail Adams arrived in London—the same year that brother Stephen's Othello doomed his career. She reconquered the stage at the Royal Theatre in Drury Lane, replacing the ignominy of bad reviews with portraits and encomia written by noble patrons.[65] This effusion of painted canvases, poetic manuscripts, playbills, and press clippings projected her character as blank, white, unmarred. This mysterious achievement—a woman entering the public realm, submitting to characterization, and emerging unsullied—fascinated Abigail Adams. Given that she was in London in a character she dreaded—the public figure of a diplomat's wife—it is especially intriguing that she should first see Siddons in *Othello.* The uses of ink and cosmetics to publicize Desdemona's suspect virtues offered Adams and Siddons a programmatic demonstration of the full array of character tools deployed by and against women in Anglo-American relations. Siddons had become a master of characterization; she cultivated a reputation sturdy enough that it would not be swallowed by this doomed and defiled character.

Siddons nurtured a "star image" which established her unmarked character by importing her children into her theatrical career. In *Heavenly Bodies,* the film scholar Richard Dyer uses the term "star image" to encompass "everything that is publicly available about stars. [Performances,] the promotion of those and of the star through public appearances . . . interviews, biographies and coverage in the press of the star's doings and 'private' life."[66] Dyer describes this all-encompassing "image" as "extensive" and also notes the interaction between the media industries, with their advantage in producing and disseminating content about the star, and audiences, who "select from the complexity of the image the meanings and feelings, the variations, inflections, and contradictions that work for them."[67] Abigail Adams was precisely this selective fan. She viewed Siddons as peerless in moving between creating characters and maintaining her reputation. The means of this magic was Siddons's incorporation of a proper, modest womanhood into her star image.

In the early 1780s, after strengthening her acting technique on the provincial circuit in Bath, Siddons departed for a triumphant return to Drury Lane. Nabby reported the story thusly:

> She told the Company one Evening that She had three very powerfull reasons for Leaving them, to go to London. They were sufficient in her Mind and she hoped would satisfy them all. If the Company would permit She would offer them the Night following. The Next Eve the House was much crouded when the Curtain was drawn up. Mrs. Siddons came upon the stage Leading in her three Children, made a Curtsey to the Audience and retired amid the general Applause of the Company who were so much pleased with this Compliment Paid to their sensibility and generossity that they made no objections to her Leaving them so much for her own advantage.[68]

Nabby tells a story that centers on Siddons's way of resolving potential criticisms for failing to stay put. Relocating to London for fame and financial "advantage" would certainly open a woman to suspicions of poor character—the kind that led to Desdemona's demise. By importing her children into her public life, Siddons established her good character, signaling that her public prominence did not suppress her proper motherly attributes.[69] Thus, she was able to continue exceeding the boundary of the domestic, traveling from one locale to another and from domestic enclosure to public stages. Rather than having her unusually public career distract from the proper direction of all maternal energies to her child(ren), Siddons transformed the stage into part of her maternal duty. Whether accurate or apocryphal, the story was a part of Siddons's star image that captivated Nabby, who was, like her mother, an attentive student of the strategies that could ruin or redeem white female character.[70]

Considering the eighteenth-century penchant for plays featuring fallen women, Siddons's star image was particularly useful.[71] The star could transgress—outstripping Macbeth's martial spirit in killing Duncan's guards or running

Joshua Reynolds's famous portrait of Sarah Siddons. Amid the clouds, this fair-skinned angel is above slander. Indeed, her contemplation of some object or ideal away from the viewer denotes that she pursues a goal beyond money—and thus avoids the then commonplace charge that actresses are prostitutes. *Mrs. Siddons as the Tragic Muse,* Sir Joshua Reynolds, 1784, oil on canvas. (Huntington Art Museum, San Marino, Calif.)

away with a blackamoor as Desdemona did—because her characters paid the price of their lives. Audiences rarely suspected that Siddons's convincing performances indicated personal familiarity with the character's anguish. Rather, they attributed them to her noble pity for women more wayward than she. Siddons continued importing her idealized offstage self onstage until the end of her career. During her final season, she was appearing in her signature role of Lady Macbeth for the last time. The audience applauded so loudly after Lady Macbeth's sleepwalking scene that the play could not go on. The curtain came down and when it rose again, Siddons was onstage in her own clothing. She addressed the audience for eight minutes, expressing her gratitude.[72] These injections of her own life story into her stage business ensured that the Siddons-ness of her characters could never be forgotten. Sarah Siddons would never be submerged in these characters, no matter what tragedies befell them.

To avoid the Shakespearean women's accrual of marks against their character, Abigail Adams drew upon the same repertoire of symbolic practices employed by Siddons to enhance the brilliance of her white character. Siddons's performances served to confirm and systematize what Abigail Adams had already intuited about the maintenance of white character. As the art historian Heather McPherson observes: "Siddons understood that her dramatic reputation hinged upon her natural pallor and emotional authenticity, which became correlates of her tragic genius."[73] In other words, Siddons linked—or exploited the cultural associations that linked—her unpainted face, a naturalistic performance style (for that period), and artistic reputation.

In her letters, Abigail Adams seemed aware that her fanatical devotion to Siddons might endanger the product of building and defending American national character. This intense adoration of Britain's leading star might indicate the comparative paucity of cultural attainment in the New Republic. However, through a careful triangulation of the French and British theatre cultures, Adams made admiration of Siddons an index of an unblemished American character. Shortly after settling in London, she wrote Thomas Jefferson, her theatre companion in Paris: "After having been accustomed to [the stages] of France, one can have little realish for the cold, heavy action, and uncouth appearence of the English stage. This would be considered as treason of a very black dye, but I speak as an American." After this winking reminder of US independence, Adams confessed that a Siddons might "reconcile" her to the English stage, but this would be done, apparently, by virtue of her likeness to actors from France, America's ally.[74] Adams would *not* be reconciled to being English, nor would she accept the "very black dye" of journalists portraying her entire clan as traitors to England. After all, her tastes demonstrated loyalty to the United States, the country she claimed as her own. With that question settled, Adams was free to borrow from Siddons's strategies of character management, using motherhood to maintain the whiteness of personal and national character.

Abigail Adams's White Rigging and Cargo

Considering the amount and severity of the objections she raised and the obstacles she encountered in the geographical and social transplantation, one wonders how Abigail Adams managed to make the trek from being an abandoned mother in Massachusetts to being an American ambassador's wife in Europe. Adams knew she needed the proper equipment, accessories, and frame of mind to undertake these simultaneous geographic and social relocations. Her keen awareness becomes all the more apparent in her intriguing deployment of nautical metaphors to describe her apparel. For someone who stated with but the lightest veneer of indirection that she would only board a ship once more in her life (i.e., to return to the United States), Abigail eagerly applied the nautical metaphor of rigging to her preparations for her first audience with England's Queen Charlotte sans John:

> The ceremony of presentation here is considerd as indispensable. . . . One is
> obliged here to attend the circles of the Queen which are held in Summer one
> a fortnight, but once a week the rest of the year, and what renders it exceedingly
> expensive is, that you cannot go twice the same Season in the same dress, and a
> Court dress you cannot make use any where else. I directed my Mantua Maker to
> let my dress be elegant but plain as I could possibly appear with Decency, accord-
> ingly it is white Lutestring coverd and full trimd with white Crape festoond with
> lilick ribbon and mock point lace, over a hoop of enormus extent. There is only a
> narrow train of about 3 yard length to the gown waist, which is put into a ribbon
> upon the left side, the Queen only having her train borne, ruffel cuffs for married
> Ladies thrible lace ruffels a very dress cap with long lace lappets two white plumes
> and a blond lace handkerchief, *this is my rigging.* I should have mentiond two
> pearl pins in my hair earings and necklace of the same kind.[75]

The language that Abigail used to describe this scaffolding of lace, ruffles, and hoops derived from the sea voyage, during which she had taken a keen interest in the ship's rigging. She wrote her older sister, "I have made a great acquisition, I have learnt the Names and places of all the masts and sails; and the Captain compliments me by telling me that he is sure I know well enough how to steer to take a trick at Helm." Demurring, Abigail flagged her feminine character: "I may do pretty well in fair weather, but tis your masculine Spirits that are made for Storms." At the same time, her metaphors suggested a comparison she would make explicit in figuring the dress as rigging: "I love the tranquil scenes of Life; nor can I look forward to those in which tis probable I shall soon be engaged."[76] As much as she hated sea travel, she did not view landing in London as re-establishing equilibrium. Rather, she anticipated rough social currents.

Once disembarked, Adams did not hesitate to translate her newly acquired nautical knowledge to steer her course. She imagined—and had her dressmaker construct—a sartorial apparatus that could carry her through the most unsettling social ceremonies. *White lutestring and crepe . . . lilac ribbon . . . and mock point lace over an enormous hoop: This is my rigging.* Abigail saw herself as a vessel crossing the treacherous seas of postcolonial relations between the United States and Britain, rigged with reams of white fabric, carrying the precious cargo of her chaste, unmarried adult daughter.[77] This white rigging and cargo constituted the crux of Abigail's self-presentation to her female kin back in the States and to the queen.[78]

Adams sought to appropriate as much of this proper, maternal civilized character as possible, while curtailing the tendency for women to become emblems of consumption, reduced to the same disposable status as the commodities they wore. Adams's search for "elegance" and "plain[ness]" still on the proper side of decency differentiated her from both figures such as the overdressed English lady and the bare-chested Indian woman. Adams was fashioning something new: a white female emblem of the estranged British Creoles who formed the United States. Suspended in the uncharted midst of a formation of shameless Frenchwomen, chauvinistic Englishwomen, unblushing negresses, and untamed squaws, Abigail Adams was in rough water, indeed. The rigging of chaste, white American motherhood—as exemplified by letters in which she drew attention to the character of other nations' women, and a white dress that tempered cosmopolitan consumption with New England modesty—kept her from sinking as she became a living white female symbol of the nation.

To turn a phrase of Iago's, I have argued in this chapter that a "flag and sign" of white character made the *Abigail Adams* a recognizable and seaworthy vessel in the turbulent waters of Anglo-American political relations after US independence (I.i.156). Adams presented a dignified and reputable American womanhood to audiences both at home and abroad through several whitening gestures that emphasized modesty and maternity as national virtues. Her self-representation required theatrical models admired and dreaded and epistolary skills that countered, in the private realm, the British press's smears of the Adamses.

Through her engagements with the figure of Desdemona and the actress playing her, Adams absorbed and refined tactics to surmount the perils of being a woman out of place. While this story could certainly be told without reference to *Othello,* the fact that Adams quotes from and speaks of it on numerous occasions throughout her correspondence makes it a useful lens through which to understand how she navigated an Atlantic economy that derived character—reputation and social status—by assessing texts and bodies. The story demonstrates the media and maneuvers necessary to construct a reputable white US-American womanhood that could circulate internationally. The various shifts of location during these years of Adams's life—as well as her employment of different media and appearances in different venues—indicate the required character fluency required for a woman to achieve and maintain an authoritative position in a transnational, transatlantic white interpretive community.

Despite the consolidation of race as a legal category that had occurred in the late seventeenth century and the emergence of what would come to be called scientific racism in the late eighteenth, Adams could not rely upon her whiteness as a stable identity, obvious to any viewer. Rather, she had to reconstruct it for each medium and in each location. Her position within or locked outside a white interpretive community—possessing or bereft of good character—varied as she moved from province to metropole and found herself reflected in British newspapers or private correspondence. Emphasizing whiteness turned out to be the most effective way to supersede suspicions about the character of women and of Americans.

Adams's story has fascinating connections to what came before and what was to come. There is a remarkable continuity between her predicament and the one Aphra Behn faced. A professional writer, Behn was able to invent a supreme position for herself in her fictionalized colonial outpost. Adams could expect no such deference in the metropole but could make herself the heroine of her familiar letters. Having created a white heroine in print who would not receive the darkening touch of the stage moor, Behn could identify with a black heroine—even experiment with having a black African double, Onahal, the witty old woman who helps the royal lovers and wins herself a young male consort in the process. Adams, to the contrary, never risked such an association. Her dress and spectatorship were posed against any potential comparisons of US Americans to Native Americans. Under unique pressures in the metropole, Abigail Adams could not engage in the long tradition of playing Indian.[79] She had to play it very white indeed.

As white women became increasingly able to participate as subjects in Atlantic commerce, the possibility of a cross-racial alliance narrowed. White women gained literacy and self-possession through ordeals both grand and minor, but their entry into a white interpretive community was predicated on aligning with slaveholding empires. Behn was already elegizing the resultant loss of a potential cross-racial alliance with women of color in 1688. Although Adams was by no means a representative white woman, it is intriguing that in her own encounters with *Othello,* she never attempted to redeem Desdemona. Even an imagined identification with the blackened Desdemona was either unavailable or to no avail.

For the scholar looking to the high scientific racism on the horizon, Adams's story is a reminder that racial identification remained fluid, contingent, relative, and negotiable—and remains so, always. Whatever the prevailing legal or scientific regime, the materials and reading protocols of vernacular racial reckoning remain available and consequential in the massive part of life not governed by experts. The cases in part 2 of this book focus on Native (Cherokee) and Haitian dissenters from the tenets of white interpretive community and the remarkable resiliency of the fraternal bond between white men who desired so much to hoard the benefits of social mobility in the Atlantic World.

❧ Part III

Crises of White Interpretive Fraternity

Interlude

Legends of Inept Spectatorship

In the first chapter, I quoted a 1709 letter from the Earl of Egmont, who worked himself up into frothy anger, denouncing women who were apparently unmoved by Thomas Betterton's portrayal of the moor of Venice. He wrote that such women "are capable of marrying again before their husbands are cold, of trampling on a lover when dying at their feet, and are fit to converse with tygers only."[1] For the earl, an insufficient identification with the tragic hero who murders his wife bespeaks a woman who should be banished from the marriage market and sent to the jungle for animal companionship. Abigail Adams felt enjoined to show disgust rather than sympathy when she took in *Othello* from her box seat at Drury Lane seventy-five years later. Although the expected affects differed, the stakes were equivalent. The wrong response could result in exclusion from a common white future. While these instances concern the surveillance of women's responses, quite a few stories entail the overinvolvement of *men* in *Othello*'s audience. The trove seems inexhaustible.

Consider this vignette:

> Mr. Edwin Booth says that the most genuine compliment he ever received was on the occasion of his playing Iago for the first time at Grass Valley, then a new mining camp. The audience, which had not seen a play for years, was so much incensed at his apparent villainy that they pulled out their "shooters" in the middle of the third act and began blazing away at the stage. Othello had the tip of his nose shot off at the first volley, and Mr. Booth only escaped by rolling over and over up the stage and disappearing through a trap-door. A speech from the manager somewhat calmed the house; but even then Mr. Booth thought it best to pass the night in the theatre, as a number of the most elevated spectators were making strenuous efforts to turn out and lynch "the infernal sneaking cuss," as they called him.[2]

In this tale, Booth positions himself as an ambassador, bringing elite theatre west from its flourishing eastern home to a culturally barren California mining town. He scores a double victory, each prong of which is based on a different kind of theatrical know-how. First, he claims to have convinced the audience who had fallen out of the habit of dramatic spectatorship that he embodied Iago, a villain deceiving a great and honorable man, a man so vile he deserves death. Second, he knew the architecture of the playhouse well enough to roll himself to a trapdoor in the midst of the shoot-out. This story simply could not work if it were set in London or indeed on the Eastern Seaboard of the United States. It asks the listener to imagine a mob that betrays its failures to rise to a standard of urbane whiteness in the low dialect of "the most elevated spectators" who call Iago an "infernal sneaking cuss."[3] Booth and his auditors bond through recounting and crediting a bit of apocrypha. Mutual suspicion would surely undo this pact between a liar and his creditors but for the western rubes. Yet, the fraternal bond thrives because each side finds a flattering image of themselves reflected from the mirror of the dupe out West.

Scholars of *Othello* have often flattered themselves in the abundant lore of unruly audiences. However, a parallel development in cinema studies should give pause. The distinction between savvy and credulous viewers has received significant attention in the "founding myth" of cinema.[4] Louis Lumière's pioneering silent short *L'Arrivée d'un train en gare de La Ciotat* (c. 1896–97), depicts the rather mundane occurrence of a train's arrival. Film historians delight in recounting a shocked audience: "In *L'Arrivée d'un train*, the locomotive, coming from the background of the screen, rushed toward the spectators, who jumped up in shock, as they feared getting run over."[5] The film scholar Martin Loiperdinger demonstrates that, in gleeful retellings of this tale, film historians have "circulate[d] a generally agreed-upon rumor . . . [but] ha[ve] provided neither evidence nor even references to contemporary sources" to substantiate it.[6] Two films followed fast on the heels of Lumière's, depicting rural filmgoers' terrified by moving pictures of a train.[7] It appears that the sole corroboration of the legend of frightened rubes at the movie house comes from the film industry itself.

Why would cinema need to manufacture this origin story? Loiperdinger says that the legend of the deceptively real moving picture is an indispensible testament to "the affective power" of the medium. I would add that the figure of the rube serves as a foil, highlighting the fleet intelligence that distinguishes film's "knowing audience" from its "naïve spectators"[8] The rube was invented to conceal the fact that film's urban producers and consumers also invest in the ephemera of moving pictures. In a capitalist mentality, those who invest in that which does not profit them are suspect. Given this similarity, it becomes urgent to establish one group as connoisseurs, a status that only comes into view against the backdrop of a corresponding population of dupes. In other words, the category of the "knowing audience" cannot exist without invoking "naïve spectators." The figure of the media illiterate is too useful to be relinquished. For those who profit from telling it, the story of the dupe's error can be neither substantiated nor disbelieved. Thus, the story survives as a social fact, despite its origin in pure fabrication. Although *Othello* did not inaugurate a new medium, it has spawned equally dubious stories of credulous, misbehaving spectators. Loiperdinger's analysis of the then-new medium of cinema offers a framework in which to analyze the apocryphal tales of viewers who prove themselves fools at *Othello*. By these lights, legends of inept spectatorship at *Othello* seem to serve theatre culture and even academic Shakespeare study by staging the criteria for membership in white interpretive community—namely, believing a flattering lie.

Traveling from the western frontier of the United States to the slaveholding South, we arrive at another celebrated, unsubstantiated tale of overinvestment in *Othello*. In a polemic against neo-classicist drama, the French Romanticist Stendhal insists that spectators derive "a dramatic pleasure" from violations of the unities of time, place, and action. Such divergences produce, he says, "that degree of illusion necessary for profound emotion."[9] When *Othello* changes location from Venice to Cyprus and the time that elapses for characters is longer than that which elapses for the audience, such disjunctures, he claims, distinguish performance from reality and create an opportunity for applauding the actor's art rather than the character's act. In the course of his argument, Stendhal casts his mind far from his Parisian environs to conjure a flawed spectator to serve as the model for credulity wrought from excessive immersion:

> Last year (August 1822) a soldier who was standing guard in the theatre in Baltimore, upon seeing Othello, in the fifth act of the tragedy of that name, about to kill Desdemona, cried out: "It will never be said that in my presence a damned nigger killed a white woman." At the same moment the soldier shot at the actor who was playing Othello and broke his arm. Not one year passes but what the newspapers report similar incidents. Now that soldier was entertaining an illusion: he believed in the reality of what was happening on the stage.[10]

As Stendhal never calls the man anything but a soldier, a reader might conclude that the author attributes the violation of decorum and credulousness—as much as the marksman's aim—to the guard's military profession. Despite Stendhal's assertion that such stories were common, I can find no mention of such an event in any nineteenth-century newspaper in the United States or Britain.[11] Untethered from corroboration and sometimes even from Stendhal, Shakespeareans and philosophers have repeated this tale for two centuries, retaining its national and regional markers while also working significant twists on its coordinates.[12]

Considering the spectator's state of mind during *Othello,* the philosopher Stanley Cavell omits Stendhal as a source and treats the narrative not as a historical incident but as a risible fable shared among the cultured. "The usual joke is about the Southern yokel who rushes to the stage to save Desdemona from the black man."[13] Perhaps Cavell forgot the specifics of Stendhal's vignette, which involves an armed soldier who fires from his guard post instead of ascending the stage and employs a much more blunt epithet for Othello than "the black man."[14] In any case, a potentially dignified soldier reappears here as a country bumpkin, who demonstrates his gullibility rather than asserting his honor with a clean shot.

Dympna Callaghan relies upon Cavell in her pathbreaking study of racial and gender impersonation on early modern English stages. She notes Cavell's apparent circumvention of the tale's charged racial atmosphere, contending that "Cavell's yokel" is "not simply a naïve spectator" but "a racist [one] whose fear of miscegenation inhibits his ability to distinguish between dramatic representation and reality."[15] Yet, adding that this fabricated spectator is not only gullible but racist traffics in its own racial imagination—of a rural southern bigot. In creating this ever-more-specific personage, Callaghan imbues what may be a figure invented for philosophical speculation with accessible motivations. To correct Cavell's evasion of the specter of racism, Callaghan must repeat her philosophical forebears' reliance on presumptions about race, class, and region, making a plausible human of what may have always been no more than an airy conceit.

The Stendhal fable, then, serves to highlight those white spectators who, by virtue of their credulity, fall out of a white interpretive community. Those who reject or laugh at the Baltimore soldier and the southern yokel indicate that they are better prepared for the slippery mediations that attend modern urban life. Abigail Adams as depicted in the previous chapter—shuddering with revulsion in her seat, yet not intervening in the live enactment that disturbed her—embodies this ideal spectator who recognizes a mediation but also responds within bounds of decorum. In the twentieth and twenty-first centuries, spectators like Adams serve as a resource for psychologists and philosophers attempting to grasp the complexities of aesthetic experience. If *Othello* generates real experiences of titillation and torture for its audience, why do they not tackle Othello, spirit Desdemona away, or strangle Iago? This question helped to generate the notion of "psychical distance" in the early decades of the twentieth century, disputed vigorously by Stanley Cavell midcentury, and revised by David Fenner as "aesthetic investment" early in the twenty-first.[16] Yet, this approach hinges on individual psychology and omits the social forces that form it—a grave omission when a white interpretive community attempts to monopolize the determination of meaning, justice, and worth. Few could afford to be laughed out of such a collective, and provoking laughter is the aim of all these legends of over-reaction to *Othello*.

While many scholars have noted the abundance of tales of interrupted *Othellos*, few have observed that tales distribute the sophistication required to resist this urge according to social divisions. In a bravura essay, Laurie Maguire argues that Shakespeare's corpus invites an undifferentiated audience to cross the boundary between plays and the real world through three techniques: deploying comic characters who cannot find the line between them, announcing that the play's "characters and events belong in a fiction," and drawing attention to dramatic artifice such as "cues, forgetting lines, stage costumes, . . . and other theatrical trappings."[17] Beyond the fact that her examples draw from Shakespeare's tragedies and comedies but exclude his many history plays, I would also question the homogeneous audience she posits. Spectators, she claims, are "responding to the influence" of Iago, "the door-keeper . . . who polices the boundary between truth and non-truth" when "like Desdemona, we/they confuse the worlds of life and drama."[18] Why should Desdemona be all spectators' point of identification? And why is Iago the supreme doorkeeper in all of Shakespeare? One could argue that *Macbeth*'s witches function as Iago does—conjuring up schemes in darkness, revealing them in equivocal language, refusing demands for clarification. However, the stories about *Macbeth* cluster around actors' bad luck rather than around audience members' efforts to prevent the lamentable murders of Duncan, Banquo, or Lady Macduff and her son.

Yet, even if we exclude *Macbeth*, the lore surrounding *Othello* does not allow for a unified theatrical experience that we/they share with Desdemona. Although the Venetian lady marries after having come under the spell of Othello's self-narration, historical viewers like Abigail Adams and her son John Quincy expressed disapproval and revulsion at her choice.[19] These negative affects indicate a refusal to be enchanted by the one whom she finds spellbinding—in short, a refusal of immersion in the world of the play. Formal aspects of Shakespearean dramaturgy cannot ensure that Desdemona and her judgmental audiences operate in a reality that has the same aesthetic and social rules. In addition, I would contend that laughable stories of overinvested audience members make sure that the slash in Maguire's "we/they" does not merge the two terms but disconnects them. The tales work by assuming *we* who hear them know better than *they* who erred, whether *they* be western pioneers, southerners, yokels, racists, soldiers, or miners. Their missteps create and authorize the East Coast Brahmin, the liberal northerner, the scholar, and the urbane philosopher—in short, the dominant members of the white interpretive community of this book's title. Therefore, I would offer a friendly amendment to Maguire: *Othello* has spawned legends in which spectators' demonstrations of acute or blinkered vision slot them within positions of expertise marked out by the play's socially striated dramatis personae.

The two chapters in this section feature interpretive crises spun off from the centrifugal force *Othello* has generated. The first is an apocryphal story of a high-ranking Cherokee woman who interrupted a performance of *Othello* for fear—a Virginia newspaper tells us—that actors fighting with unsheathed swords might truly injure one another. Both amateur and academic theatre historians have recounted this purported mistake so often that it might well be considered a founding myth of American theatre history. Of course, the interrupted *Othello* in Williamsburg does not involve a brand-new medium, as in the case of moving pictures on a screen. Instead, it narrates the introduction of a supposedly unfamiliar medium to the Native peoples of the Americas. In the case of the *Othello* at Williamsburg, the entire region of Virginia is potentially a zone of rubes. Therefore, it becomes an advantage for white colonists—and their subsequent descendants among American theatre historiographers—to make a distinction between their investment in theatre and that of Native people. If the rural bumpkin helped to establish the "affective power" of cinema and the discernment of its creators and connoisseurs, I would argue that the story of the Cherokee empress's mistake did much the same for Virginia colonists. In the penultimate chapter of *Inkface*, I consider this unnamed and mistitled woman's likely aim—to reassert the jurisdiction of Cherokee women over the disposition of captives. She did not require a fine appreciation of Shakespearean verse or of eighteenth-century stagecraft for her purposes. Instead, she seems to have been part of a community that circulated acute observations about the tools and tactics of English imperialism, including the pastime of watching Indians watch English plays.

The second interpretive crisis involves the error of a semifictional white character: Herman Melville's sea captain Amasa Delano, whose misperceptions guide the exquisitely elongated torture of "Benito Cereno" (1855). When they installed Melville in the literary canon in the 1920s, literary critics viewed Delano as a white Othello: a noble, trusting man deceived by treacherous slaves who were incarnations of evil. Since the Civil Rights Movement, Delano has become a useful gull, a shorthand in literary circles for a "romantic racialism" in which African character is imagined to be that of the loyal, affectionate pet.[20] Very little scholarship has interrogated this turn from sympathetic alignment with the American dolt to knowing condemnation and even ridicule of him. In the final chapter, I argue that in evaluating Delano's ability to decipher (black) character, even antiracist critics have reinforced a precondition of white interpretive authority—namely, that African persons' bodies are subject to the reading protocols of the black-and-white page, while European persons have the potential to stand apart from it as expert readers.

In fleeting moments, Melville does force white paper and white readers into the foreground, enmeshed in the same scene of reading as black ink and blackened people. However, these flashes are depicted as nullifications of the social contract and even the New Testament—as, in short, portents of the end of the world. Despite Melville's gloomy conclusion, the only hope remains in forcing those whites exempted from meaningful scrutiny into the field of interpretation on an equal footing. Breaking up that monopoly over legitimate interpretation could make possible a redistribution of property, pleasure, and protection.

4

The Cherokee *Othello*

Treating with "The Base Indian"

In November of 1752, the Board of Trade wrote the lieutenant governor of Virginia to repeat that it was "of the greatest importance" to establish "friendship" with local Indians "without a fresh instruction from his Majesty."[1] Although Robert Dinwiddie had only been in the seat for one year, he had attained the plum post of governor of England's oldest North American colony after service in two other colonial administrative posts. He knew his charge and needed no reminders. Before he received their correspondence, he had already penned this summation of all he had accomplished to further the Crown's interests:

> Some time since, the emperor of the Cherokees, his empress and only son, two of his generals, and attendants came to this city.... I bid them welcome and assured them of civil entertainment. His errand I found was to cultivate a friendship and encourage a trade from this government to his nation. I told him it was too great a distance from this, as he had come 700 miles, and recommended to them to continue their trade with South Carolina, which is within 100 miles of his nation, but he gave me to understand there was some uneasiness and disputes between him and the governor of South Carolina; I advised him to make up these differences and live in friendship with that colony for the future, and I would use my interest with the governor to establish the same. I told him I had not power over our traders to direct them in their commerce, but would acquaint them of the friendship, protection and encouragement he was pleased to provide them.
>
> I ordered for him, empress, son, generals, and attendants some fine cloths and a handsom [*sic*] present. They went away highly pleased and fully determined to keep up strict friendship and fidelity with the British nation in general and this government in particular.[2]

Having painted himself as a skillful navigator of imperial, intercolonial, and international relations, Dinwiddie offered apologies for a lengthy communiqué and concluded.

Although this meeting did not result in any official shift in Anglo-Cherokee relations, it generated a newspaper report that has become one of the foundational tales in Anglo-American theatre history. Dinwiddie did not specify the nature of the "civil entertainment" he offered to the Cherokee envoy, but the colony's sole (state-funded) newspaper, the *Virginia Gazette,* reversed his emphasis. In place of closed-door trade negotiations, the newspaper presents a public weekend of pomp for the embassy, as well as a fireworks celebration for the king's birthday. At its center is an occasion for Indian Watching in a double sense—Cherokees watching a performance of *Othello* and Englishmen watching the Indian spectators:

> The Emperor of the Cherokee Nation with his Empress and their Son the young Prince, attended by several of his Warriors and great Men and their Ladies, were received at the Palace by his Honour the Governor, attended by such of the Council as were in Town and several other Gentlemen, on Thursday, the 9th Instant, with all the Marks of Civility and Friendship, and were that Evening entertained, at the Theatre, with the Play (The Tragedy of Othello) and a Pantomime Performance, which gave them great surprise, as did the fighting with naked Swords on the Stage, which occasioned the Empress to order some about her to go and prevent their killing one another. The Business of their coming is not yet made publick; but it is said to relate to the opening and establishing a Trade with this Colony, which they are very desirous of.[3]

Interpretation of this disturbance hinges on the so-called Cherokee empress's knowledge and intentions.[4] If her culture had no equivalent for stage

News item concerning the Cherokees' visit with the governor of Virginia in 1752. "Williamsburg, November 17," *Virginia Gazette,* November 17, 1752. (Special Collections, John D. Rockefeller Jr. Library, Colonial Williamsburg Foundation)

performance, then she was necessarily unprepared for theatrical simulation and foolishly panicked about a swordfight that would never have ended in real bloodshed.[5] Conversely, if the Cherokees were familiar with British plays—or a similar performance tradition in their own culture—then the newspaper article fabricates an incident or falls prey to the kind of misapprehension that it suggests is proper to unsophisticated Indians.[6]

Although we lack firsthand accounts from Cherokees about their responses to the British, the English accounts yield suspicious patterns that cast doubt on their reliability. These sources reveal that, by the 1752 performance in Virginia, watching Indians had become an established pastime for Atlantic Britons. Pocahontas had been a guest of James I, attending Ben Jonson's masque *The Vision of Delight* at court in 1617. John Chamberlain, a London gentleman, wrote to England's ambassador at the Hague: "The Virginian woman Poca-huntas . . . hath ben with the King and graciously used, and both she and her assistant *well placed at the maske.*"[7] It appears that this first theatrical embassy was structured so that the English could view an Indian woman watching a performance in which urban London was presented as a place of dissolution, which the king could order and revivify by commanding the gentry to return to the countryside.[8] It remains a mystery what she thought as a witness to this allegorical transfiguration of a local conflict. She was certainly not invited to enter into the contract between English performers and spectators, but we can be confident that she did not recognize—that is acknowledge and assent to—the imperial gesture.

There were no subsequent Indian embassies for the rest of a century riven by domestic strife in England. Yet, with the Restoration of the monarchy, these peculiar rituals were revived and magnified in public theatres for the imagined community of the nation. Playhouse spectacles, newspapers, and ballads offered the opportunity for a white English audience to scrutinize Indigenous American specimens. Like the stage moors of the seventeenth century discussed in the introduction and first chapter, these Indian guests were presumed to have readable countenances—not least because English portraits of Cherokee leaders in the mid-eighteenth century focus attention on the ink tattoos on their faces.[9]

That metaphorical textuality is, of course, not unique. Interpreting faces was a nascent science and may indeed be a human universal.[10] However, to determine that the character of an entire people includes a kind of media illiteracy, an inability to grasp the unseen (such as motives or worth), is more than any evolutionary imperative to gauge the emotional state of another individual. It is a function of inkface, in this case conveying not slavish nature or sexual dishonor but a constitutional inability to read and to know. Printed reports of Indian spectatorship—generated anywhere the British had theatres and treated with Indians—reveal Indian Watching as an activity predicated on the presumption that Indians were gullible spectators, distracted from invisible meanings and values by literal appearances. These public acts authorized and sustained the dream of a legitimate and commercially profitable empire.

A spate of eighteenth-century performances took James I's private ritual public at playhouses, on fairgrounds, and in print. The 1710 staging of an operatic version of *Macbeth* for Mohawk and Mahican guests in London popularized Indian Watching by supplementing public sightings with print reports to spread images of Indians' supposed twin responses to an advanced British culture: wonder and submission.[11] Newspapers tracked Indian delegates' movements, and printers transformed the tour into lore in romanticized ballads published for another century.[12] The performance historian Joseph Roach christened the 1710 opera the "Mohawk Macbeth," and Alden Vaughan has shown that it established a precedent that Anglo-Indian alliances would be cemented in London, where the visiting leaders' tour would include an evening of theatre.[13] When considered alongside these metropolitan rituals, the performance in Williamsburg, as well as subsequent ones in New York in the 1760s, suggests that the inclusion of command theatrical performances during Anglo-Indian summits extended beyond London. In those cities that could boast a purpose-built playhouse, British colonial officials invited Indians to the theatre and other spectacles, watched their reactions, and circulated reports that British arts left the guests awed.[14] If viewed as one of a series of restagings of the "Mohawk Macbeth," the Williamsburg summit of 1752 emerges as a "Cherokee *Othello*," a counterpart to the metropolitan sensation, scaled to the size of a smaller colonial capital with a fledgling commercial theatre and only a single newspaper. Although the Cherokee disrupters left no written record of their motivations, placing the Cherokee *Othello* in the context of an intertwined history of theatre, diplomacy, and commercial ambitions certainly illuminates colonists' predisposition to misinterpret the interruption.

Obstacles in the Scholarship

One important question is why the oft-told tale of the Cherokees' foolish inability to understand the first premise of theatre (i.e., that it is a representation and not reality) circulated so long as an unquestionable fact. While repeating the arresting vignette, nearly every scholar in US (or even hemispheric American) theatre history accepted the premise that an elite Indian diplomat's wife was incapable of understanding the difference between a staged swordfight and a real one. In the 1880s, the first historians of US-American theatre adopted the *Virginia Gazette*'s viewpoint, characterizing the empress's reported mistake as an example of the "simplicity" of "savage royalty."[15] In the intervening century and a quarter, the event has been solidified as a risible incident in the early days of American theatre—few have even noted that the Cherokees were present for treaty negotiations.[16] Robin Warren opened this century by gesturing to scholars' unquestioning acceptance of a suspicious story by noting the "implicit racist assumptions" propelling the *Gazette*'s report, but those "assumptions" remained implicit.[17] In fact, one recent overview of Shakespeare's career in British America departs from over a century of tradition in omitting the Cherokees from the first season of professional theatre offered in North America.[18] Theatre history, in general, has viewed this event outside the context of trade negotiations and, therefore, missed the larger Atlantic pattern to which it belongs. Returning to the Cherokees' interruption of *Othello,* with its brew of public spectacle, racial characterization, and imperial commerce, offers an opportunity to pinpoint the specific nature of those racist assumptions and the work they were tailored to accomplish.

Scholars outside theatre history could have offered context to help understand the cultural work of this event, but the theatrical interlude is absent from their narratives of Anglo-Indian relations in the eighteenth century. Given the wide availability of eighteenth-century newspaper reports on the amazement of Indian spectators, it is highly unlikely that these scholars did not see them. Instead, it would appear that they operated in fields structured by an unspoken axiom that theatre could not have been the site of significant political and economic thought or activity.[19] After all, the Board of Trade never officially codified theatregoing as an essential component of Anglo-Indian diplomacy. It might be, however, that theatre was such an integral part of Anglo-Indian treaty negotiations that it could be understood "without a fresh instruction from His majesty" that the "civil entertainment" offered to foreign dignitaries would include an evening of theatre—an occasion for Britons to flaunt dramatic performance as a spectacle of civilization and to generate reports of Indians' awe or credulity.[20] Throughout this book, I have been suggesting that the most stubborn aspects of racial ideology burrow deep enough to go unspoken. The unarticulated sense that an Anglo city should stage theatre and report amazement on the face of Indian spectators stands as an illustration of ideology in this sense of a standard operating procedure rather than an explicit creed.[21]

Restoring the playhouse as a frequent, meaningful site of treaty negotiations would illuminate mental components of the eighteenth-century struggles scholars study: the contested incorporation of the Cherokees into the capitalist world system, the British Empire's forced reorganization of autonomous Cherokee villages into a tribal state, the attendant transformation of Cherokee gender systems, and the South Carolina monopoly on the Cherokee trade.[22] These transformations did not just *occur;* they had to be dreamed and the dream sustained in the face of competing visions and unruly reali-ties.[23] Theatre—and the broader field of ritualized action and interpretation to which it belongs—offered the tantalizing hope that stock characters were not just a spectator's imaginative indulgence of actors but reliable models for interpreting and predicting human behavior.[24] Performance culture did not merely *reflect* broader historical contexts, it also served as the mental store of character types that people used to make sense of offstage interactions.

The mutually reinforcing boundaries of nation and period have also pre-vented investigation of the Cherokee *Othello*. Although they discuss British antecedents for racial impersonation, Americanists typically begin their in-quiries into the interplay between racial thinking and performance culture in the early national period, with emphasis falling on the nineteenth century.[25] Furthermore, they have held that both colonial and Early Republican drama borrowed heavily from London fare and, thus, reflected a world "some three thousand miles away, and at times, a century removed" from the particulari-ties of life in North America.[26] One of the foremost scholars in the resurgent field of colonial American theatre, Odai Johnson, notes the absence of North American types onstage: "the (white) poor, enslaved Africans, Dutch mer-chants, native Indians, and backwoods frontiersmen."[27] He concludes that the history of these populations and that of the colonial stage "were ideologically and materially utterly unchanged" by each other.[28] Of Indians, in particular, he writes that "though they were the subject of all the gaze of London, in the British theatre of colonial America, [American Indians were] literally incon-ceivable, impossibly beyond and below the threshold of representation."[29]

Scholars of early American theatre have had to fight against the longstanding myth that the only story to tell of colonial American theatre is of its repression. Johnson's painstaking and imaginative research into archives and archaeology have helped to rescue the field from obscurity. Consequently, I hear a note of lament in Johnson's claim that there can be no place for race in the study of colonial American theatre—a fear that the impossibility of discussing such a pressing topic might insulate the field from other vital conversations in early American studies. Yet, that outcome is not inevitable. Scholars of early mod-ern and eighteenth-century British culture have shown the centrality of the empire as source of both concrete and imaginative materials in London.[30] The colonial stage did feature players and plays from the metropole, but those plays were inflected by England's imperial ambitions—and the players knew they had to appeal to their local audiences.[31] With these dynamics in mind, Jenna Gibbs posits an Atlantic frame that challenges the geographic and tem-poral boundaries of theatre history by addressing "the tensions between the regional factors peculiar to each locale and the transatlantic themes of debate common to [them]."[32]

In this light, the "ideological and material" traffic between the Cherokees and North American theatre did not entirely "belong to the [nineteenth] century."[33] Events such as the Cherokee *Othello* suggest that concrete differences of time and place were warped inside the playhouse, where a colonial viewer was "caught . . . between his sense of spectatorial distance from the actions onstage and the constant invitations by both performer and script to identify with those actions."[34] That identification would have entailed imaginatively recasting Mediterranean stories like *Othello* in local terms, not paying strict fidelity to the stated ethnicities of the characters represented onstage. Neither the scripts nor the staged performances would have posed a great obstacle to this work of identification, for, as Jeffrey Richards notes, ethnic types were portrayed "with gross inaccuracies, measured against flesh-and-blood" people.[35] We have already seen a racial category peculiar to the theatre in *Mr. Moore's Revels*, which I analyzed in the introduction—an Oxford masque in which moor, negro, and "sutty-visaged Indian" were all names for the same stage type. Consequently, in a performance like *Othello*, London's "dull moor" (V.ii.225) could become Virginia's Cherokee empress, even though local Indians were not directly portrayed onstage.[36]

One need not assume that identification adhered to any strict legal, economic, or scientific distinctions among races. The milieu of the theatre helps show that emulation, rivalry, and traffic between colony and metropole kept identifications circulating and in flux. Still, a circum-Atlantic archive of print propaganda about Indian habits as spectators and economic thinkers suggests that theatre was a site where some dispersed Britons animated racialized characters to participate in fantastic stories wherein Indian wealth would be transferred to British hands. Neither ethnographic accuracy nor adherence to distinctions now accepted between black and Indian mattered. Perceptions of racial difference did not proceed from lived interactions or observations; rather, they structured a dream narrative that Britons were desperate to live.

In what follows, I take the cue to pursue an anthropological approach to Atlantic culture in Joseph Roach's aphorism "Historians ought to attend to the 'deep play' in the stock plays."[37] Extending beyond play scripts, Kathleen Wilson adds that "attention to performance can reveal novel aspects of social and political relations that scholars would otherwise ignore."[38] These scholars suggest that theatre cannot be seen as passive, a mere reflection of political and economic thought and action determined in more serious, objective realms. The past subjects we are studying considered the playhouse a site of economic thinking and diplomatic activity; our disciplinary protocols have kept us from seeing what could and did go unsaid with them.[39] The requisite attention to theatre as an enterprise that produced fictive participants in social exchange leads deeper into both *Othello* and the rumored trade negotiations, linking the newspaper account with multiple parties' political calculations. A new look at the Cherokee *Othello*—as well as its genealogy and repercussions—reveals a racialized theatre that made it possible for some to dream successful intercolonial and imperial schemes and for others to disrupt those dreams.

In the context of *Inkface,* this incident provides a view of the processes by which a white interpretive community was formed and disrupted. The play, transatlantic newspaper reports of the trade summit, and the correspondence of colonial governors formed nonidentical but intertwined schemas of Anglo-Atlantic economic accumulation—projects that were disrupted when a Cherokee woman intervened at the site of their convergence to reassert Cherokee sovereignty and Cherokee women's political prerogatives. Although her success was not permanent, for a moment the political and imaginative elements of a British commercial dream were held in suspension while both stage and imperial actors attempted to get back "on book"—to return to a script of the Americas as a site for white enrichment.

While the previous chapters in this book have considered white women's engagements with the blackened figure of Desdemona, the final two focus more on the utility of inkfaced dupes for white men seeking to garner an exclusive hold on the spoils of empire. Consequently, the emphasis shifts from a gendered notion of honor to intellectual sophistication as a racial marker. Desdemona's time on stage accomplished the cultural work of making it possible for audiences to behave as if sexual shame appears as a mark on a woman's face. Similarly, the revelation of stage moors—and the invocation of Indians—as media illiterates enabled an operating assumption that these populations would pose no barrier to imperial accumulation mediated by letters, numbers, and ceremonial acts. Despite this shift, gender remains on the agenda here, just as racial hierarchy and authority were always operative in the previous chapters. In fact, the Cherokee empress's orders to halt the play reassert Native sovereignty *through* a demonstration of Cherokee women's political prerogatives within that polity.[40]

However, none of these engagements become visible until the playhouse is taken seriously as a site of Anglo-Indian diplomacy and *Othello* as a mediator (rather than as a reflection) of those interactions. In the theatregoers' world, the knowledge of letters and of commodity value is conceived of as a white racial property. Similarly, to the extent that "race" is the product of a reading of the body, it stands to reason that the culture that can properly interpret theatre will also be able to know and articulate racial character. As such, the Cherokee *Othello* proves a meaningful episode in the racialization of literacy itself.

Othello and Indian Baseness: Genealogy and Theory

One of the strange coincidences in this chapter is that the very play that the Cherokees attempted to halt ends with a line about Indians' incapacity. The *Virginia Gazette*'s report of the Cherokee empress's error recalls a figure Shakespeare's blackfaced moor references in his famous, suicidal monologue.[41] Having foolishly murdered a wife he wrongly judged adulterous, Othello compares his mistake to that of the "*base Indian* [who] threw a pearl away / Richer than all his tribe" (V.ii.363–64).[42] In Shakespeare, as in the newspaper report, errors in assessing human character are yoked to economic errors. As spectators stare at Desdemona's wasted body onstage, Othello's monologue asks them to envision a jewel, discarded by an Indian who does not know its priceless value. It is crucial to note that both the moor and the Indian make a theatrical mistake as well—if one remembers that *theatre* comes from the Greek verb *theasthai,* meaning "to see" or "to look."[43] By conflating the errors of the jealous husband and the carelessly wasteful Indian, Shakespeare aligns theatrical gullibility and economic ignorance for his audiences. *Othello* collapses—or, perhaps, has no need to recognize—what are in other times and circumstances commonsense ethnic and disciplinary distinctions. In Shakespeare's conception of baseness, black, moor, and Indian can be one, as can theatrical misperception and economic error.[44]

While the "base Indian" is held up to scorn in *Othello* for his inability to apprehend a pearl's unseen value, Karl Marx returned to this same jewel to demystify capitalism's inaccessible, imaginary forms of value.[45] "No chemist," he quipped, "has ever discovered exchange value either in a pearl or a diamond."[46] Marx aimed to demonstrate that the exchange value "of material objects belongs to them independently of their material properties." What Iago calls an "essence that's not seen" (IV.i.16) has its counterpart in exchange value, "a fantastic form different from" the "ordinary, sensuous thing" (mis)represented in, as, and through the universal equivalent of money.[47] At a conceptual level, the theatre and the capitalist economy align here. In an economic culture based on the fetish of exchange value, when participants gather in a theatre of impersonation and deception, the actor speaks for Marx's mute commodity to ask the implicit question: *What do you take me for?*[48]

As Jean-Christophe Agnew and subsequent scholars have noted, the seventeenth- and eighteenth-century playhouse was a literal site of economic transaction among patrons, players, and prostitutes, while the stage itself offered opportunities to reflect upon these transactions by depicting them.[49] Theatregoing, therefore, became an exercise in the kinds of character assessment necessary in a capitalist system in which the participants in an exchange made bonds with strangers based on a notoriously unstable money form.[50] At present, few scholars have considered that the capacities for character assessment and economic savvy were not only conjoined but also, crucially, presented as beyond the capacities of races deemed primitive.[51] In other words, the invention of whiteness was not purely a legal or scientific phenomenon but a folk anthropological distinction between the anticipated beneficiaries of Atlantic ventures and those who had to lose.[52] It is worth considering the production of racial essence, exchange value, and theatrical character as not only interwoven but also interdependent aspects of imperial fantasies of wealth transfer in the early modern period and eighteenth century.

Rather than retroactively justifying the empire's racial hierarchy, the figure of the base Indian arguably enabled the pursuit of a commercial empire from the start.[53] To recast Gary B. Nash's formulation about "friendly" Indians, "it was only a . . . [base] Indian who *could* be a trading Indian."[54] Nash identifies the "desire to trade" as the cultural engine, providing a "special incentive . . . for seeing the Indian as something more than an intractable savage."[55] I would add that the image of a hostile, violent Indian posed a practical but not an ideological threat to commercial empire. Though certainly not as convenient as the "friendly" Indian, the belligerent Indian was still a recognizable type. Britons could plan to trade with the former and to eliminate the latter through warfare. On an ideological level, the greatest threat would have been an Indian whose nature and motivations the British felt they could not capture, an Indian who undermined Britons' confidence in their means of apprehending and representing visible and invisible realities. The base, undiscerning Indian was fabricated to serve in fantasies of the Americas as a space of unreciprocated exchange. Consequently, the figure challenges attempts to ground it in the imperial ideology of one era or one nation. Indeed, it appears that various Europeans interpreted their encounters with Indians in anticipation of the extractive economy they aimed to establish in the Americas.

In the 1970s and early 1980s, scholars of Shakespeare's sources traced the financially incompetent Indian to the second of three works on America by Richard Eden, a London imprint of 1553, in which the four voyages of the Italian explorer Amerigo Vespucci appear in condensed form. Eden retained a passage about the Indians' ignorance of the value of pearls, gold, and other treasures: "As for Golde, Pearles, precious stones, jewelles, and suche other thinges, which we in Europa esteme as pleasures and delicates, they sette noughte by."[56] This reference and others like it firmly locate base Indians not on the Indian subcontinent but in the Americas and establish a characteristic blindness to value as a pan-ethnic distinction. In Vespucci's formulation, "we in Europa," regardless of language or nation, can see inherent economic value, while all Indians, irrespective of ethnic particularities, cannot. Early modernists have found several other texts—both roughly contemporaneous with *Othello* and from subsequent decades—that revive this stock character.[57]

As Peter Hulme notes in his study of early Caribbean encounters between Europeans and Indigenous peoples, the economically illiterate Indian appears in the narration of the inaugural moment of contact, mythologized in Christopher Columbus's first journal. Hulme's translation reads: "Because I recognized that they were people who would be better freed [from error] and converted to our Holy Faith by love than by force—to some of them I gave red caps, and glass beads which they put on their chests, and many other things of small value, in which they took so much pleasure and became so much our[s] . . . that it was a marvel." Hulme portrays Columbus as, essentially, the first Indian Watcher. Viewing indigenes' reactions to his gifts, Columbus calculates the "warmth of the welcome" as "in excess of the value of the items distributed" and imagines a relationship in which "trade is not going to be necessary because everything and everyone will rapidly become 'our[s]'; ours to exploit as we will." The racialized figure Shakespeare would eventually name "the base Indian" is a product of a process Hulme calls "cultural economics," an "accountancy . . . lodged at the very beginning of the European colonial venture" and designed to discredit Indigenous economies of exchange and attendant ethical obligations.[58] Whatever his immediate perceptions of this first encounter, Columbus penned a retrospective account that appealed to his royal sponsors' desire to believe in the existence of a race of people whose inability to assess value was already assured as a defining trait.

The most striking attribute of the figure of the base Indian is its immediate availability. It did not take years—or even months—of uneven trade with Indigenous peoples to conclude that they could not perceive value. Rather, the project of extraction demanded this figure. The possibility of savvy or, worse, unreadable economic and political partners had to be excluded from consideration. Shrewd Indians would never consent to uneven trade. The base Indian was born of dreams of the Americas as a space of unreciprocated exchange and, consequently, proved particularly resilient in the face of Native peoples' actual behaviors. This desire was not born of long experience of Indians' economic mistakes. Rather, this racialized figure of financial incompetence was a necessary precondition, enabling Europeans to imagine an uneven exchange that remained morally legitimate. Shifting to early British America, the historian Caitlin Rosenthal encapsulates how important basic numeracy was to commercial activity and morality:

> In the expanding market economy, anyone who had to work, buy, or sell needed access to the language of numbers. Increasingly, this was everyone. . . . Once they could speak the language of numbers, they could convert measures and currencies,

compare prices, and calculate wages, all of which helped them navigate the expanding world of commerce. . . . [Numeracy] privileged and legitimated certain
varieties of exchange. As with more conventional technologies, it simultaneously
reflected and remade the market. The transactions it enabled came to seem not
just correct but fair and even moral.[59]

Technologies of racialization arguably mirror those of numeracy, both
"reflect[ing] and rema[king]" social life, "legitimat[ing]" some exchanges and
concealing both doubts and alternate social arrangements.

Having been invented out of sheer hope, the economically incompetent
Indian then became a part of Europe's gallery of imaginary characters, there
to be recast in subsequent scenarios of uneven exchange. Consequently,
one might say that the base Indian is more like a letter of the alphabet or a stage
persona in its strange relationship to historiographical time. The alphabet has
a history but we do not need to be cognizant of that history in order to wield
the characters. The "artificial persons" of the stage have a physical existence
for the duration of the performance and they exist as concepts in the memory
or in a script, but action undertaken in character is not, typically, understood
to be prosecutable. In sum, the author or the actor may be held accountable,
but the characters of the page and stage exist in a temporal space that might
be called "unreal time."[60]

As a pretext for nationalist and imperialist action, the base Indian and other
racialized figures precede that which national history can account for. For racial characters are not, originally, the product or object of state power. Like a
national language, they are a preconception enabling the significant action that
builds an imagined (and exclusive) community. In other words, they are what a
nation thinks with, a medium in which they conduct their transactions—the
imagined community is constituted first in faith in this prophecy and then
in collective action to speed its fulfillment in the flesh.[61] Karen and Barbara
Fields describe the process in defining the term "racecraft": "Real action creates evidence for the imagined thing. By that route, [the desire to believe] . . .
constantly dumps factitious evidence for itself into the real world."[62] The persistent restaging of base Indian scenarios was one of those "real actions," and
each reference to Indian baseness provided the "evidence" to sustain the desire
to believe that one could trade with this financially illiterate fantasy.[63]

The concept of racecraft offers an entry into a wishful component often
missing from more mechanistic accounts of racialization, conquest, and incorporation. Though imperial violence is certainly a historical fact, the empire, as a smoothly functioning geopolitical unit, necessarily remained a
"represent[ation of] things as yet only imagined . . . [but] ardently desired."
The author of this phrase, Angel Rama, asserts that Latin American cities

founded on the specifications of royal commands and meticulous diagrams never reconciled material reality and imperial dream. Consequently, the cities lived double lives: "on one hand, a material life inescapably subject to the flux of construction and destruction ... and the circumstantial intervention of human agency; on the other hand, a symbolic life, subject only to the rules governing the order of signs, which enjoy a stability impervious to the accidents of the physical world."[64] Though Rama was interested in letters and city planning in Spanish and Portuguese America, his remarks can be expanded to consider the manufacture and enjoyment of racial characters, such as the gullible moor and the base Indian.

Rama makes clear precisely why mediations matter: a unit within a literary, theatrical, or economic system may not correspond to reality, but it has forms, such as typeface and blackface—conventions that create an alternate, self-referential universe. Such forms, like the alphabet, tend to mediate facts rather than conform or multiply to fit them. Just as print shops ran on the supposition that they could produce an infinite array of texts by rearranging a limited set of alphanumeric characters, so theatre companies deemed their rosters of typecast actors sufficient to tell the full range of dramatic stories. As Jeffrey H. Richards notes, eighteenth-century drama tended to produce characters and plots based on conventional genres and types rather than on current events.[65] The base Indian is such an unreal character type—a product of the collective, imaginative work of racecraft, practiced in theatres and deployed in offstage character assessments. Seen in this light, it would appear that Indian Watching entailed substituting racecraft's unreal characters for the less compliant Indigenous diplomats Britons in the metropole and the colonies confronted in real historical time.

If the desire to believe in the Indian as economic dupe conditioned first contact, this race-based speculation also persisted long after Iberian dominance in the New World waned. The British repeatedly revived the base Indian, its function persisting even if its name changed or was not invoked at all. Publishers seized upon it; readers recognized it. Like Columbus and Vespucci before them, many Britons hoped to interact with this figure and to reap untold profits. As the saying goes, their hopes sprang eternal.

The Economy of the "Mohawk Macbeth": London, 1710–1713

These depictions of credulous Indians emerged as Britons were renegotiating their own relationship to the spectacle of performance. As professional theatre eclipsed the medieval play cycles, playwrights began to thematize the transactional nature of the relationship between audience and performer as a metaphor for interactions with strangers in an urban setting.[66] This insight of Jean-Christophe Agnew's has had tremendous influence, but it has not yet been observed that the two forms of calculation he identified—hedonistic and histrionic—were understood to be white racial properties. By the 1590s it was common for drama to offer Britons a time and place of ideological fantasy in which the capacities of insight and profit making were linked to each other and to racial character. Visually engaging a succession of characters with unsubtle names like Golding, Quick-Silver, and Surface taught playgoers that discerning human character and determining economic value were twin activities.[67] Meanwhile, a string of stage personae with alien names, foreign costumes, and painted black faces made laughable errors of vision, suggesting that insight into character and value was a racial property of Europeans in general—and of the British in particular.[68] Eighteenth-century Britons, then, were primed to see Indians as lacking in sight.

In 1710 London welcomed three Mohawks and a Mahican, the first Indian officials who did not make pacts in the colonies but, rather, traveled to the metropole to establish military, economic, and religious ties directly with the monarch. This summit established a formula for subsequent ceremonies, including a playhouse visit, public appearances by ambassadors, and portrayals of Indian appearance and character in a variety of media.[69] When the "Mohawk Kings" arrived at the Haymarket Theatre, the audiences demanded to see these exotic men, refusing to let William Davenant's operatic adaptation of *Macbeth* commence until the American guests had been moved from their box to seats located onstage. One account quotes the working-class "Mob" thusly: "Since we have paid our money, the Kings we will have." The reporter quipped that for such a "Mob . . . it is a maxim to *have* as much as possible for their money."[70] In accord with the etymology of *theatre* as the place to see, the means of this possession was, above all, visual.[71] Yet, Indian Watching proved as strange a commodity as stage performance itself. In both cases, the rare and exotic acquired value, despite lacking the tangibility and durability of traditional vendibles.

At the conclusion of the opera, a performer recited an epilogue written especially for the occasion. Adopting the British monarch's perspective, the epilogue reduces the four men designated as kings to supplicant foreign princes "struck with Wonder at the Monarch's Sight."[72] More important, it articulates that the journey to meet Queen Anne would culminate in submission to the empire. Unlike Caesar—who famously came, saw, and conquered—these Indians "come, and see, and wonder, and obey."[73] Cast as new magi, these kings' intuitive and inarticulate sighting of a court "so enrich'd"—in appearance and inward character—induces them to grant "the whole Globe, of Earth that Prince's right." The epilogue asks audiences to look at the Indian guests, find irrepressible "wonder" on their faces, and imagine that the kings themselves have betrayed an instinctive recognition that they should surrender their all. This manufactured look of "wonder" was first witnessed as a hope-induced hallucination at the theatre and then preserved and promulgated by print.[74]

One popular ballad in this archive casts a Mahican visitor as a sort of Othello, in love with a "fair" English lady, a "saint . . . far above me, / Altho' I am an Indian king." The literary scholar Laura Stevens presents a cogent analysis of this ballad, "The Four Indian Kings Garland," which furthers the racialized economy of sight and insight of the other documents. In this musical text, revised and reprinted for decades after the 1710 visit, the kings arrive "To report their sorrows great; / Which by France they had sustained, / To the overthrow of Trade"—a tale they recount "With all humble low submission."[75] Subsequent to this audience, one of the kings is lovestruck by the sight of a beautiful English woman. To woo her, he sends a ring, which Stevens reads as an instance of "an outrageously valuable gift" symbolizing "the transfer of treasure" from America to England.[76]

These portraits of Indians as fundamentally unprepared for mediated urban economies continued after the sensation of 1710. For example, in 1713 the Society for the Propagation of the Gospel recommended that the queen send a Yamassee "prince" home to Carolina in fine clothes, because "the Indians in Generall are most affected with that kind of garb, which is gawdy and makes the finest shew."[77] Clearly, the English had a preferred narrative in which Indian submission to imperial rule would be guaranteed by spontaneous acts of submission, prompted by the amazing spectacles of advanced European culture. There would not be another major tour by Indian diplomats until 1730, but the Indian as deficient watcher and financial incompetent had been established and would be promptly revived.

Cherokees in London: 1730

The activity of Indian Watching certainly framed England's imperial relationship with the Cherokees, which had its official start in October 1730 when seven Cherokee "Chiefs" arrived in London to formalize a treaty with the Crown.[78] Like their "Mohawk" predecessors in 1710, the Cherokees were a sensation, drawing ogling crowds and initiating an outpouring of representation, from newspapers to ballads and portraits. The archives have preserved only a portion of what was surely a wider conversation during both visits about whether or not Indians possessed the insight necessary to properly evaluate the treacherous personages and media of city life.

Newspapers cast the Cherokees as new incarnations of the humble Mohawks. The Cherokee delegates were reportedly "extreamly surprized at the Magnificence of every Thing about them" in Windsor.[79] Though they were

portrayed as "expert[s]" when they watched an archery exhibition at Three
Tuns in London, they were said to be transfixed by sleight of hand tricks at
Bartholomew Fair, exhibitions that left them "surprized" and "amazed."[80] Images of Indians unprepared for urban entertainments again led to stories of
their susceptibility to being swindled. The *Grub Street Journal* reported a gift
of rings reminiscent of that in "The Four Indian Kings' Garland":

> Friday night about 11, the Indian Prince walking in Covent Garden, was pick'd
> up by the infamous Jenny Tite, who took 2 rings off his fingers, and made off
> with them. P.—*I think the Lady for the future deserves the title of* the famous Jenny
> Tite, *on account of this amour with* his R. Highness, *who not knowing the use of
> money on these occasions, might present her with these* 2 rings. *I guess, that this*
> Prince *was not one* of the 6 Indian Chiefs, *whom Sir Alex. Cumings* chose out
> *when he was in* the Charokee mountains; *but is the 7th, who, as we find in Six
> Alexander's letter, was once before* picked up by the way.[81]

These representations of Cherokee baseness share the idea that Indians may
possess the practical knowledge of the archer, but they lack the capacity to see
beyond appearances to metaphysical essences. At best, their sight is merely a
reflex—an innate response to greatness, such as the Mohawk kings' deference
to Queen Anne. This capacity to be captivated by show produces characters
who are laughably defenseless against fraud, such as the Yamassees who are
enthralled by gawdy clothes and the Cherokee prince who loses two gold rings
to a prostitute an Englishman would have known to pay off with petty cash.

The desire that prompted the continual resuscitation of the base Indian
in theatre culture and humorous news items also pervades the structuring assumptions of the official documents of treaty negotiation. For example, the
architects of the 1730 Articles of Friendship and Commerce hoped that
the document would initiate the "transfer of treasure" from the Cherokees to
England. In that spirit, the Board of Trade informed the king's representative, the Duke of Newcastle, that "words may easily be inserted acknowledging their Dependence upon the Crown of Great Britain, which Agreement
remaining upon Record in our Office, would . . . greatly Strengthen our Title
in those Parts, even to all Lands which these People now possess."[82] The hope,
then, was that Indians would be unable to interpret the theatre of diplomacy.
Without referencing *Othello* directly, the board cast them as base Indians, not
formidable opponents or respected allies but dupes who could not resist an
exploitative economic and political relationship because they could not even
see when it was being imposed.

The gullible Indian appears again as the imagined party who participates
in the curious visual procedures for cementing the Articles of Friendship and

Commerce. Each article of the 1730 treaty is punctuated by the offering of a gift. All are notably utilitarian: striped duffles (for woolen coats), blue cloth, red cloth, guns, powder, swan shot, bullets, vermillion dye, gun flints, hatchets, spring knives, brass kettles, and belts. Yet two are particularly notable, for the English offer them in a way that is supposed to cater to Indians' perceived incapacity for abstraction. Not satisfied with a mark from the ambassadors, the committee offers "Two Pieces of Blue Cloth" so that the chiefs can "fasten it well to the Breast of Moytoy of Telliquo," as "the Great King has fasten'd one End of it to his own Breast." Then, after reciting an article that aims to marshal the Cherokees "against any Nation, whether they be White Men or Indians who shall dare to molest or hurt the English," the English give "20 Guns."[83] Imperial administrators excused this presentation of gifts—which would not have been part of a written treaty with Europeans—by saying that the exchange was required by Indian custom.

Yet, perhaps, such gifts were less a concession to Indians' alleged literal mindedness than a way to assuage English fears that these treaties failed to establish a true meeting of the minds and could not be enforced. The simple symbolism could have been designed to assure Britons that the content of the agreement could not possibly be misinterpreted, as if to say, For what purpose, other than fighting off French Indians, could they think we were giving them guns?[84] The resort to synecdoche—a mode of figuration in which a sign is a component of that which it symbolizes—probably does not indicate the poverty of Indians' signifying systems. More likely, it reveals that the English hoped that Cherokee acceptance of these gifts would constitute a binding contract when, in fact, Indian polities did not recognize the policies of enclosure that would be imposed on North American soil.[85] To overcome their own concern that these agreements across vast cultural and linguistic difference were not mutual contracts, the English represented Indians as hopelessly literal minded in their approach to symbolic representation.

Their base intellects, conveyed by their incapacity for abstract metaphor, become indicative of a racial destiny of political and economic abasement. Cherokees are depicted as erupting in spontaneous displays of submission to almost any white man. For example, Alexander Cuming, who initiated the Anglo-Cherokee alliance and arranged for the 1730 summit in London, reported that on his first arrival in one of the Cherokee villages the inhabitants laid their emperor's crown at his feet.[86] Much like Christopher Columbus, Cuming reported that Indians communicated their submission to him by signs that he faced no cultural barrier in deciphering. The text of the Articles of Friendships and Commerce, then, restages this submission by recording Cuming's gesture of laying "the Crown of your Nation, with the Scalps of your Enemies, and Feathers of Glory, in Token of your Obedience" at the

"Feet" of "the Great King George . . . by express Authority for that Purpose from . . . Moytoy." The trope of dependency continues in the translated "*Answer*" of the Cherokees to the proposed treaty of 1730: "We came hither naked and poor, as the Worm out of the Earth; but you have every thing; and we that have nothing must love you, and can never break the Chain of Friendship which is between us."[87] These scenes recall the wonder and deference the Mohawk kings were imagined to have shown Queen Anne twenty years prior—not to mention genuflections in theatre and fiction ranging from *The Tempest* and "Oroonoko" to *Robinson Crusoe*.[88] These texts aimed to endow imperial sign systems with myriad subtleties while rendering Indians as a group whose costume and gesture could not be mistaken.[89] A belief that Indians lacked semiotic sophistication likely shaped British reception of a report that Cherokees ceded land to Virginia, sealing the act not by signing a contract but by, quite literally, presenting a "Parcel of Earth" from the site to be transferred.[90]

Although calibrated to reassure British investors unsure what profit would be gained from Indian alliances, the perfect replication of Indian baseness betrays British anxiety, not confidence. For example, a bit of hesitancy is memorialized in the moment in which the Cherokees reportedly say they will sign the 1730 treaty. "We look upon you," they announce, "as if Great King George was present, and we love you, as representing the Great King."[91] To an ambitious imperial reader wanting to see the base Indian, this insistence on the presence of the king would seem to indicate poor preparation for ledgers and written edicts that "act at a distance" from their author.[92] Yet, as Birgit Brander Rasmussen has demonstrated, belts of colored wampum—the preferred means of commemorating alliances among the Indians of the Eastern Woodlands—were not an inferior technology to alphabetic texts. Wampum shares an important trait with paper documents, despite their differences: neither provides a pictorial representation of every person and object referenced.[93] As the Cherokees were drawn into more formal relations with the British Empire, ink and paper did not render wampum obsolete. Cherokees did begin to bring written treaties to conferences as props, yet they did not subordinate themselves to the authority of ink and paper. Rather, they assimilated paper documents into the ethos of wampum—a "chain of friendship," the preservation of which required in-person meetings wherein mutual obligations could be renewed and renegotiated to alleviate grievances and ensure parity.[94] The Cherokees were not overawed by the technology of alphabetic literacy in these early decades of Indian Watching. In fact, they would show themselves adept at deciphering, deploying, and contradicting the representational practices at the nexus of performance and print where racial essences and fictitious economic value were regenerated.

Williamsburg: 1751–1752

When he sat down to write to the Council of Virginia on September 18, 1751, fourteen months before the summit that produced the Cherokee *Othello*, Governor James Glen of South Carolina was furious. In the preceding months, relations with the Cherokees had deteriorated rapidly. Over the spring and summer, the governor had been informed that Cherokees had shot one trader, burned another's home to the ground (killing one person inside), and raided the stores of several others. With autumn approaching, the Cherokees had not budged in their refusal to yield up Cherokee suspects to the governor for punishment. Glen's imposition of a trade embargo failed to force the Cherokees to submit to his understanding of the 1730 accord that had inaugurated the Anglo-Cherokee alliance. Rather, as the "Friendship and Commerce" proclaimed in that treaty deteriorated into what scholars call the Panic of 1751, Cherokee representatives made a journey to seek from Virginia the goods and munitions South Carolina withheld.[95] It was this last act that prompted Governor Glen's missive to the Council of Virginia.

News of the Williamsburg trade summit reached Glen by way of a *Virginia Gazette* article detailing the dignified reception Cherokee ambassadors received on August 9 in Virginia's capital. Glen had muzzled the *South Carolina Gazette,* suppressing all coverage of the Carolina-Cherokee dispute.[96] Yet here, in another colony's newspaper, was news that neither the Cherokees nor Virginia respected the monopoly the 1730 treaty had granted to South Carolina on all economic, political, and military matters related to the Cherokees. Worse, from Glen's perspective, this disregard for South Carolina's preeminence was being publicized and, in the process, granted a certain legitimacy. That counternarrative included a claim that South Carolina had not fulfilled its promises in supplying the Cherokees. The *Virginia Gazette* printed an apparently complete account of the words exchanged between the Cherokees and Lewis Burwell, president of the Council of Virginia, including a translation of the Cherokee spokesperson's opening salvo:

Brother,

. . . Our Emperor sent us here to acquaint the Governor of *Virginia,* that when his Father was in *England,* the King directed and advised him to apply to the Governor of *Virginia* or *Carolina,* whenever the *Cherrokees* were in Want of any Thing. . . . We are instructed to inform you, that four Years ago we waited upon the Governor of *South-Carolina,* to endeavour to prevail on him to encourage a Trade between the Subjects of that Colony and the *Cherrokees,* and to supply us with Ammunition and other Necessaries, which he promised to do, but has not perform'd. . . . Moreover, the Governor of *Carolina* has furnished the *Creek Indians,* our Enemies, with Ammunition and other Necessaries, and given them very distinguishing Tokens of Kindness. Upon these Considerations our Emperor has sent us to solicit a Confirmation of your Friendship, and to desire, that you will be pleased to send white People amongst, and establish a Commerce between the King of *Great-Britain*'s Subjects, Inhabitants of this Dominion, and the *Indians* of the *Cherokee Nation.*

Aware that he lacked authority to resolve this dispute, Burwell declined to challenge South Carolina for control of the Cherokee trade. Nevertheless, he offered a present of "Two Hundred Pounds" and a subsequent gift of arms to encourage the Cherokees not to shift their allegiances from Britain to France.[97]

A week after reading news that outraged him, Glen wrote a scathing letter to the Council of Virginia. The unsubtle message was that the Virginians were unsophisticated spectators taken in by confidence artists.[98] He fumed that the suspects South Carolina wanted to try for crimes "are the People, the very identical Persons, who came with complaints to you against this Government, and whom you have received with open Arms, and Caress'd in a ver[y] extraordinary manner."[99] In a logic that should by now be familiar, this error in character evaluation led to an overly generous gift.[100] Glen castigated the Virginians for giving "very large presents . . . possibly of Arms and Ammunition" to erstwhile "Embassadors, and nobles as they are called," whose real worth, Glen alleged, was no more than "really obscure Fellows . . . who were to have been delivered up to us by their Country Men to be punished as their Crimes deserv'd." Furthermore, Glen insisted that the only proper reading of the 1730 treaty was that "the English in Carolina" had exclusive permission to "trade with the Indians and to furnish them with all manner of Goods that they want."[101] Glen's recitation of the 1730 text was meant to nullify the Cherokees' statement that George II had put supplying their tribe in the hands of either Virginia or South Carolina. Moreover, this performance aimed to restore the British to their proper position as contrivers, not targets, of dissimulation. Indians can appear savvy in Glen's letter, but Cherokee confidence artists are not presented as capable of deceiving a Briton who properly uses his superior skills of character assessment. There was no need for Indians' racial character to be fixed, as long as all variations of that character could be accounted for by English systems of representation and interpretation.

Despite this tirade, Governor Glen was stymied by those equally skilled in the empire's mediations. In the short term, he shamed the Council, who compelled William Hunter to print a corrected story in the *Virginia Gazette,* dismissing the Cherokee envoys as rogues and warning Virginians not to trade with them.[102] Nevertheless, the next year, Virginia's newly appointed lieutenant governor, Robert Dinwiddie, welcomed a visit from Amouskositte, the Cherokee emperor himself, to discuss the same proposition.

Dinwiddie's imperial acumen was well established by the time he disembarked at Yorktown, Virginia, in 1751 to take up the post of lieutenant governor. For thirty of his fifty-eight years, the Scotsman had proven tenacious in pursuing Britain's financial interests in the Americas. In recognition of his record of service—exposing embezzlers in Bermuda and maximizing royal revenue as surveyor general of the southern ports of North America—the Crown promoted him to the post of lieutenant governor of England's oldest (and still lucrative) colony.[103] As his previous postings had never required direct negotiations with North America's indigenes, Dinwiddie had much to learn in a short time about this form of diplomacy. Consequently, when the Cherokees arrived in 1752, he was no more eager than Burwell had been to initiate a trade that might antagonize South Carolina and displease the king and his ministers. As he reported to the Board of Trade, Dinwiddie did little more than Burwell, offering gifts and assurances. The most significant change, however, was in the *Virginia Gazette*'s coverage of the 1752 conference, which yielded the Cherokee *Othello* in lieu of a transcript of the emperor's entreaty.

Given that Hunter, the editor of the *Virginia Gazette*, retracted the 1751 story at the government's request, it is safe to assume that Dinwiddie directed him to suppress the content of the talks from the 1752 summit. Hunter would have been hesitant to substitute the Cherokee *Othello* anecdote for a substantive report on the trade talks if he thought such a maneuver would displease Dinwiddie. Hunter undoubtedly considered that the colonial government apportioned his salary and supplied the bulk of his business when he changed strategies from 1751.[104] His new article focused on the entertainment offered the Cherokee delegation—and their astonished response—omitting speeches entirely and relegating trade talks to the status of mere rumor. Given Glen's rebuke in 1751 and Dinwiddie's cautious reply to the Cherokees, the *Gazette*'s brief story of 1752 seems less an innocent report of a theatrical faux pas than a well-considered ruse.

Apparently, Dinwiddie and Hunter agreed that the authority of both the governor and the newspaper relied on printing stories that would not have to be retracted later. The story they agreed upon was well constructed. The Cherokee *Othello* anecdote legitimates the colonial government and its mouthpiece, even as it redacts the treaty talks to pacify Glen. Dinwiddie himself appears as a respected official who receives and entertains the allies on whom the colony's defenses—and some of its potential profits—rely. The reference to rumored trade talks signals to interested subscribers that Hunter has access to unpublished information on a pending Cherokee-Virginia alliance that his paper might eventually reveal. Cherokees appear as worthy allies—members of an organized society with a visible political and military hierarchy. At the same time, the theatrical mistake suggests they are too unsophisticated to detect or disrupt imperial projects. It may also be that the notion of a Cherokee woman, specifically, who overidentified with a theatrical scene seemed particularly credible.[105] In any case, the Cherokees' arrival in Williamsburg testifies to the power Dinwiddie holds, while not directly detracting from that of Glen, as the most memorable scene of the visit entails not the signing of a rival treaty with Virginia but an interrupted blackface play.

The players of the Hallam Company and the wider audience cannot be said to have directly colluded in Dinwiddie's and Hunter's manipulation of the press. Nevertheless, they were part of the same interpretive community. None of their recorded actions disrupt the consignment of Cherokees to the position of base interpreters. In fact, most of their actions suggest a careful management of public image to avoid being cast into that position themselves.

Despite the marginal social status of traveling actors in the middle of the eighteenth century, the troupe that came to Williamsburg from London assumed the stature of visiting representatives from a cultural center. In a prologue written for the occasion of their opening night, a Mr. Rigby (who would subsequently play the silver-tongued lover Bassanio in *The Merchant of Venice*) delivered a prologue that positioned Virginia as a late conquest for "the Muse" of drama. Charting the evolution of theatre from Athens and Rome to contemporary London, he declared "Virginia's plains" an "unknown clime"—that is, one not charted in the geography of civilization rooted in Greco-Roman antiquity. The actors become "Agents" of the dramatic Muse, in need of "kind protection" from an approving audience.[106]

As poetry, the prologue is plodding and uninventive, but as an occasional piece, it was rhetorically astute. The thespians intuited and then spoke to the hunger of colonists to be understood as members of a shared community with those in the metropolis, rather than as provincial fools. The printing of the speech suggests the local community accepted and memorialized the flattery. In addition, having the prologue printed in the newspaper spread the desire to see this company to those who had not been present. According to contemporary reports, the first season of professional theatre offered in Britain's colonies was a smash success. Two months into their run, local actor-turned-apothecary George Gilmer complained that the little cash in Virginia's tobacco-based economy "flew among this Association of indigent wretches with a lavishness you would be surprised at."[107]

As colonists handed liquid cash to transient actors, they became vulnerable to the suspicion that they had spent their money on, essentially, nothing. An evening at the theatre is but a fleeting sensation, a poor investment

in commercial terms. Nevertheless, as Odai Johnson has shown, colonial theatre was a place of "sporting," of displaying one's newly acquired fashions and,
potentially, attaining a higher social, cultural, or marital perch.[108] Colonists'
desire to treat theatre as something real, something of value, seems to have ne-
cessitated the invention of a figure even less adept, a figure that could absorb all
the shame of investing too much in the theatre. In this regard, the Cherokees
may well have served both the colonists and subsequent historiographers who
wanted to demonstrate that the colonies' separation from the metropole was
to be measured only in distance and not in aesthetic cultivation.[109]

Yet, if the *Virginia Gazette* article constructs a Cherokee empress who can
serve the functions of the base Indian, the *Executive Journals of the Council of
Colonial Virginia* show Cherokees who understood the protocols of British
diplomatic ceremony and intervened in them skillfully.[110] By 1752 Cherokee
delegates would have been quite familiar with treaty negotiations and the occasions for Indian Watching that surrounded them. In fact, the youngest envoy
to London in 1730, Attakullakulla, had grown to wield significant power in
Anglo-Indian negotiations: it was he who delivered the 1751 appeal to Virginia that so incensed Governor James Glen. Attakullakulla's manipulation of
the 1730 treaty's paternalist rhetoric indicates that—probably well before the
1750s—he had developed a potentially threatening fluency in British cultural
forms. He reportedly amassed influence among the Cherokees by speaking
of his audience with King George II. In addition to fomenting jealousy, Attakullakulla's recollections of his time in London would have informed other
Cherokee leaders about the metropolitan blend of theatre and diplomacy that
Williamsburg was trying to emulate by inviting Indians to the playhouse. Aug-
menting Attakullakulla's intelligence with their own keen observations of their
Virginia hosts, the emperor and empress expertly intervened in the symbolic
arena of public politics that Elizabeth Maddock Dillon calls the "performative
commons."[111]

If Glen said the 1751 delegates were mere rogues, the Cherokees would
send the man whom the British recognized as emperor to legitimate the asser-
tions of those who had been dismissed.[112] Showing adeptness at stagecraft, the
so-called emperor, Amouskositte, arrived brandishing the 1730 treaty, wielding the source of Glen's textual authority against him.[113] Furthermore, both
Amouskositte and the previous year's delegation showed themselves to have
no deficiency in insight. After all, their appeal to Virginia relied not on the
explicit naming of South Carolina in the 1730 treaty but rather on an implication folded into the paternalistic language rampant in that document and
in subsequent negotiations. Specifically, the Cherokees maintained that any
treaty signed with the king of England—one that referred to settlers and Indians alike as the king's children—could be extended from South Carolinians,

named in the text, to compel Virginia children, unnamed.[114] Far from being naive people who lacked the capacity to create entities and relationships that exceed the literal, the Cherokees took advantage of the metaphor of father and children the British used to frame the relationship of Cherokees and colonists to King George II.

If it is easy to see Cherokees diminished in documents where they are recorded referring to England's king as "Great King" and "Father," one need only recall that Cherokees had few dealings with this remote patriarch, compared with frequent visits to Williamsburg and Charleston.[115] Actions of the most immediate consequence for the Cherokees and the empire involved colonists and administrators designated as fellow children of the king. As in Attakullakulla's 1751 greeting, Cherokee representatives considered any "brother" equally bound to obey his king. Moreover, in relations among brothers, "white" skin did not confer compulsory power, as compulsion was not a fraternal prerogative—nor, in Cherokee understandings, even a paternal one. In treating South Carolina and Virginia as interchangeable brothers—and, later, in insisting on negotiating face-to-face with the king in London—the Cherokees produced fictive kinship in ways that repurposed English metaphors. Despite the long-held tenets of scholars who believe print revolutionized thought itself, there is no need to view this intercultural activity as an extraordinary feat. Scholars who now place print within—and not atop—a media environment would conclude that all cultures have mediations and substitutions. Therefore, the capacity for a second, metaphysical, sight need not be reserved for those with literate cultures or market economies.[116]

The empress, Amouskositte's wife, posed the most thorough challenge to English attempts to transpose their imaginary commercial empire from the stage to the real world. To be understood, her interference in the play must be unearthed from the double burial of an inauthentic title and misperceived motives.[117] In the mid-eighteenth century, the Cherokees were a collection of semiautonomous villages with no central government, most certainly no emperor, and hence no empress. However, the Cherokees did have male leaders in their red (war) and white (peace) councils.[118] Amouskositte was a leader in the peace councils. The improper titles of chief and emperor that Anglo-Virginians assigned to Attakullakulla and Amouskositte may have reflected the fact that the white council held a preeminent position over the red. Though she would not have called herself "empress," Amouskositte's wife was an influential woman, as indicated by her presence at this diplomatic summit. The evidence of Cherokee familiarity with British theatre—as well as their attention to casting and props for their audience with Virginia's governor—suggests that her reported interruption was likely a calculated intervention in the "performative commons."[119]

Amouskositte's wife was probably prepared for an evening of theatre. The Cherokees and their neighbors reportedly spoke often of their London travels, which typically included playhouse visits. A headman of the Cherokees' Creek neighbors announced the he was "never tired of hearing what Tomo Chachi tells" him about London. Adventures in London were clearly told and retold, with all the attendant expansions and variations. Cherokee visitor Attakul-lakulla was no less voluble. He reportedly boasted often of his trip to London as a way of claiming superior status over rival Cherokee leaders—of whom the empress's husband, Amouskositte, was one.[120] The empress would have been among the women of rank present at council meetings, and Attakullakulla, who objected to British attempts to exclude such women, would have freely discussed political business in their presence. Amouskositte's wife was noted as an attentive listener in these meetings, and others knew her to be a source of information on what transpired in council deliberations.[121]

Informed in these ways, an influential Cherokee woman would have been primed to notice that Williamsburg's British theatregoers were a rowdy bunch. Indeed, if these Virginians, so hungry for London theatre, behaved like their metropolitan counterparts, a Cherokee delegate would have witnessed patrons disrupting the performance, even clamoring for a better view of the Indian guests. She might have concluded that if they behaved so raucously, she was not compelled to observe the solemn decorum of an audience with British royalty or treaty signing. Regardless of the reputation of the playwright, British theatregoers were wont to vocalize assent, express political dissent, and shout instructions to performers and spectators.[122] Amouskositte's wife entered a site where Britons behaved boisterously and placed Indians in prominent positions to scrutinize their reactions to the stage performance.

The first moment in which swords appear in *Othello* would have presented this Cherokee woman with something resembling the following tableau: a single performer with black paint on his face, surrounded and waiting to be taken captive by a group of white men bearing swords. For several reasons, it seems unlikely that she would have interpreted the character of Othello as a moor, blackamoor, or Afro-Virginian. First, audiences recognize blackface performers as racially black because painted actors cite a convention, not because they resemble African people. Second, she probably spoke little to no English, and therefore the play's references to Venice, Cyprus, and Mauritania would not have conjured for her either northern or sub-Saharan Africans. Third, she might have thought of black paint as mimicry or mockery of Cherokees, because Cherokee men applied black paint to at least some sections of their faces.[123] Rather than seeing an African, then, she probably interpreted the painted figure as a surrogate Indian. To her mind, the tableau of Othello about to be seized may have read as a public reassertion of the disputed treaty proviso that the Cherokees must yield all suspects to be tried in colonial courts. "The Empress['s] . . . order[ing] some about her to go and prevent their killing one another"—as the *Gazette* reported it—may have been her way of (a) rejecting a virtual depiction of South Carolina's jurisdiction, (b) insisting that any new agreement with Virginia could not include this stipulation, or (c) asserting that any representation of Indian abduction was inappropriate to the occasion of establishing friendly relations.[124]

A high-ranking Cherokee woman would have been authorized to take advantage of the Cherokees' hypervisibility in this way, as Cherokee villages granted women authority over the disposition of captives.[125] Thus, her reported actions may have been meant to reassert the prerogatives of Cherokee women in the face of Anglo attempts to exclude women from treaty negotiations and disregard Cherokee sovereignty.[126] It hardly needs noting that all of the British imperial correspondents were men and that they expected to conduct diplomacy with Cherokee men alone. Her interruption was a vocal trespass into that fraternal realm and into the shadows of visibility in documented history. She capitalized on a colonial audience as invested in Indian Watching as were their metropolitan counterparts. Confident that many eyes would be on her, she could register her sense of propriety when it came to staged representations of acts that could plausibly occur offstage. This interruption is notable because it was at once an assertion of Cherokee culture and an adaptive response to the force and cultural forms of British empire.[127]

Given that Williamsburg's theatregoers may have clamored for the Cherokee guests to be placed onstage, like the Mohawk kings at the Haymarket, it is tempting to imagine the so-called empress very much in the midst of things. In any case, given a well-lit theatre and the absence of security guards, it is certainly possible that her companions did assume the stage.[128] Perhaps they left onstage seats or mounted the stage from seats in the audience before anyone thought the commotion was enough to warrant stopping the play. Did they stretch out their hands to signal that the action should stop or pantomime resheathing the swords? Did they shield the blackfaced character—attempt to remove him from custody? Used to interruptions, perhaps the actors improvised, urging the Cherokees to stand to the side while the painted man's trial commenced. Perhaps the Cherokees remained standing onstage while Othello pleaded his case before the Venetian Senate—it is unlikely an audience of Indian Watchers would have minded—and returned to their seats when the senators released Othello, with his wife, to depart and go fight the Turks. Whatever happened, the empress initiated an action, the significance of which was buried under the trope of Indian gullibility.[129]

If Attakullakulla brought information on British theatre to Amouskositte's wife, her actions in Williamsburg may in turn have influenced Cherokees to insert themselves more fully into the British Atlantic performative commons. It appears that Attakullakulla and other Cherokees came to expect or hope for theatre as part of diplomatic ceremony. In 1767 his delegation took in *Richard III* in New York City on their way to treaty negotiations in Albany.[130] Five months later, in April 1768, he and other Cherokee "Chiefs and Warriors" presented on the same stage what a New York newspaper called a "War Dance."[131] When placed in sequence with the 1730 tour of London and the empress's interruption, Attakullakulla's repeated visits to British Atlantic play-houses and his eventual decision to take the stage suggest that the Cherokees moved from silent spectators to interactive audience members and, finally, to stage performers. If theatre was a meaning-generating site for English specula-tors, Indians joined them in noting its utility as a locus for staging and inter-rupting visions of what relations in the Atlantic World might look like.

Given his outraged reaction to the Cherokee-Virginia talks of 1751, it is notable that Governor James Glen lodged no response to the sequel in 1752. In these years, Glen was desperate to demonstrate his effectiveness as governor to a skeptical Board of Trade in London by showing himself as the sole architect of a grand alliance between southern and northern Indians and the British.[132] The story of the Cherokees' 1751 visit to Williamsburg had been reprinted in full in the *Evening Post* of London, and he could not afford a repeat of such an embarrassment.[133] Yet it would appear that little harm could come to his reputation from the story of an interrupted play. For Governor Glen, the sub-stitution of the theatre vignette for trade talks seems to have minimized the 1752 embassy's importance.

Though Glen was satisfied enough not to demand a second retraction, sev-eral London newspapers took a different message from the Cherokee *Othello*. Assessing the Virginia report as a species of those generated from theatre vis-its at metropolitan trade summits, the *Evening Post* mistakenly concluded that the Cherokees had renewed the 1730 treaty in Williamsburg. This item was subsequently reprinted in two other London newspapers.[134] From their vantage point in London, newspaper publishers concluded that Virginia had replicated an imperial audience with Indians at a colonial site, complete with the requisite theatre sightings and newspaper reports. They either forgot or disregarded that Virginia arguably had no standing to renew a treaty that as-signed Cherokee relations to South Carolina. Metropolitan responses to the Cherokee *Othello* suggest that some in the empire's capital city did not care to distinguish between a Cherokee alliance with Virginia or South Carolina, as long as that alliance would aid in retaining British control over lucrative North American colonies against French encroachments.[135]

As Robert Dinwiddie and William Hunter hoped, the vignette of the Chero-kees' visit to the theatre made a difference. Glen seemed satisfied that portrayals of the Cherokees as gullible theatregoers had replaced the prior year's portrayal of his government's failures. Londoners concluded that any foreign embassy that included a visit to the playhouse must have culminated in the signing of a treaty, as it would have in London. For dispersed Britons, the theatre displayed the sophistication of English civilization, symbolized political legitimacy, and offered apparently simple savages to enjoy onstage and in the house. Yet, the playhouse was also a site where Indians could interrupt those fantasies with gestures that Britons seem to have willed themselves not to understand. Performances of Indian baseness were simply too compelling a spectacle and precondition for commercial activity for dispersed Britons to release them.

Although the trope of the base Indian persisted, there were occasional moments when doubts surfaced. Betraying rare unease with this stock character, London's *St. James's Chronicle* used the occasion of a 1762 embassy of Cherokees to reminisce about the 1730 visit. An article recalled Attakullakulla as one who "was shy of being stared at, and therefore always chose to go *incognito* to any public Place. 'They are welcome,' said he, once to his Interpreter, 'to look upon me as a strange Creature. They see but one, and in return give me the Opportunity to look upon Thousands.'" On the whole, the article treats Attakullakulla's shrewdness as an exceptional capacity not shared by all Indians.[136] Still, it does acknowledge a possibility that is usually suppressed: through disguise, at least one Indian could reverse the dynamics of Indian Watching and perceive more about British character than Britons could perceive of his. However, in the end, the economy is reversed, and Attakullakulla provides a spectacle of sincerity that requires no interpreter: "at his Embarking, he took hold of the last Person's Hand that met his, which happened to be an old Fisherwoman's; when wringing it hard, with Tears in his Eyes, he repeated several Times—*I tank you, I tank you, I tank you* All."[137]

Like the gendered figures of the Madonna, the whore, and the coquette, racial characters work best in coordinated systems. Europeans therefore conceived of many dichotomous racial characters between 1492 and 1752.[138] However, addressing the persistent appeal of the particular figure of the base Indian to Atlantic Britons exposes something important about the materiality, content, and chronology of racial character. In terms of materiality, this incident shows racial character to exist in the realm of both the material signifier and the immaterial signified. The Cherokee empress's apparent identification of Othello as her co-ethnic seems to have everything to do with a material practice of black face painting that she recognized. The dictates of dictionaries, travel writers, and naturalists reveal little about her methods of racial identification—or, indeed, those of the dispersed Britons.

The likeliest interpretation of her motivation and act—that it was to interrupt the symbolic staging of English jurisdiction over Cherokees—highlights the limits of the interminable scholarly debate on Othello's identity. As long as Othello's identity was produced by paint, this medium would not transparently indicate a single population. The English Othello had no home, no single natal community. The Cherokee empress seems to have conceived of him as fictive kin—a member of her polity, for the purposes of her intervention. Clearly, performance yields its own, unexpected, identifications, subject to rules other than those that govern outdated archival methods attuned only to the *OED*'s restrictive definitions of words like "Moor" with a capital M.

As for the history of race, this incident shows that racial characters, such as the black male rapist, the unrape-able Black woman, and, indeed, the base Indian occupy a strange temporality. Their existence could be as fleeting as the time of a performance. Yet, they could also recur across centuries, from Columbus's first voyage for Spain to ceremonies conducted in the name of the constitutional monarchy of post-Revolutionary England. While one dominant mode of analysis among scholars dictates that cultural field must reflect objective social relations, this form of historicism takes the scholar's period of specialization and favored archive as indicative of the shared mentality of a people. Yet, for those invested in racial projects, dreams of empire have been impossible to achieve or to relinquish across a very long Atlantic *durée.* However, those dreams could be staged in and through media that allowed the substitution of a virtual reality for a real world that was less than compliant.

In the case of the Cherokee *Othello,* the virtual reality ran on the premises that treaties were true meetings of the mind and that Native peoples agreed to their terms. Inventing the preposterous story that Cherokees were hysterical and unsophisticated obviated the need to ask what reason an influential Cherokee woman could have had to interrupt a performance of *Othello.* Unfortunately, the possibility that she could have reasons beyond the ideological framework of a colonial archive was buried in the political needs of its own time and obscured by the terms of settler-colonialist virtual reality that have obtained since.

In a justly famous essay on Aphra Behn's *Oroonoko* (the subject of my second chapter), the literary scholar Laura Brown quotes anthropologist Johannes Fabian to assert that it is possible for "the colonialist author and his characters [to] 'meet the Other on the same ground, in the same time.'" After investigating the Cherokee *Othello,* I have reservations. An author serving a "colonialist" project has a certain authority over her characters, by definition.

In her mind and on the page, she arranges the characters and determines their relationships to each other and to her authority. The mediated form of the novel seems to frustrate an egalitarian encounter, but the playhouse would not seem to yield the salutary outcomes Brown predicts either. The circulation of colonial misinterpretations of the Cherokee woman's acts suggests that even a direct confrontation will not guarantee what Brown predicts: "[the representation of] opposition in a body and a language that even the colonialist can be made to understand."[139] Even when two parties face each other in the flesh, ideological pretexts—the kind of persons and relationships one is willing to conceive—can still limit the extent to which the colonizer can see, hear, feel, or cognize opposition. In the case of "Benito Cereno," the subject of the next chapter, Herman Melville ruthlessly dismantles the bases of white character mastery but neither he nor his white characters can conceive of the liberation of black characters as anything other than the end of the world.

The enduring myth of inkface is that white people are masters of black character in whatever form it appears—as a body onstage or off, on paper, in the soul—and that blackened people are not subjects who read but natural objects of reading. These preconditions have permitted the drafting of imperial treaties and maps and the construction of racial groups to inherit the spoils. As I turn to the last chapter of the book, my final case sits near the middle of the nineteenth century, an endpoint that has caused some to question the historical logic of my project. The 1855 publication date of Herman Melville's "Benito Cereno" does not have a meaningful temporal relationship with any landmark legal ruling or the publication of any major treatise of scientific racism. Besides, the era so close to the US Civil War is considered firmly within "modernity." It can hardly be called early American and certainly not "early modern." Yet, some conventions of inkface representation remained in place—specifically, blackface performance, ink recipes, and the black-white palette of the page. In addition, "Benito Cereno" is strangely out of time. Melville backdates the action to 1799, which makes it the conclusion of what one might call a (very) long eighteenth-century analysis of inkface.

In fact, "Benito Cereno" doubles the performance of inkface: the protagonist treats blackness as the color of signification and Africans, specifically, as alphabetical characters personified; meanwhile, readers are positioned as white male experts who can access human character only through its alphabetical mediation. Two hundred fifty years after the debut of *The Moor of Venice,* Melville wrote to a readership of lay and expert white men he imagined as too comfortable in the racial relations established through inkface to observe the grave intellectual, physical, and spiritual danger occasioned by African literacy. In Melville's "Benito Cereno," the penning of the Haitian Declaration of

Independence spawned an anomalous white-authored text that tried, vainly, to signal the end of an era. Under the spell of Shakespeare's *Othello,* the American novelist staged the undoing of white mastery in a haunting message, written with the chalk of a dead white slaveholder's bones. The mutiny of black characters and the muteness of white ones would bring the ideological fantasy of inkface to a state of crisis that the colonial governors and newspapers I gathered in this chapter sought to forestall indefinitely.

5

Inkface to Chalkbones

The End of White Character Mastery in Melville's "BC"

Never let it be said that Herman Melville lacked the capacity for drama. The accidental unveiling of a skeleton beneath a ship's shrouded prow in his long tale "Benito Cereno" (1855) raises gothic terror to its highest pitch. "Benito Cereno" is, on its surface, the story of Amasa Delano, an American captain who, on August 17 of the portentous year 1799, spies a mysterious slave ship flying no colors and drifting aimlessly off the coast of Chile. Delano approaches the slaver to assist. Don Benito Cereno, a haggard Spanish aristocrat, welcomes the American aboard. Rusted iron-wrought capitals spell the ship's name, the SAN DOMINICK, across the headboard. With this allusion and the date, Melville places the subsequent action quite literally under the heading of the Haitian Revolution, which birthed the world's first black republic from the rubble of colonial slavery. On the ship's deck, disheveled white sailors mix tar while unchained Africans unravel rope or polish hatchets.

Cereno, shadowed by a small Senegalese manservant named Babo, fails to discipline the occasionally unruly Africans and withholds any direct explanation of the ship's disorderly condition. Delano vacillates between pity for and fearful suspicion of the elusive Cereno, who rebuffs the amiable American's overtures while staying close to Babo's side.[1] Delano finally despairs of befriending the sad, mysterious Spaniard and steps aboard his own ship, now anchored alongside the slaver. To his surprise, Cereno leaps after him as if, perhaps, he desired his companionship after all. Babo follows. In the increasing commotion, Delano discovers that he has misread the calm disorder of the *San Dominick* as "misrule . . . [or] tumult" when in fact the Africans have been suspended in the midst of a "ferocious, piratical revolt."[2]

Captain Delano's view has been shrouded behind his presumptions about the character of aristocrats, Spaniards, and Africans. Yet, Melville is not satisfied with exposing the impediments to Delano's perception of character. He saves the most dramatic unveiling for readers. During the ensuing battle for control of the *San Dominick,* "the fag-end [of the ship's cable], in lashing out, whip[s] away the canvas shroud about the beak, suddenly revealing, as the bleached hull sw[i]ng[s] round towards the open ocean, death for the figure-head, in a human skeleton; chalky comment on the chalked words below, '*Follow your leader*'" (228). As if this unveiling has removed a gag from his mouth, Don Benito "covering his face, wail[s] out, "'Tis he, Aranda! My murdered, unburied friend!'"

After the first four chapters of this book, this episode strikes as a shocking reversal of the racialized textual politics of *Othello*. When performed in black-face, Shakespeare's play ends with an image of Othello's dyeing kiss imprinted on Desdemona's face and his own blood proclaimed as the "period" on his final report to his commanders in Venice (V.ii.357). The dialogue and props surrounding Othello and other stage moors suggest that these black charac-ters were composed of and covered in a signifying, transferable ink. Conse-quently, stage moors and their white lovers became what I have been calling inkface characters. Stage personae who blacked up backstage or acquired black marks during performance were presented as readable people whose meaning was available to white male experts but not to themselves. Throughout this book, I have argued that these blackface plays summoned a white interpretive community into being by having them treat blackened characters as textual objects and not as potentially authoritative readers.

For six years before "Benito Cereno" appeared, Melville had been im-mersing himself in Shakespeare's collected works, where he would have come across black moors bearing letters, failing to read, imprinting their lovers with kisses, bleeding ink. Melville was the kind of thinker disposed to notice this play in Shakespeare. As the literary scholar Elizabeth Renker has shown, the novelist was obsessed with textual materials—book jackets, spelling, seals, ink (in the form of facial tattoos)—from his first essays in 1839 through his final book of poetry in 1891. *Moby-Dick* and his long tales of the 1850s are products of his engagement with Shakespeare, in whose plays Melville found a similar obsession. With the unveiling of the skeleton and chalked inscrip-tion in "Benito Cereno," Melville dramatically inverts the racial hierarchy Shakespeare bequeathed him and asks his ideal white male audience to con-front their own bodies, their very bones, being used up in textual production. Haitian revolutionary lore inspires a response to the conceit that Africans (and those they contaminate) have inky faces. Babo seems to know of the legend that the scribe who declared Haiti's independence wanted to use a Frenchman's blood for ink and his skin for parchment. The rebellious African discovers that white men have chalky bones and proclaims this gospel for the small audience of the ship.

This emblem of the white male body consumed for textual production contradicts an unspoken precondition of white authority. In conducting its daily business, a white interpretive community must assume racially blackened humans to be as serviceable as the letters of the alphabet. They can be known, arranged, figured with, counted, and counted upon. The white person who knows them is not subject to a reciprocal scrutiny from an African any more than he would consider that a printed letter might speak back to him about himself. Melville confounds these enabling axioms in "Benito Cereno," creating a mutiny of black characters—both alphabetical and African—which culminates in the dumbfounding spectacle of the skeleton and its accompanying graffiti, an emblem I will call chalkbones.

After long dallying in the familiar cognitive territory of inkface in which a white mind confidently assesses black signifiers in the world, "Benito Cereno" introduces *chalkbones,* a figure that reverses the ground of the black and white page and its presumed racial politics. Chalkbones forces white character into the foreground, stripping white men of their unseen omniscience and making their bodies—and their imagined remains—text. Furthermore, chalkbones defies white masculine pretenses to interpretive distance by making the skeleton of a slaveholding white man into textual material. As I intimated by noting the year Melville selected for the story's setting—1799—this simultaneous revolt against racial slavery and white epistemological authority constitutes the end of the eighteenth century for Melville—and, therefore, the conclusion of my project. In Melville's novella, the Haitian Revolution overwhelms its North American precedent. Consequently, *his* eighteenth century concludes not with a new nation joining an international circuit of goods and ideas but with colonial slavery and the Republic of Letters in shambles.

Placing *chalkbones* in its various Shakespearean and nineteenth-century contexts and considering what we have to learn from it are my tasks in this chapter. I will conduct my work in several sections: contrasting the scene of catechism in "Benito Cereno" with comparable scenes of the same decade and explicating the threefold challenge that Babo's graffiti poses to white literary mastery.

Catechizing in B.C.

Readers belatedly discover that Babo is both the mastermind of the revolt and the author of its signature phrase, the terse command or prophecy beneath the skeleton: *seguid vuestro jefe* (follow your leader). Melville employs an African male tutor to present a haunting new catechism to the Iberian sailors and the white fraternity Melville imagined as his readership.[3] This scene of instruction is revealed to readers in fragments of fictional court documents, cobbled from the testimony of the surviving white sailors, who, with the help of Delano's American crew, have recaptured the *San Dominick* and brought the defeated mutineers to Lima for trial. Although broken and elliptical, the documents do provide crucial pre-text—both events that precede the writing of *seguid vuestro jefe* and the premise of the ruse that deceives Captain Delano.

The deposition records the European sailors' testimony about the immediate aftermath of the mutiny before Delano has boarded the ship. During this belated prelude, Babo unveils a morbid text and instructs the sailors in a hermeneutics suited to the interpretive task. The pious Don Benito repeatedly requests the remains of his friend Don Alexandro, killed at the start of the mutiny. Babo denies the request for an excruciating three days. When this biblically resonant period has passed, he triumphantly confronts the Catholic nobleman with a faceless display on the sunrise of the fourth: "The negro Babo showed him a skeleton, which had been substituted for the ship's proper figure-head, the image of Christopher Colon . . . the negro Babo asked him whose skeleton that was, and whether, from its whiteness, he should not think it a white's, that . . . the negro Babo, coming close, said words to this effect: 'Keep faith with the blacks from here to Senegal, or you shall, in spirit, as now in body, follow your leader,' pointing to the prow" (237). Babo repeats his ritual with each of the Iberian mates who survives the mutiny. Each man "cover[s] his face," rather than look upon the skeleton or at the words that they presume were written with the bones: *seguid vuestro jefe* (237).

The hermeneutical demands of this moment are striking. Babo confirms nothing; all is insinuation. The sailors cannot know that these remains are those of Don Aranda. There is no face by which to identify the skull. Even if there were, the survivors refuse to look upon the sight. Though they proceed blindly, each man understands what Babo intimates. They understand that this skeleton represents the leader of the whites—a captain and a forerunner like the former figurehead, Christopher Columbus. His life has been extinguished, his identity removed, and his very remains consumed in the act of making him into textual material.

Babo's catechism undoes the Gospels and their good news of the risen Savior. Recall that, in the Gospel of John, the disciple Thomas demands to see Christ's pierced hands and touch the wound in his side to believe in the Resurrection. When the risen Christ offers Thomas the opportunity to touch and see, the doubter immediately calls his Savior by title: "My Lord and my God!"[4] That is, he affirms Jesus's identity. After Thomas's declaration, Christ blesses those who will believe without seeing, but Don Benito—though his forename means "blessed"—ends this tale refusing the reality of his salvation. In the time between the sea battle and the trial, the sanguine American Delano tries to convince Cereno of God's blessings: "'You are saved,' crie[s] Captain Delano, more and more astonished and pained; 'you are saved: what has cast such a shadow upon you?'" The melancholy Spaniard answers laconically, "the negro," while "unconsciously gathering his mantle about him, as if it were a pall" (246).

Although Cereno rejects any sense of salvation, he has acquired a perverse faith. Any man who can identify a faceless skeleton without so much as a glance has learned that if faith is "the evidence of things not seen," then it can be as haunting as it is hopeful.[5] Toni Morrison, a keen student of Melville, captures Don Benito's situation in a description of one of her characters who has been struck blind: "Half cursed, half blessed . . . [she was possessed of a] pure sight that damned her if she used it."[6] Thus, the performative power of *seguid vuestro jefe* far exceeds its literal command to follow your leader. Its chalky materiality prophesies the reversal of divine dispensation, the negation of the Resurrection of the body, and, therefore, a return to a time before Christ, designated by the initials of the story and its title character, B.C.

The history of criticism of Melville's novella has been one of scholars emulating the Iberian sailors, turning their faces away from the skull and the chalked graffiti to engage in protracted debate over the symbolism of blackness or Melville's attitudes toward Black people. I confronted a similar evasion in my first chapter. There, I proposed that, in calling *Othello* by its early modern stage title, *The Moor of Venice,* we might access the materiality of its performance—proliferating pages and dyeing kisses—that a relentless realism in staging and editing has obscured. In this chapter, I offer in place of the much-analyzed "Benito Cereno," a text I call "BC": a catechist's primer in which the alphabet lacks an A (or leader) and the prophecy, written by surrogate Haitian revolutionaries with a slaveholder's bones, vacates the Christian promise of salvation. "BC" becomes companion, sequel, and successor to Nathaniel Hawthorne's *Scarlet Letter,* its two black majuscules following the abiding A in the primer of US literature.

In fact, it appears that Melville invented the surname "Cereno," which does not exist in Spanish, to foreground the allegorical potential of BC. Melville wrought this tale from an episode that makes up chapter 18 of Amasa Delano's *A Narrative of Voyages.* While scholars have debated the extent and significance of Melville's alterations to his source, we remain in search of a satisfactory answer to a question about that character struggle happening at the scale of the letter: why name the story "Benito Cereno" when the third-person narration is mostly limited to Delano's perspective and when, in the source, the Spanish name is pointedly spelled "Bonito Sereno"?

"Bonito Sereno" translates roughly into "beautiful serene." It also references the bonito, a small fish related to the tuna, with dark stripes on its back. Substituting an e for the first o in the Don's name produces Benito, deriving from "blessed." Melville's alteration obscures the beauty implied by Bonito, an attractiveness that might be an unacknowledged motivation for Delano's instinctive and compelling impulse to achieve intimacy with the Spanish captain.[7] Numerous details in the story—such as references to Benedictine monks and the meditation on Providence and salvation in the coda—suggest that blessedness is woven into Melville's tale "Benito Cereno." Yet his replacing the S in "Sereno" with a C produces no such motif but, rather, nonsense. The etymology of "Cereno" yields no key, as it does not appear to be a Spanish word or proper name. This change operates solely at the level of orthography, drawing attention to the materiality of character through the sonic interchangeability of the S and the soft C. This substitution serves an even more crucial function—it ensures that the story's major characters all have initials in the alphabetical range of ABCD. In the midst of all of this alphabetical business, chalkbones replaces inkface as Herman Melville filters *Othello*'s racialized textual politics through the lore of the Haitian Revolution.[8] Before turning to a deeper reading of the novella, I want to describe the antebellum iconography that Melville's Babo interrupts with his chalked scrawl.

Race, Literacy, and Catechism in Antebellum US Culture

A little over a century passed from the Cherokees' interruption of *Othello* in colonial Virginia (the subject of the previous chapter) to Herman Melville's re-vision of *Othello* in his 1855 novella "B[enito] C[ereno]." In the interim, the United States became a nation and its printing and performance businesses boomed.[9] These businesses, of course, still depended on British approval at the high end of the cultural scale.[10] Free white children benefited from an expanding commitment to literacy education. Yet, this instruction was not merely technical. National projects such as standardizing spelling had as their aim the production of a uniform white citizenry.[11] Learning to read (English) was depicted as a cultural naturalization ceremony. By attaining biblical literacy, the swarthy—presumably Catholic, southern and eastern European—could obtain US-American whiteness as an aspect of both moral and national character. The racial coding of literacy was so ingrained—and such a powerful rhetorical shorthand—that it was employed even when all the involved pupils were of European parentage.[12]

According to nineteenth-century iconography, an imagined white reader of inkface could exit a coded blackness to join a white interpretive community with mastery over black characters—appearing in the form of inked letters and numbers or blackened persons. Indeed, literacy itself came to be represented as a whitening project in alphabetic primers. For example, in the frontispiece to the American Tract Society's 1848 *The Picture Alphabet: In Prose and Verse,* a ragamuffin with black hair and clothing creeps from the bottom

Demonstrating the racialization of southern Europeans and Catholics, a gleaming blonde Protestant girl teaches a swarthier ragamuffin how to read the Bible for herself. Frontispiece of *The Picture Alphabet: In Prose and Verse,* New York: American Tract Society, 1848. (American Antiquarian Society, Worcester, Mass.)

right quadrant of the frame toward a glowing, blonde girl holding a Bible in her lap.[13]

The American Tract Society was founded in 1825 with a mission to spread the Gospel to illiterates like this not-quite-white girl: unlettered, Catholic immigrants from Europe flocking to the rapidly expanding settler colony. By the time of the publication of *The Picture Alphabet,* nearly six hundred colporteurs were on the society's rolls, carrying Bibles and other Christian literature to the "many US citizens flung across our vast nation."[14] The link of literacy to a US citizenship then defined as exclusive to "free white person[s]" is clearly encoded in this frontispiece.[15] Sin, Catholicism, foreignness, ill-breeding—all of these are encapsulated in layers of black soot, fabric, and benighted ignorance that can be washed away by readerly immersion in the King James Bible.

The optics of inkface had become an efficient vehicle for displaying immediately both masterful and subject positions in the interpretive community. To exit subjection was to become an expert white reader, capable of participating in a republic, or even an empire, of letters.[16] In fact, it could be argued that Melville's two captains, conversing in Spanish in the shared discourse of Providence, represent a hope that white brotherhood could transcend ethnic difference, within or across nations.[17] While blackened subjects of European descent were represented as potentially able to attain that social and epistemological position—and with some speed—a different timetable and potentiality enclosed African descendants.

By the 1850s, an anti-black hierarchy was fully entrenched in the pedagogy of literacy. As the scholar E. Jennifer Monaghan cogently puts it, reading was a skill permitted the enslaved while writing was a skill reserved for the free.[18] Following Frederick Douglass, who achieved literacy through cleverness and daring, most now assume that slave owners believed that learning to read would "forever unfit [their human property] to be ... slave[s]."[19] Yet, reading instruction for the enslaved was not outlawed until 1829. Authorities would have seen no need to prohibit instruction that had biblical literacy as its immediate aim. In fact, elites generally understood the Bible to be a text that promoted deference to them.[20]

Accordingly, until 1829 each slaveholder judged the prudence or morality of offering reading instruction. Late that year, the circulation of David Walker's *Appeal* that Black people emulate the rebellious example of Haiti provoked Georgia to enact laws making it illegal to teach enslaved persons to read.[21] Walker's theology was as revolutionary as his battle cry: in the *Appeal,* he establishes himself as skillful interpreter of the central text in Christian culture and, then, of a wider remit of texts from antiquity to Thomas Jefferson's *Notes on the State of Virginia* (1785). By announcing himself as a master both of exegesis and of published prophecy, Walker threatened the authority of the white interpretive community coalescing in a post-Jacksonian country in which all white men, propertied and unpropertied, were political equals. By 1837 Alabama, Florida, Louisiana, Mississippi, North Carolina, Tennessee, and Virginia had joined Georgia in making it illegal to teach Black people to read or to write.[22] The authors of these antiliteracy laws sought not only to contain the spread of Walker's message but also to raze the image of unruly black readers from their consciousnesses.

Yet, the law was not the only way of method of barring Black people's presence in the sphere of white interpretive authority. In the face of these incursions, a romantic denial arose—one distributed across proslavery and antislavery forces. Artists propagated nostalgic imagery of bucolic domestic scenes to paper over a public sphere of increasingly bold black antislavery orators and texts. For example, Europeans in sympathy with Toussaint Louverture, the leader of the black forces in the colony of French Saint-Domingue, which became independent Haiti, wrote that he was inspired to a calm, rational revolutionary project by reading the Enlightenment writer Abbé Raynal's prophecy that a "black Spartacus" would arise to liberate Africans enslaved in the West Indies.[23]

In an image from an 1853 biography of Louverture, an artist depicts the future leader of the Haitian Revolution in a country household. His wife eyes him, ready to prepare any drink or food he may desire at table; his children are drawn to the expansive view offered by an open doorway. Louverture's gaze is fixed upon the open book on his lap. This is the artist's rendering of the moment in which Louverture reads that his fate as the "Black Spartacus" has already been written. Though he would go on to command an army, the image presents him as subordinate to the history and prophecy of the European (in this case, French) text. The white-authored text has all the agency, imprinting itself on the blank and passive mind of the black student who will perform to the letter what he could not otherwise imagine.[24] None of the images in this biography depicts Louverture at his writing desk—like the famous frontispiece of Phillis Wheatley-Peters, poised in thought—though he was, in fact, a prolific correspondent.[25] To paraphrase Jefferson's denigration of

"Toussaint Reading the Abbé Raynal's Work," from *The Life of Toussaint L'Ouverture: The Negro Patriot of Hayti,* by John R. Beard, London: Ingram, 1853. (Duke University)

Wheatley, the conferral of freedom cannot make a writer out of an African whose highest aspiration could be that of a submissive reader.[26] Even though he is already a free man envisioning the revolt he will lead to secure liberty for the enslaved, Toussaint is depicted as a reader and not the author of the future.

In the 1850s, the same decade that John R. Beard's English biography of Louverture memorialized him as a dutiful reader, cultural production in the United States sought to wish away the writerly activity of Black Freemasons, David Walker, Maria Stewart, petitioners, and the authors of the classic slave narratives by restoring scenes of black tutelage.[27] Rather than positioning black authors at writing desks with an author's tools at hand, white people—even those in political conflict with each other—converged on images of blacks as beneficiaries of reading instruction. It is an irony that these images were produced amid concerted activity meant to outlaw black literacy. That con-tradiction suggests a white supremacist investment in the idea that if Black people would simply become good readers (again), a sort of peaceful tutorial could (re)commence.[28] Though the length of this pedagogical instruction is never specified, the placid country classroom imagery does not suggest any particular hurry. In this iconography, white tutors are angelic instructors with all the time in the world to teach enslaved black readers who are forever stalled on the first letter: A.[29]

As an example, consider *Little Eva, Flower of the South,* a rebuttal to Harriet Beecher Stowe's best-selling *Uncle Tom's Cabin. Little Eva* appeared perhaps as early as 1853, just one year after the publication of Stowe's sensation.[30] Like its predecessor, this eight-page children's story features a saintly white girl named Eva who teaches the alphabet to slaves. Although this rejoinder transformed Stowe's antislavery Eva as an angel of the Peculiar Institution, the New York publication also flouted or simply ignored prevailing law by showing her as a literacy instructor. It appears that the pull of the catechizing scene was so strong that the author could not omit it. The illustration shows Eva point-ing to the letter A, an indication that the enslaved pupils have not progressed beyond the first stages of instruction. In the accompanying narration, the au-thor has the slaves abjure reading. Although Eva offers them the opportunity to read the Bible aloud, they say they prefer to hear the scriptures read in her sweet voice.

In a book like *Little Eva,* a proslavery audience could have it both ways: presenting themselves as fulfilling a Christian duty to give the enslaved the Word of God while perpetuating an image of slaves who have no need of or use for reading and writing. The enslaved characters in *Little Eva* cannot make from Christian texts the liberation theology of a David Walker. Nor will they use the skill of penmanship to petition for manumission, forge free passes, or write memoirs critical of the slave system.[31] In the figure of this luminously white girl—so unlike the American Tract Society's ragamuffin, tainted with sin, Catholicism, and foreignness—proslavery whites could imagine resuming negro instruction untroubled by incendiary words from the North or, indeed, from Haiti.

The Textual Politics of the Haitian Revolution

The lore surrounding the Haitian Declaration of Independence of January 1, 1804, shattered the frame of these scenes of benevolent literacy education. In legends circulating in Melville's time, the document was portrayed as the culmination of a revolt against a regime of white interpretive authority in which African bodies were transposed into ledgers, passes, laws and other instruments of the machinery of slavery, sadism, and capital accumulation.[32] While it has been acknowledged that the Haitian Revolution posed a radical and enduring threat to the political order of colonialism and slavery in the Atlantic World, it has sometimes escaped notice that the authors of Haitian nationhood reportedly understood declaring their liberty and independence not only as the announcement of the political status of an emergent nation and of its citizens but also as a blow against whites' monopoly on the means of representation.

Toussaint Louverture had sought to preserve Haitians' hard-won freedom from slavery while also remaining a French colony. He issued numerous acts, proclamations, and even a Constitution of 1801 to secure a political relationship he also tended through transatlantic correspondence with France. However, the ascension of Napoleon made continuing as a colony untenable, as the new emperor reversed the French revolutionary government's decree of abolition, reinstating slavery throughout France's Atlantic empire. When he sent troops to unseat Louverture and reimpose slavery, the hope for a peaceful colonial relationship, mediated by metropolitan law and transatlantic correspondence among an interracial fraternity, dissolved.

The generals who succeeded the kidnapped Louverture concluded that preserving emancipation would require a war for independence. Legend has it that at least one founder explicitly rejected the textual basis of the relationship with France. After General Dessalines rejected an earlier attempt as too tepid, Louis Félix Boisrond-Tonnerre reportedly volunteered to pen another version of a declaration of independence with this announcement: "to draw up the act of independence we [would] need the skin of a white man for parchment, his skull for an inkwell, his blood for ink, and a bayonet for a pen."[33] Although he did not use these materials in his next draft, Boisrond-Tonnerre severed the fraternal tie to France, declaring a bond among Haitian men, in defense of their wives and children from "barbarous" Frenchmen.

The angelic Little Eva from Harriet Beecher Stowe's runaway bestseller *Uncle Tom's Cabin* became so iconic that proslavery authors tried to reappropriate her for their purposes. The images here demonstrate an irony: the great Abolitionist and the defenders of the peculiar institution both sentimentalize literacy instruction, portraying a white child holding and reading the Bible, a font attended by eager black pupils who—the range of ages implies—could never be educators themselves. *Top:* "Eva Teaching the Alphabet" and "Eva Reading the Bible," from *Little Eva, Flower of the South,* c. 1853 (Duke University); *bottom:* "Little Eva Reading the Bible to Uncle Tom in the Arbor" by Hammatt Billings, from *Uncle Tom's Cabin,* 1852 (Harvard University).

Rhetorically, Boisrond-Tonnerre's 1804 declaration exceeded the US Declaration from three decades prior. The Caribbean text was more than a recital of transgressions, making a moral and philosophical justification for national independence. The US document points to the performative force of writing to dissolve some imagined bonds while forging others: "for the support of this Declaration, with a firm reliance on the protection of divine Providence, we mutually pledge to each other our Lives, our Fortunes and our sacred Honor."[34] In contrast, the Haitian Declaration makes explicit the martial project necessary to effect the declaration. The Haitian assembly vows to "give the nations a terrible but just example of . . . vengeance" against French "vultures. . . . tigers dripping with [the] blood [of spouses, siblings] and suckling infants."[35]

One month later, to preempt a takeover of the island and the reinstitution of slavery, Jean-Jacques Dessalines ordered the extermination of the remaining French population—a bloody massacre that would have provided the white corpses Boisrond-Tonnerre thought the proper medium for conveying independence. Slaveholding nations canceled the image of Haitian legislators engaged in solemn deliberation with another text of the revolution: white French blood marking the very earth.[36] For the beneficiaries of colonial slavery, the textual performance of Haitian independence was not—and could not be—a transcendent gesture that just happened to have a material basis in text. Rather, a black republic had to be the perversion of textuality, the dissolution of the hierarchy separating sovereign humans from animals and the natural environment.[37] Disregarding the bloodshed of beheaded monarchs and combatants that marked the emergence of their own enlightened/slaveholding nations, anti-black Europeans insisted that the true text of Haitian Revolution was, in fact, the one that Boisrond-Tonnerre did not prepare—that made from the destroyed white body.

Boisrond-Tonnerre's reported wish is quite blunt—that the founding document of this Black republic will be a white Frenchman's remains. His reversal serves to reveal the extent to which white nations have a dependency on the magically conjoined agencies of racialized slaves and instrumentalized letters so routinized that its operation is rarely explicit. The figures that populate this book—Africanist figures covered in ink, women described as blotted parchment—may strike the contemporary critic as fanciful figures that do not merit serious consideration. However, the reduction of a white male body to literary material restores the visceral impact of the figurative language.[38] Perhaps the Haitian Revolution was unthinkable for Europeans, in Trouillot's memorable phrase, because they refused to hail Africans as authors of the events and texts that constitute nations.[39] Romanticized scenes of tutelage like those in the previous section blotted out the full implications of the textual production among African descendants fueled by the Haitian achievement.

Melville was clearly not taken in by sentimental scenes of Africans dutifully submitting to benevolent literacy instruction as a cover for tyrannical rule. The use of white bodies as writing material in "BC" indicates that he realized that white racial mastery was under attack both in the flesh and in the print public sphere. Acknowledging the crisis, he shifts the historical Delano's story from 1805 to 1799—a date that falls within the years of the struggle for Saint Domingue but carries the additional force of a millennial reckoning.[40] For Melville, the mutiny in Saint Domingue spells the end of the eighteenth century and its project of Enlightenment spread through universal white literacy. Melville perceives his own era of the 1850s as the aftermath of a revolt that seized the means of representation and, thereby, shook the foundations of racial slavery and of white interpretive community with the same (pen) stroke.[41] When the mastermind of the slave insurrection orders Aranda killed and scrawls "follow your leader" using what he suggests are the dead white aristocrat's bones, he composes Boisrond-Tonnerre's wished-for Haitian Declaration of Independence for those brave enough to face it.

Beneath the shroud of scenes of dutiful Black readers is Babo's text, an interpretive impasse for Delano and his brothers, who seek their own new place in a pan-European brotherhood that (as Abigail Adams and the Virginia colonists profiled in my previous chapters found) is not guaranteed to English transplants in the Americas. As I turn to a deeper reading of "BC," I note that the impasse occurs at three pressure points in the procedures of white reading. First, in the symbolic system of inkface, the weight of signification falls upon Africanist figures, blackened persons, by dint of a projected cultural and material equivalence with ink. Second, consequently, this inky exterior may take legible forms, but its very conventionality makes it impossible to determine whether writing—or the African character derived from overwriting—is authentic or counterfeit. A black figure can only repeat its conventional signification. Finally, Babo's catechism forces *whiteness* into an unaccustomed position and shape, bringing it to the forefront as both chalked text and mute gesture. Through Babo's offices, Melville forces his white readers into a version of Othello's interpretive impasse: the impressions of his dyeing kisses cannot symbolize fidelity because they are culturally predetermined to be black marks against Desdemona's character; similarly, whiteness can no longer function as unmarked when the white body is made the ur-symbol.

Melville and the Mutiny of Shakespeare's Black Characters

Scholars have long known that Melville used *Othello* as the basis for "Benito Cereno." In 1952 Arthur Vogelback formulated the standard reading of the pattern Shakespeare provided the American: "Othello is brought to destruction by the evil in an unrepentant Iago; Don Benito, too, is destroyed by evil, embodied for him in the Negro [manservant], Babo."[42] While New Historicist interpretations shifted the focus from an insular conversation about literary influence to Melville's engagement with the political issue of slavery—with the successful revolt in Haiti looming particularly large—occasional returns to Shakespeare have typically followed Vogelback in seeking corresponding characters. In 1990 the critic David Leverenz dissented from the earlier New Critical consensus, suggesting that the seemingly victorious American—and not the dissipated Spanish captain—is really the Othello to Babo's Iago: "If Babo is Iago, Delano becomes an unwitting parody of Othello, prevailing through the brute strength he attributes to blacks only after he has been manipulated nearly out of his wits. . . . By the end Delano looks like a black buffoon while Babo's brain, 'that hive of subtlety,' becomes everyone's 'leader.'"[43] Leverenz's reassignment of the part of Othello relies upon a revaluation of an audience's relationship to and judgment of Iago. In Leverenz's interpretation, Iago becomes an intellectual David, defeating Othello, recast as a gargantuan oaf of a Goliath.

These interpretations miss the fact that Melville filtered *Othello* through his sense of Shakespearean inkface. On November 19, 1849, Melville saw the English star Charles Macready play Othello as part of his advertised farewell to the stage. Macready was not an imposing, physical moor in the mold of bounding, muscular rivals like Edmund Kean and, particularly, Edwin Forrest. Rather, his thin, aged figure and halting, intellectual approach arguably inspired the Spanish invalid who serves as the titular character in "BC."[44] Melville had taken Macready's part when workingmen hooted the Englishman offstage in an incident that spawned the Astor Place riots.[45] Having thus lost the chance to watch the legend in New York, Melville rushed to see Macready play the moor at the Haymarket in London.[46] The experience, described in a journal, was unsatisfying: "panted hideously. Did'nt like him very much upon the whole—bad voice, it seemed."[47] It was this incident that probably inspired Melville's experiment with a central figure both grand and enfeebled, the Spanish captain Don Benito.

When he composed "BC," Melville conjured Macready's thin and breathless Othello. If the actor, nearing retirement, was skin and bones, there was an echo for that in Haitian lore. Baron de Vastey was the secretary of Dessalines's successor, King Henry Christophe, and an early historian of Haiti. Recalling his time serving under Toussaint Louverture, Vastey wrote of the effects of the tropical climate on European soldiers: "The complexion, so late the pride, becomes haggard, wan, and discolored . . . their bodies become feeble and emaciated, and their moral and physical powers destroyed; so that the White man appears, in the eyes of the black a mere walking skeleton, disgraced by nature."[48] The fixation on white men's bones in Vastey and in Boisrond-Tonnerre's

Playbill from the night Herman
Melville saw the aged legend
Charles Macready play Othello in
1849. Haymarket Theatre Playbill,
November 19, 1849. (Houghton
Library, Harvard University)

wished-for Declaration reverberates through "BC." Thin and hoarse like
Macready, Don Benito has become "worn to a skeleton," the exemplar of a
muted white subject (171).

Although one could have arrived at "BC" and its ghastly emblem solely
through Haitian textual politics, Melville synergized the New World material with his Shakespearean reading. At this point, many scholars would turn
to Melville's engagement with Shakespeare's "dark characters" in his famous

Herman Melville based the character Don Benito on Charles Macready's Othello—notably thin and pensive, as compared to the muscular Othellos that have come down to this day. "Mr. Macready as Othello," engraving after H. Tracey, mid-nineteenth century. (Folger Shakespeare Library, Washington D.C.)

review "Hawthorne and His Mosses" (1850).[49] However, I would argue that a lesser-known moment in his correspondence provides a more exact model for Delano's exemplary predicament of a white man reading in the aftermath of Boisrond-Tonnerre's unachieved consumption of a white man's corpse as material for Haiti's founding text.

While his wife completed her postnatal convalescence in early 1849, Herman Melville spent the winter days on his father-in-law's sofa absorbed in *The Dramatic Works of William Shakspeare*.[50] During these weeks in Boston, the medium of the book afforded Melville a belated intimacy with Shakespeare, who had already been established in the eighteenth century as the preeminent Anglophone contributor to global arts and letters. On February 24, he wrote Evert Duyckinck, an editor of a jingoist American literary magazine who had become a friend. A jubilant Melville mocked his own prior ignorance of Shakespeare, which he amended after his felicitous discovery of an edition with large print:

> Dolt & ass that I am I have lived more than 29 years, & until a few days ago, never made close acquaintance with the divine William. Ah, he's full of sermons-on-the-mount, and gentle, aye, almost as Jesus. . . . And if another Messiah comes 'twill be

in Shakespeare's person.—I am mad to think how minute a cause has prevented me hitherto from reading Shakespeare. But until now, every copy that was come-atable to me, happened to be in a vile small print unendurable to my eyes which are tender as young sparrows. But chancing to fall in with this glorious edition, I now exult over it, page after page.[51]

Yet, Melville's encounter was not to remain a Sermon on the Mount for a private audience of one reader. The New York native also found his experience inside Shakespeare's text uncomfortably like being under siege. "Every letter," he wrote of the seven-volume set, "is a soldier, & the top of every 't' like a musket barrel." The "great glorious type" of this edition printed in Boston in 1837 invited the weak-eyed novelist to immerse himself in reading, then surrounded him like an enemy force with rifles aimed squarely between his eyes.[52]

Melville's scene of reading is far from the scene I anatomize in my first chapter, a scene in which Othello dictates his final dispatch to the state, using his blood as period and seal. Shakespeare offered a speaking moor who unites voice, flesh, and document in his suicide (note). Presumably, its readers could scrutinize it and determine its authenticity, its faithful representation of Othello as he is. In Melville's letter to Duyckinck, it is not the blackamoor's throat but the silent white reader's brain that is in the crosshairs. His is the body to be punctured and to bleed punctuation. White readers are not presented as masters who look down omnisciently on a miniature world of printed characters. The vaunted white male reader is suddenly of the same size as the figures he scans. The result is a white reader in peril behind enemy lines of black characters.

Before unveiling the text of whiteness at the close of "BC," Melville presents readers expected texts of black letters and submissive Africans—both in unaccustomed mutiny. In this post-Shakespearean and indeed postapocalyptic narrative, the black characters of the page are no longer un-raced riflemen; they have been specifically Africanized. As the American captain Amasa Delano boards the aimlessly drifting Spanish slave ship, he cannot blink away the sense that he is reading black text against a white backdrop. For example, when Delano scans the various zones of the ship, he notices: "the quarter-deck rose into an ample elevated poop, upon the forward verge of which, lifted . . . some eight feet above the general throng, sat along in a row, separate by regular spaces, the cross-legged figures of six other blacks; each with a rusty hatchet in his hand" (168–69). Melville introduces these "hatchet-polishers" not as people but as black "figures" sitting in a row with regular spaces between. This arrangement of evenly spaced black characters personifies the iconography of the printed page. These Africans are black letters of type come to (still) life, and they have made their reader—the striding, optimistic American captain—their "mark," their target and their dupe (168). In this moment, Delano is Melville reading Shakespeare.[53] The hatchet-wielding Africans replicate the role of the riflemen in the Duyckinck letter, hybrid creatures of human and alphanumerical components who entice but also potentially threaten to reduce the unsuspecting white male reader to reading matter.

If Delano heeded his recurring suspicion that he is viewing a "juggling play" aboard the *San Dominick,* he might have been able to detect the mutiny much sooner (212). However, he stubbornly insists on employing interpretive conventions spawned from print's black-and-white clarity. These protocols and the underlying assumption of a white monopoly on alphabetical intelligence are Delano's master interpretive codes.[54] Consequently, every "figure" he encounters is one associated with literary paraphernalia—printed rows, "stamp[s]," "impression[s]," and "hacked [seals]" (194). Delano sees the ship, in its "true character," as a page composed of suspended, noisy African figures standing atop muted white ones, as inked letters are imposed upon white paper.[55] Anticipating the academic metaphor of close reading, Melville yokes credible perception with access to character, that imagined essence indicated, more or less faithfully, through conventional signs.[56] Delano does not meet the challenge to learn how to read character outside the conventions of intelligibility imposed by print and its racialized palette.

The story's famous overture elaborating on the shades of gray enveloping the *San Dominick* does not just indicate an indistinct zone between black and white. Rather, gray indicates a color that print's hermeneutic practices will fail to detect. Print unites black and white without producing gray, as would happen when the pigments of black and white mix in the world outside the page. Further, the mixture of gray summons that other blend of black and white, the mulatto. "BC" features an interlude in which the Spanish and American captains discuss the puzzle of mulatto character, whether a "European face" hides a devilish black nature or "a little of our blood mixed with the African's, should, far from improving the latter's quality, have the sad effect of pouring vitriolic acid into black broth; improving the hue, perhaps, but not the wholesomeness" (215). In the black-and-white world Delano encounters on the *San Dominick,* the "mulatto Francesco" suggests the Oriental(ist) Othello popularized in the nineteenth century: "a tall, rajah-looking mulatto, . . . set off with a pagoda turban formed by three or four madras handkerchiefs wound about his head . . . approaching with a salaam" (214). Despite these eastern touches, Francesco "was of the first band of revolters, that he was, in all things, the creature and tool of the negro Babo" (241). Despite the gray atmosphere surrounding the ship, in the racial imaginary, mixedness is not a possibility: an intermediate brown resolves into an absolute black.[57]

Although the black-and-white epistemology of the page works to ascertain the essentially black character of the "mulatto Francesco," Melville proves less optimistic about that hermeneutic outside of the sphere of race and blood. A *massa*, it would appear from the examples of both Delano and Aranda, becomes a vulnerable mark when he becomes seduced by the reading practices of the page in a world suffused with gray.[58] Alexandro Aranda represents the assurance of the Old World aristocrat, confident in the social structure of the ancien régime, trusting even unfettered African captives to stay within "given bounds"—as if human black characters were no more than letters, with social barriers imposed as easily as conventions about page margins. Delano, as the liberal American, proposes to leave "open margin" to the Spaniard's "black-letter text" (187).

Melville's pun on "black-letter" obviously invokes the color assigned to African descendants in the system of Atlantic racial slavery.[59] At the same time, it also refers to an early baroque typeface, with elaborate black lines of varying thickness, akin to Gothic. Therefore, through its association with ornately drawn black character in "BC," Gothic signals both a genre and a typeface. It encompasses the well-known macabre elements of Melville's tale—captivity, revenge, and possible cannibalism—while also pointing to the stately African Atufal, whose first appearance is certainly that of an elaborately designed black shape: "Captain Delano's attention was caught by the moving figure of a gigantic black . . . an iron collar was about his neck, from which depended a chain, thrice wound round his body; the terminating links padlocked together at a broad band of iron, his girdle" (182).[60] The gigantic African resembles a black-letter majuscule with its seemingly excessive rings and arms. "Ranging freely" while yet bound by his chains, Atufal is a Gothic letter *A* come to life, albeit in black rather than in Nathaniel Hawthorne's favored scarlet coloring.[61]

Returning white readers to school to start over with a mobile letter *A*, Atufal's name imparts a sinister lesson. The name of Babo's co-conspirator foretells the shared fates of Aranda, the alphabet, and white authority. No one has yet observed that the name of Babo's henchman, Atufal, is not Melville's approximation of an authentic African name but a disguised spelling of the fate of all headmen: *A to fall*. Executing the prophecy in that name, the mutineers murder A[randa] and install *b* in its place—where the minuscule *b* represents Babo, "a black of small stature" (169). At the outset of "BC," Delano mistakes this revolt for "misrule"—a carnivalesque inversion of social positions. He is not entirely wrong. Melville's devilish Babo has doubly distorted alphabetical order, in removing *A* and placing minuscule before majuscule. Were "BC" an alphabet primer, it would commence: bB, cC (170, 227).[62] Babo's "pageant" is so effective in sustaining "a false gaze" because character, the basic unit of legibility for the literate, remains recognizable in "BC," but gaps and displacements impede the reading process.[63] Not to mention that a Eurocentric obsession with reading blackness mutes the white characters, the surviving Iberian sailors whom Delano ignores while trying to interpret any figure of blackness he sees.

Chalkbones

Melville pursues his own remediation of Shakespeare's inkface performance and warns his nineteenth-century contemporaries that Haiti's independence has fundamentally destabilized white authority through an implied maxim: black mutiny produces white mutes. For example, he suggests this fusion of rebellion and silence in a racialized description of the sonic atmosphere of the ship: the collective sounding of blacks and whites "in one voice" when Delano boards the ship and later the "indiscriminate wailing" of both groups.[64] As usual, Delano refers all sensory evidence to the page, where black ink and white paper merge to produce "one voice." Under the premises of inkface, though, that voice is that of ink and not of paper. Accordingly, African voices blot out European ones for much of "BC."

In another instance, Delano sees the surviving Spanish sailors as "white faces, here and there sparsely mixed in with the blacks, like stray white pawns venturously involved in the ranks of the chess-men opposed" (194). This mixture suggests the dominance of blacks on the ship and the power of the inked letter, an item that draws more readerly attention than does the surrounding or intermingled white space. If we retain Melville's metaphor of the ship deck as a "black letter-text," the Africans become ornate ink marks. Delano identifies them by type, casting each of them in a recognizable form, investing them with predetermined content, and putting them in relation to each other and to Don Benito. The intermingled Spaniards want desperately to communicate with Delano, but their bodies and gestures remain shapeless and, thus, hard to apprehend. Like the white spaces between letters, their white bodies are visible. However, within the inkface paradigm they cannot speak to Delano as they do not constitute units of meaning.

The protocols of inkface insist that blackness speaks, and Melville obliges. His Africans sit in rows in the mouth of the longboat, a "den for family groups of the blacks, mostly women and small children; who, squatting on old mats below, or perched above in the dark dome, on the elevated seats, were descried, some distance within" (205). The squatting and the perched are rows of black characters, with the variable heights of capital and miniscule letters. Occasionally, they emerge from the mouth of the den, "dividing before [Delano]" in rows so tight they can move only enough to "[twitch] each other aside" (194). Clearly, Melville intends for African persons to be alphabetical shapes, issuing from a figurative mouth large enough to emit human characters from its lips, arraying themselves in militaristic lines as tight as those of rows of print.

Yet, we would mistake Melville's experiment if our focus remained on these armed, noisy, obtrusive black characters. Beneath all the bustling busyness of "Benito Cereno" is another text entirely—not that of the mutinous Africans but that of the whites' muteness. "BC" is, in one sense, the headless alphabetical order of the African figures on the ship that the sanguine Amasa Delano is determined to decipher. His failure to properly decipher that "black-letter text" of posed African bodies represents Melville's view of a self-consciously white reader's encounter with an alphabetic primer that Babo has organized as both an apocalyptic catechism and a sinister carnival. Yet, I would argue that Melville is finally far more interested in the white platform than in the black figures.

Americanist scholars of "Benito Cereno" have been transfixed by its black characters and, therefore, unable or unwilling to read white character. Some have declared it a story of the "malign evil in man" (164), which they assign to African mutineers as much for their "ferocious, piratical revolt" as for their concealment of that capacity.[65] Others have ruled the story an encomium to the same Africans who heroically risk their lives for their liberty.[66] Still others have focused on the extracts of (fictional) court documents that Melville reproduces in his text as a way of discussing the incapacity of documentary archives to provide a definitive history of this (or any) slave revolt.[67]

However, all these approaches—even the theoretically sophisticated deconstructive emphasis on the nonreferentiality of signifiers—reproduce the cacophonous sound of black characters while ignoring the mute presence of suppressed white ones. Scholarly attempts to interpret black character in "BC" repeat Delano's fundamental error. The American captain is a reader who is fooled because, as the literary scholar Catherine Toal reveals, he "sees only blackness."[68] I would sharpen Toal's insight further: Delano can hear or interpret only black character when the scene that he has come upon requires him to attend to white characters—and to the signifying potential of white text.[69]

During an interlude during his time aboard the *San Dominick,* Delano watches an old Spanish sailor and senses the presence of evil on the ship. "If, indeed, there be any wickedness on board this ship, thought Captain Delano, be sure that man there has fouled his hand in it, even as he now fouls it in the pitch. . . . The negroes . . . joined in with the old sailor, but, as they became talkative, he by degrees became mute" (195). In the first sentence, Delano is overtaken by the fullness of inky blackness as the signifier par excellence in the world of print. He cannot make anything of the sailor *until* he sees the sailor being blackened. When Delano sees the pot of tar, his mental fog lifts. The store of anti-black discourse supplies him with metaphors and analogies for blackness that restores his certainty.[70] Yet, his preoccupation with the imagined foulness and wickedness of blackness impedes his thought as much as the voluble Africans drown out the muted white sailor.

Catherine Toal reads Melville's problem as a susceptibility to the "allegorical denigration" of blackness, that is, the clichéd association of blackness with evil.[71] In my view, this formulation misstates the impediment to Delano's perception. He is not convinced that blackness must signify *evil* but that blackness—and blackness alone—must do *all* signifying. The blithe American is indeed perfectly capable of presenting the racialized color as the height of simplicity, fidelity, joy. For example, at one moment, he is certain that Babo exemplifies the good nature of blacks: "There is something in the negro which, in a peculiar way, fits him for avocations about one's person. Most negroes are natural valets and hairdressers; taking to the comb and brush congenially as to the castinets, and flourishing them apparently with almost equal satisfaction" (208).

Delano is unperceptive because blackness so saturates his sonic and visual fields that he cannot perceive the signals of white characters, who repeatedly try to give him coded messages that Babo has them captive and may kill every white man aboard, Delano included. A reader asked to interpret the white spaces of a "black-letter text," Delano has no tools for reading white characters. In "BC," the adherent to inkface is incapable of drawing any communicative information from the blank silence of character when it appears in a white (type)face. In obsessing over Melville's attitude toward black character(s), scholars have reproduced Delano's blindness to the white text—indeed, the text of whiteness—that appears at the story's climax.

Babo's lone written words, the chalked imperative "follow your leader," achieve the status of new universal gospel, refusing a single addressee, referent, or destination. The imperative gains force from its materiality. "Follow your leader" is a thought become deed, as well as words that become flesh (well, bone) in the medium of their expression. Any reader who doubts the prophecy of death—or the Africans' ability to bring it to pass—can refer to the bones that were presumably used to write it. These written words do not refer to or describe reality; they *perform* it. That reality, specifically, is the reversal of the gospels, turning back the clock from AD to BC.

Babo's use of bones for chalk vacates the potential for the resurrection of the body. The American captain, Amasa Delano, is a hopeful man whose very initials suggest the potential for Providential intervention in history: A.D., *anno Domini*. Yet, the mutineers have written an everlasting prophecy that foretells an obliteration of the body and extinguishing of the soul.[72] This is the catechism of "BC" that neither the sailors nor the critics of "Benito Cereno" have been willing to read. It is, in short, the story of how Herman Melville recognized in the writing of Haiti's revolutionary documents the end of the epistemological hierarchy that the inkface dynamic propagated by *Othello* was designed to impose.

Melville's Shakespeare-influenced reworking of the Haitian Revolution as a slave mutiny in the Pacific Ocean is a bitter irony: a testament that white masters have lost control of their blackamoor slaves and their textual moorings at once. Set in 1799, "BC" marks the end of an era but fails to provide the salvation associated with AD. Instead, Melville implies that he and his readers live in a nineteenth century unfolding as a disenchanted time when a white interpretive community that reached its zenith in the eighteenth century's vision of a Republic of Letters lay in ruins.[73] While holding out hope that a keen white reader could exist, Melville employed Captain Delano to depict whites of the US North as too sanguine about their imperial prospects to read the proverbial writing on the crumbled walls. The satire of the gullible Yankee type gains additional heft from the fact that he is the heir of Christianity and of the Enlightenment: Bibles, dictionaries, encyclopedia, biological classifications, and glorious constitutions. For the period of his reign, Babo vacates all assurances of this textual tradition.

Throughout this book, I have been arguing that white racial hegemony had an important base of material support in *inkface,* my name for the place where blackface performance and protocols of reading meet. Inkface transforms blackened persons into alphanumeric characters subject to the codes and operations of media forms, interpretations, and values—economic and moral. This transformation into objects of characterizations is required to make blackened persons potential subjects of manipulations that will fulfill European descendants' desires for disproportionate enjoyment of property, protection, and pleasure. Of course, *Othello* did not initiate the formation of white interpretive community. However, both its internal content and its social life across two and a half centuries indicate that the play presumed, depicted, and helped perpetuate maldistribution in realms from the commercial to the sexual. The failures of black Othello, blackened Desdemona, base Indians, and provincial whites as readers revived operating assumptions about who could and could not grasp character in a world increasingly mediated by alphanumeric symbols, social types, and racial essences.

My previous chapters have tracked suspect white women, denigrated Creoles, ambitious novelists, and royal governors who claimed a share of a collective right to determine legitimate meaning and value and apportion vulnerability and protections. These were among the contentious members of what I have termed a white interpretive community. Their intramural disagreements were constant and potentially ferocious, but the combatants shared one grudging and usually unspoken premise: *Despite our differences of rank, region, gender, and class, we are the ones who will determine what constitutes a sign and how signs may be interpreted. We are the masters of black character in whatever form we conjure it.*

Herman Melville restaged *Othello* on the pages of Amasa Delano's memoir to show what the Haitians' revolutionary declaration had done to this transatlantic, pan-European synod. The African rebellion produces a decapitated alphabet—one in which the Alpha has been removed and what remains is merely a sinister mimicry of order under the miniscule *b.* Babo, in particular, literalizes the implications of a rebellious African writing for readers whose media forms have been suffused with racial meanings. Contrary to the pretense of inkface—that the bodies of all women and of nonwhite men are texts for the perusal of a white male fraternity—Babo insists that *every body* can be made into writing matter. However, his lone inscription in chalk proves more transcendent prophecy than contribution to a global sphere of letters. What an African-derived contribution might be—other than rebuke and vengeance—is not to be found in the haunting graffiti *follow your leader* (into death).

Considering this moment in her outstanding study of the ideology of race in early American literature, Dana Nelson writes: "Babo's gesture graphically affirms [that] when one gets down to the bare bones, there is *no* difference."[74] Nelson's long history of racial meanings embedded in North American letters is an important model for my own project. However, I think she errs in claiming that Babo's writing with a dead white man's bones refers to a human quality beneath racialized skin. Babo does not invoke universal humanity by using the murdered slaveholder Aranda's bones to write an inscription. Rather, his pointed insinuation overturns the relations of inkface in which white people are authors and readers and blackened people literary objects and slaves. Babo has intuited the master's presumption that Black people are covered in and filled with ink, with its implication that blackness encompasses every stratum of character, from the outside in as it were. He redeploys that presumption to compel the Iberian soldiers to conclude—by a logic they have already accepted regarding black bodies—that the bones of a white man must be as white as his skin. This act completes the undoing of white authority by making white bones into material that moors alphabetical symbols to deeds. His readers can trust his inscription because they cannot help but conclude that the availability of a white man's bones for chalk attests that the mutineers have murdered white men and will not shrink from doing so again. With inkface in mind, the full shock of Babo's revelation finally registers: the white male body has lost its distinction from those of the ink-filled moor and the white woman figured as paper.

Melville means to show the real-world counterparts of Cassio and the senators from *Othello*—those paragons of literacy—not that they, too, can be blackened but that they are *constituted by* materials that can be utterly consumed in the production of character's media of text and theatre.[75] In Haitian lore and in Melville's apocalyptic fiction, white men lose their omniscient position as masters of character and find themselves mere textual material, after all. This outcome does more than to reconfirm that Babo is a villainous African Iago, as scholars have long known. Rather, it suggests that Melville grasped intuitively that inkface was the foundation of white interpretive fraternity. He enjoyed being a part of a male homosocial community bound economically and affectively through letters.[76] Consequently, he was attuned to the subtlest of threats to that world, the real-life Jack Cades and Iagos who would destroy it. The hypercanonicity of Melville—and of "Benito Cereno," in particular—has substituted a universal audience for the intended white male readership he did not have to name in his own time. My goal has been to rescue from universalist speculation the dramatic trope he grasped and the historical audience he sought to warn.

Nevertheless, I concur with Dana Nelson's observation that Melville's narrator does not escape the "conceptual, epistemological, and representational structures that support the racist economy."[77] His interests are in inhabiting and even satirizing the perspectives possible from within the interpretive fraternity of which he is a member.[78] He aims not to re-create the interior life of a Babo but to reproduce a white male readerly experience of Babo as a black sign—undoubtedly meaningful but at once too easily grasped and utterly elusive. Toni Morrison characterized Melville as a penetrating writer whose primary interest in Africans was not as "real flesh and blood people" but as "dark symbols" or "shadows" of white characters.[79] As Nelson observes, that tactic leaves those interested in pathways to a multiracial public commons wanting.

In the unrelieved gloom of "BC," Melville does not provide an idyllic image of what egalitarian communication would look like, nor a prescription for how to achieve it. The mood, at least, is quite different from that in an intercultural encounter in *Moby-Dick*. The scholar Birgit Rasmussen says that the mystical hieroglyphs Queequeg inscribes on his coffin suggest an Indigenous American literacy that cannot be absorbed in Western writing but sits alongside it as a formidable, alternate representational system. Rasmussen writes that "while [Melville's] early work such as *Typee* registers the confrontation with Indigenous forms of literacy as a threat, his great epic *Moby-Dick* ponders instead interdependence and the possibility of commensurability. . . . [by representing 'Indian characters'] as markers of alterity and anteriority, testaments to the presence of another literary culture belonging to the continent's original inhabitants."[80] Melville's apparent respect for Indigenous literacy echoes Thomas Jefferson's pronouncement when scientific racism was in early bloom: "I am safe in affirming, that the proofs of genius given by the Indians of North America place them on a level with whites in the same uncultivated state."[81]

Yet, in "BC," New World black literacy does not resemble that of the Americas' Indigenous peoples. Creolized black literacy is alphabetical and therefore does not represent the genius of a romanticized civilization of the past. Rather, it spells the *end* of Europe's civilizing project. An African has learned the rudiments of literacy, but he employs it in savage mockery of his tutors. In an imperial Atlantic imagination, the writing of former African slaves is parodic and parasitic at best. At worst, its aims are outright murderous: to decapitate a textualized European male body, dissolve its flesh, grind even its bones for chalk with which to scrawl gratuitous, triumphal vengeance. This haunting imagery does not make Melville identical to those who tried to smother a Black Atlantic print public by outlawing literacy, but it does suggest he felt himself their "brother of the state" (I.ii.96)—a Brabantio whose terrifying "dream[s]," perhaps, were "not unlike" theirs (I.i.142).

Epilogue
Beyond White Authority

Cultural Inquests of White Literary Remains

By concluding with a comparison of Herman Melville to Brabantio, the father who would use racism as a pretext for patriarchal control over his daughter's choice of husband, I have perhaps left a door open to a set of questions from readers. Is Melville racist? Is he more racist than Shakespeare? Than Aphra Behn? How do they compare to Abigail Adams? Or to Kemble and Siddons, those stars of the eighteenth-century stage? Is the *Othello* story itself irredeemably implicated in racism?

I cannot help but suspect that these questions spring from an urge to keep the discomforts and demands that attend race out of some sacred sphere: that of the Renaissance, literature (Shakespeare's in particular), feminism, England, or the founding of the United States—to name a few arenas. Under pressure of this need to protect and defend, comparison does not make an idle distinction but separates the relatively innocent who will be cherished from the relatively culpable who will be disavowed. Anxious questions born of this need derail anti-racist efforts to repair and redress into a project of determining whether long-dead white figures could justly declare, in modern parlance, *I don't have a racist bone in my body.*[1]

Bartlett Sher, the operatic director with whom I began the book, exemplifies this process in his reported claim that "Verdi and his librettist, Arrigo Boito, were less focused on [Othello's] race than Shakespeare was."[2] For Sher, the fact that the opera omits Shakespeare's first act and its avalanche of monstrous and bestial images of Othello reduces *Otello*'s interest in race. This conclusion seems strange when we recall that Verdi and Boito called the black general "Il Ciocolatto" in their coded correspondence. The collaborators were not interested in disrupting well-established "scripts of blackness," such as the association of Africans with edible commodities.[3] However, their excision of the first act, executed to achieve unity of place (in Cyprus), now permits the Metropolitan Opera to deracinate the moor and, thereby, redeem a masterpiece of European art that dates to the height of blackface minstrelsy as an international sensation. Plucked from that context, this opera from the blackface repertoire reappears as a beautiful and affecting work that addresses human concerns. The shrewd strategy maintains the aging, white subscriber base while reaching out to nonwhite patrons with a promise that they will not be insulted in their costly seats. To be sure, the currently indestructible Shakespeare juggernaut absorbs some fire to salvage a particular production of *Otello*. Still, in the end, neither artist is irreparably harmed, as the exculpatory process can always be repeated with other artists or works substituted.

It is difficult to criticize this comparative habit, as the distinctions it produces uphold a hallowed value that persons deserve to be judged as individuals. Yet, both the aim and the process deserve scrutiny. Comparison aims to make a cultural process conform to evidentiary rules more appropriate to a trial. This insistence is strange, since there are no direct descendants of Shakespeare, Verdi, or Boito who stand to lose materially if some legitimately find their work racist. Yet, one would think by the feverish defenses offered that a trial for damages really was occurring. Accordingly, in this cultural proceeding, defenders insist that the evidence must be restricted to language with a recognized racial charge. The histories of casting and attendance are excluded—as are the material properties of the stage paint. These procedures would strike nearly anyone who majored in literature as the only way to do justice to writers—namely, to judge them by their words. However, when we recall that *Othello* and *Otello* are not merely textual but *performance* pieces, the exclusion of centuries of all-white casting, audience reactions, transferable blackface, dirty jokes, and visual caricatures no longer appears so appropriate. It becomes apparent that these restrictions of the evidence serve to exonerate beloved works, authors, or historical personages but, in the process, misrepresent the medium and efface the messy histories of blackface I have detailed.

In this book, I have taken advantage of the fact that I am relatively unencumbered by financial or sentimental ties to Shakespeare or any of the other canonical figures who appear in these pages. Consequently, I am free of the obligation to dig up the dead and conduct a cultural biopsy to determine whether they had racist bones. Having largely sidestepped that diagnostic urge, I find I have little to say to questions that demand I allocate comparative guilt. Therefore, I have resisted considering the Atlantic engagements with *Othello* I analyze as direct revelations about attitudes toward or treatment of Black people. I have avoided treating them as barometers of racial tension or direct reflections of successive epochs of either legal or scientific racism. They are not evidence of proper or improper responses to an urgent and immediate encounter with Black persons. Rather, they indicate what ambitious white subjects knew about how they might use slippery character-based media forms (i.e., writing, print, and theatre) successfully to navigate a promising but uncertain social

world. The white people in my study did not offer a program for redistributing property, pleasure, and protection—since their aim was only to survive
and prosper in a system of maldistribution. They were in precarious enough
situations that they had plenty to do in maintaining their public image, establishing their literary personae, guarding against disgrace, and seeking to
achieve and sustain economic advantage and social elevation. Yet, they were
also in secure enough positions that they did not *have* to care about whether
their work did one thing to better the life of Indigenous persons struggling to
retain sovereignty or Africans seeking universal emancipation.

It seems fitting, then, that when I looked at the correspondence, commentary, and afterlives attending each of my cases, I did not find the presence of Africans. I found white people talking to each other, exploiting the affordances
of specific media, such as epistolary correspondence, print, clothing, cosmetics, and drama. Meditations on black and white pervaded their performance
spaces and their texts, but few if any Africans were to be found, despite the recurrence of figurative language about ink and paper and attempts to personify
those materials onstage. I learned that constraining myself to these metaphors
and entertainments could produce a history of the emergence of white community and authority unobtainable by other means.

The materiality and metaphorics of the page provided a view of an aspect
of white social life that had profound racial implications but could be conducted with indifference to the presence or absence of Black people. Literacy
training engendered a white interpretive community. Its racial effects were
pervasive if not necessarily overt: the Roman alphabet and Arabic numerals
have no racial content, but the use of those systems as a kind of master code
entailed the discrediting of other symbolic systems and the peoples who used
them. Consolidation of white authority and the subordination and exclusion
of those who might challenge it could occur in the selection of a medium
and of protocols for interacting with it. Thus, white interpretive authority
was born in an act that is invisible in intellectual histories of racial ideology:
the imposition of European character systems as the official tools of meaning
making. This seizure of the means of symbolic representation entailed a long
struggle that has been ably covered by scholars of literacy encounters. For now,
I merely want to note that, from alphabetic instruction to academic and even
legal deliberation, our interpretive enterprise has been in the service of white
domination. The characters of the ledger, the page, and the stage can be made
to do other work, but only once we have acknowledged that we have not yet
severed them from that history.

Some might want to interject here that art serves precisely this function
by making people question their prejudices. The cultural historian Martin
Orkin famously claimed that the South African government "discouraged"

the teaching of *Othello* because it "oppose[d] racism" of the apartheid state, "as it has always done."[4] The scholar Emily Bartels writes that *Othello* reveals the racist strategy of "demoniz[ing] an Other as a means of securing the self." She praises it as a singular Renaissance play that "refuses, boldly and subversively, to 'close off borders' and 'concentrate' difference [in the racial Other] and that chooses to make more of the Moor."[5] Yet, such conclusions substitute the critic's analysis for reception history. First, there is nothing in the text of *Othello* that *prevents* a racist reading. Second, the first full-throated assertion that *Othello* opposes racism appears over 150 years after the play's debut. The theatre manager David Douglass successfully circumvented a ban on theatre in the colony of Rhode Island by arguing that *Othello* is not a play at all but a series of "moral dialogues" that combat vices. He identifies racism as a heretical belief the play can correct: "The father of Desdemona . . . is foolish enough to dislike the noble Moor, his son-in-law, because his face is not white, forgetting that we all spring from one root. Such prejudices are very numerous and very wrong."[6] Despite the arguments of Shakespeare's advocates, the historical conditions for the emergence of a lone anti-racist play seem absent. There was no social movement against racism to fuel or frame the composition. Audiences did not clamor for anti-racist drama as they did for revenge tragedies. And so, *Othello* would have to wait for actors and directors who risked their careers and sometimes their lives to activate an anti-racist potential that went unnoticed, or at least undocumented, for over a century.[7]

Throughout the contexts I cover in *Inkface*, *Othello* never played a decisive role in resolving a consequential matter. No racist laws or imperial battle cries in my study rely on *Othello* for their language. Nevertheless, racial hierarchy shaped the contours of how the white subjects involved conducted the business that ran through or alongside the performances they saw. That business may have been mundane in comparison to the events for which eras are named, but the urgencies and anxieties within it reveal social details at a very fine level. What I find telling is that actual, living African people could play such a miniscule role in how Europeans brought whiteness into social being.

Consider these cases:

1. In his dramatic works, Shakespeare makes no direct reference to the African population in England or to the transatlantic slave trade. When he does allude to Africa, he relies on his reading to supply a rich poetic geography of reptiles and monstrous races rather than adhering to cartographic or ethnographic facts. Therefore, his interest in stage blackness seems to consist in a preoccupation with the material properties of the paint and textiles used to achieve it. The threat of acquiring stigma hovers around any scene of contact with a moor. Shakespeare's aim seems to be experimental, as he assigns a lone blacked-up part to different players: the lead tragedian in *Othello*, a boy actor

in *Antony and Cleopatra,* a minor fool in *The Merchant of Venice,* and a more substantive comic role in the late romance *The Tempest.* The obsessive interest in sexual unions with white partners suggests that Shakespeare was playing with a stage technology rather than making a moral pronouncement on England's increasing involvement in Atlantic slavery. Nevertheless, the audiences that he summoned to think through the social possibilities of this color transfer constituted a white interpretive community in the making. If it did not definitively establish a cohesive image of black racial character, inkface plays offered a white collective an opportunity to formulate that image without input from racial subordinates deemed too foolish to participate in the process.

2. The *London Gazette's* first issue of 1685 promises a generous reward to anyone who returns a runaway "Negro about 16 years of age . . . called by the name of Othello" to his "Master," the shipbuilder and eventual navy commissioner Sir Phineas Pet.[8] Aphra Behn might have made this fugitive from the Navy Yard, marked by his "slow . . . Speech" and sumptuous, stolen "Blue Livery Suite . . . laced with Gold Galloom, and lined with Orange Colour, and the Sleeves fringed about with Silk" the basis of her revision of *Othello.* She was a Londoner who made her living by writing and, presumably, read the newspapers during the years of political instability that concluded in the Glorious Revolution that deposed her Stuart patrons. In addition, at a time of financial distress, she might have taken special notice of the promised reward and the potential for publishing a piece about the adventure. However, as I detailed in the second chapter, her feminist experiment with *Othello* did not entail her pursuit of *this* Othello's origin or destination, his original name, his quest for freedom, his loves—though her "Oroonoko" thematizes each of those concerns. This observation is not meant to chastise her but to highlight that it is rarely possible or advisable for the scholar to anchor artistic experiments with race in brute facts either of biography or of the number of English slave ships crossing the Atlantic in a given decade.[9] Behn was quite preoccupied with the signifying potential of racialized materials—especially with their implications for the possibility of women's sexual self-possession. The stage sensation *The Moor of Venice* vexed and obsessed her. The runaway Othello did not.

3. The theatre historian Odai Johnson reports that the "'Charming Sally' that brought the first London company of actors to North America was also a trading vessel that trafficked in slaves. The actors were supercargo."[10] Tantalized by this coincidence, I once tried to make the November 1752 performance of *Othello* in Williamsburg reflect the archived history of enslaved Africans and literacy education in Virginia. I expected that the reception of the performance would mirror the facts of this slaveholding society: Given the content of the play, the colonists in attendance must have mused about the captives they had just imported into their midst and feared the potential liaisons of

African men and English women. For their part, I assumed, the Cherokee delegation had to be thinking about the proviso of their treaty with George II that required them to return fleeing Africans to the Carolina authorities. Yet, the enslaved population never rose to the level of a direct statement from any of the parties involved. I had to relinquish the hypothesis that staging Othello's errors with reading aided in resolving a crisis involving the management of Afro-Virginians' acquisition of literacy. Subsequently, I cut a wealth of historically meaningful material on the Bray School, the Society for the Propagation of the Gospel, forged passes, and petitions for emancipation.[11]

4. Since I happen to share his fascination with the black characters of the alphabet, I was never tempted to yoke Melville's literary ambitions or his experiments with form to living people of African descent. However, the case that first taught me to be wary of hauling the nearest racial controversy into a topical reading of a performance involved Abigail Adams. Adams spent not a word on the play's black-white pair in several letters before the performance, but Shakespeareans and biographers have been certain that the performance triggered an indiscreet disclosure of racial animus. A recent biographer, Woody Holton, expresses perplexity at the apparent discordance of Adams's reaction to "Shakespeare's interracial romance," her stated opposition to racial slavery, and her concern for the well-being of Phoebe Abdee, an African woman Abigail's father enslaved for the duration of his life and freed in his will.[12] In an otherwise remarkable biography with new discoveries and incisive reinterpretations of Adams's gender politics, he falters on her engagement with *Othello*. In calling the play an "interracial romance," he would seem to forget that the couple's blissful moments are short-lived, as the play hurls them into a domestic tragedy by the second act. More important still, he overlooks that the performance that Adams attended featured no Africans. The recollection of every African about whom she ever made a fond or disparaging remark does not reflect the associations *she* made while watching *Othello* but *his* anxiety when facing a contemporary imperative to measure the racism in her bones.

While I lost the opportunity to write about the African people and communities I thought would figure in this project, I did learn that the racial work of blackface *Othello* did not have to adhere to the nearest African person. The implications, like Othello's paint, were communicable and could color situations that did not mirror the plot of the play. I had to put aside the hypothesis that cultural production faithfully reflects its context and instead mine the myriad ways in which artists and audiences ignored, refracted, or fled their local situation in the encounter with art. I had to see that an experience of transcendence was not always apolitical, as absorption, transport, and catharsis could provide a welcome, if temporary, reprieve from unpleasant political realities. Aesthetic form, audience enjoyment, and political struggle eventually appeared to me as vectors with different origins and ends that collided in complex and unexpected ways in the moment of performance. Race could appear anywhere temporally, as a precondition, an element, and a product of social activity under examination.

This flickering, unpredictable history of race in formation becomes obscured when the demand for historical rigor warps into an injunction to behave as a defense attorney for white subjects of the past. Endless attempts to assess their intentions occlude a view of the *effects* of living in an Atlantic World of competing European empires. In addition, they conceal that anti-racism could take much stronger forms that are rarely discussed. If the goal were not to defend the dead but to expand our knowledge and capacity to imagine other ways of living together, a comparison of Abigail Adams to the "white Indians of colonial America" or of Melville to John Brown could be illuminating.[13] While an Adams, a Jefferson, or a Montaigne penned their speculations about the character of their racial subordinates, other white people were defecting from colonial settlements or actively working to overthrow the relations of white domination. Without a knowledge of white people who rejected or opposed white authority, our understanding of both historical and contemporary options is compressed. Those who fled whiteness or fought it can turn our attention to what Black and Indigenous people thought of the European systems that attempted to subjugate them—thoughts that typically fall out of the so-called history marshaled to defend canonized whites. Although harder to locate in the victor's archive, the subaltern critique of whiteness has a history of speech, song, and movement—as well as of reading and inscription.[14]

A Final Word from Black Characters

"We are the alphabet; upon us all are constructed." This cryptic, tantalizing pronouncement about the centrality of people racialized as black in the symbolic activities and social architecture of the United States—and, I would argue, the entire Atlantic World—comes from the August 1859 address of George T. Downing to a Convention of Colored Citizens of New England. In one sense, Downing invokes quite a material (and materialist) understanding of black life. He suggests, by analogy, that if the alphabet provides the basic units of complex literary constructions, then persons of Africans replicate that role in the building of social life. In another sense, Downing implies that the fate of a society may be spelled out, with African descendants serving as the letters. Downing insists that Africans on US soil have "an inseparable, providential identity with this country."[15] The invocation of Providence suggests a divine mission to realize "a great principle, the fraternal unity of man"—that is, to achieve at once sociopolitical equality and universal salvation.

Although the major powers of the day declared that liberty was an essential element in their civic scriptures, Downing implied that the bodies of African persons were the real indexes of progress toward the day of jubilee. That embodied witness—and the petitions and memoirs that supplemented it—provided a proliferating counternarrative to religious or secular institutions that claimed to promote universal equality or Christian charity. Whether in or out of bondage, within the United States or elsewhere in diaspora, African bodies bore a kind of "hieroglyphics of the flesh," in Hortense Spillers's chilling phrase: brands, punctures, and disfigurements at the hands of those who enforce racial domination.[16] Thus, to Downing, African bodies formed an "alphabet"—that is, both an organizing principle and a pedagogical tool in instructing all persons in whether slaveocracy and God's will are compatible.

The maiming of black bodies indicated that the great majority of empowered white readers found no compelling contradiction between those hacked human forms, on the one hand, and the Christian texts and sanctified documents of the nation's founding, on the other.[17] With that framing in mind, Downing situates African bodies as esoteric texts that white men must learn to read as portents of the nation's future, as determined by an all-seeing God. *We are the alphabet,* he announces, meaning: *Read what is marked upon us, and you will learn to see your society as God judges it and, thereby, know your character and your eternal fate.*

The pedagogical utility of Downing's alphabet of African bodies becomes clear in an extended metaphor he offers: "All of the great principles of the land are brought out and discussed in connection with the Negro. But for him . . . the great principles [i.e., the issues of universal brotherhood and the rights of human nature], the great ethical school of the times, would be closed for the want of a subject." Here, Downing suggests that while the alphabet enables political debate in the modern public sphere, persons of African descent are the implicit subject of discussion. That the issue of their treatment was so unsettled and unsettling meant that ethical matters were not merely dead philosophy but subjects infused with "vitality." Downing was familiar with the Apostle Paul's discussion of life, death, and letters in Corinthians. "[God] also hath made us able ministers of the new testament; not of the letter, but of the spirit: for the letter killeth, but the spirit giveth life."[18] Through Paul, Downing theorized African persons as *living* testimony, a text neither dead nor mortifying but alive and life-giving to the nation and its inhabitants. He (re)established God as the final reader of that text and suggested that white people enroll in "the great ethical school of the times."

In so doing, Downing grasped and overturned one of the most fundamental claims of slave society—that persons of African descent were monstrous texts of a different kind. I refer, of course, to the oft-discussed "curse of Ham," in which Ham's children were designated as "blacke and loathsome, that it might remain a *spectacle* of disobedience to all the world. And of this blacke and cursed Chus came all these black Moores which are in Africa."[19] The sin of disobedience and its spectacular punishment positions human beings able to escape consignment to blackness—the world—as the readers of God's will and as the executors of His punishment through processes of subjection. Moreover, it makes social hierarchy reproducible across time, as this loathsome blackness "remain[s]," not only in that children inherit the color but also in that its meaning persists, as with any divine text, as circular, self-confirming, and eternal. There is, of course, voluminous commentary on this curse, but what scholars have overlooked is that racial slavery is not just about biological reproduction of the enslaved race but about social reproduction of the *means* of distinguishing one type of human from another. The curse of Ham solicits an audience capable of reading the "spectacle of disobedience" and ordering their society accordingly—and the Hamites are assuredly not among them.

Although Downing's favorite authority is scripture, his Americans of African descent have an uncanny relevance to the moors of the early modern stage, who are creatures of ink, fused with the black characters of the alphabet. When Tamir Rice is rendered as a threatening adult, Michael Brown as a bulletproof wrestler or demon—when such impossible characters enter the state archive as if they existed in the flesh and not just in unoriginal fabrications—the white monopoly on authority that arguably had its high point in the eighteenth century is reproduced again in our own day. When Brett Kavanaugh's credibility remains undiminished even after the Senate concedes the credibility of his accuser, Dr. Christine Blasey, the priority of white men's rank and reputation over that of white women is reaffirmed in the present. Both national and transnational reforms have failed to grasp and uproot epistemic injustice, which calls an undue distribution of property, protection, and pleasure just or inevitable. Even when framed in specifically racist language, the ramifications of epistemic injustice have always been felt beyond the boundaries of Black community. As Blasey, a modern analogue of *Othello*'s women, could easily tell us: it is not only people of African descent who suffer when the authority to characterize is dominated by a fraternal group claiming a monopoly on the means of legitimate representation.

An interpretive community's authority over legitimate representation is not merely a matter of lexicographies and guides to literary style. The ultimate aim is to maintain social relations of exploitation and domination. Much contemporary controversy over race focuses on the sphere of interpersonal expression—utterances of hate speech or of negative stereotypes—without addressing the fact that racial representations are designed to abet maldistribution. Beneficiaries of the Atlantic system have needed to conjure and control essences—exchange value, racial character, gendered honor, literary meaning—that are not universally shared. Because our character system came to us as a means of excluding both testimony and interpretation that would disrupt white domination, we cannot behave now as if literature, theatre, history, and the intellectual disciplines attached to them are neutral and universally available or desirable.

What is needed are narratives from new premises, based not in high humanism but in a lowly material fact: all of us are subjects and objects of characterization, as well as we are readers in the broadest sense of the term. The law of the page in the West has been that whiteness is not signifying material, despite its presence. People marked as black—whatever their ancestry or phenotype—have become akin to those marks, objects of scrutiny and rhetorical instruments in others' political contests. In the chapters of *Inkface,* blackened characters retained their object status. Othello's submission to state command, Desdemona's alienation from her voice, the French opera girls Abigail Adams castigated for indecency, Cherokee ambassadors amazed by the spectacle of English drama, enslaved Africans imagined as perpetually docile students of European tutors: these instances all involve a relegation of some human persons to the status of signifying object and concomitant exclusion from the business of assessing meaning and value. Meanwhile, those with a claim to an unmarked white body enjoyed both a conditional reprieve from being incorporated into the scene of reading and the fantasy of hovering above, contemplating and assessing without being subject to a reciprocal evaluation.

To authorize that returned gaze requires breaking the exclusive authority of whiteness and its protocols over the interpretive enterprise. The project will not be easy, as racial character is resolutely figurative, and therefore always simultaneously material and conceptual. In other words, whiteness is not a biological certainty but a revocable social certification. One can be granted probationary white authority through certain cultural maneuvers; one can fall out of it by acts that have nothing to do with ancestry. Therefore, those of us who wish to create multiracial democracies will have to redistribute interpretive authority to address the foundational exclusions at the inceptions of the character economy. We will have to contemplate things that would seem to make no everyday sense, such as characters—not just literary figures but actual alphanumeric marks and "hieroglyphics of the flesh"—that can turn upon their authors and interrogate them.

Regarding the potential for black character to speak, Fred Moten revisits the famous moment in Marx in which the German theorist describes what a commodity might say. The performance theorist uses the sound of Aunt Hester's screams in Frederick Douglass's slave narratives to insist that speaking commodities *existed*—a discovery with implications not only for human beings reduced to commodities but, by extension, for all that has been reduced to the status of thingness without being granted a hearing. Moten refers to "the revolutionary force of the sensuality that emerges from the sonic event Marx subjunctively produces without sensually discovering."[20] To combat epistemic injustice will require radical reciprocity and revision to admit the significance of unrecognized signs and the insights of unjustly discredited witnesses.

At present, we remain between Shakespeare and Melville—with black characters as either grist for the data mill or as transcendent prophecies. Some may have thought that, with blackface banned, Othello's occupation would be gone. But until we address this injustice at the heart of our collective distribution of social authority, the relations of inkface continue. The eighteenth century's Enlightenment project may be over, but the self-appointed masters stumble blindly forward as Melville's disenchanted nineteenth century drags on at its petty pace.

Notes

Introduction

1. Michael Church, "Otello, English National Opera, Review: A Flawless Production from David Alden," *Independent,* September 15, 2014, https://www
.independent.co.uk/arts-entertainment/classical/reviews/otello-english-national
-opera-review-flawless-production-david-alden-9733718.html. Although I recognize that opera houses were not using the cartoonish makeup of blackface minstrelsy, I use the term "blackface" as a metonym for the ensemble of codes deployed in whites' racial impersonations of dark others. See Ian Smith, "White Skin, Black Masks: Racial Cross-Dressing on the Early Modern Stage," *Renaissance Drama* 32 (2003): 33–68; Richard Blunt, "The Evolution of Blackface Cosmetics on the Early Modern Stage," in *The Materiality of Color: The Production, Circulation, and Application of Dyes and Pigments, 1400–1800,* ed. Andrea Feeser, Maureen Daly Goggin, and Beth Fowkes Tobin (Burlington: Ashgate, 2017); Farah Karim-Cooper, "The Materials of Race: Staging the Black and White Binary in the Early Modern Theatre," in *The Cambridge Companion to Shakespeare and Race,* ed. Ayanna Thompson (New York: Cambridge University Press, 2021), 17–29; Ian Smith, "The Textile Black Body: Race and 'Shadowed Livery' in The Merchant of Venice," in *The Oxford Handbook of Shakespeare and Embodiment: Gender, Sexuality, and Race,* ed. Valerie Traub (Oxford: Oxford University Press, 2016), 290–315.

2. When Verdi undertook his *Otello,* there was a rival opera of that title still in the repertoire—but Rossini's version relied on a French tale. Verdi's collaborator—the librettist, Boito—intended to distinguish their new opera from its predecessor by returning to the Shakespearean source material. See Garry Wills, *Verdi's Shakespeare: Men of the Theater* (New York: Penguin, 2011), 62, 80.

3. Sarah Hatchuel and Nathalie Vienne-Guerrin, eds., *Shakespeare on Screen: Othello* (Cambridge: Cambridge University Press, 2015).

4. Kim Hall's innovative edition of *Othello* links Shakespeare's plays to its burlesque descendants by including nineteenth-century minstrel plays as indispensable contextual materials. Hers is the only edition to do so. Kim F. Hall, ed., *Othello: Texts and Contexts* (Boston: Bedford/St. Martin's, 2006).

5. Michael Cooper, "An 'Otello' without Blackface Highlights an Enduring Tradition in Opera," *New York Times,* September 17, 2015, sec. Arts, https://www
.nytimes.com/2015/09/20/arts/music/an-otello-without-the-blackface-nods-to
-modern-tastes.html. Sher's production proceeds from the influential argument of the cultural critic Leslie Fiedler: "For Shakespeare 'black' does not primarily describe an ethnic distinction (though, of course, Othello is meant to be perceived as an African, thick-lipped as well as dusky-hued), but a difference in hue—and temperament—distinguishing from one another even what we would identify as

members of the same white race.... The blackness of Othello is, in short, primarily symbolic, signifying not that he is of a lesser breed, but rather one at the furthest possible cultural remove from the girl he loves and who loves him." See Fiedler, *The Stranger in Shakespeare* (New York: Stein and Day, 1972), 171, 173.

6. A similar whitewashing of Shakespeare's play—a move to casting white actors—would likely occur in the theatre if not for two complicating factors. First, actors of African descent would balk at losing one of the few significant Shakespearean roles for which they will be seriously considered. Second, majoritarian theatres have come to rely on *Othello* to advertise that they hire nonwhite actors and stage plays that confront topical issues such as racism and domestic violence.

7. This tactic, of course, reinforces the sense that to be human is to be white, as if some other species undertook the whole business of establishing and resisting racial hierarchies. The classical formulation of this enforced impasse between blackness and humanity is Frantz Fanon, *Black Skin, White Masks* (1952; New York: Grove Press, 1994).

8. Casey Chalk, "Circumscribing Shakespeare," *American Conservative*, February 2, 2022.

9. See William Shakespeare, *Othello*, ed. Edward Pechter, 2nd ed. (New York: W. W. Norton, 2016), xi.

10. Leslie Fiedler, "Come Back to the Raft Ag'in, Huck Honey!," *Partisan Review* 15, no. 6 (June 1948): 670 (italics in original).

11. George Vandenhoff, *Leaves from an Actor's Note-Book* (New York: D. Appleton, 1860), 109.

12. Frank Benson, *My Memoirs* (London: Ernest Bunn Limited, 1930), 218; quoted in Paul Menzer, *Anecdotal Shakespeare: A New Performance History* (New York: Bloomsbury Arden Shakespeare, 2015), 89.

13. Arthur Murphy, *The Life of David Garrick* (Dublin: B. Smith, 1801), 105 (my emphasis). The biographer's choice of "obscure" suggests concealment in a general sense, but also in the specific sense of the paint that leaves him "jet black." "Obscure" derives from the Latin *obscurus* (dark).

14. Menzer, *Anecdotal Shakespeare*, chap. 2; Brigitte Fielder, "Blackface Desdemona: Theorizing Race on the Nineteenth-Century American Stage," *Theatre Annual: A Journal of Theatre & Performance of the Americas* 70 (2017): 39–59.

15. I discuss this play more fully in chap. 1.

16. Quoted in Menzer, *Anecdotal Shakespeare*, 67.

17. I am grateful to Patricia Akhimie for sharing this image from her research. *Mr. Booth, as Othello [in Shakespeare's Othello, V, 2] Smudges the Face of the Fair Desdemona in Kissing Her*, n.d., graphic, Folger Library ART vol. a6, no. 87.

18. Ellen Terry, *The Story of My Life* (New York: Doubleday, 1908), 204; quoted in Menzer, *Anecdotal Shakespeare*, 68.

19. Julie Miller, "Maggie Smith Had No Patience for Laurence Olivier's Diva Antics," *Vanity Fair*, accessed November 11, 2019, https://www.vanityfair.com/hollywood/2018/09/maggie-smith-laurence-olivier-othello-tea-with-the-dames-joan

-plowright-judi-dench-eileen-atkins; Roger Michell, dir., *Tea with the Dames,* documentary, 2018.

20. Stuart Burge, dir., *Othello,* 1965. On the causes of audience laughter at *Othello,* see Robert Hornback, "Emblems of Folly in the First Othello: Renaissance Black-face, Moor's Coat, and 'Muckender,'" *Comparative Drama* 35, no. 1 (Spring 2001): 69–99. On the somber tone that accompanied the transfer of Shakespeare from popular to elite culture in the United States, see Lawrence Levine, *Highbrow/Lowbrow: The Emergence of Cultural Hierarchy in America* (Cambridge, Mass.: Harvard University Press, 1990), chap. 1.

21. John Coleman, *Players and Playwrights I Have Known: A Review of the English Stage from 1840 to 1880* (London: Chatto and Windus, 1888) 1:41; quoted in Lois Potter, *Othello* (New York: Manchester University Press, 2002), 31. On a bad night near the end of his career, the legendary actor Charles Macready played Othello while frail and hoarse, inspiring the title character of Herman Melville's "Benito Cereno," the subject of this book's final chapter.

22. *Othello* III.iii.357; *Macbeth* V.v.25. Both from G. Blakemore Evans et al., eds., *The Riverside Shakespeare* (Boston: Houghton Mifflin Company, 1974). Except when I need to refer to peculiarities of early modern editions, I will use Evans throughout to cite Shakespeare. On the psychic life of the white actor playing Othello, see Imtiaz Habib, "Racial Impersonation on the Elizabethan Stage: The Case of Shakespeare Playing Aaron," *Medieval and Renaissance Drama in England* 20 (2007): 17–45; Joel B. Altman, *The Improbability of Othello: Rhetorical Anthropology and Shakespearean Selfhood* (Chicago: University of Chicago Press, 2010), chap. 11.

23. Rebecca Schneider, *Performing Remains: Art and War in Times of Theatrical Reenactment* (New York: Routledge, 2011).

24. Charles Mathews, *The Life and Correspondence of Charles Mathews, the Elder, Comedian* (London: Routledge, Warne, and Routledge, 1860), 218 (italics altered from original). See also Tracy C. Davis, "Acting Black, 1824: Charles Mathews's Trip to America," *Theatre Journal* 63, no. 2 (2011): 163–89.

25. Two exceptions include the famous "photonegative Othello" of 1997 starring Patrick Stewart and an early episode of the hit sitcom *Cheers.* See Denise Albanese, "Black and White, and Dread All Over: The Shakespeare Theatre's 'Photonegative' *Othello* and the Body of Desdemona," in *A Feminist Companion to Shakespeare* (Malden, Mass.: John Wiley, 2016), 244–65; "Homicidal Ham," *Cheers* (NBC, October 27, 1983).

26. Mary Floyd-Wilson, *English Ethnicity and Race in Early Modern Drama* (New York: Cambridge University Press, 2003), 1.

27. In an essay that deserves to be better known, Charles Lower argues that scholars were hasty to proclaim the nineteenth century a "Bronze Age" in which blackened Othellos were proscribed. However, for my purposes, the precise color of the makeup is of little concern. The shade of the stage paint does not alter its transferability, and racial blackness has been ascribed to a range of hues. See Charles B. Lower, "Othello as Black on Southern Stages, Then and Now," in *Shakespeare in*

the South: Essays on Performance, ed. Philip C. Kolin (Jackson: University Press of Mississippi, 1983), 199–228.

28. Lower, "Othello as Black," 204.

29. Ayanna Thompson, *Performing Race and Torture on the Early Modern Stage* (New York: Routledge, 2007), 27 (emphasis in original). Scholars have made revelatory arguments by granting primacy to performance practice in their studies of race in early modern drama. See V. M. Vaughan, *Performing Blackness on English Stages, 1500–1800* (New York: Cambridge University Press, 2005), chap. 2; Dympna Callaghan, *Shakespeare without Women: Representing Gender and Race on the Renaissance Stage* (New York: Routledge, 2000); Robert Hornback, *Racism and Early Blackface Comic Traditions: From the Old World to the New* (New York: Palgrave Macmillan, 2018); Andrea Stevens, *Inventions of the Skin: The Painted Body in Early English Drama* (Edinburgh: Edinburgh University Press, 2013); Ian Smith, "The Textile Black Body: Race and 'Shadowed Livery' in The Merchant of Venice," in *The Oxford Handbook of Shakespeare and Embodiment: Gender, Sexuality, and Race,* edited by Valerie Traub, 290–315 (Oxford: Oxford University Press, 2016).

30. Habib, "Racial Impersonation on the Elizabethan Stage," 17.

31. Students sometimes instinctively refer to printed plays as "novels," a slip that indicates the novel's dominance among contemporary literary genres.

32. Miles Grier, "Are Shakespeare's Plays Racially Progressive?: The Answer Is in Our Hands," in *The Cambridge Companion to Shakespeare and Race,* ed. Ayanna Thompson (New York: Cambridge University Press, 2021), 237–53.

33. I. Smith, "White Skin, Black Masks," 34. On inwardness (rather than interiority) as a quality of Shakespearean characters, see Katharine Eisaman Maus, *Inwardness and Theater in the English Renaissance* (Chicago: University of Chicago Press, 1995). Accepting that Shakespeare may not have aimed for full or round characters (and that his audiences may not have expected them) requires an understanding that criteria for judging fictional characters have been unstable and evolving. See Deidre Shauna Lynch, *The Economy of Character: Novels, Market Culture, and the Business of Inner Meaning* (Chicago: University of Chicago Press, 1998); Margreta de Grazia, "Hamlet's Thoughts and Antics," *Early Modern Culture* 2 (2000), https://earlymodernculture.org/1-2/degrazia.html.

34. I. Smith, "White Skin, Black Masks," 34–35 (my emphasis).

35. Hortense J. Spillers, "Mama's Baby, Papa's Maybe: An American Grammar Book," *Diacritics* 17, no. 2 (Summer 1987): 65.

36. Toni Morrison, *Playing in the Dark: Whiteness and the Literary Imagination* (New York: Vintage Books, 1993), 6–7.

37. Jyotsna Singh, "Othello's Identity, Postcolonial Theory, and Contemporary African Rewritings of *Othello,*" in *Women, "Race," and Writing in the Early Modern Period,* ed. Margo Hendricks and Patricia Parker (New York: Routledge, 1994), 288 (my emphasis).

38. Matthieu Chapman asserts that "since the primary encounters" with Arabs and Europeans, Black Africans have been cast "immediately and without deliberation" as "the ontological Slave" and granted neither "participation in or resistance to the

varying semiotic structures of humanity." Chapman theorizes two central elements of what I am now calling inkface: the exclusion of blackened peoples from interpretive community and the availability of black flesh to serve whatever meaning-making purposes others devise for it. I depart from him only insofar as I pursue a history in which dominion is not so easily accomplished and an ongoing struggle over the means of representation can be seen.

39. Erika T. Lin, *Shakespeare and the Materiality of Performance* (New York: Palgrave Macmillan, 2012), 8.

40. Anthony Gerard Barthelemy, *Black Face, Maligned Race: The Representation of Blacks in English Drama from Shakespeare to Southerne* (Baton Rouge: Louisiana State University Press, 1987); Callaghan, *Shakespeare without Women.*

41. Callaghan, *Shakespeare without Women,* chap. 3; Morwenna Carr, "Material/Blackness: Race and Its Material Reconstructions on the Seventeenth-Century English Stage," *Early Theatre* 20, no. 1 (July 2017).

42. "Black, Adj. and n.," in *OED Online,* http://www.oed.com/view/Entry/19670. To the contrary, ink historian Thaddeus Davids suggests that blae[c]k was the word for ink itself in Scandinavian languages but does not elaborate on his related observation that "black is and always has been preferred in ordinary uses." See Thaddeus Davids, *History of Ink, Including Its Etymology, Chemistry, and Bibliography* (New York: Thaddeus Davids & Co, 1856), 9, 7.

43. *La chanson de Roland* is an eleventh-century French text that testifies to the etymological roots of blackness in ink. In *La chanson,* Saracens prove blacker than ink. Further research will determine whether medieval sources in French or English ever used ink not as a point of comparison but as a constitutional element of those racialized as black: "When Roland sees that race of infidels / —Each one of them is blacker far than ink / Their teeth the only feature that shows white." *The Song of Roland,* trans. Howard S. Robertson (London, 1972), ll. 1932–34. See discussion in Barthelemy, *Black Face, Maligned Race,* 11.

44. Ben Jonson, *The Masque of Blackness* (London, 1604), f.3, f.5, [JnB 683] [British Library MS Royal 17 B XXXI].

45. For a fuller reading, see Miles P. Grier, "Inkface: The Slave Stigma in England's Early Imperial Imagination," in *Scripturalizing the Human: The Written as the Political,* ed. Vincent L. Wimbush (New York: Routledge, 2015), 193–220. I wrote this essay pondering the serious complications that the nymphs' inky and transferable color pose for Mary Floyd-Wilson's argument that to "blacken" and to "blanch" refer to the "immediate politics" of "the union between Scotland and England" under James I. The Aethiopian nymphs, she claims, represent not Africans but "Scottish citizens . . . subject to James's" legal powers. Like Pechter, Floyd-Wilson prefers to see these nymphs with her "mind's eye." Yet, Jonson's language and the stubbornness of the paint insist on a set of African associations for the masquing women. The vehicle of a metaphor does not evaporate after its tenor is uncovered. See Floyd-Wilson, "Temperature, Temperance, and Racial Difference in Ben Jonson's *The Masque of Blackness,*" *English Literary Renaissance* 28, no. 2 (1998): 191–92. As Stevens notes, the makeup was so difficult to remove that the

women would not appear restored to whiteness until the sequel, *The Masque of Beauty.* See Stevens, *Inventions of the Skin,* 89.

46. J. P. Collier identified *Lust's Dominion* as *The Spanish Moor's Tragedy,* which Henslowe purchased from Dekker, Haughton, and Day on February 13, 1600. See Robert Dodsley et al., eds., *A Select Collection of Old Plays. In Twelve Volumes,* vol. 2 (London: S. Prowett, 1825), 311. See also Philip Henslowe, *Henslowe's Diary,* ed. Walter W. Greg (London: A. H. Bullen, 1904), 131.

47. On the necessity of galls in ink receipts (recipes) and their cultural significance, see Tanya Pollard, "Spelling the Body," in *Environment and Embodiment in Early Modern England,* ed. Mary Floyd-Wilson and Garrett A. Sullivan, Early Modern Literature in History (London: Palgrave Macmillan, 2007), 171–86; Alan Stewart, *Shakespeare's Letters* (New York: Oxford University Press, 2009), 48. On Eleazar's blackness, see the excellent Vanessa Corredera, "Complex Complexions: The Facial Signification of the Black Other in Lust's Dominion," in *Shakespeare and the Power of the Face,* ed. James A. Knapp (New York: Routledge, 2015), 93–114; I. Smith, "White Skin, Black Masks," 47.

48. John Marston et al., *Lust's Dominion, or, The Lascivious Queen: A Tragedie* (London: Printed for F.K. and are to be sold by Robert Pollard, 1657), 13. See also I. Smith, "White Skin, Black Masks," 33, 46. Smith examines the recurrence of dye; I turn the focus to the adjective "inky."

49. John R. Elliott, "Mr. Moore's Revels: A 'Lost' Oxford Masque," *Renaissance Quarterly* 37, no. 3 (October 1984): 412.

50. The most incisive and generative accounts of textile blackness are those of Ian Smith. See his "White Skin, Black Masks" and "Othello's Black Handkerchief," *Shakespeare Quarterly* 64, no. 1 (2013): 1–25.

51. Elliott, "Mr. Moore's Revels," ll. 19–20. All subsequent references appear in parentheses in the text. Though it is tempting to think of the buckram coats as an animal reference, the *OED* prefers the French form *boquerant* (for a costly and delicate fabric made of cotton or linen) to the German *bock* (for goat's hair). See "Buckram, n.," in *OED Online* (accessed November 23, 2019). Nevertheless, in a masque overflowing with puns, it is possible that all senses, including that of Othello as "black *ram* tupping . . . [a] white ewe," were in play (I.i.88–89). On tupping, see Jeffrey Masten, *Queer Philologies: Sex, Language, and Affect in Shakespeare's Time* (Philadelphia: University of Pennsylvania Press, 2016), chap. 8.

52. Barthelemy and Vitkus are notable among those who attend to the imprecision of the term "moor." In his pioneering study, Barthelemy notes that "moor" has roots in the Greek *maurus,* meaning "dark." He then focuses on depictions of black persons, as a rough synonym for sub-Saharan Africans. Vitkus takes the opposite approach, acknowledging the ethnic imprecision of "moor" but then suggesting that the proper frame for understanding Othello is not "race" but "religion." See Barthelemy, *Black Face, Maligned Race,* 8–9; Daniel Vitkus, "*Othello,* Islam, and the Noble Moor: Spiritual Identity and the Performance of Blackness on the Early Modern Stage," in *The Cambridge Companion to Shakespeare and Religion,* ed. Hannibal Hamlin (Cambridge: Cambridge University Press, 2019), 218–33.

53. Morrison insists that the Africanist presence in American letters provides in-exhaustible "service." See her *Playing in the Dark,* 8, 32, 45, passim.

54. Stevens provides an illuminating discussion of painting onstage as exposing offstage preparations; see *Inventions of the Skin,* 13. Vaughan is concerned with establishing that the material in the inkhorn was not ink; see V. M. Vaughan, *Performing Blackness on English Stages,* 12. Vaughan is almost certainly correct, but the substance was represented as an ink and thus demands interpretation as such.

55. Since the rediscovery of this masque, scholars have paid extensive attention to its repetition of the trope that Africans are especially close cousins of apes. The stage property of the inkhorn has received less attention. Kim F. Hall, "Troubling Doubles: Apes, Africans, and Blackface in Mr. Moore's Revels," in *Race, Ethnicity, and Power in the Renaissance,* ed. Joyce Green MacDonald (Cranbury, N.J.: Fairleigh Dickinson University Press, 1997), 120–44.

56. Matthieu Chapman, *Anti-Black Racism in Early Modern English Drama: The Other "Other"* (New York: Routledge, 2016), 119.

57. In *Black Shakespeare,* Ian Smith trains his focus on a white reader-critic of Shakespearean books whose interpretive protocols were "formed by a history of structural systems ranging from the slave economy and its social legacies to congressional legislation about immigration and racialized citizenship in the Unites States." Smith, *Black Shakespeare* (New York: Cambridge University Press, 2022), 33. I agree with Smith's premises, but I hope to enlarge the scope beyond the United States and to place literary interpretation in a larger system of character assessment that also included public playgoing.

58. Although he omits the red accent, I largely concur with Michel Pastoureau, who claims: "All or almost all medieval images were polychromatic. The great majority of images in the modern period, circulated in and outside of books, were black and white. This signified a cultural revolution of considerable scope not only in the domain of knowledge but also in the domain of sensibility." Michel Pastoureau, *Black: The History of a Color,* English language ed. (Princeton: Princeton University Press, 2009), 114. On the use of red in early modern print culture, see Bianca F.-C. Calabresi, "'His Idoliz'd Book': Milton Blood, and Rubrication," in *The Book in History, the Book as History: New Intersections of the Material Text. Essays in Honor of David Scott Kastan,* ed. Heidi Brayman, Jesse Lander, and Zachary Lesser (New Haven: Yale University Press, 2016), 207–32.

59. Sara B. T. Thiel, "'Cushion Come Forth': Materializing Pregnancy on the Stuart Stage," in *Stage Matters: Props, Bodies and Space in Shakespearean Performance,* ed. Annalisa Castaldo and Rhonda Knight (Vancouver: Fairleigh Dickinson University Press, 2018), 143–58.

60. James Daybell, *The Material Letter in Early Modern England* (New York: Palgrave Macmillan, 2012), 32–33; Joshua Calhoun, *The Nature of the Page: Poetry, Papermaking, and the Ecology of Texts in Renaissance England* (Philadelphia: University of Pennsylvania Press, 2020), chap. 1.

61. For a fuller reading, see Miles Grier, "Black/White," 325–33. I wish to correct an error in the earlier essay: While the Romans never acknowledge that the child has

a sex or noble lineage, his moorish father does once refer to him as a "boy . . . of royal blood." (V.i.49).

62. William Kemp, *Kemps Nine Daies Vvonder* [. . .], 1–2.

63. I thank Robert Hornback for this reference and recommend his essay. See "'Extravagant and Wheeling Strangers': Early Blackface Dancing Fools, Racial Impersonation, and the Limits of Identification," *Exemplaria* 20, no. 2 (Summer 2008): 197–222.

64. Robert Armin, *The History of the Tvvo Maids of More-Clacke* [. . .] (1609). For a discussion of Armin's emphasis on his literacy and erudition, see Tiffany Stern, *Making Shakespeare: From Stage to Page* (London: Routledge, 2004), 68.

65. The remarkable work on early modern English letters has not often considered whether letterwriting and reading assumed or summoned a white audience. See Alan Stewart and Heather Wolfe, *Letterwriting in Renaissance England* (Seattle: University of Washington Press, 2005); Lisa Hopkins, "Reading between the Sheets: Letters in Shakespearean Tragedy," *Critical Survey* 14, no. 3 (2002): 5–15; Frances N. Teague, *Shakespeare's Speaking Properties* (Lewisburg, Pa.: Bucknell University Press, 1991). One tantalizing exception: Lynn S. Meskill, "The Characters of Posterity in Jonson's *The Masque of Blacknesse* and Shakespeare's *Antony and Cleopatra*," *Huntington Library Quarterly* 73, no. 1 (March 2010): 37–56. Scholars of the conquest of the New World have been much more attentive to literacy as a tool for imperial race-making. See Walter D. Mignolo, *The Darker Side of the Renaissance: Literacy, Territoriality, & Colonization*, 2nd ed. (1995; Ann Arbor: University of Michigan Press, 2003); Joanne Rappaport and Tom Cummins, *Beyond the Lettered City: Indigenous Literacies in the Andes* (Durham: Duke University Press, 2011); Lisa Brooks, *The Common Pot: The Recovery of Native Space in the Northeast* (Minneapolis: University of Minnesota Press, 2008); Andrew Newman, "Captive on the Literacy Frontier," *Early American Literature* 38, no. 1 (2003): 31–65.

66. I. Smith, "White Skin, Black Masks," 37. Arthur Little concurs: "More often than not, Others assume a place in dominant discourse less through any kind of positivist model and more through associative thinking—and dissociative place." See his *Shakespeare Jungle Fever: National-Imperial Re-Visions of Race, Rape, and Sacrifice* (Stanford: Stanford University Press, 2000), 7.

67. Although I range beyond sonnets and emphasize the inky origins of blackness more than she does, I remain indebted to Kim Hall's field-defining, black feminist argument that English sonneteers presumed blackness ugly and then took beautifying it as a test of their poetic prowess. See her *Things of Darkness: Economies of Race and Gender in Early Modern England* (Ithaca: Cornell University Press, 1996), chap. 2.

68. Miles P. Grier, "Reading Black Characters: Staging Literacy, 1604–1855" (PhD diss., New York University, 2010), 201, 333; Carr, "Material/Blackness."

69. John Cleveland, *The Character of a London-Diurnall: With Severall Select Poems* (London: [n.p.]: 1647).

70. *The Works of George Herbert*, ed. F. E. Hutchinson (London: Oxford University Press, 1945), 209. See also Hall, *Things of Darkness*, 121–22; John T. Gilmore,

"Æthiopissæ: The Classical Tradition, Neo-Latin Verse and Images of Race in George Herbert and Vincent Bourne," *Classical Receptions Journal* 1, no. 1 (January 2009): 73–86.

71. Thomas Browne, *Pseudodoxia Epidemica, or, Enquiries into Very Many Received Tenents and Commonly Presumed Truths* (London: Printed by T.H. for E. Dod, 1646), 336. For discussion of this passage, see I. Smith, "White Skin, Black Masks," 54; Siobhán Collins and Louise Denmead, "'There Is All Africa [. . .] Within Us': Language, Generation and Alchemy in Browne's Explication of Blackness," in *"A Man Very Well Studyed": New Contexts for Thomas Browne,* ed. Kathryn Murphy and Richard Todd (Leidin: Brill, 2008), 141.

72. John Bulwer, *Anthropometamorphosis* [. . .] (London: Printed by William Hunt, 1653), 469.

73. I write to challenge Bartels, who claims that early modern English people "anxiously repeated" similar "stereotypes" about Africans, sodomites, and Jews but never gave credence to these "imaginative" projections. Her insistence that the English did not really *believe* anti-black stereotypes fuels her influential claim that race is an anachronistic frame for analysis of *Othello.* The results are visible in Emily C. Bartels, "Othello and Africa: Postcolonialism Reconsidered," *William and Mary Quarterly* 54, no. 1 (January 1997): 53; Floyd-Wilson, *English Ethnicity and Race,* chap. 6; Michael Neill, "'Mulattos,' 'Blacks,' and 'Indian Moors': Othello and Early Modern Constructions of Human Difference," *Shakespeare Quarterly* 49, no. 4 (December 1998): 361–74.

74. Little, *Shakespeare Jungle Fever,* 8.

75. Hall, *Things of Darkness.*

76. James Howell, *Epistolæ Ho-Elianæ Familiar Letters Domestic and Forren* [. . .] (London: Printed by W.H. for Humphrey Mosely, 1650), b2v (italics in original).

77. B. K. Adams, "Fair/Foul," in *Shakespeare/Text: Contemporary Readings in Textual Studies, Editing and Performance,* ed. Claire M. L. Bourne (New York: The Arden Shakespeare, 2021), 29–49.

78. Some might object that Aaron, Shakespeare's first black moor, constitutes a glaring exception to my claim. Sale and Parker argue persuasively that Aaron is the most perceptive reader in *Titus Andronicus.* Yet, as well as he understands written character, his insistence on the identical nature of his interior and exterior suggests an incapacity to dissemble. Like Othello and Caliban, he lacks the player's capacity to change his *own* character, so crucial to self-fashioning. See Carolyn Sale, "Black Aeneas: Race, English Literary History, and the 'Barbarous' Poetics of *Titus Andronicus,*" *Shakespeare Quarterly* 62, no. 1 (2011): 25–52; Patricia Parker, "Shakespeare's Sound Government: Sound Defects, Polyglot Sounds, and Sounding Out," *Oral Tradition* 24, no. 2 (2009): 359–72; Stephen Greenblatt, *Renaissance Self-Fashioning: From More to Shakespeare* (Chicago: University of Chicago Press, 1980); Joseph R. Roach, *The Player's Passion: Studies in the Science of Acting* (Ann Arbor: University of Michigan Press, 1993), chap. 1, esp. 30; Grier, "Reading Black Characters," 209–13.

79. On whiteness as a redistribution of aristocratic liberties, see Michal Jan Rozbicki, "Between Private and Public Spheres: Liberty as Cultural Property in

Eighteenth-Century British America," in *Cultures and Identities in Colonial British America,* ed. Robert Olwell and Alan Tully (Baltimore: Johns Hopkins University Press, 2006), 293–318.

80. Halpern, *The Poetics of Primitive Accumulation.*

81. Étienne Balibar, "The Nation Form: History and Ideology," *Review of the Fernand Braudel Center* 13, no. 3 (July 1990): 358.

82. Although working on a later period, Edward Said inspired many early modernists by identifying seizure of the authority to represent that established Europe's imperial knowledge and the practice of fraternal citation that sustains it. See Edward W. Said, *Orientalism* (New York: Vintage, 1979), 15. See also Israel Burshatin, "The Moor in the Text: Metaphor, Emblem, and Silence," *Critical Inquiry* 12, no. 1 (October 1985): 98–118; Josiah Blackmore, *Moorings: Portuguese Expansion and the Writing of Africa* (Minneapolis: University of Minnesota Press, 2008).

83. Across numerous stunning essays and a monograph, Hornback has demonstrated that a presumption of intellectual deficiency is fundamental to anti-black racism. Positioned as mentally deficient, blackened persons lose their capacity to participate in the social activities of valuation and interpretation that compose official social life. See, e.g., Robert Hornback, "The Folly of Racism: Enslaving Blackface and the 'Natural' Fool Tradition," *Medieval and Renaissance Drama in England* 20 (January 2007): 46–84; Hornback, "Beyond Good and Evil Symbolism: Allegories and Metaphysics of Blackfaced Folly from Augustine to Fanon," in *Racism and Early Blackface Comic Traditions: From the Old World to the New,* Palgrave Studies in Theatre and Performance History (Cham: Springer International Publishing, 2018), 71–107.

84. On the inability to separate race and religion as social categories, see Dennis Austin Britton, *Becoming Christian: Race, Reformation, and Early Modern English Romance* (New York: Fordham University Press, 2014); Leerom Medovoi, "Dogma-Line Racism: Islamophobia and the Second Axis of Race," *Social Text* 30, no. 2 (111) (June 2012): 43–74; Ambereen Dadabhoy, "Two Faced: The Problem of Othello's Visage," in *Othello: The State of Play,* ed. Lena Cowen Orlin (London: Bloomsbury, 2014), 121–48.

85. Thelwell challenges recuperative readings of classic blackface minstrelsy, arguing that white male minstrels were far more interested in ridicule and denigration than in class solidarity with Black people. See Chinua Thelwell, *Exporting Jim Crow: Blackface Minstrelsy in South Africa and Beyond* (Amherst: University of Massachusetts Press, 2020).

86. Miranda Fricker, *Epistemic Injustice: Power and the Ethics of Knowing* (Oxford: Oxford University Press, 2009), 1.

87. Ralph Ellison glosses white and black Americans as "the seer and the seen," the title he gives a group of essays that skewer schools of sociology meant to pathologize black life. See Ellison, *Shadow and Act* (New York: Random House, 1964).

88. I can only gesture at a few influential works here, representative of periodizing tendencies in the history of ideas. See Winthrop D. Jordan, *White over Black: American Attitudes toward the Negro, 1550–1812* (New York: W. W. Norton, 1977);

Stephen Jay Gould, *The Mismeasure of Man* (New York: W. W. Norton, 1996); Andrew Valls, ed., *Race and Racism in Modern Philosophy* (Ithaca, N.Y.: Cornell University Press, 2005); A. Leon Higginbotham, *In the Matter of Color: Race and the American Legal Process: The Colonial Period* (New York: Oxford University Press, 1978); Kathleen M. Brown, *Good Wives, Nasty Wenches, and Anxious Patriarchs: Gender, Race, and Power in Colonial Virginia* (Chapel Hill: University of North Carolina Press, 1996); Ibram X. Kendi, *Stamped from the Beginning: The Definitive History of Racist Ideas in America* (New York: Nation Books, 2016); Ivan Hannaford, *Race: The History of an Idea in the West* (Baltimore: Johns Hopkins University Press, 1996).

89. I am using performance to get at what scholars have to come to call "folk concepts" of race—the common sense the comes before and runs beneath expert discourses. See George T. Newberry, "A 'Folk Biology' of Racial Theory? Psychology and the Historiography of 18th-Century Race Thought," *History Compass,* October 2018, 1–11; Quayshawn Spencer, "Racial Realism II: Are Folk Races Real?," *Philosophy Compass* 13, no. 1 (January 2018).

90. Charles W. Mills, "White Ignorance," in *Race and Epistemologies of Ignorance,* ed. Shannon Sullivan and Nancy Tuana (Albany: State University of New York Press, 2007), 13–38; Lewis R. Gordon, *Bad Faith and Antiblack Racism* (Atlantic Highlands, N.J.: Humanities Press, 1995); Briana Toole, "What Lies Beneath: The Epistemic Roots of White Supremacy," in *Political Epistemology,* ed. Michael Hannon and Elizabeth Edenberg (Oxford: Oxford University Press, 2021), 76–94.

91. This line has become the most quoted of the "I Have a Dream Speech," delivered at the March on Washington for Jobs and Freedom on August 28, 1963. See Martin Luther King, Jr., *A Testament of Hope: The Essential Writings and Speeches,* ed. James M. Washington (San Francisco: Harper Collins, 2003), 217–21.

92. Although journalists employed "postracial" to proclaim the dawn of a blissful, functioning, multiracial democracy, the legal theorist Derrick Bell coined the term to describe a more unsettling resolution to the "negro problem" in the United States—selling African Americans to alien invaders to pay off the national debt. See Bell, "After We're Gone: Prudent Speculations on America in a Post-Racial Epoch," *Saint Louis University Law Journal* 34 (1990): 393–405. For a trenchant use of "postracial" as an analytic in early modern English studies, see Kyle Grady, "Othello, Colin Powell, and Post-Racial Anachronisms," *Shakespeare Quarterly* 67, no. 1 (2016): 68–83.

93. "Character, n.," in *OED Online,* pt. 9a, accessed February 6, 2018 (my emphasis). The *OED* also records an early instance of inkface, Christopher Marlowe's use of character in *1 Tamburlaine:* "Art thou but captain of a thousand horse / That by characters graven in thy brows, / And by thy martial face and stout aspect, / Deserv'st to have the leading of an host?" The very features of the brow—along with the face and comportment—become recognizable symbols of the inner desert of military promotion.

94. Mario DiGangi, *Sexual Types: Embodiment, Agency, and Dramatic Character from Shakespeare to Shirley* (Philadelphia: University of Pennsylvania Press, 2011);

Urvashi Chakravarty, "More Than Kin, Less Than Kind: Similitude, Strangeness, and Early Modern English Homonationalisms," *Shakespeare Quarterly* 67, no. 1 (2016): 14–29.

95. The sociologists Omi and Winant propose that a racial project "is simultaneously an interpretation, representation, or explanation of racial dynamics, and an effort to reorganize and redistribute resources along particular racial lines." Michael Omi and Howard Winant, *Racial Formation in the United States: From the 1960s to the 1990s,* 2nd ed. (New York: Routledge, 1994), 56. I would add that the medium of character provides the passageway between the representational and the material, as character itself encompasses abstract and particular, visible and invisible, sign and referent.

96. Patricia Akhimie, *Shakespeare and the Cultivation of Difference: Race and Conduct in the Early Modern World* (New York: Routledge, 2018). On blackness as a sonic and linguistic phenomenon, see Ian Smith, *Race and Rhetoric in the Renaissance: Barbarian Errors* (New York: Palgrave Macmillan, 2009); Jennifer Lynn Stoever, *The Sonic Color Line: Race and the Cultural Politics of Listening* (New York: New York University Press, 2016); Guthrie P. Ramsey Jr., *Race Music: Black Cultures from Bebop to Hip-Hop* (Berkeley: University of California Press, 2004); Nicholas R. Jones, *Staging Habla de Negros: Radical Performances of the African Diaspora in Early Modern Spain* (University Park: Pennsylvania State University Press, 2019); Marcyliena Morgan, *Language, Discourse and Power in African American Culture* (New York: Cambridge University Press, 2002); Garrett Albert Duncan, "Discourse, Cultural Imperialism, Black Culture and Language Research in the United States," in *Discourse as Cultural Struggle,* ed. Xu Shi (Hong Kong: Hong Kong University Press, 2006), 142–53.

97. A. L. Higginbotham, *In the Matter of Color;* Ashley Montagu, *Man's Most Dangerous Myth: The Fallacy of Race* (New York: Columbia University Press, 1945); Brown, *Good Wives, Nasty Wenches;* David R. Roediger, *How Race Survived US History: From the American Revolution to the Present* (New York: Verso, 2008).

98. On the methods by which agents sustain white supremacy as an epistemological system, see Toole, "What Lies Beneath," 85–90.

99. I. Smith, *Race and Rhetoric in the Renaissance.*

100. Vincent J. Rosivach, "Enslaving 'Barbaroi' and the Athenian Ideology of Slavery," *Historia* 48, no. 2 (1999): 129–57; Rosivach, "Agricultural Slavery in the Northern Colonies and in Classical Athens: Some Comparisons," *Comparative Studies in Society and History* 35, no. 3 (July 1993): 551–67.

101. On Britons as Roman slaves and budding imperialists in their own right, see Sale, "Black Aeneas." Although Gillies deems the term "race" anachronistic, the figure of the barbarian at the center of his study is raced—tattooed—and deemed less capable of knowledge. See John Gillies, *Shakespeare and the Geography of Difference* (New York: Cambridge University Press, 1994).

102. Karen E. Fields and Barbara J. Fields, *Racecraft: The Soul of Inequality in American Life* (New York: Verso, 2012), 25.

103. Historians who engage Shakespeare and his contemporaries have addressed theatre as a site of spectacle or as an echo of the Bible or scientific thinking but not

as a medium that made unique and necessary affordances to racial ideology. See Jordan, *White over Black,* 37–38; Kendi, *Stamped from the Beginning,* 34–37. Smallwood and Morgan invoke the stage to deem it a minor site of racial construction when compared to slave markets or double-entry books. See Stephanie E. Smallwood, *Saltwater Slavery: A Middle Passage from Africa to American Diaspora* (Cambridge, Mass.: Harvard University Press, 2007), 159; Jennifer L. Morgan, *Reckoning with Slavery: Gender, Kinship, and Capitalism in the Early Black Atlantic* (Durham: Duke University Press, 2021), 13.

104. Histories that ground the origins of race in law, science, or philosophy include Thomas F. Gossett, *Race: The History of an Idea in America* (New York: Oxford University Press, 1963); George M. Fredrickson, *The Black Image in the White Mind: The Debate on Afro-American Character and Destiny* (New York: Harper & Row, 1971); Edmund S. Morgan, *American Slavery, American Freedom* (New York: W. W. Norton, 1975); A. L. Higginbotham, *In the Matter of Color;* T. H. Breen, *Myne Owne Ground: Race and Freedom on Virginia's Eastern Shore, 1640–1676* (New York: Oxford University Press, 1982); Gould, *The Mismeasure of Man;* Hannaford, *Race;* Nicholas Hudson, "From 'Nation' to 'Race': The Origin of Racial Classification in Eighteenth-Century Thought," *Eighteenth-Century Studies* 29, no. 3 (1996): 247–64; Kirsten Fischer, *Suspect Relations: Sex, Race, and Resistance in Colonial North Carolina* (Ithaca: Cornell University Press, 2001); Robert Miles and Malcolm Brown, *Racism* (New York: Routledge, 2003); Roediger, *How Race Survived US History.*

105. Though not limited to American studies, the tenet that cultural texts reflect a social and economic context beyond them has been especially strong in that field. A few examples include Barbara Jeanne Fields, "Slavery, Race and Ideology in the United States of America," *New Left Review,* no. 181 (1990): 95–118; Stephen Greenblatt, *Shakespearean Negotiations: The Circulation of Social Energy in Renaissance England* (Berkeley: University of California Press, 1988); Amy Kaplan and Donald E. Pease, eds., *Cultures of United States Imperialism* (Durham: Duke University Press, 1993); Bartels, "Othello and Africa"; Roxann Wheeler, *The Complexion of Race: Categories of Difference in Eighteenth-Century British Culture* (Philadelphia: University of Pennsylvania Press, 2000); Shelley Streeby, *American Sensations: Class, Empire, and the Production of Popular Culture* (Berkeley: University of California Press, 2002); Alexander Saxton, *The Rise and Fall of the White Republic: Class Politics and Mass Culture in Nineteenth-Century America* (1991; New York: Verso, 2003); Katy L. Chiles, *Transformable Race: Surprising Metamorphoses in the Literature of Early America* (New York: Oxford University Press, 2014).

106. Eric Slauter, "History, Literature, and the Atlantic World," *Early American Literature* 43, no. 1 (2008): 153–86; also published in *William and Mary Quarterly* 65, no. 1 (2008): 135–66.

107. Louis Althusser, "Ideology and Ideological State Apparatuses (Notes Towards an Investigation)," in *Lenin and Philosophy and Other Essays,* trans. Ben Brewster (New York: Monthly Review Press, 2001), 114 (italics in original).

108. Althusser, "Ideology," 109.

109. Slavoj Žižek, "How Did Marx Invent the Symptom?," in *The Sublime Object of Ideology* (London: Verso, 1989), 45. See also Carla Freccero, "Ideological Fantasies," *GLQ: A Journal of Lesbian and Gay Studies* 18, no. 1 (January 2012): 47–69.

110. See Raymond Williams, *The Sociology of Culture* (Chicago: University of Chicago Press, 1995), 142.

111. Saidiya V. Hartman, "The Time of Slavery," *South Atlantic Quarterly* 101, no. 4 (2002): 757–77; Scott Lauria Morgensen, "The Biopolitics of Settler Colonialism: Right Here, Right Now," *Settler Colonial Studies* 1, no. 1 (2011): 52–76.

112. Jennifer Morgan, *Reckoning with Slavery*, chap. 3.

113. Lisa Verner, *The Epistemology of the Monstrous in the Middle Ages* (New York: Routledge, 2005).

114. On the slave's dishonor, see Orlando Patterson, *Slavery and Social Death: A Comparative Study* (Cambridge: Harvard University Press, 1982), 10–12.

115. Rosivach, "Enslaving 'Barbaroi,'" 144.

116. The most notable exception to this trope is Aaron from Shakespeare's *Titus Andronicus*. Scholars have observed his linguistic mastery. See Ian Smith, "Those 'Slippery Customers': Rethinking Race in *Titus Andronicus*," *Journal of Theater and Drama*, no. 3 (1997): 45–58; Thompson, *Performing Race and Torture*, 57–58; Parker, "Shakespeare's Sound Government," 360–61; Philip C. Kolin, "Performing Texts in *Titus Andronicus*," in *Titus Andronicus: Critical Essays*, ed. Philip C. Kolin (New York: Routledge, 2015), 255–56; Sale, "Black Aeneas," 37. However, I would argue that the unfailing consistency of Aaron's identity—from soul to body, from moment to moment, and from father to progeny—suggests an incapacity for self-improvement crucial to the upward social mobility claimed as a white property. See Grier, "Reading Black Characters," 154–55; Akhimie, *Shakespeare and the Cultivation of Difference*, 4–5.

117. I borrow the term "interpretive community" from Stanley Fish, who suggests that texts are made with the assumption of a readership comprising of "native speaker[s]" possessed of "a system of rules that each of them has somehow internalized." While Fish suggests that this "linguistic competence" functions "independently of differences in education and culture," I view interpretive community as a more fraught formation, reproduced in acts of ridiculing or banishing even native speakers who follow different protocols and reach dissenting conclusions. Where Fish follows Noam Chomsky in assuming that linguistic competency is hardwired in the brains of native speakers, I suggest that interpretive authority is determined in political contest. See Stanley Fish, *Is There a Text in This Class? The Authority of Interpretive Communities* (Cambridge, Mass.: Harvard University Press, 1982), 5.

118. Karl P. Wentersdorf, "The Time Problem in *Othello*: A Reconsideration," *Jahrbuch der Deutschen Shakespeare-Gesellschaft West*, 1985, 63–77; Graham Bradshaw, "Obeying the Time in *Othello*: A Myth and the Mess It Made," *English Studies* 73, no. 3 (1992): 211–28, https://doi.org/10.1080/00138389208598807; Steve Sohmer, "The 'Double Time' Crux in 'Othello' Solved," *English Literary Renaissance* 32, no. 2 (2002): 214–38; Carol Chillington Rutter, "Unpinning Desdemona

(Again) or 'Who Would Be Toll'd with Wenches in a Shew?,'" *Shakespeare Bulletin* 28, no. 1 (Spring 2010): 111–32.

119. Structural and poststructural linguistics made it easier to see both reference and significance in language as effects of power rather than as neutral conventions. The outpouring of work on literacy and empire, however, has tended to overlook the utility of staging literacy—either in tests of competency in reading alphabetic texts or in insinuations that certain kinds of people can be read as if they were text. In bringing the study of literacy, performance, gender, and race together, I have taken inspiration from these works not cited elsewhere: Harry Berger Jr., "Bodies and Texts," *Representations,* no. 17 (1987): 144–66; Houston A. Baker Jr., *Modernism and the Harlem Renaissance* (Chicago: University of Chicago Press, 1989); Mae G. Henderson, "(W)Riting *The Work* and Working the Rites," *Black American Literature Forum* 23, no. 4 (1989): 631–60; Alyssa Mt. Pleasant, Caroline Wigginton, and Kelly Wisecup, "Materials and Methods in Native American and Indigenous Studies: Completing the Turn," *Early American Literature* 53, no. 2 (2018): 407–44.

1. "O Bloody Period"

1. Eldred D. Jones, *Othello's Countrymen: The African in English Renaissance Drama* (Oxford: Oxford University Press, 1965).

2. Daniel J. Vitkus, "Turning Turk in *Othello:* The Conversion and Damnation of the Moor," *Shakespeare Quarterly* 48, no. 2 (July 1997): 160.

3. Knowledge is the key term in Mary Floyd-Wilson's study, which assumes that theatre reflected the speculations of ethnologists. See Floyd-Wilson, *English Ethnicity and Race,* 1–3.

4. Some seek to establish Othello's identity, either in a historical person or in a contemporary analogue. See Jerry Brotton, "Is This the Real Model for Othello?," *Guardian,* March 19, 2016, sec. Culture, http://www.theguardian.com/culture/2016/mar/19/moroccan-ambassador-london-1600-real-othello-shakespeare; Keith Hamilton Cobb, *American Moor,* New York: Methuen Drama, 2020. Kyle Grady makes subtler use of Colin Powell not to establish Othello's authenticity but to identify ambivalence as a durable feature of racialism from the seventeenth century to the present. See Grady, "Othello, Colin Powell, and Post-Racial Anachronisms."

5. Michael Neill, "Unproper Beds: Race, Adultery, and the Hideous in *Othello,*" *Shakespeare Quarterly* 40, no. 4 (December 1989): 383–412.

6. Jackman, *All the World's a Stage,* 27. I am grateful to Laura Rosenthal, who drew my attention to this play.

7. Jackman, *All the World's a Stage,* 28 (comma after "know" in original).

8. Vaughan suggests that blackface impersonation was already a cliché by the 1636 burlesque *Mr. Moore's Revels.* See V. M. Vaughan, *Performing Blackness on English Stages,* 12. In the light of Vaughan's claim, explicit references to transferable makeup in the eighteenth century suggest not a new race consciousness but

a deep familiarity with an old joke. Beyond the examples from poetry, science, and theatre I offer in the introduction, see the following ballad, in which a man pays a begging woman for sex. As she prepares for their nocturnal tryst, she mistakes a bottle of ink in his chamber for rosewater. They copulate until daylight, when he flees from what he believes to be a blackfaced devil. See *A New Delightful Ballad Called, Debauchery Scared; or, The Beggar Wench Turn'd into a Devil* [. . .] (London: Printed for JBissel at the Bible and Harp near the hospital-gate in West-smithfield, 1687). I am grateful to Brandi K. Adams for sharing the *New Delightful Ballad* with me.

9. On text as a prompt for bodily comportment and oral performance, see Sandra M. Gustafson, *Eloquence Is Power: Oratory and Performance in Early America* (Chapel Hill: University of North Carolina Press, 2000); Robin Bernstein, "Dances with Things: Material Culture and the Performance of Race," *Social Text* 27, no. 101 (December 2009): 67–94.

10. William Shakespeare, *The Tragœdy of Othello, the Moore of Venice: As It Hath Beene Diuerse Times Acted at the Globe, and at the Black-Friers, by His Maiesties Seruants* (London: printed by A. M. [Augustine Mathewes] for Richard Hawkins, and are to be sold at his shoppe in Chancery-Lane, neere Sergeants-Inne, 1630), 92. See also William Shakespeare, *A New Variorum Edition of Shakespeare: Othello,* ed. Horace Howard Furness (Philadelphia: J. B. Lippincott, 1886), 333.

The lion's share of the energy in textual work on Othello has been devoted to reconciling the versions of *Othello* in the First Folio of 1623 (F1) with that of the First Quarto of 1622 (Q1). According to the Riverside Shakespeare, "There are more than a thousand verbal variants between the two texts, aside from about 160 lines found only in F1 and some thirteen lines or part-lines unique to Q1." Q2 is typically treated as "Q1, but with additions and correction from F1," and, therefore, the potentially suggestive textual variant of "dye" (found in neither Q1 or F1) has received no attention. See, for example, Evans et al., eds., *The Riverside Shakespeare,* 1240, 1248. See also William Shakespeare, *The First Quarto of Othello,* ed. Scott McMillin, *The New Cambridge Shakespeare* (New York: Cambridge University Press, 2001); Hall, ed., *Othello,* 166–67; Shakespeare, *Othello* (2016 ed.), 125–31, 136.

11. On the critical insights that puns, homonyms, and quibbles offer to the study of Shakespeare and the surrounding culture, see Margreta De Grazia, "Homonyms before and after Lexical Standardization," *Shakespeare Jahrbusch,* 1990, 143–56; Little, *Shakespeare Jungle Fever,* 7–8; Parker, "Shakespeare's Sound Government." On the cosmetic blackness of the earliest Othellos, see (among others) V. M. Vaughan, *Performing Blackness on English Stages;* Andrew Gurr, "A Black Reversal," *Shakespeare* 4, no. 2 (July 2008): 148–56; Joel B. Altman, *The Improbability of Othello: Rhetorical Anthropology and Shakespearean Selfhood* (Chicago: University of Chicago Press, 2010).

12. Actors were likely to remember this rhymed couplet and audiences to recall their chime. Therefore, the pun would have received more repetitions than the printings of Q2, until the nineteenth century when productions began to prevent Othello

from reaching Desdemona for the final kiss. See James R. Siemon, "'Nay, That's Not next': *Othello,* V.ii in Performance, 1760–1900," *Shakespeare Quarterly* 37, no. 1 (1986): 38.

13. Edmund Sawyer, ed., *Memorials of Affairs of State* [...], vol. 2 (London: Printed by W.B. for T. Ward in the Inner-Temple-Lane, 1725), 44.

14. I am arguing that any line of descent from the black Vice figure to early modern stage Moors must account for the crucial fact that painted moors can convey their blackness in a way that masked moors cannot. See Vitkus, "*Othello,* Islam, and the Noble Moor"; L. Fiedler, *The Stranger in Shakespeare,* chap. 3.

15. The study of early modern cosmetics has been involved in theorizing race, although the ink-like aspect of the paint has not often been remarked. See Annette Drew-Bear, *Painted Faces on the Renaissance Stage: The Moral Significance of Face-Painting Conventions* (Lewisburg: Bucknell University Press, 1994); Farah Karim-Cooper, *Cosmetics in Shakespearean and Renaissance Drama* (Edinburgh: Edinburgh University Press, 2006); Farah Karim-Cooper, "'This Alters Not Thy Beauty': Face-Paint, Gender, and Race in Richard's *The English Moor,*" *Early Theatre* 10, no. 2 (July 2007): 140–49; Stevens, *Inventions of the Skin;* Carr, "Material/ Blackness."

16. Gwendolyn Brooks, "still do I keep my look, my identity . . . ," in *A Street in Bronzeville* (New York: Harper and Row, 1945), 45.

17. Wimbush argues that, by the end of the eighteenth century, England considered itself a nation with authority over interpretation of the scriptures. To be sure, performance of this authority began much earlier, with Henry VIII's establishment of the Church of England, which eventually spawned that state-sponsored publication of catechisms and the King James Bible. See Vincent L. Wimbush, *White Men's Magic: Scripturalization as Slavery* (New York: Oxford University Press, 2012), 51.

18. Mignolo, *The Darker Side of the Renaissance;* Martin Brückner, *The Geographic Revolution in Early America: Maps, Literacy, and National Identity* (Chapel Hill: University of North Carolina Press, 2006); Lauren Robertson, "'Ne'er Was Dream So Like a Waking': The Temporality of Dreaming and the Depiction of Doubt in *The Winter's Tale,*" *Shakespeare Studies* 44 (2016): 291–315; Laura Kolb, "Jewel, Purse, Trash: Reckoning and Reputation in *Othello,*" *Shakespeare Studies* 44 (2016): 230–62, 10; J. L. Morgan, *Reckoning with Slavery;* Jerry Brotton, *Trading Territories: Mapping the Early Modern World* (London: Reaktion Books, 1997).

19. Joel Fineman, "The Sound of O in *Othello:* The Real of the Tragedy of Desire," *October* 45 (Summer 1988): 77–96; Patricia Parker, "Cassio, Cash, and the 'Infidel o': Arithmetic, Double-Entry Bookkeeping, and Othello's Unfaithful Accounts," in *A Companion to the Global Renaissance: English Literature and Culture in the Era of Expansion,* ed. Jyotsna G. Singh (Chichester: Wiley-Blackwell, 2009), 223–41. See also Meskill, "The Characters of Posterity"; Erika Mary Boeckeler, "Staging the Alphabet in Shakespeare's Comedies," *Journal of the Wooden O* 14–15 (2015): 21–42.

20. Contrast with Nabil I. Matar, *Turks, Moors and Englishmen in the Age of Discovery* (New York: Columbia University Press, 1999); Floyd-Wilson, *English Ethnicity and Race,* chap. 6; Emily C. Bartels, *Speaking of the Moor: From "Alcazar" to "Othello"* (Philadelphia: University of Pennsylvania Press, 2008); Jean E. Feerick, *Strangers in Blood: Relocating Race in the Renaissance* (Toronto: University of Toronto Press, 2010); Vitkus, "*Othello,* Islam, and the Noble Moor."

21. For further discussion, see Valerie Wayne, "Historical Differences: Misogyny and *Othello,*" in *The Matter of Difference: Materialist Feminist Criticism of Shakespeare,* ed. Wayne (Ithaca: Cornell University Press, 1991), 153–80; Sean Lawrence, "The Two Faces of Othello," in *Shakespeare and the Power of the Face,* ed. James A. Knapp (New York: Routledge, 2015), 61–74.

22. Gerald Baker, "The Name of Othello Is Not the Name of *Othello,*" *Review of English Studies* 67, no. 278 (February 2016): 78 (italics in original).

23. For a bracing challenge to the consensus that black Othellos disappeared after Edmund Kean's debut in bronze, see Lower, "Othello as Black on Southern Stages."

24. John Bernard, "Theatricality and Textuality: The Example of 'Othello,'" *New Literary History* 26, no. 4 (October 1995): 942. Berger refers to Iago's audience as "supervisors." See Harry Berger Jr., "Acts of Silence, Acts of Speech: How to Do Things with Othello and Desdemona," *Renaissance Drama* 33 (2004): 6.

25. See Carol Thomas Neely, "Women and Men in *Othello:* 'What Should Such a Fool / Do With So Good a Woman?,'" in *Critical Essays on Shakespeare's "Othello,"* ed. Anthony Gerard Barthelemy, 68–90 (New York: G. K. Hall, 1994).

26. On tupping and topping Desdemona, see the outstanding Masten, *Queer Philologies,* chap. 8. The metaphor of imprinting entails a component that analyses restricted to the perspective of sexuality or animal studies may miss. See Bartels, "Othello and Africa"; Daniel Boyarin, "Othello's Penis: Or, Islam in the Closet," in *Shakesqueer: A Queer Companion to the Complete Works of Shakespeare,* ed. Madhavi Menon (Durham: Duke University Press, 2011), 254–63.

27. Compare the recipe for black tincture in V. M. Vaughan, *Performing Blackness* (11) with the ink recipes C. H. Bloy records in *A History of Printing Ink, Balls, and Rollers, 1440–1850* (London: Evelyn Adams & Mackay, 1967), 46. Eggs, too, might have been found in the stock of those cooking either ink or cosmetics. See Pastoureau, *Black,* 115; and Karim-Cooper, *Cosmetics,* 7.

28. Joseph Moxon, *Mechanick Exercises: Or, the Doctrine of Handy-Works. Applied to the Art of Printing,* vol. 2 (London: printed for Joseph Moxon on the West-side of Fleet-ditch, at the Sign of Atlas, 1683), 373. I thank Brandi K. Adams for pointing me to this passage.

29. This selection from act 5, scene 2 comes from the Second Quarto of *Othello.* I employ Q2 to highlight the use of punctuation, so different from our own. The Folio version of this text employs *five* periods in the course of the monologue as opposed to Q2's single period at the end of the speech. See Shakespeare, *The Tragœdy of Othello,* 91–92, italics in original. On the "authority" of the Q2 as

"the first 'conflat[ion]'" of Q1 and F1, see Thomas L. Berger, "The Second Quarto of Othello and the Question of Textual 'Authority,'" in *Othello: New Perspectives,* ed. Kent Cartwright and Virginia Mason Vaughan (Rutherford: Fairleigh Dickinson University Press, 1991), 26–47.

30. Shakespeare's source for *Othello* is the third story in the seventh decade of Italian writer Cinthio's *The Hecatommithi,* published in Italian in 1566 and in French in 1584. This tale is concerned with "The Unfaithfulness of Husbands and Wives." See Hall, ed., *Othello: Texts and Contexts,* 31–32.

31. For a contrasting case that the gum is "myrrh" and Othello compares himself to a Judean rather than an Indian, see Joan Ozark Holmer, "Othello's Threnos: 'Arabian Trees' and 'Indian' versus 'Judean,'" *Shakespeare Studies* 13 (January 1980): 145. The essay is well informed and thorough but emphasizes geographic consistency and empirical accuracy to the exclusion of ink's materiality and connotations. See also Rodney Stenning Edgecombe, "Ovid and the 'Medicinal Gum' in Othello V.ii," *Notes and Queries* 54, no. 3 (2007): 293–94; Geraldo U. de Sousa, *At Home in Shakespeare's Tragedies* (Burlington: Ashgate, 2010), 69–71.

32. William J. Barrow, "Black Writing Ink of the Colonial Period," *American Archivist* 11 (1948): 295.

33. Richard Hakluyt et al., eds., *The Principal Navigations, Voyages, Traffiques and Discoveries of the English Nation* [. . .], 359.

34. Thaddeus Davids, *History of Ink, Including Its Etymology, Chemistry, and Bibliography* (New York: Thaddeus Davids & Co., 1856), 18.

35. Barrow, "Black Writing Ink," 294. In fact, these acids, known as astringents, may have been the source of the slightly misplaced "medicinal" reference Shakespeare attaches to gum arabic.

36. Davids, *History of Ink,* 16.

37. Thomas Gainsford, *The Glory of England* [. . .] (London: Printed by Edward Griffin for Th: Norton and are to be sold at his shop in Pauls-Church-yard at the signe of the Kings-head, 1618), 195–96.

38. Davids, *History of Ink,* 18.

39. Barrow, "Black Writing Ink," 294. In *The Triumphs of Honor and Vertue,* the "blacke queen" India suggests a prior tanning when she calls her complexion her "natiue dye." Thomas Middleton, *The Triumphs of Honor and Vertue; a Noble Solemnitie,* [. . .] (London: Printed by N. Okes, 1622), A2. I am grateful to Brandi K. Adams for the citation.

40. See Charlotte Sussman, "The Other Problem with Women: Reproduction and Slave Culture in Aphra Behn's *Oroonoko,*" in *Rereading Aphra Behn: History, Theory, and Criticism,* ed. Heidi Hutner (Charlottesville: University Press of Virginia, 1993), 220. See also Mary Ann O'Donnell, "Aphra Behn: The Documentary Record," in *The Cambridge Companion to Aphra Behn,* ed. Derek Hughes and Janet Todd (New York: Cambridge University Press, 2006), 1–11.

41. Aphra Behn, "Oroonoko: Or, the Royal Slave," in *Versions of Blackness: Key Texts on Slavery from the Seventeenth Century,* ed. Derek Hughes (Cambridge: Cambridge University Press, 2007), 173.

42. Aphra Behn, "Oroonoko," 186.

43. Debate has occurred over whether Othello stabs himself in the throat or heart. See Furness's notes in Shakespeare, *A New Variorum Edition of Shakespeare: Othello*, 332–33.

44. Jonathan Bate, *How the Classics Made Shakespeare* (Princeton: Princeton University Press, 2019), 14.

45. See Peter Stallybrass et al., "Hamlet's Tables and the Technologies of Writing in Renaissance England," *Shakespeare Quarterly* 55, no. 4 (December 2004): 379–419. I am grateful to John Archer for first pointing me to Stallybrass and *The Spanish Tragedy*.

46. Bruce Smith also notes that names for punctuation such as point and prick refer to a gash made in paper. See his "Prickly Characters," in *Reading and Writing in Shakespeare*, ed. David Moore Bergeron (Newark: University of Delaware Press, 1996), 25–44.

47. Teague engages the question of Othello's arsenal of weapons, but she does not consider the possibility of a pen or a penknife as the final one. Teague, *Shakespeare's Speaking Properties*, 86. See also Siemon, "'Nay, That's Not Next.'"

48. The virtue of the small dagger, from a dramaturgical standpoint, is that it suits the textual declaration that Othello has been disarmed, while leaving him an undetectable weapon with which to finish himself. Julie Hankey provides an excellent summary of the means of Othello's suicide in performances for which we have direct evidence—dating to the first quarter of the nineteenth century. See William Shakespeare, *Othello*, ed. Hankey, 2nd ed. (New York: Cambridge University Press, 2005), 290–93. Only one, Tomasso Salvini, slit his throat—albeit, not with a pen or a penknife. The elaborate means the actors devised (and the ideas of African savagery they called upon to do so) could constitute an essay in themselves.

49. Jonathan Goldberg, *Writing Matter: From the Hands of the English Renaissance* (Stanford: Stanford University Press, 1990), chap. 2.

50. B. Smith, "Prickly Characters."

51. Although space will not allow a full examination here, both structuralist and poststructuralist linguistics would have much to say about the issues of reference, voice, authenticity, and authorship implicated in Othello's suicide. This discussion, of course, was primarily conducted without consultation of the special case of inkface, wherein an Africanist imagination permits the impossible: the sign that transcends the problem of representation to be that which it stands for. See Ferdinand de Saussure, *Course in General Linguistics*, trans. Roy Harris (La Salle, Ill.: Open Court, 1986); Michel Foucault, "What Is an Author?," in *Language, Counter-Memory, Practice: Selected Essays and Interviews*, ed. Donald F. Bouchard (Ithaca: Cornell University Press, 1980); Jacques Derrida, *Of Grammatology* (Baltimore: Johns Hopkins University Press, 1998); Benjamin Minor and Ayanna Thompson, "'Edgar I Nothing Am': Blackface in *King Lear*," in *Staged Transgression in Shakespeare's England*, ed. Rory Loughnane (New York: Palgrave Macmillan, 2013), 153–64. Although Othello aims to imbue the text with his

voice, his is *not* the politically rebellious use of African American vernacular that Gates finds at the heart of African American letters. See Henry Louis Gates Jr., *The Signifying Monkey: A Theory of African-American Literary Criticism* (New York: Oxford University Press, 1989).

52. My aim here has been to bring eighteenth-century studies of character into conversation with seventeenth-century scholarship—and to bring race to the center of both discussions. See Lisa Freeman, *Character's Theater: Genre and Identity on the Eighteenth-Century English Stage* (Philadelphia: University of Pennsylvania Press, 2001); Elaine McGirr, *Eighteenth-Century Characters: A Guide to the Literature of the Age* (New York: Palgrave Macmillan, 2007); Karen Newman, "Charactery," in *Essaying Shakespeare,* 111–22 (Minneapolis: University of Minnesota Press, 2009); Stephen Orgel, "Knowing the Character," *Zeitschrift für Anglistik und Amerikanistik* 40, no. 2 (1992): 124–29; Jonathan Goldberg, *Shakespeare's Hand* (Minneapolis: University of Minnesota Press, 2003).

53. B. Smith, "Prickly Characters," 30.

54. As I discuss in my final chapter, Herman Melville picks up on this motif in "Benito Cereno," in which the African mastermind of a mutiny ends the novella with his head on a pike, inserted (like Othello's quill) at the neck, converting the negro's head not into a period but into an inverted exclamation point. See Herman Melville, "Benito Cereno," in *Billy Budd, Sailor and Selected Tales,* ed. Robert Milder (New York: Oxford University Press, 1998), 247.

55. Smith, "Prickly Characters," 28.

56. Smith, "Prickly Characters," 26.

57. Fineman, "The Sound of O in Othello"; Gary Taylor and John Jowett, "Appendix II 'O' and 'Oh' in English Renaissance Dramatists."

58. Howard Felperin, *Shakespearean Representation: Mimesis and Modernity in Elizabethan Tragedy* (Princeton: Princeton University Press, 1978), 76.

59. Floyd-Wilson, *English Ethnicity and Race,* 1–2.

60. David R. Roediger, *The Wages of Whiteness: Race and the Making of the American Working Class,* rev. ed. (New York: Verso, 1999), 95.

61. Thomas Pitt Taswell-Langmead, *English Constitutional History from the Teutonic Conquest to the Present Time* (London: Stevens & Haynes, 1880), 67.

62. Walter J. Ong, *Orality and Literacy: The Technologizing of the Word* (New York: Routledge, 1991), 79.

63. Jean-Christophe Agnew, *Worlds Apart: The Market and the Theater in Anglo-American Thought, 1550–1750* (New York: Cambridge University Press, 1988), 58.

64. Adam Fox, *Oral and Literate Culture in England, 1500–1700* (New York: Clarendon Press, 2000). Fox's primary intention is to demonstrate the interpenetration of oral and print cultures, showing how print culture incorporated previously oral proverbs and contributed new rhymes and sayings to vernacular speech. I follow anthropologist Brian V. Street in arguing that orality and literacy do not appear as neutral tools but as embedded in ideological practices of contending social formations. Street, *Literacy in Theory and Practice* (New York: Cambridge University Press, 1985), 4.

65. John Perceval to Elizabeth Stockwell, September 20, 1709, Egmont *MS*, II, 240. Quoted in Mythili Kaul, *Othello: New Essays by Black Writers* (Washington, D.C.: Howard University Press, 1997), 4–5.

66. Samuel Taylor Coleridge, *Coleridge's Essays & Lectures on Shakespeare & Some Other Old Poets & Dramatists* (London: J. M. Dent; New York: E. P. Dutton, 1907), 172. See also Auden's 1947 lecture on *Othello* in W. H. Auden, *Lectures on Shakespeare,* ed. Arthur C. Kirsch (Princeton: Princeton University Press, 2019), 195–207.

67. These words have special weight because, as Neely suggests, Emilia's analysis of the unequal relations between the sexes proves the most accurate in the play. See Neely, "Women and Men in *Othello.*"

68. The idea of a personality untethered from reason was, arguably, more of the Romantics' preoccupation than it was Shakespeare's, anyway.

69. On male literary coteries, see Jeffrey Masten, "Toward a Queer Address: The Taste of Letters and Early Modern Male Friendship," *GLQ: A Journal of Lesbian and Gay Studies* 10, no. 3 (2004): 367–84.

70. Mark Thornton Burnett, *Masters and Servants in English Renaissance Drama and Culture: Authority and Obedience* (New York: St. Martin's Press, 1997).

71. I am *nearly* aligned with Reynolds and Fitzpatrick, who argue that, based on act 1, scene 1, Iago's overarching aim is to have "revenge against an unjust and capricious hierarchical institution of the state by causing the destruction of the institutor of hierarchical order (symbolized by Othello) and of its nepotistic beneficiary (Cassio)." However, I think this summation overlooks his antipathy toward the literate and his use of Desdemona as a page. See Bryan Reynolds and Joseph Fitzpatrick, "Venetian Ideology or Transversal Power?: Iago's Motives and the Means by Which Othello Falls," in *Othello: Critical Essays,* ed. Philip Kolin (New York: Routledge, 2001), 212.

72. On the disciplines of the schoolroom, see Halpern, *The Poetics of Primitive Accumulation,* chap. 1; Urvashi Chakravarty, *Fictions of Consent: Slavery, Servitude, and Free Service in Early Modern England* (Philadelphia: University of Pennsylvania Press, 2022), chap. 2.

73. For a detailed understanding of accounting in *Othello,* see Parker, "Cassio, Cash, and the 'Infidel o.'"; Kolb, "Jewel, Purse, Trash."

74. While I admire Berger and, especially, Burnett, I cannot agree with their visions of Iago as a needy actor or as a paradigmatic servant. His precise grievance—that "preferment goes by letter and affection"—deserves direct engagement for its constellation of literacy, affinity, and favoritism. See Harry Berger Jr., "Acts of Silence," 7; Burnett, *Masters and Servants,* 1, 4, 8.

75. Roger Chartier, "Jack Cade, the Skin of a Dead Lamb, and the Hatred for Writing," *Shakespeare Studies* 34 (January 2006): 77.

76. Chartier, "Jack Cade," 78. Although Iago conjoins "letter and affection," Felperin focuses solely on Iago's desire to "subordinat[e] passion to reason." See Felperin, *Shakespearean Representation,* 79.

77. David Cressy, *Literacy and the Social Order: Reading and Writing in Tudor and Stuart England* (New York: Cambridge University Press, 1980); Sanders, *Gender*

and Literacy on Stage. The final skill, arithmetic, is also part of Cassio's arsenal, a further indication of his elite status.

78. Agnew, *Worlds Apart;* Aaron Kitch, "Bastards and Broadsides in 'The Winter's Tale,'" *Renaissance Drama* 30 (January 1999): 43–71. In this regard, Shakespeare anticipates insights of both historicist and theoretical scholars—namely, that reproduction and conventionality facilitate misrepresentation.

79. While I certainly think that queer readings of Iago are viable, I do not think that the Iago of *The Moor of Venice* is attracted to Othello and sexually jealous of Desdemona. The "latent homosexual" reading came to prominence through Laurence Olivier in the middle of the twentieth century. This interpretation errs in localizing homoeroticism in him alone when the entire male social order places a premium on male homosocial relationships. Iago simply prefers the fraternity of the encampment to that of the Senate chamber. See Gayle Rubin, "The Traffic in Women," in *Toward an Anthropology of Women,* ed. Rayna R. Reiter (New York: Monthly Review Press, 1975), 157–210; Eve Kosofsky Sedgwick, *Between Men: English Literature and Male Homosocial Desire,* 30th anniversary ed. (New York: Columbia University Press, 2015).

80. The same nexus of male affection, commerce, and literacy appears in a quotation I referenced in the first section: "Letters *as* Ligaments the *World do tie,* / *Else all commerce and love 'twixt men would die.*" See James Howell, *Epistolæ Ho-Elianæ,* b2v (italics in original).

81. Neely, "Women and Men in Othello."

82. Much of the rich discussion of Desdemona's handkerchief has come to encompass its commodification, color, and symbolism, without noting the common origins of cloth napkins and linen rag paper, or that its primary colors—black, white, and red—are those of the page. See Lynda E. Boose, "Othello's Handkerchief: 'The Recognizance and Pledge of Love,'" *English Literary Renaissance* 5, no. 3 (1975): 360–74; John A. Hodgson, "Desdemona's Handkerchief as an Emblem of Her Reputation," *Texas Studies in Literature and Language* 19, no. 3 (1977): 313–22; Virginia Mason Vaughan, *Othello: A Contextual History* (New York: Cambridge University Press, 1997), 33; Will Fisher, "Handkerchiefs and Early Modern Ideologies of Gender," *Shakespeare Studies* 28 (January 2000): 199; Natasha Korda, *Shakespeare's Domestic Economies: Gender and Property in Early Modern England* (Philadelphia: University of Pennsylvania Press, 2002), chap. 4; I. Smith, "Othello's Black Handkerchief."

83. On alphabetical and other symbolic components of textiles, see Susan Frye, *Pens and Needles: Women's Textualities in Early Modern England* (Philadelphia: University of Pennsylvania Press, 2011), 120, 126, 177, 178; Janelle Jenstad, "Paper, Linen, Sheets: Dinesen's 'The Blank Page' and Desdemona's Handkerchief," in *Approaches to Teaching Shakespeare's Othello,* ed. Peter Erickson and Maurice Hunt (New York: Modern Language Association, 2005), 198–200.

84. Othello refers to them as his "noble and approved good masters" (I.iii.77).

85. Villain still retained the sense of serf in the seventeenth century. Since only Roderigo has identified himself by name to Brabantio, the use of "senator" as a derogatory term

seems a non sequitur, coming from someone of Brabantio's own status. This eruption of antielitism reveals the depth of Iago's animus toward the Senate. On villeinage, see Edward P. Cheyney, "The Disappearance of English Serfdom," *English Historical Review* 15, no. 57 (January 1900): 20–37; R. H. Hilton, "Freedom and Villeinage in England," *Past and Present*, 1965, 3–19; Paul R Hyams, *King, Lords and Peasants in Medieval England: The Common Law of Villeinage in the Twelfth and Thirteenth Centuries* (Oxford: Clarendon Press, 1980); J. Hatcher, "English Serfdom and Villeinage: Towards a Reassessment," *Past and Present*, 1981, 3–39.

86. On writing and the state after the French Revolution, see Ben Kafka, *The Demon of Writing: Powers and Failures of Paperwork* (Brooklyn: Zone Books, 2012).

87. Korda, *Shakespeare's Domestic Economies*.

88. The etymological link between text and textile was clearer then when the most common, affordable form of paper was made not from wood pulp but from linen rags.

89. "The Great Sir Laurence," *LIFE Magazine*, May 1, 1964, 80A–105.

90. Smith argues that Othello's speech is virtuosic. I would say that the acts of deference in the speech—including the facts that he waits until bidden to speak and that he does not directly refute Brabantio's charge—argue against Othello's linguistic mastery. Moreover, eloquence seems to me to require willfulness and guile, a capacity for self-division that Othello lacks. See I. Smith, *Race and Rhetoric in the Renaissance*, 139.

91. It is arguable that Iago has been ignorant of the operations of social capital, since he thought he would earn promotion through accomplishments and sponsorship. Othello has ignored "three great ones of the city" who doffed their caps and vouched for Iago (I.i.8).

92. On the juridical search for the inward-facing aspects of persons, see Maus, *Inwardness and Theater*. On credit as an economy of belief, see Craig Muldrew, *The Economy of Obligation: The Culture of Credit and Social Relations in Early Modern England* (New York: Palgrave Macmillan, 1998); Theodore B. Leinwand, *Theatre, Finance and Society in Early Modern England* (New York: Cambridge University Press, 1999).

93. Compare to Bartels, "Othello and Africa," 63–64.

94. Scholarly focus on skepticism in *Othello* has revolved around Othello's suspicion of Desdemona. The Senate's resolution of its doubts about the Turkish attack on Cyprus—and of Othello's seizure of Desdemona—has not been deemed emblematic of the larger motif. See Stanley Cavell, "Epistemology and Tragedy: A Reading of *Othello*," *Daedalus* 108, no. 3 (July 1979): 27–43; Cavell, *Must We Mean What We Say?: A Book of Essays*, 2nd, updated ed. (1969; New York: Cambridge University Press, 2008); Cavell, *Disowning Knowledge in Seven Plays of Shakespeare*, 2nd ed. (New York: Cambridge University Press, 2003); Naomi Scheman, "Othello's Doubt/Desdemona's Death: The Engendering of Skepticism," in *Engenderings: Constructions of Knowledge, Authority, and Privilege* (New York: Routledge, 1993), 57–74; Maus, *Inwardness and Theater*.

95. Peter Erickson helpfully identifies a white interpretive community in *Othello*. I would add that the imagined *incapacity* of nonwhite persons to interpret the page makes that white interpretive community conceivable in the first place, despite the internal fissures of that volatile grouping. See "Images of White Identity in *Othello*," in *Othello: New Critical Essays*, ed. Philip C. Kolin (New York: Routledge, 2013), 133–45. See also Benedict Anderson, *Imagined Communities: Reflections on the Origin and Spread of Nationalism*, rev. ed. (New York: Verso, 1991); Vincent L. Wimbush, ed., *Misreading America: Scriptures and Difference* (New York: Oxford University Press, 2013), 11–14.

96. Agnew, *Worlds Apart*.

97. John Leon Lievsay, *The Elizabethan Image of Italy* ([Washington]: Folger Shakespeare Library, 1979); Shaul Bassi, *Shakespeare's Italy and Italy's Shakespeare: Place, "Race," Politics* (New York: Palgrave Macmillan, 2016).

98. To answer with the historical fact that Venice employed foreigners to lead their armies is to sidestep the question, since it does not explain the Senate's abrupt rejection of Brabantio's suit nor their equally abrupt removal of Othello as general.

99. Here, as in *Coriolanus*, there is a pun on voice and vote, which both originate in the Latin *vox*. The implication, then, is that Brabantio can potentially sway twice as many senators to vote with him as the Duke can.

100. Under the rules of coverture, rape was not a crime against a woman's person but against her father's property. Arthur Little remarks upon the relationship between *raptus* (bride theft) and rape. See Little, *Shakespeare Jungle Fever*, 87.

101. Leslie Fiedler asserted that Othello plays the role of witch in this scene—one usually reserved for women. While Fiedler is right to highlight the accusations of witchcraft, the mythical potency of paper recurs more often and arises at more crucial moments. See Fiedler, *The Stranger in Shakespeare*, 141–42.

102. John Gillies is, to my mind, needlessly hesitant to call ethnocentric geography a racial system. Nevertheless, his book remains a classic. See Gillies, *Shakespeare and the Geography of Difference*.

103. Scholars who reject the notion that race was operative in the seventeenth century insist that religion and rank were the operative social determinants. However, Brabantio's objection to being ruled by Othello's children relies upon the notion that there is something in his nature—something communicable to his children, though their mother is Venetian—that permanently excludes them from participating in the government of Venice. Viewed as essential and transmissible, this difference overrides the fact that Othello is a descendant of the nobility and, if Iago can be believed, a converted Christian. Skeptics of the racial analytic include Theodore W. Allen, *The Invention of the White Race: The Origin of Racial Oppression in Anglo-America* (New York: Verso, 1997); April Lee Hatfield, "A 'Very Wary People in Their Bargaining' or 'Very Good Marchandise': English Traders' Views of Free and Enslaved Africans, 1550–1650," *Slavery & Abolition* 25, no. 3 (2004): 1–17; Derek Hughes, ed., *Versions of Blackness: Key Texts on Slavery from the Seventeenth Century* (Cambridge: Cambridge University Press, 2007).

104. For analysis of race and kinship in the early modern Atlantic, see (among many) Dawn Peterson, *Indians in the Family: Adoption and the Politics of Antebellum Expansion* (Cambridge, Mass.: Harvard University Press, 2017); Chakravarty, "More Than Kin, Less Than Kind"; J. L. Morgan, *Reckoning with Slavery*.

105. On the value of virginity, see Katherine Gillen, *Chaste Value: Economic Crisis, Female Chastity and the Production of Social Difference on Shakespeare's Stage* (Edinburgh: Edinburgh University Press, 2017).

106. As early as the 1750s, theatre impresarios seeking to avoid bans on theatre as encouraging vice used the Duke's proclamation "If virtue no delighted beauty lack, your son-in-law is far more fair than black" as evidence that *Othello* encouraged a Christian universalism that disregards color. However, the Duke's lines actually emphasize color, creating a hypothetical situation in which Othello's virtues render him simultaneously white and beautiful. Blackness is, in this formulation, the "lack" of virtue—far from an colorblind statement, the Duke's sentence *depends* on a black-white polarity. See Hall, "Beauty and the Beast of Whiteness."

107. Editorial work on early modern literature has long revolved around both real and imagined authorial papers—foul drafts and fair, corrected copies. Feminist scholars and historians of print have considered the social life of those metaphors. See J. W. Saunders, "The Stigma of Print: A Note on the Social Bases of Tudor Poetry," *Essays in Criticism* 1, no. 2 (April 1951): 139–64; Steven W. May, "Tudor Aristocrats and the Mythical 'Stigma of Print,'" *Renaissance Papers* 10 (1980): 11–18; Daniel Traister, "Reluctant Virgins: The Stigma of Print Revisited," *Colby Quarterly* 26, no. 2 (1990): 75–86; Wendy Wall, "Reading for the Blot: Textual Desire in Early Modern English Literature," in *Reading and Writing in Shakespeare,* ed. David Moore Bergeron (Newark: University of Delaware Press, 1996), 131–59; Olga L. Valbuena, "'The Dyer's Hand': The Reproduction of Coercion and Blot in Shakespeare's Sonnets," in *Shakespeare's Sonnets: Critical Essays,* ed. James Schiffer (New York: Routledge, 2013), 325–46; Mitchell M. Harris, "The Expense of Ink and Wastes of Shame: Poetic Generation, Black Ink, and Material Waste in Shakespeare's Sonnets," in *The Materiality of Color: The Production, Circulation, and Application of Dyes and Pigments, 1400–1800,* ed. Andrea Feeser, Maureen Daly Goggin, and Beth Fowkes Tobin (Burlington: Ashgate, 2017).

108. Kim F. Hall's work continues to be foundational to the study of fairness as a trope implicated in white supremacist hierarchy: Hall, *Things of Darkness,* chap. 2; Hall, "'These Bastard Signs of Fair': Literary Whiteness in Shakespeare's Sonnets," in *Post-Colonial Shakespeares,* ed. Ania Loomba and Martin Orkin (New York: Routledge, 1998), 64–83. See also Karim-Cooper, *Cosmetics in Shakespearean and Renaissance Drama,* 7–8, 11; Gary Taylor, *Buying Whiteness: Race, Culture, and Identity from Columbus to Hip Hop* (New York: Palgrave Macmillan, 2005), 32–39.

109. Nabil Matar and Daniel Vitkus, among others, have taught the field about relations between the English and the Ottoman Empire around the turn of the seventeenth century. I do not, however, think they have established that either plot or characterization in *Othello* would have to display fidelity to political

realities or printed information about Turks. See Vitkus, "Turning Turk in *Othello*"; Matar, *Turks, Moors and Englishmen;* Vitkus, "*Othello,* Islam, and the Noble Moor."

110. *OED,* Quirk n.1, 3.a. Vickers observes that quirk is a "rhetorical conceit," in her pioneering analysis of the blazon, but overlooks its material manifestation as a curlicue, a flourish on the page. See Nancy J. Vickers, "This Heraldry in Lucrece' Face," *Poetics Today* 6, no. 1/2 (1985): 171; Vickers, "'The Blazon of Sweet Beauty's Best': Shakespeare's *Lucrece,*" in *Shakespeare and the Question of Theory,* ed. Geoffrey H. Hartman and Patricia Parker (London: Routledge, 1986), 103. See also James Calderwood, "Appalling Property in *Othello,*" *University of Toronto Quarterly* 57, no. 3 (March 1988): 362.

111. Brigitte Fielder has produced an outstanding study of blackened Desdemonas in the nineteenth century. I am arguing that this phenomenon occurred much earlier and is also inextricable from the history of print literacy, as the overlay of signifying black on the white surface of paper. See Fielder, "Blackface Desdemona."

112. Although Cassio's kisses do not leave black marks, the conceit requires black ink as the sign of defilement. The term "obscure" (from the Latin for "dark") provides Iago the necessary symbolic blackness.

113. As I mentioned in the introduction, Maggie Smith turns "upstage" away from the camera in the two public scenes in which Othello kisses or strikes her. See Stuart Burge, dir., *Othello,* BHE Films, National Theatre of Great Britain Production, 1966.

114. Ong, *Orality and Literacy,* chap. 3; Greenblatt, *Renaissance Self-Fashioning,* chap. 6.

115. On the irretrievable nature of spoken words as compared to the recoverable nature of text, see Ong, *Orality and Literacy,* 32.

116. On pitch as a black resin and agent of defilement, see Thompson, *Performing Race and Torture,* 56. For cognitive approaches, see Greenblatt, *Renaissance Self-Fashioning,* chap. 6; Reynolds and Fitzpatrick, "Venetian Ideology or Transversal Power?"; Paul Cefalu, "The Burdens of Mind Reading in Shakespeare's *Othello:* A Cognitive and Psychoanalytic Approach to Iago's Theory of Mind," *Shakespeare Quarterly* 64, no. 3 (Fall 2013): 265–94, 393; Edward Pechter, "'Iago's Theory of Mind': A Response to Paul Cefalu," *Shakespeare Quarterly* 64, no. 3 (Fall 2013): 295–300, 393.

117. Sadowski suggests that Iago simply wants Cassio demoted and needs for Othello to survive as a mark. While I align with much of this reading, I think it neglects the extent to which Othello and Desdemona personify ink and paper. See Piotr Sadowski, "'Do It Not with Poison': Iago and the Killing of Desdemona," *Shakespeare Quarterly* 71, no. 3–4 (December 2020): 242–43.

118. On Othello's precarious "sufficiency," see Akhimie, *Shakespeare and the Cultivation of Difference,* 51–52.

119. On the transferability of moors' makeup, see V. M. Vaughan, *Performing Blackness on English Stages;* Grier, "Reading Black Characters"; Stevens, *Inventions of*

the Skin; Carr, "Material/Blackness"; Richard Blunt, "The Evolution of Blackface Cosmetics on the Early Modern Stage," in *The Materiality of Color: The Production, Circulation, and Application of Dyes and Pigments, 1400–1800,* ed. Andrea Feeser, Maureen Daly Goggin, and Beth Fowkes Tobin (Burlington: Ashgate, 2017).

120. Peter R. Moore, "Shakespeare's Iago and Santiago Matamoros," *Notes and Queries* 43, no. 2 (June 1996): 162–63.

121. Joseph Roach demonstrates that a quicksilver constitution was central to early modern notions of acting. See Roach, *The Player's Passion,* 41ff.

122. It is also possible that he lost himself (his "I") some time ago. Emilia, after all, cannot recognize her husband in the liar that confronts her in the play's final scene. On self and identity in Shakespeare, see Joel Fineman, *The Subjectivity Effect in Western Literary Tradition: Essays toward the Release of Shakespeare's Will* (Cambridge, Mass.: MIT Press, 1991); Linda Charnes, *Notorious Identity: Materializing the Subject in Shakespeare* (Cambridge, Mass.: Harvard University Press, 1993).

123. On the punitive ends of bureaucratic identity, see Michel Foucault, "What Is an Author?," in *Language, Counter-Memory, Practice: Selected Essays and Interviews,* ed. Donald F. Bouchard (Ithaca: Cornell University Press, 1980). In Herman Melville's "Benito Cereno" (1855), the subject of my fifth and final chapter, a handkerchief-bearing African repeats Iago's refusal to provide narration for the archive.

124. Calderwood writes that the tragedy of *Othello* stems from "the tendency of the seemingly fixed and irreplaceable to metamorphose into the transient and repeatable." James L. Calderwood, *The Properties of "Othello"* (Amherst: University of Massachusetts Press, 1989), 101. Other outstanding analyses of repetition in *Othello* include Robert Hornback, "'Speak[ing] Parrot' and Ovidian Echoes in *Othello:* Recontextualizing Black Speech in the Global Renaissance," in *Othello: The State of Play,* ed. Lena Cowen Orlin (London; Bloomsbury, 2014), 63–94; Simon Palfrey and Tiffany Stern, *Shakespeare in Parts* (Oxford: Oxford University Press, 2007), 227–37.

125. "Mooring, n.1," in *OED Online,* accessed August 22, 2019, http://www.oed.com /view/Entry/121980.

126. Emily Bartels argues that preposition *of* in "the Moor of Venice" suggests that Othello is included in Venetian society, a man who is not "out of place" but at home with its codes of conduct. I read the "of" as indicative of possession: Othello is but an instrument of the senators he calls his "very noble and approv'd good masters" (I.iii.77). See Bartels, *Speaking of the Moor,* 156.

127. On the predicaments of early modern servants, see Burnett, *Masters and Servants in English Renaissance Drama and Culture;* Urvashi Chakravarty, "Livery, Liberty, and Legal Fictions," *English Literary Renaissance* 42, no. 3 (September 2012): 365–90; Elizabeth Rivlin, "Service and Servants in Early Modern English Culture to 1660," *Journal of Early Modern Studies,* no. 4 (2015): 17–41; Akhimie, *Shakespeare and the Cultivation of Difference,* chap. 2.

128. Animal language accumulates around Othello. Others describe him or he envisions himself as a ram, horse, toad, dog, and ass. See Alexander G. Gonzalez, "The Infection and Spread of Evil: Some Major Patterns of Imagery and Language in 'Othello,'" *South Atlantic Review* 50, no. 4 (November 1985): 35–49.

Interlude: Desdemona's Guilt, or "The Farce of Dead Alive"

1. Wall, "Reading for the Blot."
2. Wayne, "Historical Differences."
3. Orlando Patterson, *Slavery and Social Death: A Comparative Study* (Cambridge, Mass.: Harvard University Press, 1982), 13.
4. On the impossible sentence, see comments by both Jan Kott and Jacques Derrida in Richard A. Macksey and Eugenio Donato, eds., *The Structuralist Controversy: The Languages of Criticism and the Sciences of Man,* 40th anniversary ed. (Baltimore: Johns Hopkins University Press, 2007), 146, 155–56.
5. *Morning Chronicle and London Advertiser* (London), Saturday, September 10, 1785, issue 5093.
6. *Morning Post and Daily Advertiser* (London), Monday, September 12, 1785, issue 3932.
7. First quoted in Latin in Geoffrey Tillotson, "Othello and The Alchemist at Oxford in 1610," *Times Literary Supplement,* July 20, 1933. The original Latin text, and the English translation used here, are from Evans et al., eds., *The Riverside Shakespeare,* 1852.
8. John Quincy Adams, "Misconceptions of Shakspeare upon the Stage," *New-England Magazine* 9 (1835): 439.
9. Adams, "Misconceptions of Shakspeare," 438.
10. On the duality of *Othello* as farce and tragedy, see also M. D Bristol, "Charivari and the Comedy of Abjection in *Othello,*" *Disorder and the Drama,* edited by Mary Beth Rose (Evanston: Northwestern University Press, 1991), 3; Shelia Rose Bland, "How I Would Direct *Othello,*" in *Othello: New Essays by Black Writers,* ed. Mythili Kaul (Washington, D.C.: Howard University Press, 1997), 29–44.
11. William Shakespeare, *Othello,* ed. Julie Hankey, 2nd ed., Shakespeare in Production (New York: Cambridge University Press, 2005), 276.
12. For discussion of cues in *Othello* (though focused on a different scene), see Palfrey and Stern, *Shakespeare in Parts,* 242–55. For more on the aesthetic effects and racial genealogy of the echo, see Hornback, "Speak[ing] Parrot."
13. On the farcical elements of Othello, see Thomas Rymer, *A Short View of Tragedy* [...] (London: Richard Baldwin, 1693), chap. 7; Bristol, "Charivari and the Comedy of Abjection in *Othello*"; Hornback, "Emblems of Folly in the First Othello," chap. 3; Korda, *Shakespeare's Domestic Economies,* chap. 4.
14. The great exception, of course, is that audiences tend to laugh at Othello, as the mark of clever Iago's confidence game. Grier, "Are Shakespeare's Plays Racially Progressive?," 239.

15. *Oracle and Public Advertiser* (London), Wednesday, March 22, 1797, issue 19 577.

16. *Oracle and Public Advertiser,* Tuesday, April 4, 1797, issue 19 588. Steevens collaborated with Dr. Johnson and then issued his own magisterial editions of Shakespeare. It is not surprising that in an era in which actors and editors collaborated to establish Shakespeare as England's national poet that they should have concerned themselves with improbabilities in his plays. It is possible that—as Thomas Southerne's *Oroonoko* drew on *Othello* for its interracial uxoricide—so, too were eighteenth-century *Othellos* influenced by the stage business in Southerne's popular play, in which the moor stabs his white wife.

17. Joseph Moxon, *Mechanick Exercises,* vol. 2 (London: Printed for Joseph Moxon on the West-side of Fleet-ditch, at the Sign of Atlas), 372 (my emphasis). I thank Brandi K. Adams for this reference.

18. Rymer, *A Short View of Tragedy,* 139.

19. One brilliant discussion of the earliest *Othello*'s dual tone is Hornback, "Emblems of Folly in the First Othello."

20. On the racial implications of fair and foul within the context of print culture, see B. K. Adams, "Fair/Foul."

21. I emphasize that there is no formal, legal finding of guilt. Still, I would argue that the potential that Othello and Desdemona could produce "bond-slaves and pagans" with a claim to Senate seats provides the *unwritten* reasons for the Duke's unorthodox decisions, such as permitting Desdemona to follow Othello to war and firing Othello the moment the war is won. Unofficially, they have been exiled from Venice. On the rules governing women's presence in theatres of war, see V. M. Vaughan, *Othello: A Contextual History,* 18–20, 266, 291–99.

22. I borrow the term "ultra-white" from Royster's excellent study of the pale, dark, and medium hues in *Titus Andronicus.* See: Francesca T. Royster, "White-Limed Walls: Whiteness and Gothic Extremism in Shakespeare's *Titus Andronicus,*" *Shakespeare Quarterly* 51, no. 4 (December 2000): 432–55.

23. With a potentially misleading stamp on her face, Desdemona begins to resemble the counterfeit coin. Katherine Gillen would note that Desdemona's chastity represents the problem of determining economic value in early capitalism when confronted with "a conflict between intrinsic value and value constituted externally, either through appearance, public opinion or the laws of supply and demand." Gillen, *Chaste Value,* 12.

24. Although he did not consider the racial implications of the page, Kiefer forms an important pillar of this project, as one of the first to establish how thoroughly early modern plays relied upon books, reading, and the ideas surrounding each. See Frederick Kiefer, *Writing on the Renaissance Stage: Written Words, Printed Pages, Metaphoric Books* (Newark: University of Delaware Press, 1996).

25. Maguire notes that Roderigo and Desdemona both speak after appearing dead. I would argue that their shared association with (and reduction to) paper permits this postmortem speech. Indeed, Roderigo speaks even after his last reported utterance through the stream of letters found in his pocket. See Laurie Maguire, "*Othello,* Theatre Boundaries, and Audience Cognition," in *Othello: The State of Play,* ed. Lena Cowen Orlin (London: The Arden Shakespeare, 2014), 23.

26. This kind of marginalia could have been understood as a form of graffiti. See Juliet Fleming, "Wounded Walls: Graffiti, Grammatology, and the Age of Shakespeare," *Criticism* 39, no. 1 (Winter 1997): 1–30; Jason Scott-Warren, "Reading Graffiti in the Early Modern Book," *Huntington Library Quarterly* 73, no. 3 (September 2010): 363–81.

27. This duality is appropriate to a character whose first line is "I do perceive here a divided duty." Earle Hyman also considers this a telling introduction to Desdemona, but for very different reasons. See Hyman, "Othello: Or Ego in Love, Sex, and War," in *Othello: New Essays by Black Writers,* ed. Mythili Kaul (Washington, D.C.: Howard University Press, 1997), 23–28.

28. Consider the scholarly controversy over whether print publication stigmatized the author. See Daniel Traister, "Reluctant Virgins: The Stigma of Print Revisited," *Colby Quarterly* 26, no. 2 (1990): 75–86.

29. I thank Jeffrey Masten for mentioning the issue of the source of writing in a conversation.

30. See Lawrence, "The Two Faces of Othello." Lawrence tracks occasions for reading faces in *Othello* with patience and insight. However, he turns toward Levinas to discuss the face of the Other in general terms, leaving unexamined the specifics of early modern stagecraft, in which the stage moor is unique in bearing a transferable black stigma and is also a member of a race of failed readers.

31. I want to extend foundational work on the blackness and blackening of Desdemona by following it to its origins in ink. See Lara Bovilsky, *Barbarous Play: Race on the English Renaissance Stage* (Minneapolis: University of Minnesota Press, 2008), chap. 1; Menzer, *Anecdotal Shakespeare,* chap. 2; B. Fielder, "Blackface Desdemona."

32. I contend that Desdemona's relationship to writing is perhaps more pertinent to this scene than Iago's incapacity to speak a courtly language of love. See Karl F. Zender, "The Humiliation of Iago," *Studies in English Literature, 1500–1900* 34, no. 2 (Spring 1994): 323.

33. In reality, ink has to be directed toward the page, but Shakespeare reverses the agency in having papery Desdemona "seriously incline" toward the ink-colored Othello (I.iii.146).

34. The hypothesis that Othello experiences a "double-time" plot can be discarded if a cultural injunction to read black marks on Desdemona as emblems of sexual impropriety drives his suspicion despite the temporal implausibility of the acts. See Sohmer, "The 'Double Time' Crux"; Wall, "Reading for the Blot"; Valbuena, "'The Dyer's Hand.'"

35. Emily Bartels argues that Desdemona has mastered poses of submission that consistently authorize her to pursue her desires for the duration of the play. I would agree that Desdemona's poses succeed in act 1. However, I find that she becomes increasingly alienated from her own voice as Othello takes his impressions of her (marked) character to speak for her. See Bartels, "Strategies of Submission: Desdemona, the Duchess, and the Assertion of Desire," *Studies in English Literature, 1500–1900* 36, no. 2 (Spring 1996): 417–33.

2. "Be Thus When Thou Art Dead"

1. When they seized control of the government and abolished the monarchy, the Puritans banned theatre as licentious (and also, perhaps, because their Royalist opponents were holding meetings in playhouses). Legend has it that when the ban on public theatre was lifted with the Restoration of the monarchy, Desdemona was the first part played by a woman rather than a cross-dressing boy. Elizabeth Howe, *The First English Actresses* (New York: Cambridge University Press, 1992), 19.

2. I rely here, as I did in chapter 1, on the spelling memorialized in the 1630 quarto of *Othello.*

3. I am borrowing from Goffman's sociological work suggesting that stigma is a social fiction that scripts interactions in ways that resemble the theatrical. See Erving Goffman, *Stigma: Notes on the Management of Spoiled Identity* (Englewood Cliffs, N.J.: Prentice-Hall, 1963). While I admire Jeffrey Wilson's revival of Goffman, I focus on the painful, nontransferable attribution of stigma synchronically, while he argues that "taken through time, the individual is able to play both parts in the normal-deviant drama." See Jeffrey R. Wilson, "'Savage and Deformed': Stigma as Drama in *The Tempest,*" *Medieval and Renaissance Drama in England* 31 (2018): 150. For an illuminating contrast that acknowledges the synchronic specificity of stigma as a race-making mark imposed through the physical discipline of "pinched" laborers, see Akhimie, *Shakespeare and the Cultivation of Difference,* chap. 4.

4. Drew-Bear, *Painted Faces on the Renaissance Stage;* Karim-Cooper, *Cosmetics in Shakespearean and Renaissance Drama;* Carr, "Material/Blackness."

5. If, indeed, Behn found *Othello* galling, the taste in her mouth would have put her in mind of ink. Scholars have noted that certain prescriptions recommended the patient consume ink or its medicinal ingredients, such as gall. See Harris, "The Expense of Ink"; Steffen, "Globalizing Nature."

6. Lynda Boose, "The Pornographic Aesthetic of Shakespeare's Othello," in *Women, Violence, and English Renaissance Literature: Essays Honoring Paul Jorgensen,* ed. Paul A Jorgensen, Linda Woodbridge, and Sharon A Beehler (Tempe: Arizona Center for Medieval and Renaissance Studies, 2003), 251, 250, 252.

7. Behn's attempts to redeem Desdemona run contrary to scholars' claims that "eighteenth-century women writers seem to have identified less with (white, female) Desdemona than with Othello himself"—not to mention the analogy made between Behn as a disempowered white woman and Oroonoko as an enslaved person. See Catherine Gallagher, *Nobody's Story: The Vanishing Acts of Women Writers in the Marketplace, 1670–1820* (Berkeley: University of California Press, 1995), 82; Jacqueline Pearson, "Blacker than Hell Creates: Pix Rewrites *Othello,*" in *Broken Boundaries: Women and Feminism in Restoration Drama,* ed. Katherine M. Quinsey (Lexington: University Press of Kentucky, 1996), 14–15; David Wallace, *Premodern Places: Calais to Surinam, Chaucer to Aphra Behn* (Oxford: Wiley-Blackwell, 2004), 259.

8. Srinivas Aravamudan, *Tropicopolitans: Colonialism and Agency, 1688–1804* (Durham: Duke University Press, 1999), 29–31.

9. Some scholars position Behn as generating Abolitionist sentiment in Britain. Those scholars would seem to forget that Oroonoko's famous speech indicting slavery would have been best known to British Abolitionists in the early nineteenth century from stage versions and not from Behn's text. See Laura J. Rosenthal, "*Oroonoko:* Reception, Ideology, and Narrative Strategy," in *The Cambridge Companion to Aphra Behn,* ed. Derek Hughes and Janet Todd (Cambridge: Cambridge University Press, 2004), 155; Pearson, "Blacker than Hell Creates," 29.

10. Aravamudan, *Tropicopolitans,* 31–32. The encounter with archives and historiography has sharpened and improved literary studies. Historians who fail to consult literary scholarship have made avoidable errors of fact concerning the plot and genre of Behn's novella. See Kendi, *Stamped from the Beginning,* 60; and A. T. Vaughan *Transatlantic Encounters,* 143.

11. William C. Spengemann, "The Earliest American Novel: Aphra Behn's *Oroonoko,*" *Nineteenth-Century Fiction* 38, no. 4 (March 1984): 384–414; Katharine M. Rogers, "Fact and Fiction in Aphra Behn's *Oroonoko,*" *Studies in the Novel* 20, no. 1 (Spring 1988): 1–15; Firdous Azim, *The Colonial Rise of the Novel* (London: Routledge, 1993); Gallagher, *Nobody's Story;* Oddvar Holmesland, "Aphra Behn's *Oroonoko:* Cultural Dialectics and the Novel," *ELH* 68, no. 1 (2001): 57–79; Michael McKeon, *The Origins of the English Novel, 1600–1740* (Baltimore: Johns Hopkins University Press, 2002); Emily Hodgson Anderson, "Novelty in Novels: A Look at What's New in Aphra Behn's 'Oroonoko,'" *Studies in the Novel* 39, no. 1 (Spring 2007): 1. In an excellent essay on the ways that three versions of "Oroonoko" establish white innocence and imperial hegemony simultaneously, Suvir Kaul says that Behn "stag[es] ethnographic dramas of reciprocity"—a metaphor that does not lead to Behn's relation to the drama. See Kaul, "Reading Literary Symptoms," 83.

12. Laura Brown, *Ends of Empire: Women and Ideology in Early Eighteenth-Century English Literature* (Ithaca: Cornell University Press, 1993); Aravamudan, *Tropicopolitans;* Thomas Cartelli, *Repositioning Shakespeare: National Formations, Postcolonial Appropriations* (New York: Routledge, 1999); Albert J. Rivero, "Aphra Behn's *Oroonoko* and the 'Blank Spaces' of Colonial Fictions," *SEL Studies in English Literature 1500–1900* 39, no. 3 (1999): 443–62; Joanna Lipking, "'Others,' Slaves, and Colonists in *Oroonoko,*" in *The Cambridge Companion to Aphra Behn,* ed. Derek Hughes and Janet Todd (Cambridge: Cambridge University Press, 2004), 166–87; Rosenthal, "Oroonoko"; Adam R. Beach, "Anti-Colonist Discourse, Tragicomedy, and the 'American' Behn," *Comparative Drama* 38, no. 2/3 (Summer 2004): 213–33; H. M. Zahid Iqbal and Munawar Iqbal Ahmad, "Othering the 'Otherself': Aphra Behn's Oroonoko in the Perspective of Postcolonial Critical Theory," *Science International* 26, no. 2 (June 2014): 933–38.

13. Bolter and Grusin focus on new, digital media in their discussion of remediation as a combination of hypermediation (which draws attention to the material form of media) and immediacy (which creates the impression that the medium has disappeared). They acknowledge that neither of these phenomena is exclusive to the present. However, my usage still differs from theirs. I am interested, as they

are, in hypermediation, but I think Behn's re-mediation is not always designed to produce immediacy. While the form of the novel does tend to simulate immediate access to her narrator's thoughts, Behn's interest in ink, marble, jet, and stone can also render the novella's Africanist characters as remote art objects. See J. David Bolter and Richard A. Grusin, *Remediation: Understanding New Media* (Cambridge, Mass: MIT Press, 1999). On how novels produce access to thought, see Nancy Armstrong, *How Novels Think: The Limits of Individualism from 1719–1900* (New York: Columbia University Press, 2006). On the novel as a technology for impeding psychological access to racial Others, see Said, *Orientalism;* Dana D. Nelson, *The Word in Black and White: Reading "Race" in American Literature, 1638–1867* (New York: Oxford University Press, 1994).

14. Aphra Behn, "Oroonoko: Or, the Royal Slave. A True History," in *Versions of Blackness: Key Texts on Slavery from the Seventeenth Century,* ed. Derek Hughes (Cambridge: Cambridge University Press, 2007), 133. Except as noted, subsequent quotations are from the Hughes edition and cited in the text in parentheses.

15. Gallagher, *Nobody's Story,* 1995; Anston Bosman, "Renaissance Intertheater and the Staging of Nobody," *ELH* 71, no. 3 (October 2004): 559–85.

16. On the term protofeminist, see Angela Y. Davis, *Blues Legacies and Black Feminism: Gertrude "Ma" Rainey, Bessie Smith, and Billie Holiday* (New York: Vintage, 1999); Basuli Deb, "Transnational Complications: Reimagining *Oroonoko* and Women's Collective Politics in the Empire," *Frontiers: A Journal of Women Studies* 36, no. 1 (2015): 33.

17. On the irrefutable nature of text, see Ong, *Orality and Literacy,* 79.

18. Aphra Behn, *The Dutch Lover a Comedy Acted at the Dvkes Theatre / Written by Mrs. A. Bhen [Sic]* (London: Printed for Thomas Dring, at the Sign of the Harrow at Chancery-lane end, over against the Inner Temple Gate in Fleet-street, 1673), A2. See also Jessica Munns, "'Good, Sweet, Honey, Sugar-Candied Reader': Aphra Behn's Foreplay in Forewords," in *Rereading Aphra Behn: History, Theory, and Criticism,* ed. Heidi Hutner (Charlottesville: University Press of Virginia, 1993), 44–64.

19. I am inclined to conclude that these two positions are not as distinct as Gallagher has them, in their content or in their associations with separate genres. Both partake of what Wayne Koestenbaum has described as the diminished empire that is the jurisdiction of the queen as opposed to the king. See Gallagher, *Nobody's Story,* chaps. 1–2; Wayne Koestenbaum, *The Queen's Throat: Opera, Homosexuality, and the Mystery of Desire* (New York: Da Capo, 2001).

20. Lauren Berlant, "The Queen of America Goes to Washington City: Harriet Jacobs, Frances Harper, Anita Hill," *American Literature* 65, no. 3 (September 1993): 549.

21. Although written in the register of deference, Behn's preface anticipates Mark Twain's famous "Notice," threatening his reader with legal consequences at the outset of *Adventures of Huckleberry Finn:* "Persons attempting to find a motive in this narrative will be prosecuted; persons attempting to find a moral in it will be banished; persons attempting to find a plot in it will be shot." See *Adventures of Huckleberry Finn,* ed. Thomas Cooley, 3rd ed. (New York: W. W. Norton, 1999), 4.

22. Spengemann, "The Earliest American Novel."

23. Rogers, "Fact and Fiction in Aphra Behn's *Oroonoko*"; L. Brown, *Ends of Empire;* Holmesland, "Aphra Behn's *Oroonoko*"; McKeon, *The Origins of the English Novel;* Joseph M. Ortiz, "Arms and the Woman: Narrative, Imperialism and Virgilian Memoria in Aphra Behn 'Oroonoko,'" *Studies in the Novel* 34, no. 2 (Summer 2002): 119.

24. The observation entered scholarship earlier but became a commonplace in criticism in the 1990s. See Thomas Southerne, *Oroonoko,* ed. Maximillian E. Novak and David Stuart Rodes (Lincoln: University of Nebraska Press, 1976), xxi, xxxvii, xli, 124; Barthelemy, *Black Face, Maligned Race,* 174–81; Laura J. Rosenthal, "Owning Oroonoko: Behn, Southerne, and the Contingencies of Property," *Renaissance Drama,* new ser., 23 (1992): 47; Margaret W. Ferguson, "Transmuting Othello," in *Cross-Cultural Performances: Differences in Women's Re-Visions of Shakespeare,* ed. Marianne Novy (Urbana: University of Illinois Press, 1993), 15–49; Pearson, "Blacker than Hell Creates," 14–15; Joyce Green MacDonald, "Race, Women, and the Sentimental in Thomas Southerne's 'Oroonoko,'" *Criticism* 40, no. 4 (October 1998): 555–70; Cartelli, *Repositioning Shakespeare,* chap. 6; Celia R. Daileader, *Racism, Misogyny, and the Othello Myth: Inter-Racial Couples from Shakespeare to Spike Lee* (New York: Cambridge University Press, 2005), chap. 2; Mita Choudhury, "Race, Performance and the Silenced Prince of Angola," in *A Companion to Restoration Drama* (Malden, Mass.: John Wiley, 2013), 161–76.

25. For an overview of and proposed solution to the play's implausible pace and calendar, see Sohmer, "The 'Double Time' Crux."

26. After quoting some passages that allude to *Othello,* Daileader argues that Thomas Southerne's 1695 play *Oroonoko* owes much more to Shakespeare than does Behn's novella. However, Daileader does not include the many allusions Behn makes to *Othello* or consider that Behn's engagement exceeds the textual to include the materials Shakespeare uses to characterize his personae. See Daileader, *Racism, Misogyny, and the Othello Myth,* 57.

27. Hughes notes that, among Restoration playwrights, Behn had 25 percent more premieres than her nearest male competitors, Dryden and Durfey. See Derek Hughes, "Aphra Behn and the Restoration Theatre," in *The Cambridge Companion to Aphra Behn,* ed. Janet Todd and Derek Hughes (New York: Cambridge University Press, 2004), 80.

28. Dolors Altaba-Artal, *Aphra Behn's English Feminism: Wit and Satire* (Selinsgrove: Susquehanna University Press, 1999), 19; Janet Todd, *Aphra Behn: A Secret Life* (London: Bloomsbury, 2017).

29. *The Rover, Sir Patient Fancy,* and *Abdelazar* all elicited charges of literary theft. See Helen M. Burke, "The Cavalier Myth in *The Rover,*" in *The Cambridge Companion to Aphra Behn,* ed. Janet Todd and Derek Hughes (Cambridge: Cambridge University Press, 2004), 118.

30. See Susie Thomas, "This Thing of Darkness I Acknowledge Mine: Aphra Behn's 'Abdelazer, or, The Moor's Revenge,'" *Restoration: Studies in English Literary*

Culture, 1660–1700 22, no. 1 (April 1998): 19. See also Todd, *Aphra Behn,* 217, 243, 249, 262.

31. Gallagher, *Nobody's Story,* 56–57; Hughes, "Aphra Behn and the Restoration Theatre," 72; Todd, *Aphra Behn,* 243.

32. Behn had not, however, abandoned writing for the stage. She still had her first discipline in mind, mentioning her "new comedy" in the text of "Oroonoko." For a compact view of how Behn operated in the markets of theatre, manuscript, and print, see Catherine Ingrassia, "Aphra Behn and the Profession of Writing in the Restoration and Early Eighteenth Century," in *A Companion to British Literature,* ed. Robert De-Maria, Heesok Chang, and Samantha Zacher (Oxford: John Wiley, 2014), 49–61.

33. Janet Todd, *Aphra Behn Studies* (New York: Cambridge University Press, 1996); Maureen Duffy, *The Passionate Shepherdess: Aphra Behn, 1640–1689* (London: Jonathan Cape, 1977); Mary Ann O'Donnell, "Aphra Behn: The Documentary Record," in *The Cambridge Companion to Aphra Behn,* ed. Derek Hughes and Janet Todd (New York: Cambridge University Press, 2006), 1–11; Maureen Duffy, "My Life with Aphra Behn," *Women's Writing* 19, no. 2 (May 2012): 238–47.

34. Jonathan Elmer, *On Lingering and Being Last: Race and Sovereignty in the New World* (New York: Fordham University Press, 2008), 49.

35. Aphra Behn, *The Dutch Lover: A Comedy,* A5, sig A6.

36. Rymer, *A Short View of Tragedy,* 92, 145–46.

37. Roland Barthes, "The Death of the Author," in *Image-Music-Text,* translated by Stephen Heath, New York: Hill and Wang, 1978; Michel Foucault, "What Is an Author?," in *Language, Counter-Memory, Practice: Selected Essays and Interviews,* edited by Donald F. Bouchard, Ithaca: Cornell University Press, 1980.

38. The term "versioning" comes from reggae culture. For more on this aesthetic practice, see Paul Gilroy, *The Black Atlantic: Modernity and Double Consciousness* (Cambridge, Mass: Harvard University Press, 1993), 95; Tricia Rose, *Black Noise: Rap Music and Black Culture in Contemporary America* (Hanover, N.H.: University Press of New England, 1994), 86, 90; Sonjah Niaah, "'Ace' of the Dancehall Space: A Preliminary Look at U Roy's Version and Subversion in Sound," *Social and Economic Studies* 55, no. 1–2 (2006): 167–89; Leif Sorensen, "Dubwise into the Future: Versioning Modernity in Nalo Hopkinson," *African American Review* 47, no. 2/3 (2014): 267–83, 446.

39. Some dismiss Behn's portrayal of Oroonoko as a slave-for-love as a cliché. For example, see Rosenthal, "Owning Oroonoko," 45. However, this figure is more than merely a vestige of the chivalric tale. In *Othello,* Desdemona is "subdu'd / even to the very quality" of Othello (I.iii.250–51). Behn may indeed draw upon clichés of the romance, but she does so to reverse the gendered politics of enslavement in *Othello.* In fact, according to Chakravarty's argument, Oroonoko is paradoxically free when love's slave, since he serves Imoinda willingly. For more on willing service as an indication of the servant's freedom, see the groundbreaking Chakravarty, *Fictions of Consent.*

40. "Point Lace, n. and Adj.," in *OED Online,* http://www.oed.com/view/Entry/146642#eid29406041. See also Gallagher, *Nobody's Story,* 72.

41. On clothing as second skin, see Anne Anlin Cheng, "Skins, Tattoos, and Susceptibility," *Representations* 108, no. 1 (November 2009): 98–119; Sean Metzger, *Chinese Looks: Fashion, Performance, Race* (Bloomington: Indiana University Press, 2014); Charlotte Ickes, "The Sartorial and the Skin: Portraits of Pocahontas and Allegories of English Empire," *American Art* 29, no. 1 (March 2015): 82–105.

42. Although I admire the work done to vivify the contexts of colonial Surinam, English attitudes toward the Coromanti, and seventeenth-century English political conflicts, I find that the first controlling context for Behn's novel is not the real world but the virtual reality supplied by *Othello*. For a sampling of old and new historicist approaches to "Oroonoko," see Spengemann, "The Earliest American Novel"; Pumla Dineo Gqola, "'Where There Is No Novelty, There Can Be No Curiosity': Reading Imoinda's Body in Aphra Behn's 'Oroonoko or, the Royal Slave,'" *English in Africa* 28, no. 1 (May 2001): 105–17; Lipking, "'Others,' Slaves, and Colonists in 'Oroonoko'"; Wallace, *Premodern Places,* chap. 6; Derek Hughes, ed., *Versions of Blackness: Key Texts on Slavery from the Seventeenth Century* (Cambridge: Cambridge University Press, 2007).

43. Joyce Green MacDonald, "Race, Women, and the Sentimental in Thomas Southerne's 'Oroonoko,'" *Criticism* 40, no. 4 (October 1998): 555–70; MacDonald, "The Disappearing African Woman: Imoinda in 'Oroonoko' after Behn," *ELH* 66, no. 1 (April 1999): 71–86.

44. Julie A. Carlson, "Race and Profit in English Theatre," in *The Cambridge Companion to British Theatre, 1730–1830,* ed. Jane Moody and Daniel O'Quinn (New York: Cambridge University Press, 2007), 175–88.

45. Thomas Southerne, *Oroonoko,* 4.

46. On the iconic importance of the bed in *Othello,* see Neill, "Unproper Beds"; Arthur L. Little Jr., "'An Essence That's Not Seen': The Primal Scene of Racism in *Othello,*" *Shakespeare Quarterly* 44, no. 3 (October 1993): 304–24.

47. In the end, Southerne's Imoinda places her hands atop Oroonoko's, helping him to complete the stabbing that he repeatedly hesitates to execute. Imoinda's contribution to her death would seem to fulfill Desdemona's statement that she herself is responsible for her death while also smoothing out the contradictions between a woman's sense of self-possession and her status as male property. See Thomas Southerne, *Oroonoko: A Tragedy as It Is Acted at the Theatre-Royal, by His Majesty's Servants. Written by Tho. Southerne* (London: Printed for H. Playford in the Temple-Change [. . .], 1696), 83.

48. Desdemona, of course, does deny Othello's charge of adultery, beg him to spare her life, and (in some productions), physically resist him. However, she also refuses to name him as her murderer in her shocking post-death speech. Every stage of Imoinda's collaboration in her execution, therefore, emphasizes Desdemona's self-abnegation to become the paragon of a dutiful wife. Unlike Southerne and the other male playwrights, Behn will make her black Imoinda simultaneously obedient and commanding.

49. V. M. Vaughan, *Othello: A Contextual History;* Vaughan, "Race Mattered: *Othello* in Late Eighteenth-Century England," *Shakespeare Survey* 51 (1998): 57–66.

244 Notes to Pages 80–81

50. George Schuyler, "The Negro-Art Hokum," *Nation*, June 16, 1926. This phrase also accords with Virginia Mason Vaughan's assessment of gallant eighteenth-century Othellos. See her *Othello: A Contextual History* and "Race Mattered."

51. On the figure of the "sable Venus," see Barbara Bush, "'Sable Venus,' 'She Devil' or 'Drudge'? British Slavery and the 'Fabulous Fiction' of Black Women's Identities, c . 1650–1838," *Women's History Review* 9, no. 4 (December 2000): 761–89; Nicholas Hudson, "The 'Hottentot Venus,' Sexuality, and the Changing Aesthetics of Race, 1650–1850," *Mosaic* 41, no. 1 (March 2008): 19–41; Regulus Allen, "'The Sable Venus' and Desire for the Undesirable," *Studies in English Literature, 1500–1900* 51, no. 3 (2011): 667–91. On the whitening of Imoinda, see MacDonald, "Race, Women, and the Sentimental"; MacDonald, "The Disappearing African Woman."

52. Nussbaum's thesis that concerns around Imoinda shaped Behn's aesthetic choices contradicts Southerne's aforementioned suspicion that Behn had a special affection for Oroonoko.

53. Felicity Nussbaum, *The Limits of the Human: Fictions of Anomaly, Race and Gender in the Long Eighteenth Century* (New York: Cambridge University Press, 2003), 172. Compare to Barthelemy, who argues that Southerne created a "conventional" plot with an interracial couple he knew would "heighten dramatic tension." See Barthelemy, *Black Face, Maligned Race*, 176.

54. Joseph Roach, "Celebrity Erotics: Pepys, Performance, and Painted Ladies," *Yale Journal of Criticism* 16, no. 1 (Spring 2003): 211–30; Felicity Nussbaum, "Actresses and the Economics of Celebrity, 1700–1800," in *Theatre and Celebrity in Britain, 1660–2000*, ed. Mary Luckhurst and Jane Moody (New York: Palgrave Macmillan, 2005), 148–68.

55. V. M. Vaughan, *Performing Blackness on English Stages*, chap. 4; Daileader, *Racism, Misogyny, and the Othello Myth*, 31–43.

56. Here, I extend the subtle argument of Lara Bovilsky from rhetorical and figurative blackening of women's sexuality to the stage business by which Desdemona did, indeed, become tainted. See *Barbarous Play*, chap. 1.

57. Numerous scholars have been engaged in the work of recovering these women's lives, strategies, and cultural significance. See Robyn Asleson, ed., *Notorious Muse: The Actress in British Art and Culture, 1776–1812* (New Haven: Paul Mellon Centre for British Art, 2003); Elizabeth Eger, "Spectacle, Intellect and Authority: The Actress in the Eighteenth Century," in *The Cambridge Companion to the Actress*, ed. Maggie B. Gale and John Stokes (Cambridge: Cambridge University Press, 2007), 33–51; Nussbaum, "Actresses and the Economics of Celebrity"; Shearer West, "Siddons, Celebrity and Regality: Portraiture and the Body of the Ageing Actress," in *Theatre and Celebrity in Britain, 1660–2000*, ed. Mary Luckhurst and Jane Moody (New York: Palgrave Macmillan, 2005), 191–213; Fiona Ritchie, "Shakespeare and the Eighteenth-Century Actress," *Borrowers and Lenders: The Journal of Shakespeare and Appropriation* 2, no. 2 (Fall/Winter 2006); Clare McManus, "Women and English Renaissance Drama: Making and Unmaking 'The All-Male Stage,'" *Literature Compass* 4, no. 3 (2007): 784–96; Laura J. Rosenthal,

"Entertaining Women: The Actress in Eighteenth-Century Theatre and Culture," in *The Cambridge Companion to British Theatre, 1730–1830,* ed. Jane Moody and Daniel O'Quinn (New York: Cambridge University Press, 2007), 159–74; Laura Engel, "The Muff Affair: Fashioning Celebrity in the Portraits of Late-Eighteenth-Century British Actresses," *Fashion Theory: The Journal of Dress, Body & Culture* 13, no. 3 (2009): 279–98; Felicity Nussbaum, *Rival Queens—Actresses, Performance, and the Eighteenth-Century British Theater* (Philadelphia: University of Pennsylvania Press, 2010); Helen E. M. Brooks, "Negotiating Marriage and Professional Autonomy in the Careers of Eighteenth-Century Actresses," *Eighteenth-Century Life* 35, no. 2 (2011): 39–75; Natasha Korda, "Insubstantial Pageants: Women's Work and the (Im)Material Culture of the Early Modern Stage," *Shakespeare* 7, no. 4 (December 2011): 413–31; Danielle Spratt, "'Genius Thus Munificently Employed!!!': Philanthropy and Celebrity in the Theaters of Garrick and Siddons," *Eighteenth-Century Life* 37, no. 3 (September 2013): 55–84.

58. Bovilsky, *Barbarous Play,* chap. 1.

59. It is easy enough for a woman to triumph in a comedy. Arguably, the comic plot is where women and feminine values are likeliest to prevail. See Linda Bamber, *Comic Women, Tragic Men: A Study of Gender and Genre in Shakespeare* (Stanford: Stanford University Press, 1992).

60. The term re-vision is Adrienne Rich's, meant to describe feminist reworkings that challenge the fundamental premises and political asymmetries of patriarchal texts. See the discussion of it in Marianne Novy, *Cross-Cultural Performances: Differences in Women's Re-Visions of Shakespeare* (Urbana: University of Illinois Press, 1993).

61. Analyzing "Oroonoko" purely as a novel, Rosenthal identifies a "subtle and unstable" distinction between the young Behn who participates in the narrative and the Behn who is the author of the text. I think that this very distinction may have been suggested as a way to subvert *Othello*'s plot against a Desdemona who does not write. See Rosenthal, "Oroonoko," 157.

62. To be clear, my sense is not that Behn pursues an intersectional feminist project. Rather, I want to suggest that she did have an interest in redeeming universal Woman from sexual slander, a political predicament that she did not derive from knowledge of women throughout the globe but extrapolated from European societies. I make no claim that Behn supported African and Indigenous women in Surinam, but I also do not see that she sets Imoinda up as a rival. Imoinda is not a flesh-and-blood African woman, occupying a historical position that could be in conflict with the historical person Aphra Behn. Rather, she is a literary experiment with an always already black Desdemona and, therefore, an instrument in Behn's rewriting of *Othello*. Imoinda is, in this framework, a figure for the possibility of female liberty and not a political foe.

63. Janet M. Todd, *The Secret Life of Aphra Behn* (New Brunswick: Rutgers University Press, 1997), 1.

64. Todd, *The Secret Life of Aphra Behn;* Duffy, *The Passionate Shepherdess.*

65. Todd, *Aphra Behn,* 59; Rogers, "Fact and Fiction in Aphra Behn's Oroonoko," 1–2; O'Donnell, "Aphra Behn: The Documentary Record," 2–3.

66. Gallagher famously considered the various authorial guises Behn employed, including "newfangled whore" and "author-monarch." See Gallagher, *Nobody's Story*, 1995.

67. Behn's mother and sister are also present in the story, but the young narrator implies that she is first among this trio of women. The three women move and think as a unit (perhaps meant to be for the martyred Oroonoko what Mary, Martha, and Mary were to the crucified Christ); the young narrator directs all of their movements. She never has to defer to the authority of her mother or sister, because they never raise an objection.

68. See L. J. Rosenthal, "Owning Oroonoko," for an incisive account of the contingencies of this property.

69. On the *bios-graphe,* see Hortense J. Spillers, "The Crisis of the Negro Intellectual: A Post-Date," *Boundary 2* 21, no. 3 (October 1994): 67; Jana Evans Braziel, *Caribbean Genesis: Jamaica Kincaid and the Writing of New Worlds* (Albany: SUNY Press, 2009), 14; Rebecka Rutledge Fisher, *Habitations of the Veil: Metaphor and the Poetics of Black Being in African American Literature* (Albany: SUNY Press, 2014), 81.

70. In chapter 1, I discuss Iago's opposition to writing. He decries that "preferment now goes by letter and affection" and ridicules the *"bookish* theoric" of war common to his rival the "arithmetician" Cassio and the "togèd consuls" of Venice's deliberating Senate.

71. A representative passage, excoriating the governor and the council as common rogues: "the Governor taking *Trefry,* about some pretended earnest Business, a Day's Journey up the River, having communicated his Design to one *Banister,* a wild *Irish* Man, one of the Council, a Fellow of absolute Barbarity, and fit to execute any Villany, but rich; he came up to *Parham,* and forcibly took *Cæsar,* and had him ... whipp'd" (72).

72. Recall that the senators first appear contemplating written reports on their colonial outpost and that the play ends with Othello dictating a final report to them on his own death.

73. One could think of Portia masquerading as the doctor of law in *The Merchant of Venice,* or almost any other of Shakespeare's female characters in male garb.

74. Betsy Erkkila, "Does the Republic of Letters Have a Body?," *Early American Literature* 36, no. 1 (2001): 115–26; Michael Warner, *The Letters of the Republic: Publication and the Public Sphere in Eighteenth-Century America* (Cambridge, Mass.: Harvard University Press, 2006). This argument forms an interesting contrast with that of Sandra Gustafson, who notes that in the context of religious and political disputes, inspired oratory was the weapon of choice for the disempowered, while elites insisted on the authority of text. See Gustafson, *Eloquence Is Power.* It may be that Gustafson's opposition of print to orality may need to be revised in light of Dillon's call to enlarge the scope from a (print) public sphere to a "performative commons." See Elizabeth Maddock Dillon, *New World Drama: The Performative Commons in the Atlantic World, 1649–1849* (Durham: Duke University Press, 2014).

75. Those forms could embody or produce cultural or social capital. On the forms of capital, see Pierre Bourdieu, "The Forms of Capital," in *Handbook of Theory and Research for the Sociology of Education,* ed. John G. Richardson, trans. Richard Nice (Westport, Conn.: Greenwood Press, 1986), 241–58.

76. Hughes also notes that the young narrator relies on Plutarch's "biographies of Greek and Roman politicians." See Hughes, ed., *Versions of Blackness,* xxiii–xxiv.

77. On the mutilation of bodies in Behn's text as emblematic of the historical violence of colonialism, see Kaul, "Reading Literary Symptoms," 83–84.

78. Discussion of this passage is ubiquitous. The question is typically whether this description qualifies as racist or not. See, for example, Barry Weller, "The Royal Slave and the Prestige of Origins," *Kenyon Review* 14, no. 3 (1992): 70; Brown, *Ends of Empire,* 35; Kim F. Hall, "Beauty and the Beast of Whiteness: Teaching Race and Gender," *Shakespeare Quarterly* 47, no. 4 (1996): 469; Wallace, *Premodern Places,* 258; Emily M. N. Kugler, *Sway of the Ottoman Empire on English Identity in the Long Eighteenth Century* (Boston: Brill, 2012), 151; Derek Hughes, "Blackness in Gobineau and Behn: Oroonoko and Racial Pseudo-Science," *Women's Writing* 19, no. 2 (May 2012): 212ff. Gallagher considers Oroonoko's blackness the inky sign of his commodification. I am indebted to her discussion of Oroonoko's skin and of Imoinda's as a cloth, but I would add that the pre-text of *Othello* and the rust color of inks of poor quality must also be brought to bear on "Oroonoko." See Gallagher, *Nobody's Story,* 65–73. Yang makes passing reference to Gallagher and to ink, but her project is to shift the focus from ink to lacquer, from literature to the realm of material culture. See Chi-Ming Yang, "Asia Out of Place: The Aesthetics of Incorruptibility in Behn's Oroonoko," *Eighteenth-Century Studies* 42, no. 2 (2009): 238, 252n28.

79. See also Lawrence, "The Two Faces of Othello."

80. Royster, "White-Limed Walls." See also Sale, "Black Aeneas."

81. The European prototypes for Oroonoko and Imoinda indicate how little Behn was interested in historical Africans when it came to her doomed lovers. Her attempts to describe relations among colonists, Indigenous people, and the unnamed majority of the enslaved Africans may have some ethnographic verity, but the hero and heroine seem most useful to her as idealized figures.

82. Racialized complexion never aligns with color qua color, as racial complexion always carries additional connotations of relative morality, purity, intellectual capacity, and aesthetic value. Scholars such as Hughes misapprehend the history and utility of racialism by insisting that skin color must be the prime indicator of difference and that negative qualities must be attributed. Compare Hughes, *Versions of Blackness;* Hall, "Beauty and the Beast of Whiteness."

83. In light of this intertextual interest in sculpture, the fact that the white female narrator's home rests on "a vast Rock of white Marble," would seem to suggest that white women are not to be the subjects of statuary but to live atop the material for making it.

84. A discussion of whether such an ancient code governed behavior, or merely served as an ideological justification for the rule of the segment that could claim honor, must be bracketed for now. On Oroonoko as avatar of Charles I, see L. Brown, *Ends of Empire.*

85. Gallagher, *Nobody's Story,* 62–66.

86. Barrow, "Black Writing Ink of the Colonial Period," 291–307. See also Charles Blagden, "Some Observations on Ancient Inks, with the Proposal of a New

Method of Recovering the Legibility of Decayed Writings. By Charles Blagden, M. D. Sec. R. S. and F. A. S.," *Philosophical Transactions of the Royal Society of London* 77 (1787): 452.

87. On the durability, pervasiveness, and figurative uses of black printers' ink, see Pastoureau, *Black*.

88. Margaret W. Ferguson, "Juggling the Categories of Race, Class, and Gender: Aphra Behn's *Oroonoko*," in *Women, "Race," and Writing in the Early Modern Period*, ed. Margo Hendricks and Patricia Parker (New York: Routledge, 1993), 209–24.

89. Here, I extend the argument regarding lacquer, so beautifully explicated in Yang, "Asia Out of Place," 238ff.

90. See also Ortiz, "Arms and the Woman."

91. Scholars of *The Winter's Tale* are well aware that Shakespeare reworks this theme in the opposite direction in this late play. In the final act, the jealous King Leontes sees a statue of the wife he imprisoned on suspicion of infidelity (and whom he believed dead). The statue returns to life and the two are reconciled.

92. Neely, "Women and Men in Othello," 133ff.; Ruth Vanita, "'Proper' Men and 'Fallen' Women: The Unprotectedness of Wives in Othello," *Studies in English Literature, 1500–1900* 34, no. 2 (April 1994): 341–56; Elizabeth Gruber, "Erotic Politics Reconsidered: Desdemona's Challenge to Othello," *Borrowers and Lenders: The Journal of Shakespeare and Appropriation* 3, no. 2 (Spring/Summer 2008).

93. Sanders, *Gender and Literacy*.

94. A discourse decrying female vanity, prostitution, and theatrical performance has been well documented by scholars. Shirley Nelson Garner, "'Let Her Paint an Inch Thick': Painted Ladies in Renaissance Drama and Society," *Renaissance Drama* 20 (1989): 123–39; Annette Drew-Bear, *Painted Faces on the Renaissance Stage: The Moral Significance of Face-Painting Conventions* (Lewisburg: Bucknell University Press, 1994); Karim-Cooper, *Cosmetics in Shakespearean and Renaissance Drama;* Edith Snook, *Women, Beauty and Power in Early Modern England: A Feminist Literary History* (London: Palgrave Macmillan, 2011).

95. Gallagher, *Nobody's Story*, 72.

96. Ferguson also called Behn's book "a safe-sex substitute for the potentially mutinous but also economically valuable black slave child Oroonoko might have had with [his wife] Imoinda—or indeed with Aphra Behn." Ferguson, "Transmuting Othello," 37. Although she is not interested in Behn's intertextual relationship to Shakespeare, Catherine Gallagher famously argued that blackness in Oroonoko is the color of monarchy, exchangeability, and—most important for this chapter—ink. See Gallagher, *Nobody's Story*, 56, 60, 66. From Gallagher's and Ferguson's insights, it becomes clear that Behn's interest in *Othello* included the play's insistence that its primary personages should be understood as personifications of ink and paper.

97. Ferguson, "Transmuting Othello," 37.

98. Juliet Fleming, "The Renaissance Tattoo," *RES: Anthropology and Aesthetics,* no. 31 (Spring 1997): 34–52; Jane Caplan, ed., *Written on the Body: The Tattoo in*

European and American History (London: Reaktion, 2000); Sujata Iyengar, *Shades of Difference: Mythologies of Skin Color in Early Modern England* (Philadelphia: University of Pennsylvania Press, 2004).

99. C. P. Jones, "Stigma: Tattooing and Branding in Graeco-Roman Antiquity," *Journal of Roman Studies* 77 (1987): 139–55.

100. Susanna Elm, "'Pierced by Bronze Needles': Anti-Montanist Charges of Ritual Stigmatization in Their Fourth-Century Context." *Journal of Early Christian Studies* 4 (1996): 414–15.

101. MacDonald, "Race, Women, and the Sentimental in Thomas Southerne's 'Oroonoko.'"

102. L. Brown, *Ends of Empire,* chap. 2.

103. Wayne, "Historical Differences," 169–70. See also Boose, "'Let It Be Hid,'" 249, 251; B. K. Adams, "Fair/Foul."

104. Ben Jonson, *The Masque of Blackness,* f. 4v.

105. See Hall, *Things of Darkness,* chap. 2.

106. Behn, *Oroonoko, and Other Writings,* 73.

107. On Imoinda's agency in consenting to the abortion, see Deb, "Transnational Complications," 48–49.

108. In an air from a popular opera, an Englishman sings of sailing to America to woo "a foreign fair quite black." Her color and her barbaric style ("a feather grace[s] her nose") make her too unattractive to arouse sexual mistrust in this masculinist reworking of the *Othello* story. "With jealousy I ne'er shall burst; / Who'd steal my bone of bone-a? / A white Othello, I can trust / A dingy Desdemona." George Colman, *Inkle and Yarico* [...] (London: G.G.J. and J. Robinson, 1792), 55.

109. Nussbaum, *The Limits of the Human,* 219. Compare to Gary Taylor, who argues that the European male complexion tended to be represented in visual art as naturally ruddy. According to Taylor, until the eighteenth century, whiteness was associated the natural or enhanced complexion of women, or male coloring altered by humoral disturbance. Taylor, *Buying Whiteness: Race, Culture, and Identity from Columbus to Hip Hop,* Signs of Race (New York: Palgrave Macmillan, 2005), 37–38. Gallagher focuses on blackness as the color indicating vendability—when ascribed to Oroonoko and all African captives. I concur, in part. Though Imoinda, too, is sold as a slave in a racialized traffic, her inviolability does suggest a self-possession that exceeds the market. Gallagher, "Nobody's Story," 76–77.

110. Ferguson, "Transmuting Othello," 35; Stephanie Athey and Daniel Cooper Alarcon, "Oroonoko's Gendered Economies of Honor/Horror: Reframing Colonial Discourse Studies in the Americas," *American Literature* 65, no. 3 (September 1993): 415; Susan Z. Andrade, "White Skin, Black Masks: Colonialism and the Sexual Politics of Oroonoko," *Cultural Critique,* no. 27 (Spring 1994): 206.

111. Eve Sanders would note that Behn tutors Oroonoko and Imoinda according to a theory of two complementary genders. The tutor reads a presumably unlettered Oroonoko lives of the Romans to encourage him to emulate the deeds of great men, while aiming to inculcate passivity in Imoinda by reading her stories of nuns. Behn insinuates herself into the male profession of literacy instruction

(as Oroonoko's tutor) and indeed into the African couple's sexual economy, since fate does allow her book to replace the African child as the only surviving "issue" of Oroonoko's life. On the gendering of literacy, see Sanders, *Gender and Literacy on Stage.* On the child as copy of the father, see Margreta de Grazia, "Imprints: Shakespeare, Gutenberg and Descartes," in *Alternative Shakespeares,* ed. Terence Hawkes, New Accents (London: Routledge, 1996), 2:65–96; Aaron Kitch, "Bastards and Broadsides in 'The Winter's Tale,'" *Renaissance Drama* 30 (January 1999): 43–71.

112. Among others, see Violetta Trofimova, "The Variety of Male Desire in Aphra Behn's Prose Fiction," *Interactions* 18, no. 1 (2009): 135–42; and from *Rereading Aphra Behn,* ed. Hunter: Ruth Salvaggio, "Aphra Behn's Love: Fiction, Letters, and Desire," 253–72; Susan Green, "Semiotic Modalities of the Female Body in Aphra Behn's *The Dutch Lover,*" 121–50; Jane Spencer, "'Deceit, Dissembling, All That's Woman': Comic Plot and Female Action in *The Feigned Cortesans,*" 86–101; Ros Ballaster, "'Pretences of State': Aphra Behn and the Female Plot," 187–211.

113. Richard Kroll, "'Tales of Love and Gallantry': The Politics of Oroonoko." *Huntington Library Quarterly* 67, no. 4 (2004): 573–605, 691; Ortiz, "Arms and the Woman"; Anita Pacheco, "Royalism and Honor in Aphra Behn's Oroonoko," *Studies in English Literature, 1500–1900* 34, no. 3 (July 1994): 491–506. See also L. Brown, *Ends of Empire;* and McKeon, *The Origins of the English Novel.*

114. Given Behn's aforementioned penchant for sly indirection, Imoinda's condescension to Oroonoko might be intended as sincere authorial statement, while the corrective that the gods were doing Imoinda an honor could be a flattering addendum to disarm chauvinist male readers. In general, I think "Oroonoko" is a far funnier text than scholars have imagined. On the fetishism of "Oroonoko," see Aravamudan, *Tropicopolitans,* 32. On the idea that Imoinda is "enslaved" to Oroonoko, see Ferguson, "Juggling the Categories of Race, Class and Gender," 169.

115. Oroonoko here revises Desdemona, who famously "saw Othello's visage in his mind." In this passage, Oroonoko does not have access to Imoinda's mind. Rather, he binds himself to maintain *his* idea of her in *his* mind and *his* heart eternally—a rather saccharine promise that becomes a significant reversal in gender-power in intertextual comparison.

116. Cf. Ros Ballaster, "New Hystericism: Aphra Behn's *Oroonoko:* The Body, the Text, and the Feminist Critic," in *New Feminist Discourses: Critical Essays on Theories and Texts,* ed. Isobel Armstrong (New York: Routledge, 1992), 2:283–95; Ferguson, "Transmuting Othello."

117. Aravamudan observes that this literary service to a noble patron is inescapably and everywhere undercut by the logic of racial slavery that reduces Oroonoko to a commodity and a pet. Aravamudan, *Tropicopolitans,* chap. 1.

118. The Book of Common Prayer asserts that "[God's] seruiue is perfecte fredome." *The booke of the common prayer and administracion of the Sacramentes* [. . .] (London, 1549). sig. A4r. For commentary on how the seeming paradox of freedom in service authorized fictions that servants consented to coerced and involuntary labor, see Chakrvarty, *Fictions of Consent.*

119. Kaul argues that the novel "enables the ideological innocence of the white imperial subject." I take the point, but I think the novel also points to alternatives, such as female empire in the realm of love. See Kaul, "Reading Literary Symptoms," 83.
120. O'Donnell, "Aphra Behn."
121. Othello assumes that Emilia's "function" is to guard the door for illicit lovers. See IV.ii.27, specifically, but also Emilia's labors in the intimate sphere throughout IV.ii and IV.iii.
122. L. J. Rosenthal, "Oroonoko."
123. L. Brown, *Ends of Empire,* chap. 2.
124. Toni Morrison, *Jazz* (New York: Vintage, 1992), 161.
125. Rosenfeld tracks the responsibility to secure an alternative to Othello's murder of Desdemona as it circulates through the cast, ending with Shakespeare as the author. Although I think that genre is an absent agent in her account, I am intrigued by the suggestion and suspect Behn may have detected this agency and emulated it in "Oroonoko." See Colleen Ruth Rosenfeld, "Shakespeare's Nobody," in *Othello: The State of Play,* ed. Lena Cowen Orlin (New York: Bloomsbury Arden Shakespeare, 2014), 268–71.

3. "Pale as Thy Smock"

1. Abigail Adams to Elizabeth Shaw, March 4, 1786. All correspondence (except as noted) in *Founding Families: Digital Editions of the Papers of the Winthrops and the Adamses,* ed. C. James Taylor (Boston: Massachusetts Historical Society, 2007), http://www.masshist.org/ff/. This online collection does not provide the manuscripts but the extensive transcriptions and footnotes of L. H. Butterfield, et al., eds., *The Adams Papers: Adams Family Correspondence,* vols. 1–4 (Cambridge, Mass.: Belknap Press of Harvard University Press, 1963–73); and Richard Alan Ryerson, et al., eds. *Adams Family Correspondence,* vols. 5–6 (Cambridge, Mass.: Belknap Press of Harvard University Press, 1993).
2. Marvin Rosenberg, *The Masks of Othello: The Search for the Identity of Othello, Iago, and Desdemona by Three Centuries of Actors and Critics* (Newark: University of Delaware Press, 1961); Edward Pechter, *Othello and Interpretive Traditions* (Iowa City: University of Iowa Press, 1999); Lois Potter, *Othello* (New York: Manchester University Press, 2002).
3. James Boaden, *Mrs. Sarah Siddons,* vol. 2 (London: Edinborough Press, 1826), 106–11; Thomas Campbell, *Life of Mrs. Siddons* (E. Wilson, 1834), 59–62.
4. Abigail Adams to Elizabeth Shaw, March 4, 1786; Abigail Adams 2nd to John Quincy Adams, September, 24, 1785. These superlative statements should be understood in context. Mother and daughter had not seen very many actresses yet, but they also had much more experience as theatregoers than the female kin to whom they wrote.
5. Abigail Adams to John Adams, March 31, 1776, Braintree, Mass. This letter has become famous as a protofeminist salvo with its threat of (white) women's rebellion against male tyranny. Edith B. Gelles tempered that view, interpreting Adams

as a staunch adherent to the doctrine of separate spheres for men and women. See *First Thoughts: Life and Letters of Abigail Adams* (New York: Twayne, 1998), chap. 2. A recent biography repositions Adams as a quiet radical, who maintained her economic independence and provided for other women in her circle to do the same. See Woody Holton, *Abigail Adams* (New York: Simon and Schuster, 2009), esp. 411–12. See also Elaine Forman Crane, "Abigail Adams, Gender Politics, and 'The History of Emily Montague': A Postscript," *William and Mary Quarterly*, 3rd ser., 64, no. 4 (2007): 839–44.

6. Holton, *Abigail Adams;* Tilden G. Edelstein, "Othello in America: The Drama of Racial Intermarriage," in *Interracialism: Black-White Intermarriage in American History, Literature, and Law,* ed. Werner Sollors (New York: Oxford University Press, 2000), 356–69.

7. Goffman, *Stigma;* Patricia Akhimie and Bernadette Andrea, eds., *Travel and Travail: Early Modern Women, English Drama, and the Wider World* (Lincoln: University of Nebraska Press, 2019).

8. Mythili Kaul, "Background: Black or Tawny? Stage Representations of Othello from 1604 to the Present," in *Othello: New Essays by Black Writers* (Washington, D.C.: Howard University Press, 1997), 1–19; Edelstein, "Othello in America." As a biographer, Woody Holton is not particularly interested in a context or genealogy of Adams's racial thought. He compares her attitudes toward and treatment of Black people with those of her family and neighbors. See Holton, *Abigail Adams,* xv, 225–26, 304–6. While Edith B. Gelles has pursued the analysis of gender in granular detail, her analysis of Adams's whiteness across three biographies is scant. See her *Portia: The World of Abigail Adams* (Bloomington: Indiana University Press, 1995); *First Thoughts; Abigail Adams: A Writing Life* (New York: Routledge, 2002); *Abigail and John: Portrait of a Marriage* (New York: William Morrow, 2009).

9. Lynn Withey, *Dearest Friend: A Life of Abigail Adams* (New York: Free Press, 1981); Phyllis Lee Levin, *Abigail Adams: A Biography* (New York: St. Martin's Press, 1987); Rosemary Skinner Keller, *Patriotism and the Female Sex: Abigail Adams and the American Revolution* (Brooklyn: Carlson, 1994); Gelles, *Portia;* Holton, *Abigail Adams.*

10. For a thorough explanation of sixteenth-century regulations regarding the presence of women in military camps, see V. M. Vaughan, *Othello: A Contextual History,* 37, 46–47. The fact that "most English regulations were firm against the presence of *any* women at camp," explains the play's insistent linking of Desdemona's joining the camp to her death. Although living in a different time, Abigail Adams faced an analogous choice of minding domestic chores or crossing the sea to join her husband on a man's mission in a foreign land.

11. Abigail Adams to Mary Smith Cranch, October 6, 1766.

12. See Abigail Adams to James Lovell, December 15, 1777, *Adams Family Correspondence,* 2:376.

13. From their arrival in Massachusetts Bay in 1669, the Adams line had yielded constables, tithingmen, ensigns, selectmen, and deacons. These middling offices in the

court, church, and military were bested on every front by Abigail Adams's maternal line, the Quincys. For a comparison of the families' respective positions, see Levin, *Abigail Adams,* 8.

14. For an excellent history of the changes in the structure and procedures of the court system as told through the history of courthouse architecture, see Carl Lounsbury, *The Courthouses of Early Virginia: An Architectural History* (Charlottesville: University of Virginia Press, 2005).

15. See John Adams diary, January 15, 10, 1768, Adams Family Papers: An Electronic Archive, Massachusetts Historical Society, http://www.masshist.org/digitaladams/. *Diary and Autobiography of John Adams,* transcribed and ed. L. H. Butterfield, vol. 1. (Cambridge, Mass.: Harvard University Press, 1961).

16. Damning theatre for alleged displays of immorality and for providing a space for frivolous and vicious behavior, Puritan New England adhered to the same Cromwellian codes that closed the playhouses in England during the Interregnum. In practice, this ban seems to have extended only to public plays. John Adams, an aspiring elite studying at Harvard, participated in such plays as *Cato* during his time there. Harvard's "closet" plays escaped prosecution, for at least two reasons: These performances did not involve itinerant actors playing for money but sons of legislators playing for their social peers. Moreover, Harvard could justify these activities as practice in the art of rhetoric, that combination of public speaking and logic. Scholars have found no record of the students' undertaking *Othello* at Harvard. Therefore, John would seem to have a reading familiarity with the text and not that of a performer or audience member.

   Jason Shaffer provides some information regarding John's theatrical career at Harvard; see *Performing Patriotism: National Identity in the Colonial and Revolutionary American Theater* (Philadelphia: University of Pennsylvania Press, 2007), 46–47. He provides contemporary justifications for college plays as grooming for orators and "excellent training for Pulpit, Bar, or Senate" (111–12). See his chap. 4, "A School for Patriots."

17. John Adams diary, January 15, 30, 1768. Charles Francis Adams, in editing the diary, corrected his grandfather's mistake: Brabantio does not characterize Othello thusly. It is failed suitor Roderigo who worries Brabantio by suggesting that his daughter has tied her virtue and fortune in "an extravagant, wheeling stranger of here and everywhere."

18. Having not attended university and being the daughter of a devout minister, Abigail was even less likely to have seen *Othello* performed in Massachusetts than was John.

19. Abigail Adams to Mary Smith Cranch, October 6, 1766.

20. For the mnemonic practices of eighteenth-century women, see Susan M. Stabile, *Memory's Daughters: The Material Culture of Remembrance in Eighteenth-Century America* (Ithaca: Cornell University Press, 2004). On Adams's habit of copying and adapting her reading materials in her letters, see Crane, "Abigail Adams, Gender Politics."

21. David Douglass was both lead tragedian and manager of his own theatre company. His advertisement for *Othello* is reproduced in full in William T. Hastings,

"Shakespeare in Providence," *Shakespeare Quarterly* 8, no. 3 (Summer 1957): 335–51.

22. Indeed, to marry Othello is simultaneously to be moored—connected to a moor—and unmoored from one's family line.

23. Rymer, *Short View of Tragedy;* John Quincy Adams, "Misconceptions of Shakspeare upon the Stage," *New-England Magazine* 9 (1835): 435–40.

24. John Quincy was already in Europe, though attending school rather than residing with John. Abigail and the three other children remained in Massachusetts, though when she and Nabby departed, the two younger boys were left with Abigail's younger sister, Elizabeth Cranch, whose husband was a schoolmaster. See Gelles, *Portia,* 114.

25. On this choice of pen name as Abigail's insistence on her proper femininity despite having assumed masculine duties, see Gelles, *Portia,* xviii, 31, 47.

26. Holton, *Abigail Adams,* 105ff.

27. Frances Teague, *Shakespeare and the American Popular Stage* (New York: Cambridge University Press, 2006), 13–15.

28. Gelles, *Portia,* 106; E. Jennifer Monaghan, "Literacy Instruction and Gender in Colonial New England," *American Quarterly* 40, no. 1 (March 1988): 18–41; Monaghan, *Learning to Read and Write in Colonial America* (Amherst: University of Massachusetts Press, 2007).

29. On the conflation of body and text, especially for women, see Wall, "Reading for the Blot"; Karen Sánchez-Eppler, *Touching Liberty: Abolition, Feminism, and the Politics of the Body* (Berkeley: University of California Press, 1993), chap. 3. Gelles offers extensive commentary on Charles Adams's editing practice, including the selection and correction of texts to emphasize the importance and propriety of his family. See Gelles, *Portia,* 175n2. The irony there is that while Adams's letters were meant to challenge the print record of Tory libels, she resisted their publication because her spelling and indiscretion would not reflect well upon her character either. See *Portia,* 2.

30. Abigail Adams to Mary Smith Cranch, June 24, 1785.

31. Abigail Adams to Cotton Tufts, August 18, 1785. The editors of the *Adams Family Correspondence* note Abigail's keen memory for the Tories' phrasing. "J[ohn] A[dams] was identified as 'the same person who was proscribed as a REBEL,' in the *Daily Universal Register* of 9 June. On 10 June the same newspaper stated that his reception at Court had been 'cool,' and on 14 June it reported: 'It is whispered the celebrated Dr. Price is political father confessor to the new Plenipo, and has already given him absolution.' Similar attacks and attempts to discredit [John Adams] appear in the *Daily Universal Register* of 6, 21 and 22 July" (n. 3, 283). This list does not include the source for the mockery of Abigail Adams's carriage.

32. Gelles provides the insult against Abigail, but its sense is obscured by the way it is excerpted. See *First Thoughts,* 103.

33. McGirr, *Eighteenth-Century Characters,* chap. 8.

34. For more on the racialized "fictive ethnicity" that undergirds national identity, see Balibar, "The Nation Form," 349–50.

35. Katy L. Chiles, *Transformable Race: Surprising Metamorphoses in the Literature of Early America* (New York: Oxford University Press, 2014).

36. Abigail Adams to Mary Smith Cranch, June 24, 1785.

37. Abigail Adams to John Adams, November 20, 1783.

38. Abigail Adams to Mary Smith Cranch, June 24, 1785.

39. Eve Tavor Bannet, "Printed Epistolary Manuals and the Transatlantic Rescripting of Manuscript Culture," *Studies in Eighteenth Century Culture* 36, no. 1 (2007): 13–32.

40. Abigail Adams to Mary Smith Cranch, February 20, 1785.

41. Wheeler famously argues that an emphasis on lineage, nationality, and custom makes eighteenth-century "race" incommensurable with biological divisions of humanity. See Roxann Wheeler, *The Complexion of Race: Categories of Difference in Eighteenth-Century British Culture* (Philadelphia: University of Pennsylvania Press, 2000). However, I follow Kathleen Wilson in emphasizing the power "to group"—and not the nomenclature or criteria—as an ability to characterize by a common essence and deem this the most crucial force for scholars to monitor. "To look for the grounds of identity-formation in the eighteenth century may also cast a searching light on the instability and unpredictability of those intersections of history, culture, and agency where people group themselves as well as where they are grouped." Wilson, *The Island Race: Englishness, Empire and Gender in the Eighteenth Century* (New York: Routledge, 2002), 2.

42. Sujata Iyengar, *Shades of Difference: Mythologies of Skin Color in Early Modern England* (Philadelphia: University of Pennsylvania Press, 2004) chaps. 4–5.

43. *The Times,* Monday, June 20, 1785, p. 2, issue 150, col C. A subsequent article reminds readers that the proscribed Adams was not John Adams but his cousin Samuel. As late as 1785, the spelling "die" persists as a homophone for our "dye." See the introduction and first chapter of this book for dye in *Othello.*

44. Wilson, *The Island Race,* 21.

45. E. McClung Fleming, "Symbols of the United States: From Indian Queen to Uncle Sam," in *Frontiers of American Culture,* ed. Ray B. Brown et al. (West Lafayette: Purdue University Press, 1968), 3, 6, 9.

46. Fleming, "Symbols of the United States," 6.

47. Philip Joseph Deloria, *Playing Indian* (New Haven: Yale University Press, 1999), 28–31; Fleming, "Symbols of the United States"; Rayna Green, "The Pocahontas Perplex: The Image of Indian Women in American Culture," *Massachusetts Review* 16, no. 4 (October 1975): 28–31.

48. Viola Hopkins Winner, "Abigail Adams and 'The Rage of Fashion,'" *Dress* 28 (2001): 64–76.

49. Abigail Adams to Mercy Otis Warren, September, 5, 1784.

50. Abigail Adams 2nd to Lucy Cranch, June 23, 1785.

51. Abigail Adams to Elizabeth Shaw Peabody, September 15, 1785.

52. Abigail Adams to Elizabeth Shaw Peabody, March 4, 1786.

53. There is some question as to whether Mary Cranch, whom Gelles describes as the most pious of Abigail's sisters, was a part of this circle of women. It is perhaps

notable that Adams directs all her letters on Siddons to her younger sister. However, the fact that Nabby wrote of Siddons to Mary's daughter Lucy, who was unmarried and living with her mother, suggests that the Adams women may not have tried to hide their enjoyment of theatre from Mary Cranch.

54. Using a still-prevalent methodology, Edelstein interprets Abigail's horrified response to Othello's touching Desdemona in 1785 as part of a spirit also reflected in a Massachusetts law, adopted the next year, banning interracial marriage but condoning interracial fornication. Edelstein does not account for the legislature's seemingly contradictory responses to marriage and fornication or the numerous particulars of Adams's situation: her dislocation from Massachusetts, the fact that (as a woman) she would not have been eligible to serve in this legislature, and the strain she felt from the scrutiny of being a visible representative of the new nation to hostile onlookers in London. If the legal frame is seen to determine the construction of race in every field, the relationship of legal institutions to other aspects of society cannot be gleaned. The practices law seeks to standardize and regulate disappear from view if only the legal proclamation makes history. See Edelstein, "Othello in America," 357–58.

55. Joseph Haslewood, *The Secret History of the Green-Room: Containing Authentic and Entertaining Memoirs of the Actors and Actresses in the Three Theatres Royal,* vol. 2 (J. Owen, 1795), 248; quoted in Menzer, *Anecdotal Shakespeare,* 67.

56. On the ways that Othello's coupling with Desdemona is figured as a rape, see Little, *Shakespeare Jungle Fever,* chap. 2. In the first chapter of *Inkface,* I discuss the Second Quarto of *Othello,* which offers "dye" at this crucial moment, and enumerate the uses of puns.

57. Shakespeareans have produced important work on the figure of the white woman sullied by sexual contact with a blackamoor. See Karen Newman, "And Wash the Ethiop White," in *Shakespeare Reproduced: The Text in Ideology and History,* ed. Jean E. Howard and Marion F. O'Connor (New York: Methuen, 1987), 143–62; Patricia Parker, "Murder in Guyana," *Shakespeare Studies* 28 (2000): 169–74; Parker, "Black Hamlet: Battening on the Moor," *Shakespeare Studies* 31 (2003): 127–67. Bovilsky has the most thorough consideration, though she treats Desdemona's blackness as rhetorical rather than theatrical. See Bovilsky, *Barbarous Play,* chap. 1.

58. Abigail Adams to William Stephens Smith, September 1785.

59. One contemporary critic thought John Kemble's Othello of 1787 "the *finished picture* of a master." The critic noted "his *dress,* a *robe* and *turban,* were not only beautiful in themselves, but aided the *character,* and better told the tale." See "Drury-Lane. Tuesday. Othello," *World and Fashionable Advertiser* (London), Thursday, January 25, 1787, issue 22. This Orientalizing gesture seems designed to placate Negrophobes by shifting the signifiers surrounding blackface, although I doubt it would have soothed Abigail Adams, who, I contend, was more concerned with color transfer than with Othello's precise racial identity. Scholars might take note of Kemble's costuming as another step toward Kean's decision to opt for a tawny Moor.

60. Charles Beecher Hogan, ed., *The London Stage, 1660–1800,* part 5: *1776–1800: A Calendar of Plays, Entertainment & Afterpieces Together with Casts, Box-Receipts and Contemporary Comment* (Carbondale: Southern Illinois University Press, 1968), 782, 821, 828.

61. Siddons was subject to some rumor and speculation late in her career. My point is that Adams perceived her as possessing an unsullied reputation and admired her for that achievement.

62. Gelles refers to the Smith sisters' letters as an example of "kin work"—women's ritual labor designed to maintain family connection across distance. See *Portia,* 123. To my mind, the work of the sisters' letters goes beyond "recreating the context of their daily lives and achiev[ing] intimacy" (124). Gelles contends that the Adams women accepted the separate feminine sphere and operated within it, but these letters flout enclosure within the home and share vicarious experiences of a wide world.

63. Abigail Adams to Elizabeth Shaw, September 15, 1785, in *Adams Family Correspondence,* 361. My argument that Abigail's discomfort arises suddenly from seeing the play staged is based on this letter.

64. Sir Pigott, Sarah Siddons, and Frances Soame, "Supplementary Egmont Papers. Vol. IIIA. Memoranda on Sarah Siddons by Frances Soame; Bef. 1809. Includes Details of Mrs Siddon's Career (Ff. 1–23), with a List of Her Roles, 1782–1789 (Ff. 24–25v Rev.). Also a Copy of Her Letter to Mr. Pigott," 1782. See also Abigail Adams 2nd to Lucy Cranch, June 23, 1785.

65. Hugh Downman, *Poems to Thespia* (Exeter: printed by WGrigg, 1781); *The Siddoniad; A Poetical Essay* (London, 1785); *The Siddoniad a Characteristical and Critical Poem. Most Respectfully Inscribed to the Honourable Mrs. O'Neil* (Dublin, 1784); *The Beauties of Mrs. Siddons or, a Review of Her Performance of the Characters of Belvidera, Zara, Isabella, Margaret of Anjou, Jane Shore,-And Lady Randolph; in Letters from a Lady of Distinction, to Her Friend in the Country* (London, 1786); Heather McPherson, "Picturing Tragedy: Mrs. Siddons as the Tragic Muse Revisited," *Eighteenth-Century Studies* 33, no. 3 (April 2000): 401–30.

66. Richard Dyer, *Heavenly Bodies: Film Stars and Society,* 2nd ed. (New York: Routledge, 2004), 2. Scholars who work on the long eighteenth century largely agree that this type of celebrity began in the period they study. See Roach, "Celebrity Erotics"; Nussbaum, "Actresses and the Economics of Celebrity"; Margaret J. M. Ezell, "Late Seventeenth-Century Women Writers and the Penny Post: Early Social Media Forms and Access to Celebrity," in *Material Cultures of Early Modern Women's Writing,* ed. Patricia Pender and Rosalind Smith, Early Modern Literature in History (London: Palgrave Macmillan, 2014), 140–58.

67. Dyer, *Heavenly Bodies,* 4.

68. Abigail Adams 2nd to Lucy Cranch, June 23, 1785. As above, my interest is not in the accuracy of the story, but in the fact that Adams recounted it to her female kin as true.

69. See Dror Wahrman's discussion of the shift in the last two decades of the eighteenth century from a conception of motherhood as a choice to an ideal of motherhood as a natural instinct and social obligation. Wahrman, *The Making of the*

Modern Self: Identity and Culture in Eighteenth-Century England (New Haven: Yale University Press, 2006), chap. 1.

70. For an excellent discussion of Siddons's strategies for maintaining an unmarked reputation, see Emily Hodgson Anderson, "Celebrity Shylock," *PMLA* 126 (October 2011): 238–39.

71. On the popularity of plays with fallen women, see Patricia K. Twining, *The Plays and the Playgoers: 18th Century as a Reflection of Its Audience* (Williamsburg: Colonial Williamsburg Foundation), 17ff.

72. Robert Shaughnessy, "Siddons, Sarah (1755–1831)," *Oxford Dictionary of National Biography,* ed. H. C. G. Matthew and Brian Harrison (Oxford: Oxford University Press, 2004).

73. See Heather McPherson, "Tragic Pallor and Siddons," *Eighteenth-Century Studies* 48, no. 4 (2015): 480. See also Joseph Roach, "Patina: Mrs. Siddons and the Depth of Surfaces," in *Notorious Muse: The Actress in British Art and Culture, 1776–1812,* ed. Robyn Asleson (New Haven: Yale University Press, 2003), 195–209.

74. See Abigail Adams to Thomas Jefferson, August 12, 1785, in *Adams Family Correspondence,* 6:263.

75. Abigail Adams to Mary Smith Cranch, June 24, 1785 (my emphasis).

76. The discussion of sea navigation and gender can be found in Abigail Adams to Mary Cranch, July 8, 1784.

77. Several scholars have noted Abigail's interventions in her daughter's romantic affairs during these years. Holton, in fact, suggests that the elder Abigail was involved in covering up her daughter's new suitor, to quiet any gossip about how quickly Nabby had moved on from the man she left in Massachusetts, playwright Royall Tyler. Holton, *Abigail Adams,* 224; Paul C. Nagel, *The Adams Women: Abigail and Louisa Adams, Their Sisters and Daughters* (Cambridge, Mass.: Harvard University Press, 1999), chap. 6.

78. Given that receipts (i.e., recipes) for paints used to enhance white complexion were available in publications to an increasing number of women (when compared to those in the time of Elizabeth I), we can assume that Abigail Adams added a layer of white powder and paint to the skin, complementing the folds of white fabric. See Kathy Lee Peiss, *Hope in a Jar: The Making of America's Beauty Culture* (New York: Metropolitan Books, 1998).

79. Deloria, *Playing Indian.*

Interlude: Legends of Inept Spectatorship

1. John Perceval to Elizabeth Stockwell, September 20, 1709, Egmont *MS,* II, 240. Quoted in Mythili Kaul, *Othello: New Essays by Black Writers* (Washington, D.C.: Howard University Press, 1997), 4–5.

2. Quoted in Menzer, *Anecdotal Shakespeare,* 94. From Folger Shakespeare Library Scrapbook B.21.1, "Forrest, Edwin."

3. This story reappears with suspiciously similar language in a biography of Edwin Forrest: "While [Forrest] was enacting the part of Iago to the Othello of

Edmund Kean in Albany one night, a stalwart canal-boatman was seated in the pit, so near the stage that he rested his elbow on it close to the footlights. Iago, in the scene where he had wrought so fearfully on the jealousy of the Moor, crossed to the stage near the boatman, and, as he passed, the man looked savagely at him and hissed through his teeth while grinding them together, 'You damned lying scoundrel, I would like to get hold of you after this show is over and wring your infernal neck!'" This tale triangulates with the two others in this interlude. The curse "damned" chimes with Stendhal's "un maudit nègre" while Kean's transformation of the boatman's threat into a "high . . . compliment," matches the opening of the Booth anecdote. See William Rounseville Alger, *Life of Edwin Forrest, the American Tragedian*, vol. 2 (Philadelphia: J. B. Lippincott, 1877), 477.

4. Martin Loiperdinger, "Lumiere's Arrival of the Train: Cinema's Founding Myth," trans. Bernd Elzer, *Moving Image* 4, no. 1 (2004): 89–118.

5. Georges Sadoul, *Geschichte der Filmkunst* (1956; Frankfurt am Main: Fischer, 1982), 27.

6. Loiperdinger, "Lumiere's Arrival of the Train," 91.

7. Edwin S. Porter, dir., *Uncle Josh at the Moving Picture Show;* Robert W. Paul, dir., *The Countryman's First Sight of the Animated Pictures.*

8. Loiperdinger, "Lumiere's Arrival of the Train," 92, 91. Early modernists have argued that theatre professionals of that era celebrated their own power, asserted that they were artisans rather than vagabonds, and distinguished their work from the informal economy of women. See, for example, Paul Yachnin, "'The Perfection of Ten': Populuxe Art and Artisanal Value in 'Troilus and Cressida,'" *Shakespeare Quarterly* 56, no. 3 (2005): 306–27; Gillen, *Chaste Value*, 16; Korda, "Women in the Theater."

9. Stendhal, *Racine and Shakespeare* (1823), trans. Guy Daniels (New York: Crowell-Collier, 1962), 17.

10. Stendhal, *Racine and Shakespeare*, 22.

11. Scholars have paid little heed to the conclusion C. Wesley Bird reached after reviewing the Baltimore theatre records of 1821 and 1822, as well as those of New York, Boston, and Washington, D.C.: "We conclude, then, that 'the Baltimore incident' did not occur. Stendhal may have been misinformed. Or, a rumor, emanating from the hostile reception accorded . . . English players at Paris (August–September, 1822) may have served as the basis for an exaggerated *Othello* story whose locale was subsequently transposed to America, and to a city in America where tension between whites and negroes might conceivably be extreme." See Bird, "Stendhal's 'Baltimore Incident.' A Correction," *Modern Language Notes* 61, no. 2 (1946): 119.

12. See William Shakespeare, *Othello*, ed. Hankey, 5; Pechter, *Othello and Interpretive Traditions*, 12; Maguire, "Othello, Theatre Boundaries, and Audience Cognition," 27; David E. W. Fenner, "In Celebration of Imperfection," *Journal of Aesthetic Education* 38, no. 2 (2004): 72–73.

13. Cavell, *Must We Mean What We Say?*, 301.

14. Cavell's "black man" would have been "un noir," but Stendhal employs a derogatory term associated with slavery in the charged original: "un maudit nègre." See Stendhal, *Racine et Shakespeare* (1854; Oxford: Clarendon Press, 1907), 8.

15. Callaghan, *Shakespeare without Women*, 2.

16. Edward Bullough, "'Psychical Distance' as a Factor in Art and as an Aesthetic Principle," *British Journal of Psychology* 5 (1912): 87–117; Cavell, *Must We Mean What We Say?*; David E. W Fenner, "In Celebration of Imperfection," *Journal of Aesthetic Education* 38, no. 2 (2004): 67–79.

17. Maguire, "*Othello,* Theatre Boundaries, and Audience Cognition," 35, 36.

18. Maguire, "*Othello,* Theatre Boundaries, and Audience Cognition," 38.

19. For discussion of John Quincy Adams's and Abigail Adams's responses to *Othello,* see the first interlude and chapter 3 of this book, respectively.

20. George M. Fredrickson, *The Black Image in the White Mind: The Debate on Afro-American Character and Destiny* (New York: Harper & Row, 1971), chap. 4.

4. The Cherokee *Othello*

1. "Bd. of Trade to Lt. Governor Robert Dinwiddie," November 29, 1752, S.R. 845, Public Record Office (PRO) CO 5/1366, pp. 516–33; Virginia Colonial Records Project (VCRP), microfilm, John D. Rockefeller Jr. Library (JDRL), Williamsburg, VA.

2. "Letter from Robert Dinwiddie to Board of Trade," December 10, 1752, S.R. 849, PRO CO 5/1370, reel 32, fol. 128ro, VCRP, microfilm, JDRL.

3. "Williamsburg, November 17," *Virginia Gazette,* November 17, 1752, [2].

4. The Cherokees did have an intricate social structure but they did not have an emperor or empress. These titles are inventions of English negotiators who wanted to elevate the particular Cherokees with whom they dealt. On the crowning of the first Cherokee emperor, see Alden T. Vaughan, *Transatlantic Encounters: American Indians in Britain, 1500–1776* (New York: Cambridge University Press, 2006), 140. On Cherokee social structure more broadly, see Fred O. Gearing, "Priests and Warriors: Social Structures for Cherokee Politics in the 18th Century," *American Anthropologist* 64, no. 5, part 2 (October 1962): 1–112.

5. *Othello* has sometimes been the occasion of near fatal injuries. The Cherokee woman who interrupted might have known that feigned violence can result in unintentional harm. I am grateful to Paul Menzer, who generously provided me with the following anecdote, in which Charles Macready reportedly just avoided killing his costar in act 5 of a nineteenth-century performance: "Instead of passing the sword behind the back of Iago, Macready, miscalculating his distance, energetically drove its point through the doublet close to the very skin of Mr. J. Smith (Iago.) The latter gentleman feeling the cold steel pass in actual contact with his skin, suddenly placed his hand on the spot to feel for blood, imaging that he was wounded. On undressing, he found that there were double openings in his dress even unto the shirt; the sword having made a complete transit. It is not always safe to be opposed to an energetic actor." See Folger Shakespeare Library B.130.9 Theatrical Clippings.

6. The irony of this last proposition has gone unremarked.

7. Karen Robertson, "Pocahontas at the Masque," *Signs* 21, no. 3 (April 1996): 553. The addressee was Dudley Carleton, who wrote of his concerns about the transfer of black makeup from Queen to Spanish ambassador during Jonson's *The Masque of Blackness*. See my chapter 1.

8. Leah Sinanoglou Marcus, "'Present Occasions' and the Shaping of Ben Jonson's Masques," *ELH* 45, no. 2 (1978): 201.

9. *The Chiefs of the Cherokee,* copperplate engraving by Isaac Basire, after a painting by Markham; *Outacite, King of the Cherokees,* engraving on paper, after Joshua Reynolds, 1762.

10. Richard Saunders, *Saunders Physiognomie, and Chiromancie, Metoposcopie* [. . .] (H. Bragis, 1671); Barbara M. Benedict, "Reading Faces: Physiognomy and Epistemology in Late Eighteenth-Century Sentimental Novels," *Studies in Philology* 92, no. 3 (Summer 1995): 311; Martin Porter, *Windows of the Soul: Physiognomy in European Culture, 1470–1780* (New York: Oxford University Press, 2005); Christopher J. Lukasik, *Discerning Characters: The Culture of Appearance in Early America* (Philadelphia: University of Pennsylvania Press, 2010).

11. Troy Bickham contends that the British public lacked imperial ambitions and, therefore, assimilated the Iroquois visitors of 1710 into a generic category of exotics, while producing more accurate views of the Cherokee visitors in 1762, after the need for Indian allies in securing the North American empire against the French became clearer. Despite Britons' attempts to achieve geographic and demographic accuracy, they also continued to produce and indulge in imaginative depictions of Indians as awestruck, gullible subjects of the Crown. I will argue below that racial characterizations do not wait on evidence but serve to generate scenarios that can be anticipated and turned to advantage. Having been generated without evidence—indeed, as a way of framing any subsequent evidence—no amount of evidence will necessarily uproot them. See Troy O. Bickham, *Savages within the Empire: Representations of American Indians in Eighteenth-Century Britain* (New York: Oxford University Press, 2005), 23–31.

12. See John G. Garratt, *The Four Indian Kings* (Ottawa: Public Archives, 1985).

13. Roach, *Cities of the Dead,* 161–72; A. T. Vaughan, *Transatlantic Encounters,* chaps. 7–8. Given Pocahontas's prominent placement in 1617, it is possible that eighteenth-century performances were not inaugurating but reviving a formula for Indian embassies.

14. For a list of diplomats from the Mediterranean and Atlantic Worlds who received royal invitations to London theatres from 1700 to 1710, see Roach, *Cities of the Dead,* 161. On Amerindian visits to London theatres and shows from 1710 to 1765, see A. T. Vaughan, *Transatlantic Encounters,* 126, 142–43, 158–59, 171–72. Indian visits to British American theatres will be discussed below.

15. George Overcash Seilhamer, *History of the American Theatre: Before the Revolution* (Philadelphia: Globe Printing House, 1888), 42.

16. For theatre historians' faithful reports of the interrupted *Othello,* see Charles Edgar Lewis Wingate, *Shakespeare's Heroines on the Stage,* vol. 2 (New York: Thomas Y.

Crowell, 1895), 328; Arthur Hornblow, *A History of the Theatre in America from Its Beginnings to the Present Time,* vol. 1 (Philadelphia: J. B. Lippincott, 1919), 87; Hugh F. Rankin, *The Theater in Colonial America,* 2nd ed. (Chapel Hill: University of North Carolina Press, 1965), 57; Charles Harlen Shattuck, *Shakespeare on the American Stage: From the Hallams to Edwin Booth* (Washington, D.C.: Folger Shakespeare Library, 1976), 9; F. H. Londré and D. J. Watermeier, *The History of North American Theater: The United States, Canada and Mexico, from Pre-Columbian Times to the Present* (New York: Continuum International, 2000); Peter G. Buckley, "Paratheatricals and Popular Stage Entertainment," in *The Cambridge History of American Theatre,* ed. Don B. Wilmeth and Christopher Bigsby (New York: Cambridge University Press, 2006), 431–32; Alden T. Vaughan and Virginia Mason Vaughan, *Shakespeare in America* (New York: Oxford University Press, 2012), 22–23. Of these, Rankin and Buckley alone note the occasion of the treaty negotiations, though both still conclude that the Cherokees mistook the staged swordfight for a real one.

Biographers and local historians have also conceded the accuracy of the 1752 *Gazette* article. Relevant biographies include John Richard Alden, *Robert Dinwiddie: Servant of the Crown* (Charlottesville: University Press of Virginia, 1973), 18; Walter Stitt Robinson, *James Glen: From Scottish Provost to Royal Governor of South Carolina,* Contributions in American History 165 (Westport: Greenwood Press, 1996), 95. Pertinent local histories are Lyon Gardiner Tyler, *Williamsburg, the Old Colonial Capital* (Richmond: Whittet & Shepperson, 1907), 230; Jane Carson, *Colonial Virginians at Play* (Charlottesville: University Press of Virginia, 1965), 94.

17. Robin Ogier Warren, "Acting Feminine on the South's Antebellum and Civil War Stages" (PhD diss., University of Georgia, 2005), 3.

18. See Teague, *Shakespeare and the American Popular Stage,* 18. Joseph Quincy Adams also left the incident out of his lecture "Shakespeare and American Culture," which he delivered at the opening of the Folger Shakespeare Library in Washington, D.C., in 1932. North America's Indigenous populations could not possibly contribute to the case he was trying to make for the transmission of Anglo-Saxon culture to the United States. See Joseph Quincy Adams Jr., "Shakespeare and American Culture," in *Shakespeare in America: An Anthology from the Revolution to Now,* ed. James Shapiro (New York: Library of America, 2014), 418–35.

19. Over the last century, the relevant issue of the *Virginia Gazette* has been transcribed, reprinted, set on microfilm, and made freely available on the internet.

20. Virginia's Executive Council uses four words—"entertained with great civility"—that offer no more direct information than do Dinwiddie's two. See Wilmer Hall, ed., *Executive Journals of the Council of Colonial Virginia,* vol. 5, 1739–54 (Richmond: Virginia State Library, 1945), 413.

21. On the relationship between public policy and cultural play, see Little, *Shakespeare Jungle Fever,* 8.

22. See Wilma A. Dunaway, "The Southern Fur Trade and the Incorporation of Southern Appalachia into the World-Economy, 1690–1763," *Review of the Fernand*

Braudel Center 17, no. 2 (April 1994): 215–42; Wilma A. Dunaway, "Incorporation as an Interactive Process: Cherokee Resistance to Expansion of the Capitalist
World-System, 1560–1763," *Sociological Inquiry* 66, no. 4 (Fall 1996): 455–70;
W. Neil Franklin, "Virginia and the Cherokee Indian Trade, 1673–1752," *East Tennessee Historical Society's Publications,* no. 4 (January 1932): 3–21; Gearing, "Priests
and Warriors"; Theda Perdue, *Cherokee Women: Gender and Culture Change,
1700–1835* (Omaha: University of Nebraska Press, 1998); David H. Corkran, *The
Cherokee Frontier: Conflict and Survival, 1740–62* (Norman: University of Okla-
homa Press, 1962); Gregory Evans Dowd, "The Panic of 1751: The Significance of
Rumors on the South Carolina-Cherokee Frontier," *William and Mary Quarterly,*
3rd ser., 53, no. 3 (July 1996): 527–60; M. Thomas Hatley, *The Dividing Paths:
Cherokees and South Carolinians through the Era of Revolution* (New York: Oxford
University Press, 1992); W. Stitt Robinson, ed., *Virginia Treaties, 1723–1775,* vol. 5,
Early American Indian Documents: Treaties and Laws, 1607–1789 (Washington,
D.C.: University Publications of America, 1983); Robinson, ed., *North and South
Carolina Treaties, 1654–1756,* vol. 13, *Early American Indian Documents: Treaties
and Laws, 1607–1789* (Washington, D.C.: University Publications of America,
2001).

23. Karen Robertson also uses the language of dreams to structure her analysis of the
writings of English men on Pocahontas. See her "Pocahontas at the Masque," 577,
580.

24. Numerous scholars address the question of the relationship between belief
in the theatre's artificial persons and the credibility of those with whom one
trades. See Agnew, *Worlds Apart;* Craig Muldrew, *The Economy of Obligation;*
Aaron Kitch, "The Character of Credit and the Problem of Belief in Middleton's City Comedies," *SEL Studies in English Literature 1500–1900* 47, no. 2
(2007): 403–26.

25. Eric Lott, *Love and Theft: Blackface Minstrelsy and the American Working Class*
(New York: Oxford University Press, 1995); Dale Cockrell, *Demons of Disorder:
Early Blackface Minstrels and Their World* (New York: Cambridge University
Press, 1997); Deloria, *Playing Indian;* David R. Roediger, *The Wages of White-
ness: Race and the Making of the American Working Class,* rev. ed. (New York:
Verso, 1999); Jeffrey H. Richards, *Drama, Theatre, and Identity in the American
New Republic* (New York: Cambridge University Press, 2005); Tavia Nyong'o, *The
Amalgamation Waltz: Race, Performance, and the Ruses of Memory* (Minneapolis:
University of Minnesota Press, 2009).

26. Agnew, *Worlds Apart,* 150.

27. Odai Johnson, *Absence and Memory in Colonial American Theatre,* 235.

28. Johnson, *Absence and Memory,* 235.

29. Johnson, *Absence and Memory,* 232. Compare Johnson's claims about the impact
of geography on theatre culture's interest in racial difference with the work of
Roach, *Cities of the Dead;* Kathleen Wilson, *Island Race;* Kathleen Wilson, ed., *A
New Imperial History: Culture, Identity and Modernity in Britain and the Empire,
1660–1840* (New York: Cambridge University Press, 2004); Carlson, "Race and

264 Notes to Pages 141–144

Profit in English Theatre"; Jane Moody, "Dictating to the Empire: Performance and Theatrical Geography in Eighteenth-Century Britain," in *The Cambridge Companion to British Theatre, 1730–1830,* ed. Moody and Daniel O'Quinn (New York: Cambridge University Press, 2007), 21–42.

30. For an overview of these trends, see Peter Erickson, "The Moment of Race in Renaissance Studies," *Shakespeare Studies* 26 (1998): 27–36; Kathleen Wilson, "Going Global: Empire, Identity, and the Politics of Performance," *Journal of British Studies* 44, no. 1 (January 2005): 194–203.

31. Shaffer has drawn our attention to prologues and epilogues as ways of re-inflecting stock plays for local audiences. See Jason Shaffer, *Performing Patriotism: National Identity in the Colonial and Revolutionary American Theater* (Philadelphia: University of Pennsylvania Press, 2007).

32. Jenna M. Gibbs, *Performing the Temple of Liberty: Slavery, Theater, and Popular Culture in London and Philadelphia, 1760–1850* (Baltimore: Johns Hopkins University Press, 2014), 9.

33. Johnson, *Absence and Memory,* 232, 234.

34. Shaffer, *Performing Patriotism,* 15.

35. Richards, *Drama, Theatre, and Identity,* 24.

36. Indeed, the comparison and conflation of moor and Amerindian has a storied history. See Matar, *Turks, Moors and Englishmen,* chap. 3. Quotations from *Othello* are taken from Evans et al., eds., *The Riverside Shakespeare.*

37. Roach, *Cities of the Dead,* 153. With the term "deep play," Roach is, of course, referring to the Clifford Geertz's celebrated essay "Deep Play: Notes on the Balinese Cockfight," in *The Interpretation of Cultures* (New York: Basic Books, 1973), 412–54.

38. Kathleen Wilson, "The Performance of Freedom: Maroons and the Colonial Order in Eighteenth-Century Jamaica and the Atlantic Sound," *William and Mary Quarterly,* 3rd ser., 66, no. 1 (January 2009): 49.

39. See Korda, *Shakespeare's Domestic Economies,* chap. 4.

40. For a discussion of Cherokees' use of print to reassert sovereignty during Indian Removal, see Keri Holt, "'We, Too, the People': Rewriting Resistance in the Cherokee Nation," in *Mapping Region in Early American Writing,* ed. Edward Watts, Keri Holt, and John Funchion (Athens: University of Georgia Press, 2015), 199–225.

41. Though "moor" has an uncertain geographic reference, the play's dialogue—as well as stage practice with cosmetics—leave no doubt that Othello was painted black until well into the nineteenth century. See Harold C. Goddard, *The Meaning of Shakespeare* (Chicago: University of Chicago Press, 1960), 2:73; Mythili Kaul, "Background: Black or Tawny? Stage Representations of Othello from 1604 to the Present," in *Othello: New Essays by Black Writers,* ed. Kaul (Washington, D.C.: Howard University Press, 1997), 1–19; V. M. Vaughan, *Performing Blackness on English Stages,* 93–95.

42. William Shakespeare, *The First Quarto of Othello,* ed. Scott McMillin (New York: Cambridge University Press, 2001), 148 (my emphasis). One of the most famous

textual cruxes in Shakespeare scholarship involves the discrepancy between the First and Second Quartos—in which Othello compares himself to "the base Indian"—and the First Folio—in which the comparison is to "the base Iudean" or Judaean. When considering this 1752 Williamsburg performance of *Othello,* the goal is not to establish the text that expresses authorial intent but to ascertain what was likely said onstage. In that matter, the scholar Julie Hankey reports that actors have been untroubled by the editorial controversy and opted to say Indian, with only two recorded exceptions. See Hankey, ed., *Othello,* 290 n. 343.

43. Harvey Young, *Theatre and Race* (New York: Palgrave Macmillan, 2013), 17. See also Maaike Bleeker, *Visuality in the Theatre: The Locus of Looking* (Basingstoke: Palgrave Macmillan, 2011), 2.

44. Here, I pursue two aims. First, I counter a scholarly tradition of separating Shakespeare's Indians from his moors. Second, I would like to enrich recent discussions of baseness as a property of demeaned Africanist characters by noting that base can refer to a racialized deficiency in economic thinking. See Fiedler, *The Stranger in Shakespeare;* Alden T. Vaughan, "Shakespeare's Indian: The Americanization of Caliban," *Shakespeare Quarterly* 39, no. 2 (July 1988): 137–53; Jerry Brotton, "'This Tunis, Sir, Was Carthage': Contesting Colonialism in *The Tempest,*" in *Post-Colonial Shakespeares,* ed. Ania Loomba and Martin Orkin (New York: Routledge, 1998); Julia Reinhard Lupton, "Creature Caliban," *Shakespeare Quarterly* 51, no. 1 (April 2000): 1–23; Jean E. Howard, "Is Black So Base a Hue?," in *Shakespeare in Our Time: A Shakespeare Association of America Collection,* ed. Dympna Callaghan and Suzanne Gossett (London: The Arden Shakespeare, 2016), 107–14; Ian Smith, "Speaking of Race," in *Shakespeare in Our Time,* ed. Callaghan and Gossett, 118–23.

45. For a useful overview of approaches to the question of Shakespeare's economic thought, with some mention of Marx's use of Shakespeare, see Douglas Bruster, "Was Shakespeare an Economic Thinker?," *Research in the History of Economic Thought and Methodology* 24-A (2006): 167–80.

46. Karl Marx, *Selected Writings,* ed. Lawrence H. Simon (Indianapolis: Hackett, 1994), 243.

47. Marx, *Selected Writings,* 237. Katherine Gillen describes the early modern English as plagued by "a disconcerting sense . . . that external markers of value may bear no essential relation to intrinsic value and that money might simply act as a signifier—rather than as an embodiment—of value." Both quantifiable and priceless, factual and mediated, chastity "occupies a privileged place within [early modern] drama's investigation of economic language, ideologies and practices." See Gillen, *Chaste Value,* 12, 3.

48. On the hypothetical speech of the talking commodity, see Marx, *Selected Writings,* 243. On the centrality of the fetish in European projections about primitive, non-white trading partners, see William Pietz, "The Problem of the Fetish, I," *RES: Anthropology and Aesthetics,* no. 9 (April 1985): 5–17; William Pietz, "The Problem of the Fetish, II: The Origin of the Fetish," *RES,* no. 13 (April 1987): 23–45; William Pietz, "The Problem of the Fetish, IIIa: Bosman's Guinea and the Enlightenment

Theory of Fetishism," *RES*, no. 16 (October 1988): 105–24; Wyatt MacGaffey, "African Objects and the Idea of Fetish," *RES*, no. 25 (April 1994): 123–31.

49. Agnew, *Worlds Apart*; Joseph Lenz, "Base Trade: Theater as Prostitution," *ELH* 60, no. 4 (1993): 833–55; Kirsten Pullen, *Actresses and Whores: On Stage and in Society* (New York: Cambridge University Press, 2005); McGirr, *Eighteenth-Century Characters*; Freeman, *Character's Theater*.

50. Agnew, *Worlds Apart*; Diane Cady, "The Gender of Money," *Genders*, no. 44 (2006). See also Will Fisher, "Queer Money," *ELH* 66, no. 1 (1999): 1–23.

51. For scholarship that suggests this convergence, see Kim F. Hall, "Guess Who's Coming to Dinner? Colonization and Miscegenation in 'The Merchant of Venice,'" *Renaissance Drama* 23 (January 1992): 87–111; Lindon Barrett, *Blackness and Value: Seeing Double* (New York: Cambridge University Press, 1999), 55; Carlson, "Race and Profit in English Theatre."

52. A sampling of the scholarship that emphasizes the legal production of race includes A. L. Higginbotham, *In the Matter of Color*; K. M. Brown, *Good Wives*; T. W. Allen, *The Invention of the White Race*; Roediger, *How Race Survived US History*. Alternate approaches that emphasize that racial difference was to be found in differential capacities for economic reasoning include Pietz, "The Problem of the Fetish," parts I, II, and IIIa; Korda, *Shakespeare's Domestic Economies*, chap. 4.

53. The base Indian was not the only Indian type that Europeans conceived from 1492 to 1752. See Karen Ordahl Kupperman, "Presentment of Civility: English Reading of American Self-Presentation in the Early Years of Colonization," *William and Mary Quarterly* 54, no. 1 (January 1997): 193–228; Nancy Shoemaker, *A Strange Likeness: Becoming Red and White in Eighteenth-Century North America* (Oxford: Oxford University Press, 2006). The notion that racism was a belated justification for the economic exploitation of Atlantic slavery is one of the key premises of Eric Williams, *Capitalism and Slavery* (Chapel Hill: University of North Carolina Press, 1994).

54. Gary B. Nash, "The Image of the Indian in the Southern Colonial Mind," *William and Mary Quarterly* 29, no. 2 (April 1972): 206 (italics in original).

55. Nash, "The Image of the Indian," 205.

56. Richard Eden, *The First Three English Books on America* [. . .], ed. Edward Arber ([1511?]–1555; repr., Birmingham, 1885), 37, quoted in Rodney Poisson, "Othello's 'Base Indian': A Better Source for the Allusion," *Shakespeare Quarterly* 26, no. 4 (Autumn 1975): 465.

57. Poisson, "Othello's 'Base Indian,'" 462–66, esp. 463 n. 6.

58. Peter Hulme, "Tales of Distinction: European Ethnography and the Caribbean," in *Implicit Understandings: Observing, Reporting, and Reflecting on the Encounters between Europeans and Other Peoples in the Early Modern Era*, ed. Stuart B. Schwartz (Cambridge: Cambridge University Press, 1994), 157–97, 157 ("Because I recognized"), 159 ("warmth"), 159–60 ("trade"), 159 ("cultural"). Scholars have shown that establishing an empire meant rewriting Africans and American Indians in the numerical, cartographic, alphabetic, and economic systems of Europe. See Immanuel Wallerstein, "From Feudalism to Capitalism: Transition or Transitions?"

Social Forces 55, no. 2 (1976): 273–83; Patricia Crain, *The Story of A: The Alphabetization of America from "The New England Primer" to "The Scarlet Letter"* (Stanford: Stanford University Press, 2000); Mignolo, *The Darker Side of the Renaissance;* Brückner, *The Geographic Revolution in Early America;* Stephanie E. Smallwood, *Saltwater Slavery: A Middle Passage from Africa to American Diaspora* (Cambridge, Mass.: Harvard University Press, 2007); Birgit Brander Rasmussen, *Queequeg's Coffin: Indigenous Literacies and Early American Literature* (Durham: Duke University Press, 2012).

59. I would add that the apparent justice of capitalist market relations consists not only in exonerating market relations but also in restricting ethical discussion to market relations. See C. Rosenthal, "Numbers for the Innumerate," 531.

60. I borrow, and perhaps reinflect, the phrase from Fred Moten's unpublished manuscript "Black Kant." The field of performance studies has largely been organized around the notion that performance is an ephemeral object, inherently opposed to archival text. Two key entries of the many that elaborate this discussion are Diana Taylor, *The Archive and the Repertoire: Performing Cultural Memory in the Americas* (Durham: Duke University Press Books, 2003); Rebecca Schneider, *Performing Remains: Art and War in Times of Theatrical Reenactment* (New York: Routledge, 2011). On the author as a subject of state punishment, see Foucault, "What Is an Author?"

61. W. J. T. Mitchell, *Seeing Through Race* (Boston, Mass.: Harvard University Press, 2012), 12–13.

62. Fields and Fields, *Racecraft,* 22. I alter the Fields sisters' phrasing because I suspect that the desire to believe is the engine here rather than "belief" itself, as they put it. Toni Morrison remarks upon the need to believe: "there are old, old men, and old, old women running institutions, governments, homes all over the world who *need* to believe in their racism and need to have the victims of racism concentrate all their creative abilities on them." This phrasing shifts scholarly inquiry from the question of whether our predecessors believed racist things they said to pinpointing the urgency of maintaining the social arrangements that the purported belief sustains. Those who participate in such arrangements need not do so consciously or sincerely to sustain the dance. They only need to accept the implicit operating principles. See Toni Morrison, "A Humanist View," in *Public Dialogue on the American Dream Theme,* ed. Keisha E. McKenzie, Black Studies Center Public Dialogue (Portland, Ore: Portland State University Library, 1975).

63. The playhouse would be a fitting site for the pursuit of such baseless desire, as Odai Johnson says playgoers "could not practically afford" theatre but "purchased and patronized [it] against all sense beyond its singular driving desire." Johnson, *Absence and Memory,* 61.

64. Angel Rama, *The Lettered City,* ed. and trans. John Charles Chasteen (Durham: Duke University Press, 1996), 8.

65. Richards, *Drama, Theatre, and Identity,* 5, 143–44.

66. Agnew, *Worlds Apart.*

67. Excellent cultural histories have analyzed the concurrent development of pro-
fessional theatre and capitalist culture in England. Leinwand addresses Quick-
Silver and Golding, from the play *Eastward Hoe* (1605). See his *Theatre, Finance
and Society in Early Modern England,* 44–54; Geo[rge] Chapman, Ben Jonson, and
Joh[n] Marston, *Eastward Hoe: As It was playd in the Black-friers* (London, 1605).
Lisa Freeman analyzes the Surfaces from *School for Scandal* (1777). See Freeman,
"The Social Life of Eighteenth-Century Comedy," in *The Cambridge Companion
to British Theatre, 1730–1830,* ed. Jane Moody and Daniel O'Quinn (Cambridge:
Cambridge University Press, 2007), 75–79; Richard Brinsley Sheridan, *The School
for Scandal* (London, 1777).

68. Theatre historian Robert Hornback argues that folly was the distinguishing trait
of blackfaced characters from the sixteenth through the nineteenth centuries.

69. Scholars such as Alden Vaughan and Richmond Bond provide an invaluable evidentiary base for studies of Indian visits to London. However, their work leaves
open the question of the *need* that prompted the production of these documents
of Indian Watching. A. T. Vaughan, *Transatlantic Encounters;* Richmond P. Bond,
Queen Anne's American Kings (New York: Octagon Books, 1974); Garratt, *The
Four Indian Kings.* A notable exception to these accounts is Hinderaker's investigation of the efflorescence of cultural production around the Four Kings' visit
and their contribution to the "imaginative construction of empire." See Eric
Hinderaker, "The 'Four Indian Kings' and the Imaginative Construction of the
First British Empire." *William and Mary Quarterly,* 3rd ser., 53, no. 3 (July 1996):
487–526.

70. John Genest, *Some Account of the English Stage, from the Restoration in 1660 to 1830,*
Vol. II (Bath: H.E. Carrington, 1832), 451 (my emphasis). See also Bond, *Queen
Anne's American Kings,* 4, 98–99.

71. "Theatre | Theater, n.," in *OED Online,* accessed May 28, 2019, http://www.oed
.com/view/Entry/200227.

72. Pierre Danchin, ed., *The Prologues and Epilogues of the Eighteenth Century:
First Part: 1701–1720* (Nancy, France, 1990), 2:470 ("struck"), quoted in Roach,
Cities of the Dead, 166. Timothy J. Shannon argues that "an Indian king visited
the royal court as an equal, not as a supplicant." See Shannon, "'This Wretched
Scene of British Curiosity and Savage Debauchery': Performing Indian Kingship
in Eighteenth-Century Britain," in *Native Acts: Indian Performance, 1603–1832,* ed.
Joshua David Bellin and Laura L. Mielke (Lincoln: University of Nebraska Press,
2012), 202. Yet the imperial project was to grant "political sovereignty" so that
Indian kings could be perceived as "effective allies and agents of the Crown in the
empire-building process." See Hinderaker, "The 'Four Indian Kings,'" 488.

73. Bond, *Queen Anne's American Kings,* 4.

74. Danchin, *Prologues and Epilogues,* 2:470, quoted in Roach, *Cities of the Dead,* 167
("enrich'd"), 166 ("whole Globe"). On the coordination of ephemeral performance
and textual memorabilia, see Julie Stone Peters, *Theatre of the Book, 1480–1880:
Print, Text, and Performance in Europe* (New York: Oxford University Press, 2000).

75. "The Four Indian Kings Garland; Being a Faithful and true Account how the powerful charms of a beautiful Lady conquer'd the Heart of one of the Four Indian Kings" (Hull, n.d.) part 1, lines 4–6.

76. Laura M. Stevens, "'Spare His Life to Save His Soul': Enthralled Lovers and Heathen Converts in 'The Four Indian Kings Garland,'" in *Atlantic Worlds in the Long Eighteenth Century: Seduction and Sentiment,* ed. Toni Bowers and Tita Chico (New York: Palgrave Macmillan, 2012), 97–113.

77. A. T. Vaughan, *Transatlantic Encounters,* 134. Gaudy West Indian Creoles were stock eighteenth-century characters. While the tacky white planter and his wife needed their taste corrected, Indigenous persons were rendered as either incorrigible or requiring a far more extensive re-education. Examples include Richard Steele, "Brunetta and Phillis," *The Spectator,* June 1, 1711; Richard Cumberland, *The West Indian: A Comedy as It Is Performed at the Theatre Royal in Drury-Lane* (London: Printed for W. Griffin, 1771).

78. "Monday, *Sept. 21,*" *Grub Street Journal* (London), September 24, 1730, [2].

79. "Journal of Sir Alexander Cuming (1730)," in *Early Travels in the Tennessee Country, 1540–1800,* ed. Samuel Cole Williams (Johnson City, Tenn., 1928), 129; see also A. T. Vaughan, *Transatlantic Encounters,* 138.

80. A. T. Vaughan, *Transatlantic Encounters,* 142 ("expert[s]"); "Monday, *Sept 7,*" *Grub Street Journal,* September 10, 1730, [2] ("urprised").

81. "Monday, *Sept. 21,*" *Grub Street Journal,* September 24, 1730, [2].

82. Ja[mes] Brudenell, M[artin] Bladen, and T[homas] Pelham, "Board of Trade to the Duke of Newcastle about Authorization for a Cherokee Treaty," August 20, 1730, doc. 34, in Alden T. Vaughan, ed., *Early American Indian Documents: Treaties and Laws, 1607–1789* (Washington, D.C.: University Publications of America, 1979), 13:135; see also Vaughan, *Transatlantic Encounters,* 145.

83. *Evening Post* (London), October 6–8, 1730, [3] ("Two pieces," "against," "20 guns"), [2] ("fasten").

84. By way of comparison, see A. T. Vaughan, *Transatlantic Encounters,* 146–47.

85. Colin G. Calloway, *Pen and Ink Witchcraft: Treaties and Treaty Making in American Indian History* (New York: Oxford University Press, 2013), 44. I am grateful to the poet Ryan Black for informative conversations on synecdoche and other modes of figuration.

86. *Daily Journal* (London), October 8, 1730, [2].

87. *Evening Post,* October 6–8, 1730, [2] ("Crown"), [3] ("*Answer*"), [4] ("hither").

88. For analysis of this imperial literature, see Peter Hulme, *Colonial Encounters: Europe and the Native Caribbean, 1492–1797* (New York: Routledge, 1992), chaps. 3, 5; L. Brown, *Ends of Empire,* chap. 2; Aravamudan, *Tropicopolitans,* chap. 1; Cartelli, *Repositioning Shakespeare,* chaps. 4, 6.

89. Greenblatt, *Renaissance Self-Fashioning,* chap. 6; Stephen Greenblatt, *Learning to Curse: Essays in Early Modern Culture* (New York: Routledge, 1990), chap. 1.

90. "Charles-Town, July 31," *Virginia Gazette,* September 19, 1755, [2].

91. *Evening Post,* October 6–8 1730, [3].

92. Keith Robson, "Accounting Numbers as 'Inscription': Action at a Distance and the Development of Accounting," *Accounting, Organizations and Society* 17, no. 7 (October 1992): 691.

93. Rasmussen, *Queequeg's Coffin.*

94. See Roach, *Cities of the Dead,* 137–38; Calloway, *Pen and Ink Witchcraft,* 6, 12, 14, 16, 48. On the battle between fixed text and unruly speech in early America, see the excellent work of David Murray, *Forked Tongues: Speech, Writing and Representation in North American Indian Texts* (Bloomington: University of Indiana Press, 1991); Alessandro Portelli, *The Text and the Voice: Writing, Speaking, and Democracy in American Literature* (New York: Columbia University Press, 1994); Jane Kamensky, *Governing the Tongue: The Politics of Speech in Early New England* (New York: Oxford University Press, 1998); Gustafson, *Eloquence Is Power.*

95. Franklin, "Virginia and the Cherokee Indian Trade"; Corkran, *The Cherokee Frontier;* James C. Kelly, "Notable Persons in Cherokee History: Attakullakulla," *Journal of Cherokee Studies* 3, no. 1 (Winter 1978): 2–34; Thomas A. Strohfeldt, "Warriors in Williamsburg: The Cherokee Presence in Virginia's Eighteenth Century Capital," *Journal of Cherokee Studies* 11, no. 1 (Spring 1986): 4–18; Dowd, "The Panic of 1751."

96. Dowd, "The Panic of 1751."

97. "To which the Chief of them return'd the following ANSWER," *Virginia Gazette,* August 16, 1751, [2].

98. For analysis of race-based expectations and eighteenth-century cons, see David Waldstreicher, "Reading the Runaways: Self-Fashioning, Print Culture, and Confidence in Slavery in the Eighteenth-Century Mid-Atlantic," *William and Mary Quarterly* 56, no. 2 (April 1999): 243–72; Shannon, "'This Wretched Scene.'"

99. W. L. Hall, *Executive Journals of the Council of Colonial Virginia,* 5:357.

100. For a kindred analysis of the economic costs of being taken in by confidence men's performances, see Waldstreicher, "Reading the Runaways."

101. W. L. Hall, *Executive Journals,* 5:357 ("very large"), 355 ("English").

102. "A Letter from the Governor of *South-Carolina,*" *Virginia Gazette,* October 31, 1751, [2]. For the council's instructions to Hunter, see W. L. Hall, *Executive Journals,* 5:364.

103. Alden, *Robert Dinwiddie,* 7–12.

104. Evidence of the close cooperation of the newspaper and government appears in the diary of council member John Blair; see "Diary of John Blair," *William and Mary Quarterly* 8, no. 1 (1899): 9–13. For a discussion of Hunter's progovernment editorial stance, see *Encyclopedia Virginia Online,* s.v. "William Hunter (d. 1761)," by David Rawson, Virginia Foundation for the Humanities, July 19, 2011, http://www.encyclopediavirginia.org/Hunter_William_d_1761.

105. Natasha Korda finds an inability to properly value objects a point of articulation between characterizations of white women and of racial others in early modernity. See Korda, *Shakespeare's Domestic Economies,* chap. 4. Meanwhile, Catherine Gallagher finds evidence after the 1760s that English women readers' were selected as

exemplifying the perils of overidentification with characters in novels. See Gallagher, "Nobody's Story," 274–75.

106. See *Virginia Gazette,* September 22, 1752, 3.

107. George Gilmer to Walter King, November 14, 1752, Letter Book of Dr. George Gilmer, 1752, Colonial Williamsburg Foundation, Special Collections.

108. Johnson, *Absence and Memory,* 64. The thrill and the danger of Abigail Adams's visit to Drury Lane comes from this very visibility of the audience.

109. Leonard Tennenhouse, *The Importance of Feeling English: American Literature and the British Diaspora, 1750–1850* (Princeton: Princeton University Press, 2007).

110. "At a Council held August the Ninth 1751," in W. L. Hall, *Executive Journals,* 5:349–52, 413–15.

111. Dillon, *New World Drama,* 14. Dillon offers the embodied, unruly "performative commons" as an alternative to the print public sphere, purportedly characterized by disembodied, rational argumentation. Interventions in this embodied arena do not require the capacity to write or access to a willing press. Consequently, the range of participants is broader than the body of literate white men who tried to constitute the national public in the more circumscribed sphere of print.

112. By way of comparison, see W. Stitt Robinson's assertion that Amouskositte tried to lend Attakullakulla retroactive legitimacy by claiming he authorized the 1751 trip to Williamsburg. Robinson, *James Glen,* 95.

113. With this interpretation, I hope to offer antecedents to the story of Cherokees' adaptation and revision of the instruments and ideologies of "European literacy." See Barry O'Connell, "Literacy and Colonization: The Case of the Cherokees," in *A History of the Book in America,* ed. Robert A. Gross and Mary Kelley, vol. 2: *An Extensive Republic: Print, Culture, and Society in the New Nation, 1790–1840* (Chapel Hill: University of North Carolina Press, 2010), 496–97.

114. For an engrossing discussion of contested understandings of familial terms, see Calloway, *Pen and Ink Witchcraft,* 24–25. For kindred work on seventeenth-century Massachusetts, see Jenny Hale Pulsipher, *Subjects unto the Same King: Indians, English, and the Contest for Authority in Colonial New England* (Philadelphia: University of Pennsylvania Press, 2005), 19–20.

115. A. T. Vaughan, *Transatlantic Encounters,* 147. By way of comparison, see Vaughan's focus on the British authors' craftiness, which seems to reify an authoritative text that the Cherokees treated as part of a relationship maintained by ongoing negotiation (146–47).

116. For Indian leaders' demands to bypass colonial governors and have an audience with the king, see Evans, "Notable Persons in Cherokee History: Ostenaco" 48; Kelly, "Notable Persons in Cherokee History: Attakullakulla," 8. On improvisation as a European capacity, see Greenblatt, *Renaissance Self-Fashioning,* chap. 6. For a more reciprocal view, see Richard White, *The Middle Ground: Indians, Empires, and Republics in the Great Lakes Region, 1650–1815* (New York: Cambridge University Press, 1991); Joshua David Bellin, *Medicine Bundle: Indian Sacred Performance and American Literature, 1824–1932* (Philadelphia: University of Pennsylvania Press, 2008); Joanne Rappaport and Tom Cummins, *Beyond the*

Lettered City: Indigenous Literacies in the Andes (Durham, N.C.: Duke University Press, 2011); Rasmussen, *Queequeg's Coffin;* Jeffrey Glover, *Paper Sovereigns: Anglo-Native Treaties and the Law of Nations, 1604–1664* (Philadelphia: University of Pennsylvania Press, 2014); Matt Cohen and Jeffrey Glover, eds., *Colonial Mediascapes: Sensory Worlds of the Early Americas* (Lincoln: University of Nebraska Press, 2014). Walter J. Ong famously argued that script and print alone enable abstraction, sequence, classification, extensive comparison, and explanation. Ong has been challenged by subsequent anthropologists. See Ong, *Orality and Literacy;* Brian V. Street, *Literacy in Theory and Practice* (New York: Cambridge University Press, 1985); Jack Goody, *The Interface between the Written and the Oral* (New York: Cambridge University Press, 1987); Brian V. Street, ed., *Cross-Cultural Approaches to Literacy* (New York: Cambridge University Press, 1993).

117. Charles H. Shattuck confidently places the interruption in the extensive, wounding swordfight of the second act of *Othello.* Yet, given that Shakespeare was not treated as sacred text, the actors may well have engaged in a bit of crowd-pleasing swordplay in the second scene of act 1 when swords are drawn to capture Othello. The empress may have had more reason to intervene in the arrest of the sole character painted black than in the later fight between whites. See Shattuck, *Shakespeare on the American Stage,* 9.

118. Gearing, "Priests and Warriors," 23–26. Raymond D. Fogelson notes that women might have been understood as "pink," as mediators between red and white councils. See Fogelson, "Cherokee Notions of Power," in *The Anthropology of Power: Ethnographic Studies from Asia, Oceania, and the New World,* ed. Fogelson and Richard N. Adams (New York: Academic Press, 1977), 185–94.

119. Though the story of the interrupted *Othello* cannot be verified, it seems unlikely—given the embarrassing retraction of the previous year—that Dinwiddie and Hunter would have risked fabricating a story that a subscriber who had been in the audience could refute. Whether the interruption occurred or not, the *Virginia Gazette* turned the Cherokee visit into a familiar story of Indian error at the theatre.

120. "Talk taken . . . from the mouths of Chekelli Mico or King & Chief of the upper and lover Creeks . . . to the Saltzburgere, and Sundry Gentlemen and Freeholders of the Said town and Province of Georgia," June 11, 1735, manuscript of vol. 14200, Letters from Georgia, June 1732–June 1735, Egmont (Sir John Perceval) Papers, University of Georgia, Athens, 8. Unable to compete with Attakullakulla's stories, rival leader Ostenaco insisted in the 1760s that he be sent to England to raise his own status. Evans, "Notable Persons in Cherokee History: Ostenaco," esp. 44. See also Kelly, "Notable Persons in Cherokee History: Attakullakulla," 3, 8, 10.

121. For Attakullakulla, see Hatley, *The Dividing Paths,* 149; for Amouskositte's wife, 108.

122. For more details on unruly behavior at playhouses, see Twining, *The Plays and the Playgoers,* 5–15; Jim Davis, "Spectatorship," in *The Cambridge Companion to British Theatre, 1730–1830,* ed. Jane Moody and Daniel O'Quinn (New York: Cambridge University Press, 2007), 57–69.

123. Henry Timberlake, *The Memoirs of Lieut. Henry Timberlake* (London, 1765), 37. See also Perdue, *Cherokee Women*, 30. Practices such as tattooing and face painting cross ethnic affiliations, giving them the potential to trouble the fixed position Matthieu Chapman ascribes to black Africans as the sole and permanent abjected group in the English imagination. See Chapman, *Anti-Black Racism in Early Modern English Drama*, 30.

124. "Williamsburg, November 17," *Virginia Gazette*, November 17, 1752, [2].

125. Gearing, *American Anthropologist*, 64:26; Perdue, *Cherokee Women*, 38–39.

126. On native women's influence in treaty negotiations, see Calloway, *Pen and Ink Witchcraft*, 17–19; Perdue, *Cherokee Women*, 55. I thank Sarah Crabtree for asking me the crucial question of whether gender had anything to do with the empress's interruption.

127. Hatley notes that Cherokees listened to speakers in silence and complained when colonists interrupted. If he is correct, then the Cherokee woman's disruption was novel. See Hatley, *Dividing Paths*, 11.

128. Johnson, *Absence and Memory*, 69.

129. Historian Dawn Peterson noted that the likelihood that the colonial newspaper fabricated this event is especially low, since they probably would not have attributed political agency to a Cherokee woman. Personal communication.

130. This New York event was another classic occasion of eighteenth-century Indian Watching. A great concourse of people gathered at the playhouse and found the Cherokees superficial viewers who observed the play with "Seriousness and Attention" but could only express "Surprize and Curiosity." See "New-York Dec 17," *Pennsylvania Gazette*, December 24, 1767, quoted in Seilhamer, *History of the American Theatre*, 219.

131. "By Permission of his Excellency the Governor," *New-York Journal; or, The General Advertiser*, April 7, 1768, [3]; see also Odai Johnson and William J. Burling, *The Colonial American Stage, 1665–1774: A Documentary Calendar* (Madison, N.J.: Farleigh Dickinson University Press, 2001), 300; Johnson, *Absence and Memory*, 232–33.

132. Joshua Piker, *The Four Deaths of Acorn Whistler: Telling Stories in Colonial America* (Cambridge, Mass.: Harvard University Press, 2013), 46–47.

133. *Evening Post*, January 2–4, 1752, [1].

134. *Evening Post*, March 17–20, 1753, [4]; *Old England's Journal* (London), March 24, 1753, [3]; *Read's Weekly Journal; or, British Gazetteer* (London), March 24, 1753, [3].

135. Julie Flavell, *When London Was Capital of America* (New Haven: Yale University Press, 2010).

136. It is possible that the alleged gullibility of American indigenes stems from their designation as "blacks." During the 1730 visit, at least one newspaper felt the need to specify that emissaries were "all blacks." *Weekly Journal, or The British Gazetteer*, June 27, 1730: "On Monday last the Indian King, and the Prince, and five of the chiefs of his Court (all blacks) were introduced to his Majesty at Windsor, the King had a scarlet jacket on, but all the rest were naked, except an apron about their middles, and a horse's tail hung down behind; their faces, shoulders, &c. were

painted and spotted with red, blue, and green, &c. they had bows in their hands, and painted feathers on their heads."

137. You know who, "To the Printer of The St. James's Chronicle," *St. James's Chronicle; or, the British Evening-Post* (London), August 7–10, 1762, [5].

138. See Kupperman, "Presentment of Civility."

139. L. Brown, *Ends of Empire,* 63.

5. Inkface to Chalkbones

1. On homoerotic aspects of this relationship, see Daniel Hannah, "Queer Hospitality in Herman Melville's 'Benito Cereno,'" *Studies in American Fiction* 37, no. 2 (2010): 181–201.

2. Herman Melville, "Benito Cereno," in *Billy Budd, Sailor and Selected Tales,* ed. Robert Milder (New York: Oxford University Press, 1998), 227. All subsequent citations are in parentheses in the text.

3. Within the tale, European sailors are the sole persons called to read Babo's inscription. Melville's attitudes toward the literary marketplace suggest that he imagined a sophisticated white male readership. See Charlene Avallone, "The Company of Women Authors," in *A Companion to Herman Melville,* ed. Wyn Kelley (Oxford: Blackwell, 2006), 313–26.

4. John 20:28.

5. Hebrews 11:1. For examination of Melville's study of the Bible, see Mark Heidmann, "The Markings in Herman Melville's Bibles," *Studies in the American Renaissance,* January 1990, 341–98.

6. Toni Morrison, *Paradise,* reprint ed. (New York: Vintage, 2014), 248. For Morrison's analyses of Melville, see Toni Morrison, "Unspeakable Things Unspoken: The Afro-American Presence in American Literature," *Michigan Quarterly Review* 18, no. 1 (Winter 1989): 140–45; Morrison, "The Official Story: Dead Man Golfing," in *Birth of a Nation'hood: Gaze, Script, and Spectacle in the O. J. Simpson Case,* ed. Morrison and Claudia Brodsky Lacour (New York: Pantheon, 1997), vii–x, xxvii–xxviii.

7. On the bonito as a deadly fish, see Max Putzel, "The Source and the Symbols of Melville's 'Benito Cereno,'" *American Literature* 34, no. 2 (1962): 204. On the homosocial desire tying the two captains, see Hannah, "Queer Hospitality in Herman Melville's 'Benito Cereno.'"

8. Sidney Kaplan, "Herman Melville and the American National Sin: The Meaning of 'Benito Cereno,'" *Journal of Negro History* 41, no. 4 (October 1956): 311–38; Carolyn L. Karcher, *Shadow over the Promised Land: Slavery, Race, and Violence in Melville's America* (Baton Rouge: Louisiana State University Press, 1980); Eric J. Sundquist, *To Wake the Nations: Race in the Making of American Literature* (Cambridge, Mass.: Harvard University Press, 1993); Ezra F. Tawil, "Captain Babo's Cabin: Stowe, Race and Misreading in 'Benito Cereno,'" *Leviathan* 8, no. 2 (May 2013): 37–51.

9. Robert A. Gross and Mary Kelley, eds., *A History of the Book in America,* vol. 2: *An Extensive Republic: Print, Culture, and Society in the New Nation, 1790–1840,* 1st ed.

(Chapel Hill: University of North Carolina Press, 2010); Adrian Johns, "The Book in, and as, American History," *New England Quarterly* 84, no. 3 (September 2011): 496–511; Scott E. Casper et al., eds., *A History of the Book in America,* vol. 3: *The Industrial Book, 1840–1880* (Chapel Hill: University of North Carolina Press, 2007); Heather S. Nathans, *Early American Theatre from the Revolution to Thomas Jefferson: Into the Hands of the People* (New York: Cambridge University Press, 2003).

10. Joseph Rezek, *London and the Making of Provincial Literature: Aesthetics and the Transatlantic Book Trade, 1800–1850* (Philadelphia: University of Pennsylvania Press, 2015); Lawrence Levine, *Highbrow/Lowbrow: The Emergence of Cultural Hierarchy in America* (Cambridge, Mass.: Harvard University Press, 1990).

11. Jill Lepore, *A Is for American: Letters and Other Characters in the Newly United States* (New York: Vintage, 2003).

12. One could also say that although racial whiteness was operative in distinction from non-Europeans, there was no guarantee of pan-European affinity.

13. American Tract Society, *The Picture Alphabet: In Prose and Verse* (New York: Published by the American Tract Society, 150 Nassau-Street, New York, 1848).

14. American Tract Society, "Early History of the American Tract Society," accessed September 5, 2011, http://www.atstracts.org/atshistory.html.

15. H.R. 40, Naturalization Bill, March 4, 1790.

16. Warner, *The Letters of the Republic;* Eve Tavor Bannet, *Empire of Letters: Letter Manuals and Transatlantic Correspondence, 1688–1820* (Cambridge: Cambridge University Press, 2005).

17. On Spanish as the language of the captains' intimacy, see Jesse Alemán, "The Age of US Latinidad," in *Timelines of American Literature,* ed. Cody Marrs and Christopher Hager (Baltimore: Johns Hopkins University Press, 2019), 159–69.

18. E. Jennifer Monaghan, "Reading for the Enslaved, Writing for the Free: Reflections on Liberty and Literacy," *Proceedings of the American Antiquarian Society* 108, no. 2 (January 1999): 309–41.

19. Frederick Douglass, *Narrative of the Life of Frederick Douglass, An American Slave, Written by Himself* (Boston: The Anti-Slavery Office, 1845), 33.

20. Gustafson, *Eloquence Is Power.*

21. David Walker, *Walker's Appeal in Four Articles; Together with a Preamble, to the Coloured Citizens of the World, But in Particular, and Very Expressly, to Those of the United States of America, Written in Boston, State of Massachusetts, September 28, 1829,* 3rd ed. (Boston: David Walker, 1830).

22. For this legal history, see Monaghan, "Reading for the Enslaved," 331–34.

23. Aravamudan, *Tropicopolitans;* Marlene Daut, *Tropics of Haiti: Race and the Literary History of the Haitian Revolution in the Atlantic World, 1789–1865* (Liverpool: Liverpool University Press, 2015).

24. Eve Sanders discusses the ideally passive female reader produced by early modern literacy instruction. It would seem that Native and African readers are slotted into the same position as white women are. See her *Gender and Literacy on Stage.* On the resonances between student and slave in the early modern English classroom, see Chakravarty, *Fictions of Consent.*

25. Philippe R. Girard, "Un-Silencing the Past: The Writings of Toussaint Louver-ture," *Slavery & Abolition* 34, no. 4 (December 2013): 663–72; "The Toussaint Louverture Internet Archive," accessed June 9, 2020, https://www.marxists.org /reference/archive/toussaint-louverture/index.htm. Girard, it must be said, has a disturbing tendency to blame Haitians, and Louverture in particular, for decisions made by Napolean. His work, though archivally sound, is marred by a desire to exculpate France that disorders the chronology and causality he offers.

26. Referring not only to baptism but also to biblical literacy instruction, Jefferson wrote: "Religion indeed has produced a Phyllis Whately; but it could not produce a poet." Thomas Jefferson, *Notes on the State of Virginia* (Philadelphia: Printed and sold by Prichard and Hall, in Market Street, between Front and Second Streets, 1788), 150.

27. Prince Saunders, ed., *Haytian Papers.: A Collection of the Very Interesting Proc-lamations, and Other Official Documents; Together with Some Account of the Rise, Progress, and Present State of the Kingdom of Hayti* (London: Printed for W. Reed, law bookseller, no. 17, Fleet Street, 1816); Prince Hall, *A Charge, Delivered to the African Lodge, June 24, 1797, at Menotomy. By the Right Wor-shipful Prince Hall.; Published by the Desire of the Members of Said Lodge* (1797); Maria W. Stewart, *Meditations from the Pen of Mrs. Maria W. Stewart: (Widow of the Late James W. Stewart) Now Matron of the Freedman's Hospital, and Pre-sented in 1832 to the First African Baptist Church and Society of Boston, Mass* (Washington, D.C.: Enterprise Publishing Company, 1879); Eric Gardner, "'You Have No Business to Whip Me': The Freedom Suits of Polly Wash and Lucy Ann Delaney," *African American Review* 41, no. 1 (April 2007): 33–50; Loren Schweninger, *Appealing for Liberty: Freedom Suits in the South* (New York: Oxford University Press, 2018). The phrase "scenes of tutelage" is a tribute to Hartman. See Saidiya V. Hartman, *Scenes of Subjection: Terror, Slavery, and Self-Making in Nineteenth-Century America* (New York: Oxford University Press, 1997).

28. Scott Saul contends that debates, however fierce, often occur on a "shared . . . field of argument." See Saul, *Freedom Is, Freedom Ain't: Jazz and the Making of the Six-ties* (Cambridge, Mass.: Harvard University Press, 2005), xii.

29. By subjecting white people to catechizing by an African, Melville's "BC" serves as a riposte to this contemporary alphabetical literature as if to say: "The Afri-cans have proceeded beyond A, the first lesson. Through subsequent lessons B and C, like Shylock, they intend to 'better the instruction' of the evils we have taught them."

30. I refer to the publication of the complete text. *Uncle Tom's Cabin* had, of course, appeared in serial form in *The National Era* in 1851.

31. Thomas N. Ingersoll, "'Releese Us out of This Cruell Bondegg': An Appeal from Virginia in 1723," *William and Mary Quarterly* 51, no. 4 (1994): 777–82; John Sekora, "'Mr. Editor, If You Please': Frederick Douglass, My Bondage and My Freedom, and the End of the Abolitionist Imprint," *Callaloo* 17, no. 2 (April 1994): 608–26; Antonio T. Bly, "'Pretends He Can Read': Runaways and Literacy

in Colonial America, 1730–1776," *Early American Studies: An Interdisciplinary Journal* 6, no. 2 (2008): 261–94.

32. Hortense Spillers's early work on gender and Atlantic slavery entwined property law with sexual abuse, emphasizing both economic schemes and the sheer vulnerability of the captive body. See Spillers, "Mama's Baby, Papa's Maybe: An American Grammar Book," *Diacritics* 17, no. 2 (July 1987): 65–81. The recent economic (re)turn in slavery studies has sometimes emphasized the economic to the exclusion of the sadistic. Yet, a comprehensive accounting of slave society requires that we remember the accrual of possessions that lack economic value or even tangible form.

33. Thomas Madiou, *Histoire d'Haiti* (Port-au-Prince: Imprimerie de J. Courtois, 1847), 114, David Patrick Geggus, *Haitian Revolutionary Studies* (Bloomington: Indiana University Press, 2002), 208. Madiou's text appeared some forty years after independence and, therefore, sits uneasily at the intersection of national myth and historical fact.

34. "Declaration of Independence: A Transcription," National Archives, Kew, November 1, 2015.

35. "Haitian Declaration of Independence" (January 1, 1804), CO 137/111/1, National Archives, Kew.

36. For a study of divided reactions to the earlier Constitution of 1801 printed in white US-American newspapers, see Michael J. Drexler and Ed White, "The Constitution of Toussaint: Another Origin of African American Literature," in *The Haitian Revolution and the Early United States: Histories, Textualities, Geographies,* ed. Elizabeth Maddock Dillon and Michael Drexler (Philadelphia: University of Pennsylvania Press, 2016), 211–31. For reactions to the governments of Toussaint and, especially, his successors, see Daut, *Tropics of Haiti;* Chelsea Stieber, *Haiti's Paper War: Post-Independence Writing, Civil War, and the Making of the Republic, 1804–1954* (New York: New York University Press, 2020); Tabitha McIntosh and Grégory Pierrot, "Capturing the Likeness of Henry I of Haiti (1805–1822)," *Atlantic Studies* 14, no. 2 (April 2017): 127–51; Grégory Pierrot, "'Our Hero': Toussaint Louverture in British Representations," *Criticism* 50, no. 4 (2008): 581–607.

37. Nancy Stepan, "Race and the Return of the Great Chain of Being, 1800–50," in *The Idea of Race in Science: Great Britain 1800–1960,* ed. Nancy Stepan, St Antony's/Macmillan Series (London: Palgrave Macmillan, 1982), 1–19; Henry Louis Gates, "Editor's Introduction: Writing 'Race' and the Difference It Makes," *Critical Inquiry* 12, no. 1 (1985): 1–20.

38. Bartels suggests that scholars should not take English imagery concerning Africans too seriously, as it "had an obvious imaginative edge." I suspect that the equally imaginative musings of Boisrond-Tonnerre regarding a white body would not strike the white critic as harmless or hypothetical. See Bartels, "Othello and Africa," 53.

39. Michel-Rolph Trouillot, *Silencing the Past: Power and the Production of History* (Boston: Beacon Press, 1995); Alyssa Goldstein Sepinwall, "Still Unthinkable?:

The Haitian Revolution and the Reception of Michel-Rolph Trouillot's *Si-lencing the Past,*" *Journal of Haitian Studies* 19, no. 2 (2013): 75–103.

40. Amasa Delano, *Narrative of Voyages and Travels in the Northern and Southern Hemispheres: Comprising Three Voyages Round the World; Together with a Voyage of Survey and Discovery, in the Pacific Ocean and Oriental Islands.* (Boston: E. G. House, 1817); Harold H. Scudder, "Melville's 'Benito Cereno' and Captain Delano's Voyages," *PMLA* 43, no. 2 (June 1928): 502–32.

41. Many scholars have noted that Melville's story restages the Haitian Revolution. My addition to this scholarship is that Melville conceives of the overthrow of colonial slavery not only as a historical event but also as a textual one. See Eric J. Sundquist, *To Wake the Nations: Race in the Making of American Literature* (Cambridge, Mass.: Harvard University Press, 1993); Maggie Montesinos Sale, *The Slumbering Volcano: American Slave Ship Revolts and the Production of Rebellious Masculinity* (Durham: Duke University Press, 1997); Jonathan Beecher, "Echoes of Toussaint Louverture and the Haitian Revolution in Melville's 'Benito Cereno,'" *Leviathan* 9, no. 2 (2007): 43–58.

42. Arthur L. Vogelback, "Shakespeare and Melville's 'Benito Cereno,'" *Modern Language Notes* 67, no. 2 (February 1952): 115.

43. David Leverenz, *Manhood and the American Renaissance* (Ithaca: Cornell University Press, 1990), 94.

44. See Dennis Berthold, "Class Acts: The Astor Place Riots and Melville's 'The Two Temples,'" *American Literature* 71, no. 3 (1999): 433; Alan Ackerman Jr., *The Portable Theater and the Nineteenth-Century Stage* (Baltimore: Johns Hopkins University Press), 108–9.

45. Berthold, "Class Acts."

46. The Haymarket was also the site where the "Mohawk Kings" saw an operatic *Macbeth* and where Miss Woolery, playing a strangled Desdemona, broke character to look about because an audience member shouted "fire!" See my interlude at the beginning of part 2 and chap. 5, respectively.

47. Herman Melville, *Journals,* ed. Howard C. Horsford, vol. 15 of *The Writings of Herman Melville* (Evanston: Northwestern University Press; Chicago: The Newberry Library, 1989), 22. I retain Melville's misspelling of didn't. There is some question as to whether Melville wrote "panted" or "painted." While many scholars choose "painted," I think it is possible that Melville wrote "panted," considering his emphasis on Macready's hoarse voice.

48. Pompée Valentin de Baron Vastey, *Reflexions on the Blacks and Whites. Remarks upon a Letter Addressed by M. Mazères . . . to J. C. L. Sismonde de Sismondi, Containing Observations on the Blacks and Whites, the Civilization of Africa, the Kingdom of Hayti . . . Translated . . . by W. H. M. B.* (Liverpool: J. Hatchard, 1817), 26. Mia Bay writes that an excerpt from this text appeared on February 14, 1829, in *Freedom's Journal,* a newspaper published in Melville's hometown. Although a ten-year-old Melville would not likely have purchased the newspaper, it is the kind of passage that he would not forget if he encountered it as a child or chanced upon it later. See Bay, *The White Image in the Black Mind: African-American Ideas about*

White People, 1830–1925 (New York: Oxford University Press, 2000), 242n36. Whether Melville saw this specific article or not, Marlene Daut has established that Vastey's ten prose works were translated and disseminated globally and that newspaper editors in the US North and Abolitionists globally were "intimately familiar" with him. See Daut, "Un-Silencing the Past: Boisrond-Tonnerre, Vastey, and the Re-Writing of the Haitian Revolution," *South Atlantic Review* 74, no. 1 (Winter 2009): 56n12.

49. Space will not permit a full engagement with Melville's ruminations on "blackness" or Puritanical gloom in Hawthorne, culminating in an implicit comparison to Hamlet, Timon, Lear, and Iago, whom Melville calls mad Shakespearean truthtellers, or "dark characters." See Herman Melville, "Hawthorne and His Mosses," in *The Piazza Tales: And Other Prose Pieces, 1839–1860,* ed. Harrison Hayford and Merton M. Sealts (Evanston: Northwestern University Press, 1987), 243–44. There seems to be no scholarly commentary on the fact that Melville did *not* count Caliban, Othello, Aaron, Morocco, or Cleopatra among Shakespeare's "dark characters." He did make some marginal notes in *Antony and Cleopatra* and clearly borrowed lines, props, and conceits from *Othello* and *Titus Andronicus.* See Hubert H. Hoeltje, "Hawthorne, Melville, and 'Blackness,'" *American Literature* 37, no. 1 (March 1965): 41–51; Collamer M. Abbott, "Melville's Hawthorne and His Mosses," *Explicator* 49, no. 4 (Summer 1991): 214; Ellen Weinauer, "Hawthorne and Race," in *A Companion to Herman Melville,* ed. Wyn Kelley (Oxford: Blackwell, 2006), 327–41; Michael J. Colacurcio, "'Artificial Fire': Reading Melville (Re-) Reading Hawthorne," *Nathaniel Hawthorne Review* 33, no. 1 (2007): 1–22.

50. Oliver William Bourn Peabody et al., *The Dramatic Works of William Shakspeare: With a Life of the Poet and Notes, Original and Selected,* Open Collections Program at Harvard University, Reading (Boston: Hilliard, Gray, and Co., 1837), http://nrs.harvard.edu/urn-3:FHCL.HOUGH:3326934.

51. Herman Melville, *The Writings of Herman Melville: Correspondence,* ed. Lynn Horth (Evanston: Northwestern University Press; Chicago: The Newberry Library, 1993), 119. See also Hershel Parker, *Herman Melville: A Biography,* vol. 1: *1819–1851* (Baltimore: Johns Hopkins University Press, 2005), 616.

52. Melville, *Correspondence,* 119.

53. Noting the irony, ambiguity, and profundity of Melville's late fiction, scholars align Melville with the narrator of "BC." Yet, Melville did call himself a "dolt and ass" in his letter to Duyckinck on first reading Shakespeare. Rather than dismissing Melville's identification with the gullible American captain Delano, it would be more accurate to see Melville's position in "BC," like Aphra Behn's in "Oroonoko," as mobile.

54. My goal is to provide firmer textual grounding for insights such as those of Peggy Kamuf, who notes "the strange power of writing [in 'Benito Cereno'] to bring figures out of blankness. . . . It is . . . first of all writing that comes on stage as suddenly as a sun god and begins to narrate." See her stimulating "Melville's Credit Card," in *The Division of Literature: Or the University in Deconstruction* (Chicago: University of Chicago Press, 1997), 201.

55. Melville offers the image of a black atop white on "the *ample oval* of the *shield-like stern-piece*, intricately carved with the arms of Castile and Leon, medallioned about by groups of mythological or *symbolical devices;* uppermost and central of which was a dark satyr in a mask, holding his foot on the prostrate neck of a writhing figure, likewise masked" (167).

56. On close reading, see John Guillory, "Close Reading: Prologue and Epilogue," *ADE Bulletin,* 2010, 8–14; Barbara Herrnstein Smith, "What Was 'Close Reading'?: A Century of Method in Literary Studies," *Minnesota Review,* no. 87 (2016): 57–75. On the logic of character, see J. Hillis Miller, *Ariadne's Thread: Story Lines* (New Haven: Yale University Press, 1995), 55ff.

57. See Guy A. Cardwell, "Melville's Gray Story: Symbols and Meaning in 'Benito Cereno,'" *Bucknell Review* 8, no. 3 (1959): 154–67; Delia Steverson, "'Everything Gray': Polygenism and Racial Perception in Herman Melville's 'Benito Cereno,'" *Journal of American Culture* 40, no. 2 (June 2017): 169–77.

58. Melville's tale remains ambivalent about whether or not racial character can be read according to the protocols of the page. While Delano and Aranda are incorrect to cast Africans as unarmed alphabetical characters, the "Barbadoes planter" who insists that "mulattos" must be assessed in terms of a European exterior and a dark interior proves correct (215).

59. Melville seems aware of Iberians' inaugural position in making commodities and signifiers fit for the processes of New World slavery. For arguments that Spain supplied the language of blackness and the obsession with blood that shaped Atlantic racial classification and status, see María DeGuzmán, *Spain's Long Shadow: The Black Legend, Off-Whiteness, and Anglo-American Empire* (Minneapolis: University of Minnesota Press, 2005); Eric Griffin, *English Renaissance Drama and the Specter of Spain: Ethnopoetics and Empire* (Philadelphia: University of Pennsylvania Press, 2009); Noemie Ndiaye, "Aaron's Roots: Spaniards, Englishmen, and Blackamoors in *Titus Andronicus,*" *Early Theatre* 19, no. 2 (2016): 59–80; Emily Weissbourd, "'I Have Done the State Some Service': Reading Slavery in *Othello* through Juan Latino," *Comparative Drama* 47, no. 4 (2013): 529–51.

60. It would be impossible to cite the full array of scholarship on the gothic strain in US-American literature. Here, however, are some highlights that indicate its age and persistence: Leslie A. Fiedler, "Second Thoughts on 'Love and Death in the American Novel': My First Gothic Novel," *NOVEL: A Forum on Fiction* 1, no. 1 (October 1967): 9–11; Matt Clavin, "Race, Revolution, and the Sublime: The Gothicization of the Haitian Revolution in the New Republic and Atlantic World," *Early American Studies: An Interdisciplinary Journal* 5, no. 1 (2007): 1–29; Robert Miles, "Transatlantic Gothic," in *Transatlantic Literary Studies, 1660–1830,* ed. Eve Tavor Bannet and Susan Manning (New York: Cambridge University Press, 2011), 202–18; Sian Silyn Roberts, *Gothic Subjects: The Transformation of Individualism in American Fiction, 1790–1861* (Philadelphia: University of Pennsylvania Press, 2014).

61. For an impressive discussion of the materiality of Hawthorne's red letter, see Crain, *The Story of A,* chap. 5. Americanists will know that Melville was an ardent admirer

of Hawthorne's work, sought his companionship and, possibly, a sexual tryst. For Melville to write a "BC" as a companion and successor to Hawthorne's Scarlet A is not, therefore, surprising. On the Hawthorne/Melville relationship, see Edwin Haviland Miller, *Melville: A Biography* (New York: George Braziller, 1975); Mark Van Doren, *Nathaniel Hawthorne: A Critical Biography* (New York: Viking, 1966); Charles N. Watson, "The Estrangement of Hawthorne and Melville," *New England Quarterly* 46, no. 3 (1973) 380–402; Hershel Parker, *Herman Melville: A Biography,* vol. 1: *1819–1851* (Baltimore: Johns Hopkins University Press, 1996), chaps. 35–36; Parker, *Herman Melville: A Biography,* vol. 2: *1851–1891* (Baltimore: Johns Hopkins University Press, 2005), chaps. 1, 30.

62. On Melville's lifelong difficulty with handwriting and spelling, see Elizabeth Renker, *Strike through the Mask: Herman Melville and the Scene of Writing* (Baltimore: Johns Hopkins University Press, 1997).

63. See my first chapter for analysis of these phrases from *Othello.*

64. In light of Stoever, one might conclude that Melville finds the page the place that both blurs and re-entrenches a sonic color line. See Jennifer Lynn Stoever, *The Sonic Color Line: Race and the Cultural Politics of Listening* (New York: NYU Press, 2016).

65. R. Feltenstein, "Melville's 'Benito Cereno,'" *American Literature* 19, no. 3 (1947): 245–55; Stanley T. Williams, "'Follow Your Leader': Melville's 'Benito Cereno,'" *Virginia Quarterly Review* 23 (1947): 61–76; Vogelback, "Shakespeare and Melville's 'Benito Cereno'"; Robin Magowan, "Masque and Symbol in Melville's 'Benito Cereno,'" *College English* 23, no. 5 (February 1962): 346–51; Barry Phillips, "'The Good Captain': A Reading of 'Benito Cereno,'" *Texas Studies in Literature and Language* 4, no. 2 (July 1962): 188–97; Putzel, "The Source and the Symbols of Melville's 'Benito Cereno.'"

66. J. Schiffman, "Critical Problems in Melville's 'Benito Cereno,'" *Modern Language Quarterly* 11, no. 3 (1950): 317; Sidney Kaplan, "Herman Melville and the American National Sin: The Meaning of 'Benito Cereno,'" *Journal of Negro History* 41, no. 4 (October 1956): 311–38; Kaplan, "Herman Melville and the American National Sin: The Meaning of 'Benito Cereno,'" *Journal of Negro History* 42, no. 1 (1957): 11–37; Margaret M. Vanderhaar, "A Re-Examination of 'Benito Cereno,'" *American Literature* 40, no. 2 (May 1968): 179–91; Jean Fagan Yellin, "Black Masks: Melville's 'Benito Cereno,'" *American Quarterly* 22, no. 3 (October 1970): 678–89; Joyce Adler, "Melville's 'Benito Cereno': Slavery and Violence in the Americas," *Science & Society* 38, no. 1 (1974): 19–48; Joshua Leslie and Sterling Stuckey, "The Death of Benito Cereno: A Reading of Herman Melville on Slavery: The Revolt on Board the Tryal," *Journal of Negro History* 67, no. 4 (December 1982): 287–301; Eric J. Sundquist, *To Wake the Nations: Race in the Making of American Literature* (Cambridge, Mass.: Harvard University Press, 1993).

67. See three remarkable essays: Charles Martin and James Snead, "Reading through Blackness: Colorless Signifiers in 'Benito Cereno,'" *Yale Journal of Criticism* 4, no. 1 (1990): 231–51; Kamuf, "Melville's Credit Card"; Douglas M. Coulson,

"Distorted Records in 'Benito Cereno' and the Slave Rebellion Tradition," *Yale Journal of Law & the Humanities* 22, no. 1 (2010): 1–34. Kamuf perceptively notes the "asymmetry" of the story—that whites can commit black deeds but blacks cannot be whitened. Yet, her discussions of Don Benito's blackened memory (196) and "the sea of white ink" (201) proceed from her own metaphors, rather than Melville's.

68. Catherine Toal, "'Some Things Which Could Never Have Happened': Fiction, Identification, and 'Benito Cereno,'" *Nineteenth-Century Literature* 61, no. (2006): 55. Compare to Kamuf, who argues that "Delano is literally incapable of reading what is written in black and white; he sees only white against white, without difference, and the appearance that results is therefore literally unreadable, its differentiations or textuality effaced in a sea of whiteness." Kamuf, "Melville's Credit Card," 192.

69. Creeger does approach this question, but primarily through the oppositions of good and evil, or life and death—not ink and paper. George R. Creeger, "The Symbolism of Whiteness in Melville's Prose Fiction," *Jahrbuch für Amerikastudien* 5 (1960): 159–60. C. L. R. James observes that Delano's "cherished [beliefs] . . . about a backward people . . . were not merely false but were the direct cause of his own blindness and stupidity." While James's analysis explains Delano's misinterpretation of the mutinous blacks, it continues to ignore Delano's confrontation with white muteness. Consequently, he concludes that *Benito Cereno* is . . . a propaganda story, a mystery, written" to disprove misconceptions about Black people. See James, *Mariners, Renegades, and Castaways: The Story of Herman Melville and the World We Live In* (Hanover: University Press of New England, 2001), 111, 112.

70. Jonathan Senchyne has been one of the most acute observers of the racialization of ink and paper in nineteenth-century print culture. On the use of ink on the faces of engraved figures to "signify racial content instead of the absence implied in white paper," see Senchyne, "Bottles of Ink and Reams of Paper: Clotel, Racialization, and the Material Culture of Print," in *Early African American Print Culture,* ed. Lara Langer Cohen and Jordan Alexander Stein, Material Texts (Philadelphia: University of Pennsylvania Press, 2012), 142. On the shared qualities of white pages and white bodies in Melville's "The Paradise of Bachelors and the Tartarus of Maids," see Senchyne, *The Intimacy of Paper in Early and Nineteenth-Century American Literature* (Amherst: University of Massachusetts Press, 2019), 116–24.

71. Toal, "'Some Things Which Could Never Have Happened,'" 55.

72. Though written in chalk, the words remain impervious to the seawater, in contrast to the wrought metal letters that spell the ship's name, which have been "streakingly corroded with tricklings of copper-spike rust" (167).

73. Warner, *The Letters of the Republic.*

74. Nelson, *The Word in Black and White,* 113.

75. The phrase "character's media" is an homage to Freeman, *Character's Theater.*

76. Surveying Melville's list of eight promising American writers in "Hawthorne and His Mosses," Wallace writes, "Melville had no interest in women writers. By

comparison, Hawthorne was very generous to them." James D. Wallace, "Haw-
thorne and the Scribbling Women Reconsidered," *American Literature* 62, no. 2
(June 1990): 203. See also Robyn Wiegman, "Melville's Geography of Gender,"
American Literary History 1, no. 4 (December 1989): 735–53.

77. Nelson, *The Word in Black and White,* 127.
78. On the fraternal intimacies Melville imagined with Hawthorne via the medium of
paper, see Senchyne, *The Intimacy of Paper,* 115.
79. See Bill Moyers, "A Conversation with Toni Morrison," in *Conversations with Toni
Morrison,* ed. Danille K. Taylor-Guthrie (Jackson: University Press of Mississippi,
1994), 264.
80. Rasmussen, *Queequeg's Coffin,* 112.
81. Thomas Jefferson to Marquis de Chastellux, June 7, 1785, https://avalon.law.yale
.edu/18th_century/let27.asp. Quoted in Shannon Lee Dawdy, "Proper Caresses
and Prudent Distance: A How-To Manual from Colonial Louisiana," in *Haunted
by Empire: Geographies of Intimacy in North American History,* ed. Ann Laura
Stoler (Durham: Duke University Press, 2006), 153.

Epilogue

1. Christopher Petrella and Justin Gomer, "'Not a Racist Bone in His Body': The
Origins of the Default Defense against Racism," *Washington Post,* July 16, 2019.
2. Cooper, "An Otello without Blackface." I quote the reporter's paraphrase because
Sher's words were not published.
3. On "foodstuff metaphors" as a "commodifying script of blackness" in early modern
European performance culture, see Noémie Ndiaye, *Scripts of Blackness: Early
Modern Performance Culture and the Making of Race* (Philadelphia: University of
Pennsylvania Press, 2022), 74.
4. Martin Orkin, "Othello and the 'Plain Face' Of Racism," *Shakespeare Quarterly* 38,
no. 2 (July 1987): 184, 188.
5. Emily C. Bartels, "Making More of the Moor: Aaron, Othello, and Renaissance
Refashionings of Race," *Shakespeare Quarterly* 41, no. 4 (Winter 1990): 454.
6. William T. Hastings, "Shakespeare in Providence," *Shakespeare Quarterly* 8, no. 3
(Summer 1957): 336–37.
7. For further discussion of when and how the anti-racist potential of *Othello* has
been activated, see Grier, "Are Shakespeare's Plays Racially Progressive?"
8. "RUN away . . . Othello," *London Gazette,* January 5, 1685. I rely on Newman for
elaboration on Pet's occupation; see Simon P. Newman, "Othello: What's in a
Name?," Folger Shakespeare Library, March 14, 2023, https://www.folger.edu
/blogs/collation/othello-whats-in-a-name/.
9. The longstanding suspicion that Behn knew an enslaved man named Oroonoko
and even became his mistress begins with Thomas Southerne's preface to his play
Oroonoko. For the most recent insistence that English racism rose and fell with the
transatlantic slave trade, see Feisal G. Mohamed, "On Race and Historicism: A
Polemic in Three Turns," *ELH* 89, no. 2 (June 2022): 385–86.

10. Johnson, *Absence and Memory*, 228.

11. Antonio T. Bly, "In Pursuit of Letters: A History of the Bray Schools for Enslaved Children in Colonial Virginia," *History of Education Quarterly* 51, no. 4 (November 2011): 429–59; Bly, "Pretends He Can Read"; Bly and Tamia Haygood, *Escaping Servitude: A Documentary History of Runaway Servants in Eighteenth-Century Virginia* (Lanham, Md.: Rowman & Littlefield, 2014); Thad W. Tate and Colonial Williamsburg Foundation, *The Negro in Eighteenth-Century Williamsburg* (Williamsburg, Va.: Colonial Williamsburg Foundation, 1965); Margaret Dewey, *The Messengers: A Concise History of the United Society for the Propagation of the Gospel* (London: Mowbrays, 1975); Thomas N. Ingersoll, "'Releese Us out of This Cruell Bondegg': An Appeal from Virginia in 1723," *William and Mary Quarterly*, 3rd ser., 51, no. 4 (1994): 777–82.

12. Holton, *Abigail Adams*, 225.

13. John Brown's powerful final address is but 642 words and insists that his acts were in accord with Christian faith and also not treasonous. His relatively small literary legacy strives to demonstrate that he was not outside the white interpretive community. See "John Brown's Last Speech," *New York Times*, November 3, 1859. Those who defected from white settlements left a few, fascinating archival traces that deserve further attention. See James Axtell, "The White Indians of Colonial America," *William and Mary Quarterly* 32, no. 1 (January 1975): 55–88.

14. John Hope Franklin and Loren Schweninger, *Runaway Slaves: Rebels on the Plantation* (New York: Oxford University Press, 2000); Waldstreicher, "Reading the Runaways"; Antonio T. Bly, "Pretty, Sassy, Cool: Slave Resistance, Agency, and Culture in Eighteenth-Century New England," *New England Quarterly* 89, no. 3 (September 2016): 457–92; John Sekora, "'Mr. Editor, If You Please': Frederick Douglass, My Bondage and My Freedom, and the End of the Abolitionist Imprint," *Callaloo* 17, no. 2 (April 1994): 608–26; Grey Gundaker, *Signs of Diaspora/ Diaspora of Signs: Literacies, Creolization, and Vernacular Practice in African America*, Commonwealth Center Studies in American Culture (New York: Oxford University Press, 1998); Grey Gundaker, "Hidden Education among African Americans during Slavery," *Teachers College Record* 109, no. 7 (July 2007): 1591–1612; Gundaker, "Give Me a Sign: African Americans, Print, and Practice," in *A History of the Book in America* (Chapel Hill: University of North Carolina Press, 2015), 483–95.

15. George T. Downing, "Presidential Address" at New England Colored Citizens' Convention, August 1, 1859, in *The Proceedings of the Black State Conventions, 1840–1865*, ed. Philip S. Foner and George E. Walker, vol. 2 (Philadelphia: Temple University Press, 1979), 211.

16. Spillers, "Mama's Baby, Papa's Maybe," 67.

17. On civic scriptures, see Vincent L. Wimbush, ed., *Misreading America: Scriptures and Difference* (New York: Oxford University Press, 2013), 11–13.

18. Downing displays that familiarity in the previous paragraph: "The man whose devotions are disturbed by having a family of well-behaved and decently dressed

colored persons in the pew next to him may know much of the doctrines of Christianity, but is very little imbued with its spirit" (211).

19. George Best, *A True Discourse of the Late Voyages of Discouerie . . . of Martin Frobisher* (London: Henry Bynneman, 1578), sig. f3v.

20. Fred Moten, *In the Break: The Aesthetics of the Black Radical Tradition* (Minneapolis: University of Minnesota Press, 2003), 12.

Bibliography

Adams, B. K. "Fair/Foul." In *Shakespeare/Text: Contemporary Readings in Textual Studies, Editing and Performance,* edited by Claire M. L. Bourne, 29–49. New York: The Arden Shakespeare, 2021.

Adams, John Quincy. "Misconceptions of Shakspeare upon the Stage." *New-England Magazine* 9 (1835): 435–40.

Adams, Joseph Quincy, Jr. "Shakespeare and American Culture." In *Shakespeare in America: An Anthology from the Revolution to Now,* edited by James Shapiro, 418–35. New York: Library of America, 2014.

Agnew, Jean-Christophe. *Worlds Apart: The Market and the Theater in Anglo-American Thought, 1550–1750.* New York: Cambridge University Press, 1988.

Akhimie, Patricia. *Shakespeare and the Cultivation of Difference: Race and Conduct in the Early Modern World.* New York: Routledge, 2018.

Akhimie, Patricia, and Bernadette Andrea, eds. *Travel and Travail: Early Modern Women, English Drama, and the Wider World.* Omaha: University of Nebraska Press, 2019.

Albanese, Denise. "Black and White, and Dread All Over." In *A Feminist Companion to Shakespeare,* 244–65. Malden, MA: John Wiley, 2016.

Alcoff, Linda Martin. *Visible Identities: Race, Gender, and the Self.* New York: Oxford University Press, 2005.

Allen, Regulus. "'The Sable Venus' and Desire for the Undesirable." *Studies in English Literature, 1500–1900* 51, no. 3 (2011): 667–91.

Allen, Theodore W. *The Invention of the White Race: The Origin of Racial Oppression in Anglo-America.* New York: Verso, 1997.

Altaba-Artal, Dolors. *Aphra Behn's English Feminism: Wit and Satire.* Selinsgrove: Susquehanna University Press, 1999.

Altman, Joel B. *The Improbability of Othello: Rhetorical Anthropology and Shakespearean Selfhood.* Chicago: University of Chicago Press, 2010.

Andrade, Susan Z. "White Skin, Black Masks: Colonialism and the Sexual Politics of Oroonoko." *Cultural Critique,* no. 27 (Spring 1994): 189–214.

Aravamudan, Srinivas. *Tropicopolitans: Colonialism and Agency, 1688–1804.* Durham: Duke University Press, 1999.

Armin, Robert. *The History of the Tvvo Maids of More-Clacke Vvith the Life and Simple Maner of Iohn in the Hospitall. Played by the Children of the Kings Maiesties Reuels. VVritten by Robert Armin, Seruant to the Kings Most Excellent Maiestie.* London: Printed by N[icholas] O[kes] for Thomas Archer, and is to be sold at his shop in Popes-head Pallace, 1609.

Armstrong, Nancy. *How Novels Think: The Limits of Individualism from 1719–1900.* New York: Columbia University Press, 2006.

Asleson, Robyn, ed. *Notorious Muse: The Actress in British Art and Culture, 1776–1812.* New Haven: Paul Mellon Centre for British Art, 2003.

Athey, Stephanie, and Daniel Cooper Alarcon. "Oroonoko's Gendered Economies of Honor/Horror: Reframing Colonial Discourse Studies in the Americas." *American Literature* 65, no. 3 (September 1993): 415.

Baker, Gerald. "The Name of Othello Is Not the Name of *Othello.*" *Review of English Studies* 67, no. 278 (February 2016): 62–78.

Baker, Houston A., Jr. *Modernism and the Harlem Renaissance.* Chicago: University of Chicago Press, 1989.

Balibar, Étienne. "The Nation Form: History and Ideology." *Review of the Fernand Braudel Center* 13, no. 3 (July 1990): 329–61.

Ballaster, Ros. "New Hystericism: Aphra Behn's *Oroonoko:* The Body, the Text, and the Feminist Critic." In *New Feminist Discourses: Critical Essays on Theories and Texts,* edited by Isobel Armstrong, 2:283–95. New York: Routledge, 1992.

Bamber, Linda. *Comic Women, Tragic Men: A Study of Gender and Genre in Shakespeare.* Stanford: Stanford University Press, 1992.

Bannet, Eve Tavor. *Empire of Letters: Letter Manuals and Transatlantic Correspondence, 1688–1820.* Cambridge: Cambridge University Press, 2005.

Barrett, Lindon. *Blackness and Value: Seeing Double.* New York: Cambridge University Press, 1999.

Barrow, William J. "Black Writing Ink of the Colonial Period." *American Archivist* 11, no. 4 (October 1948): 291–307.

Bartels, Emily C. "Making More of the Moor: Aaron, Othello, and Renaissance Refashionings of Race." *Shakespeare Quarterly* 41, no. 4 (Winter 1990): 433.

———. "Othello and Africa: Postcolonialism Reconsidered." *William and Mary Quarterly* 54, no. 1 (January 1997): 45–64.

———. *Speaking of the Moor: From "Alcazar" to "Othello."* Philadelphia: University of Pennsylvania Press, 2008.

———. "Strategies of Submission: Desdemona, the Duchess, and the Assertion of Desire." *Studies in English Literature, 1500–1900* 36, no. 2 (Spring 1996): 417–33.

Barthelemy, Anthony Gerard. *Black Face, Maligned Race: The Representation of Blacks in English Drama from Shakespeare to Southerne.* Baton Rouge: Louisiana State University Press, 1987.

Barthes, Roland. "The Death of the Author." In *Image-Music-Text,* translated by Stephen Heath. New York: Hill and Wang, 1978.

Bate, Jonathan. *How the Classics Made Shakespeare.* Princeton: Princeton University Press, 2019.

Behn, Aphra. *The Dutch Lover a Comedy Acted at the Dvkes Theatre / Written by Mrs. A. Bhen [Sic].* London: Printed for Thomas Dring, at the Sign of the Harrow at Chancery-lane end, over against the Inner Temple Gate in Fleet-street, 1673.

———. "Oroonoko: Or, the Royal Slave." 1688. In *Versions of Blackness: Key Texts on Slavery from the Seventeenth Century,* edited by Derek Hughes, 119–89. Cambridge: Cambridge University Press, 2007.

Bell, Derrick. "After We're Gone: Prudent Speculations on America in a Post-Racial Epoch." *Saint Louis University Law Journal* 34 (1990): 393–405.

Benedict, Barbara M. "Reading Faces: Physiognomy and Epistemology in Late Eighteenth-Century Sentimental Novels." *Studies in Philology* 92, no. 3 (Summer 1995): 311.

Berger, Harry, Jr. "Bodies and Texts." *Representations,* no. 17 (1987): 144–66.

Berlant, Lauren. "The Queen of America Goes to Washington City: Harriet Jacobs, Frances Harper, Anita Hill." *American Literature* 65, no. 3 (September 1993): 549.

Bernard, John. "Theatricality and Textuality: The Example of 'Othello.'" *New Literary History* 26, no. 4 (October 1995): 931–49.

Bickham, Troy O. *Savages within the Empire: Representations of American Indians in Eighteenth-Century Britain.* New York: Oxford University Press, 2005.

Blackmore, Josiah. *Moorings: Portuguese Expansion and the Writing of Africa.* Minneapolis: University of Minnesota Press, 2008.

Blair, John. "Diary of John Blair." *William and Mary Quarterly* 8, no. 1 (July 1899): 1–17.

Bland, Shelia Rose. "How I Would Direct *Othello.*" In *Othello: New Essays by Black Writers,* edited by Mythili Kaul, 29–44. Washington, D.C.: Howard University Press, 1997.

Blunt, Richard. "The Evolution of Blackface Cosmetics on the Early Modern Stage." In *The Materiality of Color: The Production, Circulation, and Application of Dyes and Pigments, 1400–1800,* edited by Andrea Feeser, Maureen Daly Goggin, and Beth Fowkes Tobin. Burlington: Ashgate, 2017.

Boeckeler, Erika Mary. *Playful Letters: A Study in Early Modern Alphabetics.* Iowa City: University of Iowa Press, 2017.

Bolter, J. David, and Richard A. Grusin. *Remediation: Understanding New Media.* Cambridge, Mass: MIT Press, 1999.

Bonilla-Silva, Eduardo. *Racism without Racists: Color-Blind Racism and the Persistence of Racial Inequality in America.* New York: Rowman & Littlefield, 2006.

The booke of the common prayer and administracion of the Sacramentes, and other rites and Ceremonies of the Churche: after the vse of the Churche of England. London, 1549.

Boose, Lynda. "'Let It Be Hid': The Pornographic Aesthetic of Shakespeare's *Othello.*" In *Women, Violence, and English Renaissance Literature: Essays Honoring Paul Jorgensen,* edited by Paul A Jorgensen, Linda Woodbridge, and Sharon A Beehler. Tempe: Arizona Center for Medieval and Renaissance Studies, 2003.

Bosman, Anston. "Renaissance Intertheater and the Staging of Nobody." *ELH* 71, no. 3 (October 2004): 559–85.

Bourdieu, Pierre. "The Forms of Capital." In *Handbook of Theory and Research for the Sociology of Education,* edited by John G. Richardson, translated by Richard Nice, 241–58. Westport, Conn.: Greenwood Press, 1986.

Bovilsky, Lara. *Barbarous Play: Race on the English Renaissance Stage.* Minneapolis: University of Minnesota Press, 2008.

Boyarin, Daniel. "Othello's Penis: Or, Islam in the Closet." In *Shakesqueer: A Queer Companion to the Complete Works of Shakespeare,* edited by Madhavi Menon, 254–63. Durham: Duke University Press, 2011.

Braziel, Jana Evans. *Caribbean Genesis: Jamaica Kincaid and the Writing of New Worlds.* Albany: SUNY Press, 2009.

Bristol, M. D. "Charivari and the Comedy of Abjection in *Othello.*" In *Disorder and the Drama,* edited by Mary Beth Rose. Evanston: Northwestern University Press, 1991.

Britton, Dennis Austin. *Becoming Christian: Race, Reformation, and Early Modern English Romance.* New York: Fordham University Press, 2014.

Brooks, Helen E. M. "Negotiating Marriage and Professional Autonomy in the Careers of Eighteenth-Century Actresses." *Eighteenth-Century Life* 35, no. 2 (2011): 39–75.

Brooks, Lisa. *The Common Pot: The Recovery of Native Space in the Northeast.* Minneapolis: University of Minnesota Press, 2008.

Brotton, Jerry. "Is This the Real Model for Othello?" *Guardian,* March 19, 2016, sec. Culture. http://www.theguardian.com/culture/2016/mar/19/moroccan-ambassador-london-1600-real-othello-shakespeare.

———. "'This Tunis, Sir, Was Carthage': Contesting Colonialism in *The Tempest.*" In *Post-Colonial Shakespeares,* edited by Ania Loomba and Martin Orkin. New York: Routledge, 1998.

———. *Trading Territories: Mapping the Early Modern World.* London: Reaktion Books, 1997.

Brown, Kathleen M. *Good Wives, Nasty Wenches, and Anxious Patriarchs: Gender, Race, and Power in Colonial Virginia.* Chapel Hill: University of North Carolina Press, 1996.

Brown, Laura. *Ends of Empire: Women and Ideology in Early Eighteenth-Century English Literature.* Ithaca: Cornell University Press, 1993.

Browne, Thomas. *Pseudodoxia Epidemica, or, Enquiries into Very Many Received Tenents and Commonly Presumed Truths.* London: Printed by T.H. for E. Dod, 1646.

Brückner, Martin. *The Geographic Revolution in Early America: Maps, Literacy, and National Identity.* Chapel Hill: University of North Carolina Press, 2006.

Bruster, Douglas. "Was Shakespeare an Economic Thinker?" *Research in the History of Economic Thought and Methodology* 24-A (2006): 167–80.

Bulwer, John. *Anthropometamorphosis: Man Transform'd: Or, the Artificiall Changling Historically Presented [. . .].* London: Printed by William Hunt, 1653.

Burge, Stuart, dir. *Othello.* BHE Films, National Theatre of Great Britain Production, 1965.

Burke, Helen M. "The Cavalier Myth in *The Rover.*" In *The Cambridge Companion to Aphra Behn,* edited by Janet Todd and Derek Hughes, 118–34. Cambridge: Cambridge University Press, 2004.

Burshatin, Israel. "The Moor in the Text: Metaphor, Emblem, and Silence." *Critical Inquiry* 12, no. 1 (October 1985): 98–118.

Bush, Barbara. "'Sable Venus,' 'She Devil' or 'Drudge'? British Slavery and the 'Fabulous Fiction' of Black Women's Identities, c. 1650–1838." *Women's History Review* 9, no. 4 (December 2000): 761–89.

Cady, Diane. "The Gender of Money." *Genders,* no. 44 (2006). https://www.colorado.edu/gendersarchive1998-2013/2006/12/01/gender-money.

Callaghan, Dympna. *Shakespeare without Women: Representing Gender and Race on the Renaissance Stage.* New York: Routledge, 2000.

Cardwell, Guy A. "Melville's Gray Story: Symbols and Meaning in 'Benito Cereno.'" *Bucknell Review* 8, no. 3 (1959): 154–67.

Carlson, Julie A. "Race and Profit in English Theatre." In *The Cambridge Companion to British Theatre, 1730–1830,* edited by Jane Moody and Daniel O'Quinn, 175–88. New York: Cambridge University Press, 2007.

Carr, Morwenna. "Material/Blackness: Race and Its Material Reconstructions on the Seventeenth-Century English Stage." *Early Theatre* 20, no. 1 (July 2017).

Cartelli, Thomas. *Repositioning Shakespeare: National Formations, Postcolonial Appropriations.* New York: Routledge, 1999.

Chakravarty, Urvashi. *Fictions of Consent: Slavery, Servitude, and Free Service in Early Modern England.* Philadelphia: University of Pennsylvania Press, 2022.

———. "More Than Kin, Less Than Kind: Similitude, Strangeness, and Early Modern English Homonationalisms." *Shakespeare Quarterly* 67, no. 1 (2016): 14–29.

Chalk, Casey. "Circumscribing Shakespeare." *American Conservative,* February 2, 2022. https://www.theamericanconservative.com/articles/circumscribing-shakespeare/.

Chamberlain, John. *The Letters of John Chamberlain.* Edited by Norman Egbert McClure. Vol. 2. Philadelphia: American Philosophical Society, 1939.

Chapman, Matthieu. *Anti-Black Racism in Early Modern English Drama: The Other "Other."* New York: Routledge, 2016.

Cheng, Anne Anlin. "Skins, Tattoos, and Susceptibility." *Representations* 108, no. 1 (November 2009): 98–119.

Choudhury, Mita. "Race, Performance and the Silenced Prince of Angola." In *A Companion to Restoration Drama,* 161–76. Malden, Mass.: John Wiley, 2013.

Church, Michael. "Otello, English National Opera, Review: A Flawless Production from David Alden." *Independent,* September 15, 2014. https://www.independent.co.uk/arts-entertainment/classical/reviews/otello-english-national-opera-review-flawless-production-david-alden-9733718.html.

Cmiel, Kenneth. *Democratic Eloquence: The Fight for Popular Speech in Nineteenth-Century America.* Berkeley: University of California Press, 1990.

Cobb, Keith Hamilton. *American Moor.* New York: Methuen Drama, 2020.

Cockrell, Dale. *Demons of Disorder: Early Blackface Minstrels and Their World.* New York: Cambridge University Press, 1997.

Collins, Siobhán, and Louise Denmead. "'There Is All Africa [. . .] Within Us': Language, Generation and Alchemy in Browne's Explication of Blackness." In *"A Man Very Well Studyed": New Contexts for Thomas Browne,* edited by Kathryn Murphy and Richard Todd, 127–48. Leiden: Brill, 2008.

Colman, George. *Inkle and Yarico: An Opera, in Three Acts. As Performed at the Theatres-Royal in Covent-Garden and the Hay-Market. First Acted (in the Hay-Market) on Saturday, August 11, 1787.* London: G.G.J. and J. Robinson, 1792.

Cooper, Michael. "An 'Otello' without Blackface Highlights an Enduring Tradition in Opera." *New York Times,* September 17, 2015, sec. Arts. https://www.nytimes.com

/2015/09/20/arts/music/an-otello-without-the-blackface-nods-to-modern-tastes .html.

Corredera, Vanessa. "Complex Complexions: The Facial Signification of the Black Other in Lust's Dominion." In *Shakespeare and the Power of the Face,* edited by James A. Knapp, 93–114. New York: Routledge, 2015.

Crain, Patricia. *The Story of A: The Alphabetization of America from "The New England Primer" to "The Scarlet Letter."* Stanford: Stanford University Press, 2000.

Dadabhoy, Ambereen. "Two Faced: The Problem of Othello's Visage." In *Othello: The State of Play,* edited by Lena Cowen Orlin, 121–48. London: Bloomsbury, 2014.

Daileader, Celia R. *Racism, Misogyny, and the Othello Myth: Inter-Racial Couples from Shakespeare to Spike Lee.* New York: Cambridge University Press, 2005.

Davis, Angela Y. *Blues Legacies and Black Feminism: Gertrude "Ma" Rainey, Bessie Smith, and Billie Holiday.* New York: Vintage, 1999.

———. *Women, Race & Class.* New York: Vintage, 1983.

Daybell, James. *The Material Letter in Early Modern England: Manuscript Letters and the Culture and Practices of Letter-Writing, 1512–1635.* New York: Palgrave Macmillan, 2012.

Deb, Basuli. "Transnational Complications: Reimagining Oroonoko and Women's Collective Politics in the Empire." *Frontiers: A Journal of Women Studies* 36, no. 1 (2015): 33.

De Grazia, Margreta. "Homonyms before and after Lexical Standardization." *Shakespeare Jahrbusch,* 1990, 143–56.

———. "Imprints: Shakespeare, Gutenberg and Descartes." In *Alternative Shakespeares,* edited by Terence Hawkes, 2:65–96. New Accents. London: Routledge, 1996.

DeGuzmán, María. *Spain's Long Shadow: The Black Legend, Off-Whiteness, and Anglo-American Empire.* Minneapolis: University of Minnesota Press, 2005.

Deloria, Philip Joseph. *Playing Indian.* New Haven: Yale University Press, 1999.

Derrida, Jacques. *Of Grammatology.* Baltimore: Johns Hopkins University Press, 1998.

DiGangi, Mario. *Sexual Types: Embodiment, Agency, and Dramatic Character from Shakespeare to Shirley.* Philadelphia: University of Pennsylvania Press, 2011.

Dillon, Elizabeth Maddock. *New World Drama: The Performative Commons in the Atlantic World, 1649–1849.* Durham: Duke University Press, 2014.

Dodsley, Robert, John Payne Collier, Octavius Gilchrist, and Isaac Reed, and John Payne, eds. *A Select Collection of Old Plays. In Twelve Volumes.* Vol. 2. London: S. Prowett, 1825.

Drew-Bear, Annette. *Painted Faces on the Renaissance Stage: The Moral Significance of Face-Painting Conventions.* Lewisburg, Pa.: Bucknell University Press, 1994.

Duffy, Maureen. *The Passionate Shepherdess: Aphra Behn, 1640–1689.* London: Jonathan Cape, 1977.

Duncan, Garrett Albert. "Discourse, Cultural Imperialism, Black Culture and Language Research in the United States." In *Discourse as Cultural Struggle,* edited by Xu Shi, 142–53. Hong Kong: Hong Kong University Press, 2006.

Edelstein, Tilden G. "Othello in America: The Drama of Racial Intermarriage." In *Interracialism: Black-White Intermarriage in American History, Literature, and Law,* edited by Werner Sollors, 356–69. New York: Oxford University Press, 2000.

Edgecombe, Rodney Stenning. "Ovid and the 'Medicinal Gum' in *Othello* V.ii." *Notes and Queries* 54, no. 3 (2007): 293–94.

Eger, Elizabeth. "Spectacle, Intellect and Authority: The Actress in the Eighteenth Century." In *The Cambridge Companion to the Actress,* edited by Maggie B. Gale and John Stokes, 33–51. Cambridge: Cambridge University Press, 2007.

Ellison, Ralph. *Shadow and Act.* New York: Random House, 1964.

Elmer, Jonathan. *On Lingering and Being Last: Race and Sovereignty in the New World.* New York: Fordham University Press, 2008.

Engel, Laura. "The Muff Affair: Fashioning Celebrity in the Portraits of Late-Eighteenth-Century British Actresses." *Fashion Theory: The Journal of Dress, Body & Culture* 13, no. 3 (2009): 279–98.

Erickson, Peter. "The Moment of Race in Renaissance Studies." *Shakespeare Studies* 26 (1998): 27–36.

Evans, G. Blakemore, Harry Levin, Herschel Baker, Anne Barton, Hallet Smith, Marie Edel, and Frank Kermode, eds. *The Riverside Shakespeare.* Boston: Houghton Mifflin, 1974.

Fanon, Frantz. *Black Skin, White Masks.* 1952. New York: Grove Press, 1994.

Feerick, Jean E. *Strangers in Blood: Relocating Race in the Renaissance.* Toronto: University of Toronto Press, 2010.

Ferguson, Margaret W. "Juggling the Categories of Race, Class and Gender: Aphra Behn's *Oroonoko.*" *Women's Studies* 19, no. 2 (August 1991): 159–81.

———. "Transmuting Othello." In *Cross-Cultural Performances: Differences in Women's Re-Visions of Shakespeare,* edited by Marianne Novy, 15–49. Urbana: University of Illinois Press, 1993.

Ferguson, Roderick A. *Aberrations in Black: Toward a Queer of Color Critique.* Minneapolis: University of Minnesota Press, 2004.

Fielder, Brigitte. "Blackface Desdemona: Theorizing Race on the Nineteenth-Century American Stage." *Theatre Annual: A Journal of Theatre & Performance of the Americas* 70 (2017): 39–59.

Fiedler, Leslie. "Come Back to the Raft Ag'in, Huck Honey!" *Partisan Review* 15, no. 6 (June 1948): 664–71.

———. *The Stranger in Shakespeare.* New York: Stein and Day, 1972.

Fields, Karen E., and Barbara J. Fields. *Racecraft: The Soul of Inequality in American Life.* New York: Verso, 2012.

Fineman, Joel. "The Sound of O in *Othello:* The Real of the Tragedy of Desire." *October* 45 (Summer 1988): 77–96.

Fish, Stanley. *Is There a Text in This Class? The Authority of Interpretive Communities.* Cambridge, Mass.: Harvard University Press, 1982.

Fisher, Rebecka Rutledge. *Habitations of the Veil: Metaphor and the Poetics of Black Being in African American Literature.* Albany: SUNY Press, 2014.

Fisher, Will. *Materializing Gender in Early Modern English Literature and Culture.* Cambridge: Cambridge University Press, 2006.

———. "Queer Money." *ELH* 66, no. 1 (1999): 1–23.

Fisher, Zachary. "'Drops Tears as Fast as the Arabian Trees': Othello's Tears and the Weeping Trees of Acacia and Myrrh. A Corrective Gloss to Most Modern Editions of Shakespeare.—Shaping Sense." Accessed August 5, 2013. http://senseshaper.com /drops-tears-as-fast-as-the-arabian-trees-othellos-tears-and-the-weeping-trees-of -acacia-and-myrrh-a-corrective-gloss-to-most-modern-editions-of-shakespeare/.

Flavell, Julie. *When London Was Capital of America.* New Haven: Yale University Press, 2010.

Fleming, Juliet. "Wounded Walls: Graffiti, Grammatology, and the Age of Shakespeare." *Criticism* 39, no. 1 (Winter 1997): 1–30.

Floyd-Wilson, Mary. *English Ethnicity and Race in Early Modern Drama.* New York: Cambridge University Press, 2003.

Foucault, Michel. "What Is an Author?" In *Language, Counter-Memory, Practice: Selected Essays and Interviews,* edited by Donald F. Bouchard. Ithaca: Cornell University Press, 1980.

Fox, Adam. *Oral and Literate Culture in England, 1500–1700.* New York: Clarendon Press, 2000.

Freeman, Lisa A. *Character's Theater: Genre and Identity on the Eighteenth-Century English Stage.* Philadelphia: University of Pennsylvania Press, 2001.

———. "The Social Life of Eighteenth-Century Comedy." In *The Cambridge Companion to British Theatre, 1730–1830,* edited by Jane Moody and Daniel O'Quinn, 73–86. New York: Cambridge University Press, 2007.

Fricker, Miranda. *Epistemic Injustice: Power and the Ethics of Knowing.* Oxford: Oxford University Press, 2009.

Gainsford, Thomas. *The Glory of England, or A True Description of Many Excellent Prerogatiues and Remarkeable Blessings, Whereby She Triumpheth Ouer All the Nations of the World* [. . .]. London: Printed by Edward Griffin for Th: Norton and are to be sold at his shop in Pauls-Church-yard at the signe of the Kings-head, 1618.

Gallagher, Catherine. "Nobody's Story: Gender, Property, and the Rise of the Novel." *Modern Language Quarterly* 53, no. 3 (September 1992): 263–77.

———. *Nobody's Story: The Vanishing Acts of Women Writers in the Marketplace, 1670–1820.* Berkeley: University of California Press, 1995.

Garratt, John G. *The Four Indian Kings.* Ottawa: Public Archives, 1985.

Gates, Henry Louis, Jr. "Editor's Introduction: Writing 'Race' and the Difference It Makes." *Critical Inquiry* 12, no. 1 (1985): 1–20.

———. *The Signifying Monkey: A Theory of African-American Literary Criticism.* New York: Oxford University Press, 1989.

Gearing, Fred O. "Priests and Warriors: Social Structures for Cherokee Politics in the 18th Century." *American Anthropologist* 64, no. 5, part 2 (October 1962): 1–112.

Geertz, Clifford. *The Interpretation of Cultures.* New York: Basic Books, 1973.

Gibbs, Jenna M. *Performing the Temple of Liberty: Slavery, Theater, and Popular Culture in London and Philadelphia, 1760–1850.* Baltimore: Johns Hopkins University Press, 2014.

Gillen, Katherine. *Chaste Value: Economic Crisis, Female Chastity and the Production of Social Difference on Shakespeare's Stage.* Edinburgh: Edinburgh University Press, 2017.

Gillies, John. *Shakespeare and the Geography of Difference.* New York: Cambridge University Press, 1994.

Gilroy, Paul. *The Black Atlantic: Modernity and Double Consciousness.* Cambridge, Mass: Harvard University Press, 1993.

Goffman, Erving. *Stigma: Notes on the Management of Spoiled Identity.* Englewood Cliffs, N.J.: Prentice-Hall, 1963.

Goldberg, Jonathan. *Shakespeare's Hand.* Minneapolis: University of Minnesota Press, 2003.

Gordon, Lewis R. *Bad Faith and Antiblack Racism.* Atlantic Highlands, N.J.: Humanities Press, 1995.

Gould, Stephen Jay. *The Mismeasure of Man.* New York: W. W. Norton, 1996.

Gqola, Pumla Dineo. "'Where There Is No Novelty, There Can Be No Curiosity': Reading Imoinda's Body in Aphra Behn's 'Oroonoko or, the Royal Slave.'" *English in Africa* 28, no. 1 (May 2001): 105–17.

Grady, Kyle. "Othello, Colin Powell, and Post-Racial Anachronisms." *Shakespeare Quarterly* 67, no. 1 (2016): 68–83.

Greenblatt, Stephen. *Renaissance Self-Fashioning: From More to Shakespeare.* Chicago: University of Chicago Press, 1980.

Grier, Miles P. "Are Shakespeare's Plays Racially Progressive?: The Answer Is in Our Hands." In *The Cambridge Companion to Shakespeare and Race,* edited by Ayanna Thompson, 237–53. Cambridge: Cambridge University Press, 2021.

———. "Black/White." In *Shakespeare/Text: Contemporary Readings in Textual Studies, Editing and Performance,* edited by Claire M. L. Bourne, 319–42. New York: The Arden Shakespeare, 2021.

———. "Having Their Cake . . . and Outlawing It, Too: How the War on Terror Expands Racial Profiling by Pretending to Erase It." *Politics and Culture,* no. 1 (2006). https://politicsandculture.org/2009/10/02/miles-parks-grier-having-their-cake-and-outlawing-it-too-2/.

———. "Inkface: The Slave Stigma in England's Early Imperial Imagination." In *Scripturalizing the Human: The Written as the Political,* edited by Vincent L. Wimbush, 193–220. New York: Routledge, 2015.

———. "Reading Black Characters: Staging Literacy, 1604–1855." PhD dissertation, New York University, 2010.

Griffin, Eric. *English Renaissance Drama and the Specter of Spain: Ethnopoetics and Empire.* Philadelphia: University of Pennsylvania Press, 2009.

Gundaker, Grey. *Signs of Diaspora/Diaspora of Signs: Literacies, Creolization, and Vernacular Practice in African America.* New York: Oxford University Press, 1998.

Gurr, Andrew. "A Black Reversal." *Shakespeare* 4, no. 2 (July 2008): 148–56.

Gustafson, Sandra M. *Eloquence Is Power: Oratory and Performance in Early America.* Chapel Hill: University of North Carolina Press, 2000.

———. "Textual Media in Early American Studies." *Early American Literature* 41, no. 2 (2006): 347–64.

Habib, Imtiaz. "Racial Impersonation on the Elizabethan Stage: The Case of Shakespeare Playing Aaron." *Medieval and Renaissance Drama in England* 20 (2007): 17–45.

Hakluyt, Richard, George Bishop, Robert Barker, Ralph Newbery, Charles Howard Nottingham, and Robert Cecil Salisbury, eds. *The Principal Navigations, Voyages, Traffiqves and Discoveries of the English Nation: Made by Sea or Ouer-Land, to the Remote and Farthest Distant Quarters of the Earth, at Any Time within the Compasse of These 1600 Yeres* [...]. Imprinted at London: By George Bishop, Ralph Newberie, and Robert Barker, 1599.

Hall, Kim F. "Beauty and the Beast of Whiteness: Teaching Race and Gender." *Shakespeare Quarterly* 47, no. 4 (1996): 461–75.

———. "Guess Who's Coming to Dinner? Colonization and Miscegenation in 'The Merchant of Venice.'" *Renaissance Drama* 23 (January 1992): 87–111.

———, ed. *Othello: Texts and Contexts.* Boston: Bedford/St. Martin's, 2006.

———. *Things of Darkness: Economies of Race and Gender in Early Modern England.* Ithaca: Cornell University Press, 1996.

Halpern, Richard. *The Poetics of Primitive Accumulation: English Renaissance Culture and the Genealogy of Capital.* Ithaca: Cornell University Press, 1991.

Hannaford, Ivan. *Race: The History of an Idea in the West.* Baltimore: Johns Hopkins University Press, 1996.

Hannah, Daniel. "Queer Hospitality in Herman Melville's 'Benito Cereno.'" *Studies in American Fiction* 37, no. 2 (2010): 181–201.

Harris, Mitchell M. "The Expense of Ink and Wastes of Shame: Poetic Generation, Black Ink, and Material Waste in Shakespeare's Sonnets." In *The Materiality of Color: The Production, Circulation, and Application of Dyes and Pigments, 1400–1800,* edited by Andrea Feeser, Maureen Daly Goggin, and Beth Fowkes Tobin. Burlington: Ashgate, 2017.

Hastings, William T. "Shakespeare in Providence." *Shakespeare Quarterly* 8, no. 3 (Summer 1957): 335–51.

Hatchuel, Sarah, and Nathalie Vienne-Guerrin, eds. *Shakespeare on Screen: Othello.* Cambridge: Cambridge University Press, 2015.

Hatfield, April Lee. "A 'Very Wary People in Their Bargaining' or 'Very Good Marchandise': English Traders' Views of Free and Enslaved Africans, 1550–1650." *Slavery & Abolition* 25, no. 3 (2004): 1–17.

Henderson, Mae G. "(W)Riting *The Work* and Working the Rites." *Black American Literature Forum* 23, no. 4 (1989): 631–60.

Henslowe, Philip. *Henslowe's Diary.* Edited by Walter W. Greg. London: A. H. Bullen, 1904.

Herbert, George. *The Works of George Herbert.* Edited by F. E. Hutchinson. London: Oxford University Press, 1945.

Higginbotham, A. Leon. *In the Matter of Color: Race and the American Legal Process: The Colonial Period.* New York: Oxford University Press, 1978.

Higginbotham, Derrick. "Women/Animals/Slaves: Race and Sexuality in Wycherley's *The Country Wife*." In *Early Modern Black Diaspora Studies: A Critical Anthology*, edited by Cassander L. Smith, Nicholas R. Jones, and Miles P. Grier, 37–61. New York: Palgrave Macmillan, 2018.

Hogan, Charles Beecher, ed. *The London Stage, 1660–1800*, part 5: *1776–1800: A Calendar of Plays, Entertainment & Afterpieces Together with Casts, Box-Receipts and Contemporary Comment*. Carbondale: Southern Illinois University Press, 1968.

Holmesland, Oddvar. "Aphra Behn's *Oroonoko*: Cultural Dialectics and the Novel." *ELH* 68, no. 1 (2001): 57–79.

Holt, Keri. "'We, Too, the People': Rewriting Resistance in the Cherokee Nation." In *Mapping Region in Early American Writing*, edited by Edward Watts, Keri Holt, and John Funchion, 199–225. Athens: University of Georgia Press, 2015.

Holton, Woody. *Abigail Adams*. New York: Simon and Schuster, 2009.

"Homicidal Ham." Episode of *Cheers*. NBC, October 27, 1983.

Hopkins, Lisa. "Reading Between the Sheets: Letters in Shakespearean Tragedy." *Critical Survey* 14, no. 3 (2002): 5–15.

Hornback, Robert. "Emblems of Folly in the First Othello: Renaissance Blackface, Moor's Coat, and 'Muckender.'" *Comparative Drama* 35, no. 1 (Spring 2001): 69–99.

———. "'Extravagant and Wheeling Strangers': Early Blackface Dancing Fools, Racial Impersonation, and the Limits of Identification." *Exemplaria* 20, no. 2 (Summer 2008): 197–222.

———. "The Folly of Racism: Enslaving Blackface and the 'Natural' Fool Tradition." *Medieval and Renaissance Drama in England* 20 (January 2007): 46–84.

———. *Racism and Early Blackface Comic Traditions: From the Old World to the New*. New York: Palgrave Macmillan, 2018.

———. "Speak[Ing] Parrot and Ovidian Echoes in *Othello*: Recontextualizing Black Speech in the Global Renaissance." In *Othello: The State of Play*, edited by Lena Cowen Orlin, 63–94. London: Bloomsbury, 2014.

Howard, Jean E. "Is Black So Base a Hue?" In *Shakespeare in Our Time: A Shakespeare Association of America Collection*, edited by Dympna Callaghan and Suzanne Gossett, 107–14. London: The Arden Shakespeare, 2016.

Howe, Elizabeth. *The First English Actresses*. New York: Cambridge University Press, 1992.

Howell, James. *Epistolæ Ho-Elianæ Familiar Letters Domestic and Forren Divided into Sundry Sections, Partly Historicall, Politicall, Philosophicall, Vpon Emergent Occasions*. London: Printed by W.H. for Humphrey Mosely . . . , 1650.

Hudson, Nicholas. "The 'Hottentot Venus,' Sexuality, and the Changing Aesthetics of Race, 1650–1850." *Mosaic* 41, no. 1 (March 2008): 19–41.

———. "From 'Nation' to 'Race': The Origin of Racial Classification in Eighteenth-Century Thought." *Eighteenth-Century Studies* 29, no. 3 (1996): 247–64.

Hughes, Derek. "Aphra Behn and the Restoration Theatre." In *The Cambridge Companion to Aphra Behn*, edited by Janet Todd and Derek Hughes, 29–45. New York: Cambridge University Press, 2004.

———. "Blackness in Gobineau and Behn: *Oroonoko* and Racial Pseudo-Science." *Women's Writing* 19, no. 2 (May 2012): 204–21.

———, ed. *Versions of Blackness: Key Texts on Slavery from the Seventeenth Century.* Cambridge: Cambridge University Press, 2007.

Hulme, Peter. *Colonial Encounters: Europe and the Native Caribbean, 1492–1797.* New York: Routledge, 1992.

Ickes, Charlotte. "The Sartorial and the Skin: Portraits of Pocahontas and Allegories of English Empire." *American Art* 29, no. 1 (March 2015): 82–105. https://doi.org/10.1086/681656.

Ingrassia, Catherine. "Aphra Behn and the Profession of Writing in the Restoration and Early Eighteenth Century." In *A Companion to British Literature,* edited by Robert DeMaria, Heesok Chang, and Samantha Zacher, 49–61. Oxford: John Wiley, 2014.

Jackman, Isaac. *All the World's a Stage; a Farce in Two Acts; as It Is Performed at the Theatre-Royal, in Drury-Lane.* 3rd ed. London: printed for J Wilkie, No71, St Paul's Church-Yard, 1777.

James, C. L. R. *Mariners, Renegades, and Castaways: The Story of Herman Melville and the World We Live In.* Hanover: University Press of New England, 2001.

Johnson, Odai. *Absence and Memory in Colonial American Theatre: Fiorelli's Plaster.* New York: Palgrave Macmillan, 2006.

Jones, C. P. "Stigma: Tattooing and Branding in Graeco-Roman Antiquity." *Journal of Roman Studies* 77 (1987): 139–55.

Jones, Nicholas R. *Staging Habla de Negros: Radical Performances of the African Diaspora in Early Modern Spain.* University Park: Pennsylvania State University Press, 2019.

Jordan, Winthrop D. *White over Black: American Attitudes toward the Negro, 1550–1812.* New York: W. W. Norton, 1977.

Karim-Cooper, Farah. *Cosmetics in Shakespearean and Renaissance Drama.* Edinburgh: Edinburgh University Press, 2006.

———. "The Materials of Race: Staging the Black and White Binary in the Early Modern Theatre." In *The Cambridge Companion to Shakespeare and Race,* edited by Ayanna Thompson, 17–29. Cambridge: Cambridge University Press, 2021.

———. "'This Alters Not Thy Beauty': Face-Paint, Gender, and Race in Richard Brome's *The English Moor.*" *Early Theatre* 10, no. 2 (July 2007): 140–49.

Kaul, Mythili. "Background: Black or Tawny? Stage Representations of Othello from 1604 to the Present." In her *Othello: New Essays by Black Writers,* 1–19. Washington, D.C.: Howard University Press, 1997.

Kaul, Suvir. "Reading Literary Symptoms: Colonial Pathologies and the Oroonoko Fictions of Behn, Southerne, and Hawkesworth." *Eighteenth-Century Life* 18, no. 3 (November 1994): 80–96.

Kemp, William. *Kemps Nine Daies Vvonder Performed in a Daunce from London to Norwich. Containing the Pleasure, Paines and Kinde Entertainment of William Kemp Betweene London and That Citty in His Late Morrice* [. . .]. London: Printed by E. A[llde] for Nicholas Ling, and are to be solde at his shop at the west doore of Saint Paules Church, 1600.

Kendi, Ibram X. *Stamped from the Beginning: The Definitive History of Racist Ideas in America*. New York: Nation Books, 2016.

Kiefer, Frederick. *Writing on the Renaissance Stage: Written Words, Printed Pages, Metaphoric Books*. Newark: University of Delaware Press, 1996.

Kitch, Aaron. "Bastards and Broadsides in 'The Winter's Tale.'" *Renaissance Drama* 30 (January 1999): 43–71.

——. "The Character of Credit and the Problem of Belief in Middleton's City Comedies." *SEL Studies in English Literature 1500–1900* 47, no. 2 (2007): 403–26.

Koestenbaum, Wayne. *The Queen's Throat: Opera, Homosexuality, and the Mystery of Desire*. New York: Da Capo, 2001.

Kolb, Laura. "Jewel, Purse, Trash: Reckoning and Reputation in *Othello*." *Shakespeare Studies* 44 (2016): 230–62.

Kolin, Philip C. "Performing Texts in *Titus Andronicus*." In *Titus Andronicus: Critical Essays*, edited by Kolin, 251–61. New York: Routledge, 2015.

Korda, Natasha. "Insubstantial Pageants: Women's Work and the (Im)Material Culture of the Early Modern Stage." *Shakespeare* 7, no. 4 (December 2011): 413–31.

——. *Shakespeare's Domestic Economies: Gender and Property in Early Modern England*. Philadelphia: University of Pennsylvania Press, 2002.

——. "Women in the Theater." In *The Oxford Handbook of Early Modern Theatre*, edited by Richard Dutton, 456–73. Oxford: Oxford University Press, 2011.

Kugler, Emily M. N. *Sway of the Ottoman Empire on English Identity in the Long Eighteenth Century*. Boston: Brill, 2012.

Lawrence, Sean. "The Two Faces of Othello." In *Shakespeare and the Power of the Face*, edited by James A. Knapp, 61–74. New York: Routledge, 2015.

Leinwand, Theodore B. *Theatre, Finance and Society in Early Modern England*. Cambridge: Cambridge University Press, 1999.

Lenz, Joseph. "Base Trade: Theater as Prostitution." *ELH* 60, no. 4 (1993): 833–55.

Lin, Erika T. *Shakespeare and the Materiality of Performance*. New York: Palgrave Macmillan, 2012.

Lipking, Joanna. "'Others,' Slaves, and Colonists in 'Oroonoko.'" In *The Cambridge Companion to Aphra Behn*, edited by Derek Hughes and Janet Todd, 166–87. Cambridge: Cambridge University Press, 2004.

Little, Arthur L., Jr. "'An Essence That's Not Seen': The Primal Scene of Racism in *Othello*." *Shakespeare Quarterly* 44, no. 3 (October 1993): 304–24.

——. *Shakespeare Jungle Fever: National-Imperial Re-Visions of Race, Rape, and Sacrifice*. Stanford: Stanford University Press, 2000.

Loiperdinger, Martin. "Lumiere's Arrival of the Train: Cinema's Founding Myth." Translated by Bernd Elzer. *Moving Image* 4, no. 1 (2004): 89–118.

Lower, Charles B. "Othello as Black on Southern Stages, Then and Now." In *Shakespeare in the South: Essays on Performance*, edited by Philip C. Kolin, 199–228. Jackson: University Press of Mississippi, 1983.

Lukasik, Christopher J. *Discerning Characters: The Culture of Appearance in Early America*. Philadelphia: University of Pennsylvania Press, 2010.

Lupton, Julia Reinhard. "Creature Caliban." *Shakespeare Quarterly* 51, no. 1 (April 2000): 1–23.

Lynch, Deidre Shauna. *The Economy of Character: Novels, Market Culture, and the Business of Inner Meaning.* Chicago: University of Chicago Press, 1998.

MacDonald, Joyce Green. "The Disappearing African Woman: Imoinda in 'Oroonoko' after Behn." *ELH* 66, no. 1 (April 1999): 71–86.

———. "Race, Women, and the Sentimental in Thomas Southerne's 'Oroonoko.'" *Criticism* 40, no. 4 (October 1998): 555–70.

MacGaffey, Wyatt. "African Objects and the Idea of Fetish." *RES: Anthropology and Aesthetics,* no. 25 (April 1994): 123–31.

Macksey, Richard A., and Eugenio Donato, eds. *The Structuralist Controversy: The Languages of Criticism and the Sciences of Man.* 40th anniversary ed. Baltimore: Johns Hopkins University Press, 2007.

Maguire, Laurie. "*Othello,* Theatre Boundaries, and Audience Cognition." In *Othello: The State of Play,* edited by Lena Cowen Orlin. The Arden Shakespeare. London: Bloomsbury, 2014.

Marcus, Leah Sinanoglou. "'Present Occasions' and the Shaping of Ben Jonson's Masques." *ELH* 45, no. 2 (1978): 201.

Marlowe, Christopher. *Tamburlaine the Great Who, from a Scythian Shephearde, by His Rare and Woonderfull Conquests, Became a Most Puissant and Mightye Monarque* [. . .]. London: Printed by Richard Ihones: at the signe of the Rose and Crowne neere Holborne Bridge, 1590.

Marston, John, Thomas Dekker, William Haughton, and John Day. *Lust's Dominion, or, The Lascivious Queen: A Tragedie.* London: Printed for F.K. and are to be sold by Robert Pollard, 1657.

Marx, Karl. *Selected Writings.* Edited by Lawrence H. Simon. Indianapolis: Hackett, 1994.

Masten, Jeffrey. *Queer Philologies: Sex, Language, and Affect in Shakespeare's Time.* Philadelphia: University of Pennsylvania Press, 2016.

Matar, Nabil I. *Turks, Moors and Englishmen in the Age of Discovery.* New York: Columbia University Press, 1999.

Maus, Katharine Eisaman. *Inwardness and Theater in the English Renaissance.* Chicago: University of Chicago Press, 1995.

McGirr, Elaine M. *Eighteenth-Century Characters: A Guide to the Literature of the Age.* New York: Palgrave Macmillan, 2007.

McKeon, Michael. *The Origins of the English Novel, 1600–1740.* Baltimore: Johns Hopkins University Press, 2002.

McManus, Clare. "Women and English Renaissance Drama: Making and Unmaking 'The All-Male Stage.'" *Literature Compass* 4, no. 3 (2007): 784–96.

Medovoi, Leerom. "Dogma-Line Racism: Islamophobia and the Second Axis of Race." *Social Text* 30, no. 2 (111) (June 2012): 43–74.

Melville, Herman. "Hawthorne and His Mosses." In *The Piazza Tales: And Other Prose Pieces, 1839–1860,* edited by Harrison Hayford and Merton M. Sealts, 239–53. Evanston: Northwestern University Press, 1987.

———. "Benito Cereno," in *"Billy Budd, Sailor" and Selected Tales,* edited by Robert Milder. New York: Oxford University Press, 1998.

Menzer, Paul. *Anecdotal Shakespeare: A New Performance History.* New York: Bloomsbury Arden Shakespeare, 2015.

Meskill, Lynn S. "The Characters of Posterity in Jonson's *The Masque of Blacknesse* and Shakespeare's *Antony and Cleopatra.*" *Huntington Library Quarterly* 73, no. 1 (March 2010): 37–56.

Metzger, Sean. *Chinese Looks: Fashion, Performance, Race.* Bloomington: Indiana University Press, 2014.

Michell, Roger, dir. *Tea with the Dames.* Documentary. DVD, 2018.

Mignolo, Walter D. *The Darker Side of the Renaissance: Literacy, Territoriality, & Colonization.* 1995. 2nd ed. Ann Arbor: University of Michigan Press, 2003.

Miller, Julie. "Maggie Smith Had No Patience for Laurence Olivier's Diva Antics." *Vanity Fair,* September 25, 2018. Accessed November 11, 2019. https://www.vanityfair.com/hollywood/2018/09/maggie-smith-laurence-olivier-othello-tea-with-the-dames-joan-plowright-judi-dench-eileen-atkins.

Mills, Charles W. "White Ignorance." In *Race and Epistemologies of Ignorance,* edited by Shannon Sullivan and Nancy Tuana, 13–38. Albany: State University of New York Press, 2007.

Mitchell, W. J. T. *Seeing Through Race.* Cambridge, Mass.: Harvard University Press, 2012.

Monaghan, E. Jennifer. "Reading for the Enslaved, Writing for the Free: Reflections on Liberty and Literacy." *Proceedings of the American Antiquarian Society* 108, no. 2 (January 1999): 309–41.

———. "'She Loved to Read in Good Books': Literacy and the Indians of Martha's Vineyard, 1643–1725." *History of Education Quarterly* 30, no. 4 (January 1990): 492–521.

Montagu, Ashley. *Man's Most Dangerous Myth: The Fallacy of Race.* New York: Columbia University Press, 1945.

Morgan, Jennifer L. *Reckoning with Slavery: Gender, Kinship, and Capitalism in the Early Black Atlantic.* Durham: Duke University Press, 2021.

Morgan, Marcyliena. *Language, Discourse and Power in African American Culture.* Cambridge: Cambridge University Press, 2002.

Morrison, Toni. "A Humanist View." In *Public Dialogue on the American Dream Theme,* edited by Keisha E. McKenzie. Portland: Portland State University Library, 1975. http://mackenzian.com/wp-content/uploads/2014/07/Transcript_PortlandState_TMorrison.pdf.

———. *Playing in the Dark: Whiteness and the Literary Imagination.* New York: Vintage, 1993.

Moxon, Joseph. *Mechanick Exercises: Or, the Doctrine of Handy-Works. Applied to the Art of Printing.* Vol. 2. London: Printed for Joseph Moxon on the West-side of Fleet-ditch, at the Sign of Atlas, 1683.

Moyers, Bill. "A Conversation with Toni Morrison." In *Conversations with Toni Morrison,* edited by Danille K. Taylor-Guthrie, 262–75. Jackson: University Press of Mississippi, 1994.

Muldrew, Craig. *The Economy of Obligation: The Culture of Credit and Social Relations in Early Modern England.* New York: Palgrave Macmillan, 1998.

Munns, Jessica. "'Good, Sweet, Honey, Sugar-Candied Reader': Aphra Behn's Foreplay in Forewords." In *Rereading Aphra Behn: History, Theory, and Criticism,* edited by Heidi Hutner, 44–64. Charlottesville: University of Virginia Press, 1993.

Ndiaye, Noemie. "Aaron's Roots: Spaniards, Englishmen, and Blackamoors in *Titus Andronicus.*" *Early Theatre* 19, no. 2 (2016): 59–80.

———. *Scripts of Blackness: Early Modern Performance Culture and the Making of Race.* Philadelphia: University of Pennsylvania Press, 2022.

Neely, Carol Thomas. "Women and Men in *Othello:* 'What Should Such a Fool / Do with So Good a Woman?'" In *Critical Essays on Shakespeare's "Othello,"* ed. Anthony Gerard Barthelemy, 68–90. New York: G. K. Hall, 1994. Originally published in *Shakespeare Studies* 10 (January 1977): 133–58.

Neill, Michael. "'Mulattos,' 'Blacks,' and 'Indian Moors': *Othello* and Early Modern Constructions of Human Difference." *Shakespeare Quarterly* 49, no. 4 (December 1998): 361–74.

———. "Unproper Beds: Race, Adultery, and the Hideous in *Othello.*" *Shakespeare Quarterly* 40, no. 4 (December 1989): 383–412.

Nelson, Dana D. *The Word in Black and White: Reading "Race" in American Literature, 1638–1867.* New York: Oxford University Press, 1994.

Newberry, George T. "A 'Folk Biology' of Racial Theory? Psychology and the Historiography of 18th-Century Race Thought." *History Compass,* October 2018, 1–11.

Newman, Andrew. "Captive on the Literacy Frontier." *Early American Literature* 38, no. 1 (2003): 31–65.

Newman, Karen. "Charactery." In her *Essaying Shakespeare,* 111–22. Minneapolis: University of Minnesota Press, 2009.

Niaah, Sonjah. "'Ace' of the Dancehall Space: A Preliminary Look at U Roy's Version and Subversion in Sound." *Social and Economic Studies* 55, no. 1–2 (2006): 167–89.

Novy, Marianne. *Cross-Cultural Performances: Differences in Women's Re-Visions of Shakespeare.* Urbana: University of Illinois Press, 1993.

Nussbaum, Felicity. "Actresses and the Economics of Celebrity, 1700–1800." In *Theatre and Celebrity in Britain, 1660–2000,* edited by Mary Luckhurst and Jane Moody, 148–68. New York: Palgrave Macmillan, 2005.

———. *Rival Queens—Actresses, Performance, and the Eighteenth-Century British Theater.* Philadelphia: University of Pennsylvania Press, 2010.

O'Connell, Barry. "Literacy and Colonization: The Case of the Cherokees." In *A History of the Book in America,* vol. 2: *An Extensive Republic: Print, Culture, and Society in the New Nation, 1790–1840,* edited by Robert A. Gross and Mary Kelley, 495–515. Chapel Hill: University of North Carolina Press, 2010.

O'Donnell, Mary Ann. "Aphra Behn: The Documentary Record." In *The Cambridge Companion to Aphra Behn,* edited by Derek Hughes and Janet Todd, 1–11. Cambridge: Cambridge University Press, 2006.

Ong, Walter J. *Orality and Literacy: The Technologizing of the Word.* New York: Routledge, 1991.

Orgel, Stephen. "Knowing the Character." *Zeitschrift für Anglistik und Amerikanistik* 40, no. 2 (1992): 124–29.

Orkin, Martin. "Othello and the 'Plain Face' of Racism." *Shakespeare Quarterly* 38, no. 2 (July 1987): 166–88. https://doi.org/10.2307/2870559.

Ortiz, Joseph M. "Arms and the Woman: Narrative, Imperialism and Virgilian 'Memoria' in Aphra Behn's 'Oroonoko.'" *Studies in the Novel* 34, no. 2 (Summer 2002): 119–40.

Palfrey, Simon, and Tiffany Stern. *Shakespeare in Parts.* Oxford: Oxford University Press, 2007.

Parker, Patricia. "Cassio, Cash, and the 'Infidel o': Arithmetic, Double-Entry Bookkeeping, and Othello's Unfaithful Accounts." In *A Companion to the Global Renaissance: English Literature and Culture in the Era of Expansion,* edited by Jyotsna G. Singh, 223–41. Chichester: Wiley-Blackwell, 2009.

———. "Shakespeare's Sound Government: Sound Defects, Polyglot Sounds, and Sounding Out." *Oral Tradition* 24, no. 2 (2009): 359–72.

Pastoureau, Michael. *Black: The History of a Color.* English language ed. Princeton: Princeton University Press, 2009.

Patterson, Orlando. *Slavery and Social Death: A Comparative Study.* Cambridge, Mass.: Harvard University Press, 1982.

Paul, Robert W., dir. *The Countryman's First Sight of the Animated Pictures: A Farmer Viewing the Approaching Train on the Screen Takes to His Heels.* Silent film. 1901. http://www.imdb.com/title/tt0000350/.

Pearson, Jacqueline. "Blacker than Hell Creates: Pix Rewrites Othello." In *Broken Boundaries: Women and Feminism in Restoration Drama,* edited by Katherine M. Quinsey, 13–30. Lexington: University Press of Kentucky, 1996.

Peiss, Kathy Lee. *Hope in a Jar: The Making of America's Beauty Culture.* New York: Metropolitan, 1998.

Pietz, William. "The Problem of the Fetish, I." *RES: Anthropology and Aesthetics,* no. 9 (April 1985): 5–17.

———. "The Problem of the Fetish, II: The Origin of the Fetish." *RES: Anthropology and Aesthetics,* no. 13 (April 1987): 23–45.

———. "The Problem of the Fetish, IIIa: Bosman's Guinea and the Enlightenment Theory of Fetishism." *RES: Anthropology and Aesthetics,* no. 16 (October 1988): 105–24.

Pleasant, Alyssa Mt., Caroline Wigginton, and Kelly Wisecup. "Materials and Methods in Native American and Indigenous Studies: Completing the Turn." *Early American Literature* 53, no. 2 (2018): 407–44.

Pollard, Tanya. "Spelling the Body." In *Environment and Embodiment in Early Modern England,* edited by Mary Floyd-Wilson and Garrett A. Sullivan, 171–86. Early Modern Literature in History. London: Palgrave Macmillan, 2007.

Porter, Edwin S., dir. *Uncle Josh at the Moving Picture Show.* Silent film. 1902. http://www.imdb.com/title/tt0000414/.

Porter, Martin. *Windows of the Soul: Physiognomy in European Culture, 1470–1780.* New York: Oxford University Press, 2005.

Pratt, Mary Louise. *Imperial Eyes: Travel Writing and Transculturation.* 1992. 2nd ed. New York: Routledge, 2008.

Prendergast, Monica. "From Guest to Witness: Teaching Audience Studies in Postsecondary Theatre Education." *Theatre Topics* 18, no. 2 (September 2008): 95–106.

Pullen, Kirsten. *Actresses and Whores: On Stage and in Society.* New York: Cambridge University Press, 2005.

Rama, Angel. *The Lettered City.* Edited and translated by John Charles Chasteen. Durham: Duke University Press, 1996.

Ramsey, Guthrie P., Jr. *Race Music: Black Cultures from Bebop to Hip-Hop.* Berkeley: University of California Press, 2004.

Rappaport, Joanne, and Tom Cummins. *Beyond the Lettered City: Indigenous Literacies in the Andes.* Durham: Duke University Press, 2011.

Rasmussen, Birgit Brander. *Queequeg's Coffin: Indigenous Literacies and Early American Literature.* Durham: Duke University Press, 2012.

Rawson, David. "William Hunter (d. 1761)." In *Encyclopedia Virginia,* edited by Brendan Wolfe. Virginia Foundation for the Humanities, July 19, 2011. http://www.encyclopediavirginia.org/Hunter_William_d_1761#start_entry.

Reynolds, Bryan, and Joseph Fitzpatrick. "Venetian Ideology or Transversal Power?: Iago's Motives and the Means by Which Othello Falls." In *Othello: Critical Essays,* ed. Philip Kolin. New York: Routledge, 2001.

Rezek, Joseph. "The Racialization of Print." *American Literary History* 32, no. 3 (Fall 2020): 1–29.

Richards, Jeffrey H. *Drama, Theatre, and Identity in the American New Republic.* New York: Cambridge University Press, 2005.

Ritchie, Fiona. "Shakespeare and the Eighteenth-Century Actress." *Borrowers and Lenders: The Journal of Shakespeare and Appropriation* 2, no. 2 (Fall/Winter 2006). http://www.borrowers.uga.edu/cocoon/borrowers/request?id=781459.

Roach, Joseph R. "Celebrity Erotics: Pepys, Performance, and Painted Ladies." *Yale Journal of Criticism* 16, no. 1 (Spring 2003): 211–30.

———. *Cities of the Dead: Circum-Atlantic Performance.* New York: Columbia University Press, 1996.

———. *The Player's Passion: Studies in the Science of Acting.* Ann Arbor: University of Michigan Press, 1993.

Robertson, Karen. "Pocahontas at the Masque." *Signs* 21, no. 3 (April 1996): 551–83.

Robertson, Lauren. "'Ne'er Was Dream So Like a Waking': The Temporality of Dreaming and the Depiction of Doubt in *The Winter's Tale.*" *Shakespeare Studies* 44 (2016): 291–315.

Roediger, David R. *How Race Survived US History: From the American Revolution to the Present.* New York: Verso, 2008.

———. *The Wages of Whiteness: Race and the Making of the American Working Class.* Rev. ed. New York: Verso, 1999.

Rogers, Katharine M. "Fact and Fiction in Aphra Behn's *Oroonoko*." *Studies in the Novel* 20, no. 1 (Spring 1988): 1–15.

Rose, Tricia. *Black Noise: Rap Music and Black Culture in Contemporary America*. Hanover, N.H.: University Press of New England, 1994.

Rosenthal, Caitlin. "Numbers for the Innumerate: Everyday Arithmetic and Atlantic Capitalism." *Technology and Culture* 58, no. 2 (June 2017): 529–44.

Rosenthal, Laura J. "Entertaining Women: The Actress in Eighteenth-Century Theatre and Culture." In *The Cambridge Companion to British Theatre, 1730–1830*, edited by Jane Moody and Daniel O'Quinn, 159–74. Cambridge: Cambridge University Press, 2007.

———. "Oroonoko: Reception, Ideology, and Narrative Strategy." In *The Cambridge Companion to Aphra Behn*, edited by Derek Hughes and Janet Todd, 151–65. Cambridge: Cambridge University Press, 2004.

———. "Owning Oroonoko: Behn, Southerne, and the Contingencies of Property." *Renaissance Drama*, n.s., 23 (1992): 25–58.

Rosivach, Vincent J. "Agricultural Slavery in the Northern Colonies and in Classical Athens: Some Comparisons." *Comparative Studies in Society and History* 35, no. 3 (July 1993): 551–67.

———. "Enslaving 'Barbaroi' and the Athenian Ideology of Slavery." *Historia* 48, no. 2 (1999): 129–57.

Royster, Francesca T. "White-Limed Walls: Whiteness and Gothic Extremism in Shakespeare's *Titus Andronicus*." *Shakespeare Quarterly* 51, no. 4 (December 2000): 432–55.

Rozbicki, Michal Jan. "Between Private and Public Spheres: Liberty as Cultural Property in Eighteenth-Century British America." In *Cultures and Identities in Colonial British America*, edited by Robert Olwell and Alan Tully, 293–318. Baltimore: Johns Hopkins University Press, 2006.

Rymer, Thomas. *A Short View of Tragedy; It's Original, Excellency, and Corruption with Some Reflections on Shakespear and Other Practitioners for the Stage*. London: Richard Baldwin, 1693.

Said, Edward W. *Orientalism*. New York: Vintage, 1979.

Sale, Carolyn. "Black Aeneas: Race, English Literary History, and the 'Barbarous' Poetics of *Titus Andronicus*." *Shakespeare Quarterly* 62, no. 1 (2011): 25–52.

Sanders, Eve Rachele. *Gender and Literacy on Stage in Early Modern England*. Cambridge: Cambridge University Press, 1998.

Saunders, Richard. *Saunders Physiognomie, and Chiromancie, Metoposcopie: The Symmetrical Proportions and Signal Moles of the Body . . . with the Subject of Dreams Made Plain, Whereunto Is Added the Art of Memory* [. . .]. London: H. Bragis, 1671.

Saussure, Ferdinand de. *Course in General Linguistics*. Translated by Roy Harris. LaSalle, Ill.: Open Court, 1986.

Sawyer, Edmund, ed. *Memorials of Affairs of State in the Reigns of Queen Elizabeth and King James I: Collected (Chiefly) from the Original Papers of Ralph Winwood. Kt. Sometime One of the Principal Secretaries of State* [. . .]. Vol. 2. London: Printed by W.B. for T. Ward in the Inner-Temple-Lane, 1725.

Schneider, Rebecca. *Performing Remains: Art and War in Times of Theatrical Reenactment.* New York: Routledge, 2011.

Schuyler, George. "The Negro-Art Hokum." *Nation,* June 16, 1926.

Scott-Warren, Jason. "Reading Graffiti in the Early Modern Book." *Huntington Library Quarterly* 73, no. 3 (September 2010): 363–81.

Sedgman, Kirsty. "Audience Experience in an Anti-Expert Age: A Survey of Theatre Audience Research." *Theatre Research International* 42, no. 3 (October 2017): 307–22.

Senchyne, Jonathan. "Bottles of Ink and Reams of Paper: Clotel, Racialization, and the Material Culture of Print." In *Early African American Print Culture,* edited by Lara Langer Cohen and Jordan Alexander Stein, 140–58. Material Texts. Philadelphia: University of Pennsylvania Press, 2012.

———. *The Intimacy of Paper in Early and Nineteenth-Century American Literature.* Amherst: University of Massachusetts Press, 2019.

Sepinwall, Alyssa Goldstein. "Still Unthinkable? The Haitian Revolution and the Reception of Michel-Rolph Trouillot's Silencing the Past." *Journal of Haitian Studies* 19, no. 2 (2013): 75–103.

Shaffer, Jason. *Performing Patriotism: National Identity in the Colonial and Revolutionary American Theater.* Philadelphia: University of Pennsylvania Press, 2007.

Shakespeare, William. *The First Quarto of Othello.* Edited by Scott McMillin. The New Cambridge Shakespeare. New York: Cambridge University Press, 2001.

———. *A New Variorum Edition of Shakespeare: Othello.* Edited by Horace Howard Furness. Philadelphia: J. B. Lippincott, 1886.

———. *Othello.* Edited by Julie Hankey. 2nd ed. Shakespeare in Production. New York: Cambridge University Press, 2005.

———. *Othello.* Edited by Edward Pechter. 2nd ed. New York: W. W. Norton, 2016.

———. *The Riverside Shakespeare.* Edited by G. Blakemore Evans, Harry Levin, Herschel Baker, Anne Barton, Hallet Smith, Marie Edel, and Frank Kermode. Boston: Houghton Mifflin, 1974.

Siemon, James R. "'Nay, That's Not Next': *Othello,* V.ii in Performance, 1760–1900." *Shakespeare Quarterly* 37, no. 1 (1986): 38–51.

Smith, Bruce. "Prickly Characters." In *Reading and Writing in Shakespeare,* edited by David Moore Bergeron, 25–44. Newark: University of Delaware Press, 1996.

Smith, Ian. *Black Shakespeare.* New York: Cambridge University Press, 2022.

———. "Othello's Black Handkerchief." *Shakespeare Quarterly* 64, no. 1 (2013): 1–25.

———. *Race and Rhetoric in the Renaissance: Barbarian Errors.* New York: Palgrave Macmillan, 2009.

———. "Speaking of Race." In *Shakespeare in Our Time: A Shakespeare Association of America Collection,* edited by Dympna Callaghan and Suzanne Gossett, 118–23. London: The Arden Shakespeare, 2016.

———. "The Textile Black Body: Race and 'Shadowed Livery' in *The Merchant of Venice.*" In *The Oxford Handbook of Shakespeare and Embodiment: Gender, Sexuality, and Race,* edited by Valerie Traub, 290–315. Oxford: Oxford University Press, 2016.

———. "Those 'Slippery Customers': Rethinking Race in *Titus Andronicus.*" *Journal of Theater and Drama,* no. 3 (1997): 45–58.

———. "White Skin, Black Masks: Racial Cross-Dressing on the Early Modern Stage." *Renaissance Drama* 32 (2003): 33–68.

Sohmer, Steve. "The 'Double Time' Crux in 'Othello' Solved." *English Literary Renaissance* 32, no. 2 (2002): 214–38.

Sorensen, Leif. "Dubwise into the Future: Versioning Modernity in Nalo Hopkinson." *African American Review* 47, no. 2/3 (2014): 267–83, 446.

Sousa, Geraldo U. de. *At Home in Shakespeare's Tragedies.* Burlington: Ashgate, 2010.

Southerne, Thomas. *Oroonoko.* Edited by Maximillian E. Novak and David Stuart Rodes. Lincoln: University of Nebraska Press, 1976.

———. *Oroonoko: A Tragedy as It Is Acted at the Theatre-Royal, by His Majesty's Servants. Written by Tho. Southerne.* London: Printed for H. Playford in the Temple-Change. B. Tooke at the Middle-Temple-Gate. And S. Buckley at the Dolphin against St. Dunstan's Church in Fleet-street, 1696.

Spencer, Quayshawn. "Racial Realism II: Are Folk Races Real?" *Philosophy Compass* 13, no. 1 (January 2018): e12467.

Spengemann, William C. "The Earliest American Novel: Aphra Behn's *Oroonoko.*" *Nineteenth-Century Fiction* 38, no. 4 (March 1984): 384–414.

Spillers, Hortense J. "The Crisis of the Negro Intellectual: A Post-Date." *Boundary 2* 21, no. 3 (October 1994): 65–116. https://doi.org/10.2307/303601.

———. "Mama's Baby, Papa's Maybe: An American Grammar Book." *Diacritics* 17, no. 2 (Summer 1987): 65–81.

Spratt, Danielle. "'Genius Thus Munificently Employed!!!': Philanthropy and Celebrity in the Theaters of Garrick and Siddons." *Eighteenth-Century Life* 37, no. 3 (September 2013): 55–84.

Stallybrass, Peter, Roger Chartier, J. Franklin Mowery, and Heather Wolfe. "Hamlet's Tables and the Technologies of Writing in Renaissance England." *Shakespeare Quarterly* 55, no. 4 (December 2004): 379–419.

Steffen, William H. "Globalizing Nature on the Shakespearean Stage." PhD dissertation, University of Massachusetts, Amherst, 2019.

Stepan, Nancy. "Race and the Return of the Great Chain of Being, 1800–50." In *The Idea of Race in Science: Great Britain 1800–1960,* edited by Stepan, 1–19. St Antony's/Macmillan Series. London: Palgrave Macmillan, 1982.

Stern, Tiffany. *Making Shakespeare: From Stage to Page.* London: Routledge, 2004.

Stevens, Andrea. *Inventions of the Skin: The Painted Body in Early English Drama.* Edinburgh: Edinburgh University Press, 2013.

Steverson, Delia. "'Everything Gray': Polygenism and Racial Perception in Herman Melville's 'Benito Cereno.'" *Journal of American Culture* 40, no. 2 (June 2017): 169–77.

Stewart, Alan. *Shakespeare's Letters.* Oxford: Oxford University Press, 2009.

Stewart, Alan, and Heather Wolfe. *Letterwriting in Renaissance England.* Seattle: University of Washington Press, 2005.

Stoever, Jennifer Lynn. *The Sonic Color Line: Race and the Cultural Politics of Listening.* New York: New York University Press, 2016.

Stolberg, Michael. "A Woman Down to Her Bones: The Anatomy of Sexual Difference in the Sixteenth and Early Seventeenth Centuries." *Isis* 94, no. 2 (2003): 274–99.

Swindall, Lindsey R. *The Politics of Paul Robeson's Othello.* Margaret Walker Alexander Series in African American Studies. Jackson: University Press of Mississippi, 2010.

Taylor, Diana. *The Archive and the Repertoire: Performing Cultural Memory in the Americas.* Durham: Duke University Press Books, 2003.

Taylor, Gary, and John Jowett. "Appendix II 'O' and 'Oh' in English Renaissance Dramatists." In *Shakespeare Reshaped, 1606–1623,* 248–59. Oxford: Clarendon Press, 1993.

Teague, Frances N. *Shakespeare's Speaking Properties.* Lewisburg, Pa.: Bucknell University Press, 1991.

Tennenhouse, Leonard. *The Importance of Feeling English: American Literature and the British Diaspora, 1750–1850.* Princeton: Princeton University Press, 2007.

Thelwell, Chinua. *Exporting Jim Crow: Blackface Minstrelsy in South Africa and Beyond.* Amherst: University of Massachusetts Press, 2020.

Thomas, Susie. "This Thing of Darkness I Acknowledge Mine: Aphra Behn's 'Abdelazer, or, The Moor's Revenge.'" *Restoration: Studies in English Literary Culture, 1660–1700* 22, no. 1 (April 1998): 18–39.

Thompson, Ayanna. *Performing Race and Torture on the Early Modern Stage.* 1st ed. New York: Routledge, 2007.

——. "Two Actors on Shakespeare, Race, and Performance: A Conversation between Harry J. Lennix and Laurence Fishburne." *Shakespeare Bulletin* 27, no. 3 (2009): 399.

Todd, Janet M. *Aphra Behn: A Secret Life.* London: Bloomsbury, 2017.

——. *The Secret Life of Aphra Behn.* New Brunswick: Rutgers University Press, 1997.

Toole, Briana. "What Lies Beneath: The Epistemic Roots of White Supremacy." In *Political Epistemology,* edited by Michael Hannon and Elizabeth Edenberg, 76–94. Oxford: Oxford University Press, 2021.

Traister, Daniel. "Reluctant Virgins: The Stigma of Print Revisited." *Colby Quarterly* 26, no. 2 (1990): 75–86.

Trouillot, Michel-Rolph. *Silencing the Past: Power and the Production of History.* Boston: Beacon Press, 1995.

Twain, Mark. *Adventures of Huckleberry Finn.* Edited by Thomas Cooley. 3rd ed. New York: W. W. Norton, 1999.

Valbuena, Olga L. "'The Dyer's Hand': The Reproduction of Coercion and Blot in Shakespeare's Sonnets." In *Shakespeare's Sonnets: Critical Essays,* edited by James Schiffer, 325–46. New York: Routledge, 2013.

Valls, Andrew, ed. *Race and Racism in Modern Philosophy.* Ithaca: Cornell University Press, 2005.

Vaughan, Alden T. "Shakespeare's Indian: The Americanization of Caliban." *Shakespeare Quarterly* 39, no. 2 (July 1988): 137–53.

——. *Transatlantic Encounters: American Indians in Britain, 1500–1776.* New York: Cambridge University Press, 2006.

Vaughan, Virginia Mason. *Othello: A Contextual History.* New York: Cambridge University Press, 1997.

——. *Performing Blackness on English Stages, 1500–1800.* New York: Cambridge University Press, 2005.

———. "Race Mattered: *Othello* in Late Eighteenth-Century England." *Shakespeare Survey* 51 (1998): 57–66.

Verner, Lisa. *The Epistemology of the Monstrous in the Middle Ages.* New York: Routledge, 2005.

Vitkus, Daniel J. "*Othello,* Islam, and the Noble Moor: Spiritual Identity and the Performance of Blackness on the Early Modern Stage." In *The Cambridge Companion to Shakespeare and Religion,* edited by Hannibal Hamlin, 218–33. Cambridge: Cambridge University Press, 2019.

———. "Turning Turk in *Othello:* The Conversion and Damnation of the Moor." *Shakespeare Quarterly* 48, no. 2 (July 1997): 145–76.

Waldstreicher, David. "Reading the Runaways: Self-Fashioning, Print Culture, and Confidence in Slavery in the Eighteenth-Century Mid-Atlantic." *William and Mary Quarterly* 56, no. 2 (April 1999): 243–72.

Wall, Wendy. "Reading for the Blot: Textual Desire in Early Modern English Literature." In *Reading and Writing in Shakespeare,* edited by David Moore Bergeron, 131–59. Newark: University of Delaware Press, 1996.

Wallace, David. *Premodern Places: Calais to Surinam, Chaucer to Aphra Behn.* Oxford: Wiley-Blackwell, 2004.

Warner, Michael. *The Letters of the Republic: Publication and the Public Sphere in Eighteenth-Century America.* Cambridge, Mass.: Harvard University Press, 2006.

Wayne, Valerie. "Historical Differences: Misogyny and *Othello.*" In *The Matter of Difference: Materialist Feminist Criticism of Shakespeare,* edited by Wayne, 153–80. Ithaca: Cornell University Press, 1991.

Weissbourd, Emily. "'I Have Done the State Some Service': Reading Slavery in *Othello* through Juan Latino." *Comparative Drama* 47, no. 4 (2013): 529–51.

Weller, Barry. "The Royal Slave and the Prestige of Origins." *Kenyon Review* 14, no. 3 (1992): 65–78.

Wells, Stanley. "Boys Should Be Girls: Shakespeare's Female Roles and the Boy Players." *New Theatre Quarterly* 25, no. 02 (2009): 172–77.

West, Shearer. "Siddons, Celebrity and Regality: Portraiture and the Body of the Ageing Actress." In *Theatre and Celebrity in Britain, 1660–2000,* edited by Mary Luckhurst and Jane Moody, 191–213. New York: Palgrave Macmillan, 2005.

Williams, Eric. *Capitalism and Slavery.* Chapel Hill: University of North Carolina Press, 1994.

Williams, Raymond. *The Sociology of Culture.* 1st ed. Chicago: University of Chicago Press, 1995.

Wills, Garry. *Verdi's Shakespeare: Men of the Theater.* New York: Penguin, 2011.

Wilson, Jeffrey R. "'Savage and Deformed': Stigma as Drama in *The Tempest.*" *Medieval and Renaissance Drama in England* 31 (2018): 146–77.

Wilson, Kathleen. "Going Global: Empire, Identity, and the Politics of Performance." *Journal of British Studies* 44, no. 1 (January 2005): 194–203.

———. "The Performance of Freedom: Maroons and the Colonial Order in Eighteenth-Century Jamaica and the Atlantic Sound." *William and Mary Quarterly,* 66, no. 1 (January 2009): 45–86.

Wimbush, Vincent L. *White Men's Magic: Scripturalization as Slavery*. New York: Oxford University Press, 2012.

Winner, Viola Hopkins. "Abigail Adams and 'The Rage of Fashion.'" *Dress* 28 (2001): 64–76.

Wyss, Hilary E. *Writing Indians: Literacy, Christianity, and Native Community in Early America*. Amherst: University of Massachusetts Press, 2000.

Yachnin, Paul. "'The Perfection of Ten': Populuxe Art and Artisanal Value in 'Troilus and Cressida.'" *Shakespeare Quarterly* 56, no. 3 (2005): 306–27.

Yang, Chi-Ming. "Asia Out of Place: The Aesthetics of Incorruptibility in Behn's *Oroonoko*." *Eighteenth-Century Studies* 42, no. 2 (2009): 235–53.

Zender, Karl F. "The Humiliation of Iago." *Studies in English Literature, 1500–1900* 34, no. 2 (Spring 1994): 323.

Index

Page numbers in italics indicate illustrations.

Writing the Early Americas

Printed in the USA
CPSIA information can be obtained
at www.ICGtesting.com
LVHW051104291223
767646LV00003B/295